Causing Human Actions

Causing Human Actions

New Perspectives on the Causal Theory of Action

edited by Jesús H. Aguilar and Andrei A. Buckareff

A Bradford Book
The MIT Press
Cambridge, Massachusetts
London, England

MIT Press books may be purchased at special quantity discounts for business or sales promotional use. For information, please email special_sales@mitpress.mit.edu or write to Special Sales Department, The MIT Press, 55 Hayward Street, Cambridge, MA 02142.

This book was set in Stone Sans and Stone Serif by Toppan Best-set Premidia Limited. Printed and bound in the United States of America.

"Omissions and Causalism" by Carolina Sartorio. Copyright 2009 Wiley-Blackwell. Reproduced with Permission of Blackwell Publishing, Ltd.

"Intentional Omissions" by Randolphe Clarke. Copyright 2010 Wiley-Blackwell. Reproduced with Permission of Blackwell Publishing, Ltd.

Library of Congress Cataloging-in-Publication Data

Causing human actions : new perspectives on the causal theory of action / edited by Jesús H. Aguilar and Andrei A. Buckareff.
    p. cm.
"A Bradford Book."
Includes bibliographical references and index.
ISBN 978-0-262-01456-4 (hardcover : alk. paper)—ISBN 978-0-262-51476-7 (pbk. : alk. paper)
1. Act (Philosophy). 2. Action theory. 3. Intentionality (Philosophy).
I. Aguilar, Jesús H. (Jesús Humberto), 1962–. II. Buckareff, Andrei A., 1971–.
B105.A35C38   2010
128'.4—dc22

                                                              2010003187

10 9 8 7 6 5 4 3 2 1

Contents

Preface

This volume brings together essays by some of the leading figures working in action theory today. What unifies all of the essays is that they either directly engage in debates over some aspect of the causal theory of action (CTA) or they indirectly engage with the CTA by focusing on issues that have significant consequences for the shape of a working CTA or the tenability of any version of the CTA. Some of the authors defend this theory, while others criticize it. What they all agree on is that the CTA occupies a central place in the philosophy of action and philosophy of mind as the "standard story of action." Two of the essays in this volume have appeared elsewhere recently. (Chapters 8 and 9 by Carolina Sartorio and Randolph Clarke, respectively, previously appeared in *Noûs*. They appear with the permission of Wiley-Blackwell, and have been lightly edited for consistency.) The remaining essays appear in this volume for the first time.

Editing this volume, though not an easy task, has been a labor of love for us. We are convinced that foundational issues in the philosophy of action, such as the issues explored in this volume, deserve greater attention. It is our hope that the publication of this collection of essays will serve to elevate the prominence of the debates the essays range over in future research on human action and agency. This volume, then, is in part an effort to promote exploration of foundational issues in action theory and especially to encourage further work on the CTA by defenders and critics alike.

Work on this volume would have been more difficult if not impossible without the support of a number of people and institutions. First, Philip Laughlin, Marc Lowenthal, and Thomas Stone from MIT Press deserve a special debt of gratitude for supporting this project. Also from MIT Press, we would like to thank Judy Feldmann for her fantastic editorial work. Thanks to Wiley-Blackwell for giving us the permission to publish the essays by Carolina Sartorio and Randolph Clarke which originally appeared in *Noûs*, and to Ernest Sosa for providing some much-needed help with acquiring the permission to put these essays in our book. Second, we would like to thank the authors who contributed to this volume. This volume would not exist were it not for their efforts. Third, we would like to thank Joshua Knobe for his help in the editing process by reviewing the essays by Thomas Nadelhoffer, Josef Perner, and Johannes Roessler. His expertise in experimental philosophy and psychology far outstrips ours. His philosophical acumen with respect to all things action theoretic made him an obvious person to go to for help in reviewing these essays. Fourth, some of the work for this volume was carried out while Andrei Buckareff was a participant in the 2009 National Endowment for the Humanities Seminar on Metaphysics and Mind led by John Heil. Andrei wishes to thank the NEH for the financial support and John Heil for creating a seminar environment that afforded him the opportunity to complete some of the work on this and other projects. Fifth, thanks are due to the institutions we work at, Marist College and Rochester Institute of Technology, for their support of our work on this and other research projects. Andrei is especially thankful to Martin Shaffer, Dean of the School of Liberal Arts at Marist, and Thomas Wermuth, Vice President for Academic Affairs at Marist, for the course releases that gave him extra time to work on his research, including editing this volume. Jesús was awarded the Paul A. and Francena L. Miller Faculty Fellowship from the Rochester Institute of Technology to support part of the work involved in this volume, also in the form of course releases, something for which he is very grateful. Finally, extra special thanks are due to our families and friends for their tolerance and their support as we worked on this project. Andrei would especially like to thank his spouse, Lara Kasper-Buckareff, for her encouragement and patience with him, especially in the final weeks of working on this project. Likewise, Jesús is full of gratitude to Amy Wolf for her constant support during his work on this volume.

Jesús H. Aguilar
Rochester, New York

Andrei A. Buckareff
Poughkeepsie, New York

1 The Causal Theory of Action: Origins and Issues

Jesús H. Aguilar and Andrei A. Buckareff

Philosophy of action is often construed either broadly as including all of the problems in philosophy dealing with human action and agency or more narrowly as concerned with merely the cluster of issues that deal directly with the nature of intentional action and the explanation of action. However we characterize the philosophy of action, one theory has recently enjoyed the title of "the standard story" of human action and agency in the literature, namely, the causal theory of action (CTA).[1]

Strictly speaking, it is misleading to think of the CTA as a single theory of action. A better way to think about the CTA is in terms of a set of theories that bear a family resemblance by accepting the following schema about what makes something an action and what explains an action:

(CTA)   Any behavioral event A of an agent S is an action if and only if S's A-ing is caused in the right way and causally explained by some appropriate nonactional mental item(s) that mediate or constitute S's reasons for A-ing.[2]

If we focus on the ontological implications of this schema we can identify the source of the most significant differences among the several versions of the CTA, namely, differences over what it means to be "caused in the right way" and over what the appropriate nonactional mental item(s) is/are that should cause S's A-ing in order for S's A-ing to be an action. Similarly, if we focus on the epistemological implications of this schema, we can identify a significant difference between the CTA and other competing theories of action regarding the specific role of reasons in the explanation of action. In this way, we can use the CTA schema as a point of reference to identify the main features of the CTA, including both its ontological commitments and epistemological commitments, trace back its historical origins, and recognize the key areas of contention and development associated with this general view on action.

In this introduction we offer a brief historical examination of three key stages in the development of the CTA, namely, the *ancient classical* period represented by the work of Aristotle, the *early modern* period represented by the work of Thomas Hobbes, and the *contemporary* period represented by the work of Donald Davidson. This is to be followed by a general presentation of the main areas of debate related to contemporary versions of the CTA and a concise presentation of the contents of the chapters in this volume.

1   The Roots of the Contemporary CTA: Aristotle, Hobbes, and Davidson

All theories of action aim at providing answers to a set of foundational questions about human action and agency. These foundational questions have been articulated in the form of whether we can distinguish intentional action (such as winking) from mere behavior (such as blinking), or, as Wittgenstein famously put it, whether there is anything left over if one subtracts the fact of an arm going up from the fact of raising one's arm (Wittgenstein 1972, §621). Furthermore, the conclusions we reach in theorizing about the nature of action and agency will provide us with extra resources to address other nearby philosophical questions such as the problem of free agency, the mind–body problem, the problem of *akrasia*, and other related problems in metaphysics, moral philosophy, philosophy of law, and philosophy of mind, among other philosophical subdisciplines. Ideally, our results in action theory should also provide researchers in the behavioral and brain sciences with a broad conceptual framework for their research into human behavior.

But although the motivations for doing action theory and the benefits of working out one's ontological commitments about the nature of action are many, it has historically been a rather narrow set of concerns that have chiefly motivated philosophers to think about action. It should come as no surprise that at many points in the history of philosophy the primary motivation to theorize about the springs of action was a desire to understand the nature of moral agency. This is Alan Donagan's compelling way of formulating this crucial relationship between moral philosophy and theorizing about human action:

Since *ought* implies *can*, writings about morality presuppose much about human action. Yet although conclusions about action can defensibly be drawn from established moral theory, no moral theory can become established unless its presuppositions about action can be defended independently. (Donagan 1987, viii)[3]

When we examine the history of the philosophy of action, we find that Donagan is echoing sentiments about the importance of action theory found among many of the leading theorists in the history of philosophy; for the idea of intimately linking the possibility of morality to the possibility of action and agency has a long and prestigious genealogy, going back at least to the work of Aristotle.

1.1 Aristotle

Although Aristotle was not the first major philosopher to write about action—Plato wrote about action before him (see, e.g., the *Phaedo* 98c–99a)—to our knowledge he was the first one to think seriously about the springs of action. Furthermore, the story he told about the role of the mental in the production and explanation of action was a causal story much along the lines of the above schema of the CTA. Such a proposal may be seen as anachronistic. After all, the CTA as a proper theory of action has only been identified under that title since the 1960s.[4] Nonetheless, to the extent that Aristotle had a theory of action, his theory is clearly a progenitor of the CTA.[5]

Aristotle's commitment to a proto-CTA theory of action can be pieced together from portions of his *De anima* (DA), *De motu animalum* (Mot.), and *Nicomachean Ethics* (NE). The origin of action lies in the agent according to Aristotle (NE, Bk. III, ch. 1.20, 1111a, 23–24). Specifically, the springs of action are what we now identify as pro-attitudes.[6] For instance, he writes that, "the proximate reason for movement is desire [*ourexeos*]"[7] (Mot. 701a35; cf. DA 433a10–434a20). In NE, Aristotle distinguishes between various types of desires. Of these types of desires two are of special interest in understanding his account of the springs of action. They are the intrinsic desires for what are deemed worthwhile ends (*boulêsis*)[8] and the instrumental proximal action-triggering desires for the means to achieving the ends (*prohairesis*).[9] A simple statement of the etiology of action is found in chapter 2 of Book VI of NE:

> The origin of an action—the efficient cause, not the final cause—is *prohairesis*. The origin of *prohairesis* is another desire [*orexis*] and goal-directed reason [*eneka tinos*]. (NE, 1139a31–34)[10]

Thus, on the Aristotelian story of intentional action, (i) an agent *S* desires some end and believes that by *A*-ing she can satisfy her desire for that end; (ii) this gives rise to a desire (*prohairesis*) to *A*; and (iii) the immediate source (the efficient cause) of *S*'s subsequent *A*-ing is *S*'s desire (*prohairesis*) to *A*.

The foregoing is a rough and not uncontroversial summary of the core notions of Aristotle's account of the etiology of action inherited by later causal theories of action. Although this account is certainly a teleological one, it is also fundamentally a causal story in which the desires of an agent are doing causal work along the lines of the CTA schema.[11] Also, whether or not Aristotle is offering a complete theory of action or a proper part of a theory of action is of secondary importance compared to the fact that his account provided a causal framework for the next two millennia for thinking about the etiology and explanation of human action. It is possible to find the core elements of Aristotle's causal story about human action throughout the subsequent history of philosophical work on human agency, particularly in Great Britain after the seventeenth century and more recently among analytic philosophers and cognitive scientists after the middle of the twentieth century.[12]

1.2 Hobbes

The early modern period is very significant in the history of the CTA. Several accounts of action emerged that incorporated the new explanatory framework coming from the Scientific Revolution to the study of human beings. In particular, an analysis of the internal mental causes that lead to an action was developed within such a framework. Some accounts placed the mental causes of action squarely in the natural realm, while others placed them completely outside the realm of nature.

Among the naturalistic-oriented thinkers of this period the most influential figure is Thomas Hobbes, who as much as Aristotle is responsible for what would be christened "the causal theory of action" in the twentieth century. Although later thinkers such as John Locke, David Hume, Jeremy Bentham, John Austin, and J. S. Mill articulated accounts of human action and agency that reflect central tenets present in contemporary versions of the CTA, Hobbes's work on action captures so much of the fundamental tenets of the CTA that nowadays this theory is sometimes referred to as the "Hobbesian picture of agency" (Pink 1997; Schroeter 2004).

Despite its fundamental contribution to the CTA, Hobbes's theory of action gets very little treatment in the secondary literature on his philosophy, often mentioned as a side note in discussions of his psychology and theory of free will.[13] Although this is not the place to mend such an omission, given the centrality of Hobbes's contribution to the development of the CTA we want to at least introduce some of its key features, in particular those that still serve to identify the CTA as a distinctive theory vis-à-vis its present-day competitors.

Hobbes's theory of action is best seen in contrast with the theories of action developed by the Scholastics. Their differences notwithstanding, three of the great Scholastics, Thomas Aquinas, Duns Scotus, and Francisco Suarez, had a fair amount to say about the springs of action. Central to their theories of action was a role for an irreducible faculty of will. For instance, Aquinas when analyzing the powers of the will has this to say: "the will as an agent moves all the powers of the soul to their respective acts, except the natural powers of the vegetative part, which are not subject to our choice" (*Summa theologica* I, q. 82, a. 4 *resp*).[14] Thus, according to this view espoused by what Hobbes called "the Schools," the will is an irreducible rational faculty that is responsive to normative reasons for actions whereby an agent exercises executive control.[15]

In stark contrast to such a Scholastic view, Hobbes reduces the will. Agents are responsive to motivating reasons for action. The reasons to which they respond, the ones that move them to act, are what we nowadays identify as pro-attitudes. In fact, for Hobbes the will just is the proximal action-triggering motivational state that causes an agent to act:

In deliberation, the last appetite or aversion immediately adhering to the action, or to the omission thereof, is what we call the WILL, the act (not the faculty) of *willing*. And beasts that have *deliberation* must necessarily also have *will*. The definition of the *will* given commonly by the Schools, that it is a *rational appetite*, is not good. For if it were, there could there be no voluntary act against reason. For a *voluntary act* is that which proceedeth from the *will* and no other. But if instead of a rational appetite, we shall say an appetite resulting from a precedent deliberation, then the definition is the same that I have given here. *Will* therefore *is the last appetite in deliberating*. (Hobbes 1651/1994, 33)[16]

For Hobbes, "appetite" is roughly synonymous with "desire" and these seem like generic titles for pro-attitudes that motivate agents (*Leviathan*, Part I.2). A succinct statement of what Hobbes means by "deliberation" is found in his *Of Liberty and Necessity*, where deliberation amounts to the "alternate succession of contrary appetites" (Hobbes 1654/1999, 37).[17]

The foregoing seems to suggest that action only follows from deliberation. But Hobbes makes it clear that not all actions follow from deliberation. Some actions require no deliberation. He writes that:

I conceive that when it comes into a man's mind to do or not to do some certain action, if he have no time to deliberate, the doing it or abstaining necessarily follows the present thought he has of the good or evil consequence thereof to himself. . . . Also when a man has time to deliberate but deliberates not, because never anything appeared that could make him doubt of the consequence, the action follows his opinion of the goodness or harm of it. These actions I call *voluntary*. . . . (Ibid.)

So an agent's actions can be voluntary even in the absence of deliberation. No deliberation and no special acts of will are necessary for action. This makes the range of actions that count as voluntary much broader than others before him would allow. In fact, for Hobbes, human action just is one species of animal action, and as such it is a thoroughly natural occurrence.

Furthermore, as if there is any question about what sort of role the will plays in the etiology of action, Hobbes makes it clear that it plays a causal role in the production of action: "of voluntary actions the will is the necessary cause" (ibid., 38). Indeed, he seems to regard any event to be uncaused to be conceptually impossible or at least problematic (ibid., 39).

So, in brief, the story of action we get from Hobbes is quite straightforward. An agent *S* does *A* voluntarily if her *A*-ing is what she willed to do. And *S*'s *A*-ing occurs in virtue of her *A*-ing being caused by her will to *A*. *S*'s will is simply her final desire that terminates deliberation or, in the absence of deliberation, the strongest desire she has at the time she acts. In this way, for Hobbes, the locus of executive control over action is an agent's desire that causes her to act as she does.

1.3 Davidson

By the middle of the twentieth century and after the anticausalist hiatus motivated by the work of philosophers such as Ludwig Wittgenstein and Gilbert Ryle, the CTA reached its full maturity and emerged as the recognized "standard story of action" among contemporary action theorists. The *locus classicus* for the presentation and defense of this contemporary version of the CTA is found in Donald Davidson's work on action and agency, particularly, in his groundbreaking essay "Actions, Reasons, and Causes" (Davidson 1963/1980). We will focus on this essay, given its centrality in discussions of contemporary versions of the CTA.

Davidson makes two claims about reasons-explanations of action in "Actions, Reasons, and Causes." The first is a claim about what constitutes an agent's primary reason for action, and the second claim is about the causal role of an agent's primary reason for action. Regarding the first claim, Davidson echoes both Aristotle and Hobbes in affording pro-attitudes a central role in his account of practical reasons. His view is particularly Aristotelian in rendering beliefs an important role as well:

C1. *R* is a primary reason why an agent performed the action *A* under the description *d* only if *R* consists of a pro attitude of the agent towards actions with a certain property, and a belief that *A*, under the description *d*, has that property. (Davidson 1963/1980, 5)

According to this view, a reason for action is a belief and pro-attitude pair, and explanations in terms of reasons will mention one or both of these items.

Regarding the explanatory role of reasons, Davidson argues that the relationship between reasons and actions displays the same pattern we discern in causal explanations. Unless the relationship is causal, we are at a loss to distinguish those cases in which an agent has a reason for acting that *fails to explain* why she acts as she does, from cases where the agent's reason for acting *explains* why she acts as she does. Davidson notes that if we dispense with a reason's causal role:

Something essential has certainly been left out, for a person can have a reason for an action, and perform the action, and yet this reason not be the reason why he did it. Central to the relation between a reason and an action it explains is the idea that the agent performed the action *because* he had the reason. (Ibid., 9)

So, to borrow an example from Alfred Mele, Sebastian may have a pair of reasons for mowing his lawn this afternoon. He wants to mow the lawn when the grass is dry and he also wants his spouse, Fred, to see him mowing the lawn when Fred gets home from work in order to impress him. It turns out that Sebastian only acts for one of these reasons. Mele asks, "In virtue of what is it true that he mowed his lawn for this reason and not for the other, if not that this reason (or his having it), and not the other, played a suitable causal role in his mowing the lawn?" (Mele 1997, 240).

This explanatory problem for the noncausalist has been christened "Davidson's Challenge" in the action-theoretic literature (Ginet 2002; Mele 2003), and it is a direct challenge to anyone who rejects causalism about reasons-explanations. Mele notes that the challenge is to "provide an account of the reasons for which we act that does not treat . . . [them] as figuring in the causation of the relevant behavior" (Mele 2003, 39).

Thus, Davidson's second claim about reasons for action and their role in the explanation of action has been the main source of contention between causalists and noncausalists about reasons-explanations:

C2. A primary reason for an action is its cause. (Davidson 1963/1980, 12)

The remainder of "Actions, Reasons, and Causes" is devoted to defending C2 from possible attacks coming from noncausalists.

One may wonder where and how Davidson gets around to making any further direct claims about the nature of action itself. After all, a commitment to causalism about reasons-explanations is at most a necessary condition for a version of the CTA.

Detecting Davidson's further commitment to a version of the CTA in "Actions, Reasons, and Causes" requires that one dig around to find anything close to a statement regarding the difference that causation by reasons makes for the actional status of some event. It is not until the very end of the essay that Davidson says something about the ontological significance of his claims about reasons as causes of action.

In the last couple of pages of "Actions, Reasons, and Causes," Davidson discusses some worries expressed by A. I. Melden (1961). Melden's worries are about mental causation and causal theories of action. In fact, they prefigure more recent criticisms of the CTA based on the idea that in this theory's picture of the production of an action, the agent is essentially absent.[18] This is what Melden has to say:

> It is futile to attempt to explain conduct through the causal efficacy of desire—all *that* can explain is further happenings, not actions performed by agents. The agent confronting the causal nexus in which such happenings occur is a helpless victim of all that occurs in and to him. There is no place in this picture of the proceedings either for rational appetite or desires, or even for the conduct that was to have been explained by reference to them. (Melden 1961, 128–129)

In response, Davidson notes that Melden's view is contradictory. Specifically, Melden identifies some actions with bodily movements, allows those bodily movements to be caused, but denies that the causes of these bodily movements *qua* movements are causes of the bodily movements *qua* actions (Davidson 1963/1980, 18–19). Davidson notes that Melden attempts to remove actions from the realm of causality altogether, getting the odd result that an action is identical with a bodily movement that is caused, but the action is not itself caused (ibid., 19).

Nevertheless, something more metaphysically substantive is contained in Davidson's reply to Melden's criticism than merely pointing out a flagrant inconsistency. As part of his rejection of Melden's views, Davidson rejects a false dilemma that is presupposed in such anticausalist views, namely, that we must either be agent-causes of our actions or be mere "patients" or "victims" with respect to our actions. A third alternative is simply this: "Some causes have no agents. Among these agentless causes are the states and changes of state in persons which, because they are reasons as well as causes, constitute certain events free and intentional actions" (ibid.). We are agents in virtue of parts of ourselves causing our behavior, and those parts are our reasons. Correspondingly, our behavior is actional in virtue of being caused by our reasons.

Two further central features of Davidson's version of the CTA are present in two later seminal essays on his theory of action, "Agency" (Davidson

1971/1980) and "Intending" (Davidson 1978/1980). In "Agency" he adds that someone counts as the agent of an action if what this person does "can be described under an aspect that makes it intentional" (1971/1980, 46). In "Intending" he revises his previous view (C1) that reduced intentions to belief and pro-attitude pairs, proposing instead that intentions are irreducible executive states that figure in the etiology and control of intentional action in addition to beliefs and pro-attitudes.[19]

Clearly, Davidson had more to say about the theory of action and its explanation. But what is important for our purposes is that he, along with the likes of Aristotle and Hobbes, laid the foundations for the articulation of a CTA that has emerged as the "standard story of action" not only in action theory, but in the philosophy of mind and moral philosophy. We now turn to some key problems raised for the CTA and some proposed solutions to these problems.

2   The Contemporary Debate over the CTA

From the foregoing, we hope it is evident that there are at least two desiderata a satisfactory theory of action should satisfy. The first is a metaphysical desideratum requiring that a theory of action should provide us with a way to distinguish behavior that is actional from behavior that is not actional. This desideratum includes the need for a theory of action to tell us a story about the role of agents in controlling their actions. The second desideratum is epistemological and requires that a theory of action should provide us with the resources to explain the occurrence of an action.

Addressing the metaphysical desideratum, all versions of the CTA propose that a behavior is an action only if it is caused in the right way by some appropriate nonactional mental items. Correspondingly, an agent exercises her causal powers through the occurrence of nonactional mental events and states, that is, agent causation is reducible to causation by nonactional mental events and states. So the story of agency on the CTA is a story about some part(s) of an agent causing some intentional behavior.

With respect to the epistemological desideratum, all versions of the CTA propose that an action A's occurrence can be explained by the reasons the agent has for A-ing, and the reasons explain an agent's A-ing only if the reasons played a causal role in the etiology of the agent's A-ing. Opponents of the CTA have questioned just how well the CTA satisfies the two desiderata. In this section of the introduction we present the main metaphysical and epistemological challenges for the CTA arising from the two desiderata.

2.1 Basic Causal Deviance

Consider a much-cited example of basic causal deviance, namely, Donald Davidson's nervous climber example:

A climber might want to rid himself of the weight and danger of holding another man on a rope, and he might know that by loosening his hold on the rope he could rid himself of the weight and danger. This belief and want might so unnerve him as to cause him to loosen his hold. (Davidson 1973/1980, 79)

The example is supposed to show that it is possible to satisfy the causal conditions for an action in accordance with the CTA without the ensuing event counting as an action. The problem of basic causal deviance is thought by some to be the Achilles' heel of the CTA. Whether it proves fatal or not, what the problem shows is that any version of the CTA that merely emphasizes a ballistic role for the relevant mental causes of action is inadequate. That is to say, whether the proximal cause of action is a belief-desire pair, an intention, or some event associated with either, the causal role of the relevant mental item(s) cannot merely trigger behavior. Exactly what must be added in order for an action to occur has been one of the central issues in the debates over the CTA.

The most prominent strategies offered by CTA defenders to date have afforded intentions a central role in their responses to the problem of basic deviance. Most have emphasized the following. Either the agent's action-triggering intention must play a sustaining and guiding causal role through to the completion of the action, or an agent must acquire a separate action-guiding intention once she begins to execute her action-triggering intention that plays a sustaining and guiding role.[20] How it is that an agent guides her action via her intention that plays the relevant executive causal role has been difficult to articulate. Some prominent defenses of the CTA have argued that behavior that is actional must be responsive to the contents of a set of the agent's reasons that both cause and explain it.[21] This condition has been called the *sensitivity condition* in the literature. While many agree that meeting the sensitivity condition is necessary for action, it is not sufficient. To identify the sources of such skepticism, consider the following type of example offered by Christopher Peacocke (1979b, 87).[22]

Ichiro has had a device planted in his brain that allows a neuroscientist to detect whenever Ichiro has acquired an action-triggering intention to perform an overt action. Unbeknownst to Ichiro, two things are true of him. First, his motor areas and efferent pathways are unresponsive to his proximal intentions to perform bodily movements. Second, the neuroscientist, upon detecting the presence of an action-triggering intention, stimulates Ichiro's motor areas and efferent pathways, thereby satisfying Ichiro's intentions to execute bodily movements. When Ichiro's body moves, his movement is at least in part a causal response to the content of his reasons for action.

If Ichiro succeeds in satisfying one of his intentions in this way, at least two things prevent the outcome to count as his intentional action. First, the causal intermediary is not the normal intermediary between the mental cause of an action and its occurrence. Specifically, the causal path from the action-triggering intention to its execution involves the activities of a causal intermediary that is another agent. That is, Ichiro's bodily movement is the result of the actions of an intermediate agent who responds to the presence of Ichiro's intention, but the intermediate agent does so for her own reasons. Second, the causal pathway is less than reliable. Ichiro has enjoyed good luck since the neuroscientist happens to agree to help him in this way. This is not like having one's normal bodily pathways from an intention to its execution "cooperate" (or even having a prosthetic device serve as a causal medium). For as long as the neuroscientist does not object to the content of Ichiro's action-triggering intention, she will stimulate his motor areas and efferent pathways accordingly. However, if her reasons for action and Ichiro's reasons for action are in conflict, the neuroscientist can exercise executive control over Ichiro's bodily movements. So Ichiro is subject to the whims of the neuroscientist intervener.

Peacocke-type examples are a serious challenge to the CTA because they provide us with cases in which bodily movements are explained by the content of the mental events that cause them without such movements counting as intentional actions. In Ichiro's case, whenever the neuroscientist cooperates, he will produce bodily movements that match up with the contents of Ichiro's reasons for performing them that explain why that particular type of movement occurred, rather than another. But the fact that Ichiro's mental state content plays this causal and explanatory role is not enough to show that Ichiro is acting.

Where the difficult work needs to be done is on being clear about the types of mechanisms and states that must cause a movement in order for it to be truly actional. This means going beyond merely assigning responsiveness to the content of reasons a role in the etiology of a movement. What is needed is the shifting of attention away from *what* causes a movement and instead concentrating attention on *how* it is caused.[23]

In the present volume, the problem of basic causal deviance is taken up in the contributions from Jesús H. Aguilar, John Bishop, Michael S. Moore, and Michael Smith. The differences in their proposals notwithstanding, they agree that basic causal deviance poses a serious challenge to the CTA and deserves the attention of proponents of the CTA.

2.2 The Problem of the Absent Agent

A second challenge to the CTA is related to the theory's approach to agency. If, as the CTA proposes, a behavior is actional in virtue of how it is caused by some mental state or event, and no mental state or event seems to be identical with an agent, then it is hard to see how such behavior involves an agent who is in charge of producing and controlling it. In fact, it appears that the agent has been erased from the picture that the CTA offers about the production and control of an action, effectively making the agent an absentee in such process. This is the problem of the absent agent.

The problem of the absent agent comes in two flavors, depending on the alleged agential deficit involved in the CTA. A first version of this problem charges the CTA with making the agent a *passive* participant in the production and control of an action. The agent is still part of the picture, albeit in a very minimal way, a sort of receptacle where the relevant mental events and states that lead to an action take place.[24] A good example of this version of the problem of the absent agent is found in Melden's previously mentioned criticism of the CTA. Recall that, according to Melden, in the picture offered by this theory, "the agent confronting the causal nexus in which such happenings occur is a helpless victim of all that occurs in and to him" (Melden 1961, 128–29). The agent then becomes more like a patient or victim with respect to the flow of causally related events and states that ensue in an action.

The foregoing version of the problem of the absent agent has led some authors to propose an alternative view of action and causation, which turns out to be one of the main competitors of the CTA. This alternative view of action that gives the agent herself the capacity to directly cause the events corresponding to her actions is known as the "agent causal theory of action" (ACTA)[25] and is associated with the work of Roderick Chisholm (1966) and Richard Taylor (1966), and, more recently, Maria Alvarez and John Hyman (1998).[26]

The second version of the problem of the absent agent is more radical in its stance, charging CTA not only with turning the agent into a passive participant in the production of an action but of actually *eliminating* the agent altogether from the picture. As critics of the CTA like Jennifer Hornsby have put it, the upshot of the CTA "in any of its versions . . . is not a story of agency at all" (Hornsby 2004, 2). If this criticism is correct, the price paid by the reductive strategy embraced by the CTA is literally the abandoning of anything resembling an account of agency understood as the capacity that subjects posses to give rise to and control an action.[27]

Defenders of the CTA have offered different ways of addressing the problem of the absent agent. The two most prominent strategies involve either embellishing the standard story given by the CTA or exploiting the available resources of our best current versions of the CTA without making any substantive additions. These two strategies can be labeled "embellishment" and "revisionist" strategies, respectively.

Typically, versions of the embellishment strategy involve hierarchical or "real-self" theories of agency inspired by the work of Harry Frankfurt. Although Frankfurt is no defender of the CTA,[28] his influence on the embellishment strategy can be traced back to his work on autonomous agency. The initial statement of this view of autonomy by Frankfurt (1971/1988) was in his paper "Freedom of the Will and the Concept of a Person" and was further developed in later papers of his.[29] On this view, an agent acts autonomously when he acts from a pro-attitude that the agent endorses or identifies with. As Frankfurt notes, the sort of endorsement of or identification with a motivational state X that is indicative of autonomous agency requires that the agent wants X to be the motivational state that "moves him effectively to act" (Frankfurt 1971/1988, 10).

Michael Bratman (2000, 2001) and J. David Velleman (1992/2000) are two prominent CTA advocates of the embellishment strategy grounded on versions of hierarchical theories of agency. In the case of Bratman, the emphasis is on the inclusion of self-governing policies "that say which desires to treat in one's effective deliberation as associated with justifying reasons for action" (Bratman 2001, 309). For Velleman, the corresponding emphasis consists in explaining the main functional role played by the agent in the production of an action, namely, "that of a single party prepared to reflect on, and take sides with, potential determinants of behavior at any level in the hierarchy of attitudes" (Velleman 1992/2000, 139). According to Velleman, this functional role is found in a propositional attitude consisting in the desire to act in accordance with reasons.[30]

The differences notwithstanding, the embellishment strategies end up suggesting that what is missing in the CTA's reductionist approach to agency is some species of reflective endorsement by an agent of the mental causes of her action. That is, what the embellishment strategy offers is a version of the CTA that is more complicated in terms of the number of items involved in the production of actions expressing true agency. But the ontological upshot remains essentially the same. Surely the CTA's picture of agency has become more complex; but complexity does not imply ontological novelty. No new powers or unique phenomena that affect the executive control of agents are conferred on them with this extended metaphysical framework. Once we strip away the complex framework added to embellish this theory in the interest of giving an account of full-blooded agency, one is left with a "causal structure involving events, states, and processes of a sort we might appeal to within a broadly naturalistic psychology" (Bratman 2001, 312).[31]

It is important to note that the CTA's commitment to a metaphysically minimalist view of the items involved in the production of an action contrasts starkly not only with the mentioned effort by defenders of the ACTA to introduce a different type of causal relationship involving agents who directly cause events, but also with the CTA's other serious competitor, namely, the volitionist theory of action (VTA). According to the VTA, the way to correctly characterize action and fully incorporate the agent in the picture requires the introduction of a unique type of irreducible mental event that is essentially actional, typically a willing or a trying.[32] Because this type of actional mental event engages the agent directly, it may seem that, if anything, the VTA is ontologically more economical than the CTA particularly in the light of the modifications suggested by the embellishment strategy. And yet, the positing of an event that is intrinsically actional, unanalyzable, and whose single distinguishing feature is the "actish" phenomenological feeling that comes with it[33] introduces a different and unique type of event that is supposed to do the hard agential work. From the perspective of the CTA, the introduction by the VTA of such a unique event amounts to an unnecessary ontological enlargement, which by stipulation is identified as the place where agency takes place.

Nevertheless, some defenders of the CTA recognize that at least with respect to the commonsensical conceptual framework associated with agency, the ACTA and the VTA appear to be responding to basic assumptions involved in the adoption of reactive attitudes toward agents, particularly when agents are seen from a moral perspective. For unless the agent herself is an active participant in the production and control of the actions for which she is going to be held morally responsible and which serve as the legitimate objects of reactive attitudes, the very possibility of these fundamental practices is undermined. From this perspective, the problem of the absent agent is the challenge of making sense of an agent who occupies the central role in the story of morality and responsibility by using exclusively the sparse ontology assumed by the CTA. This type of challenge motivates a second CTA strategy to deal with the problem of the absent agent grounded on the recognition that the commonsensical conceptual framework associated with agency needs to be accommodated inside a reductive naturalist metaphysics of agency.[34] The reason this second strategy is revisionist is that it continues to exploit the available metaphysical resources of the CTA while promising to deliver the goods requested by the commonsensical conceptual framework.

Donald Davison inaugurated the revisionist effort within the CTA by accepting the conceptual irreducibility of agency while maintaining his well-known metaphysical commitment to monism, in this case taking the form of the basic ontological items proposed by this theory of action. A more recent and fully developed effort along these revisionist lines is found in the work of John Bishop, particularly in his *Natural Agency* (1989). In this book, Bishop tries to reconcile what he considers to be a fundamental tension between two competing perspectives:

> We seem committed to two perspectives on human behaviour—the ethical and the natural—yet the two can be put in tension with one another—so seriously in tension, in fact, as to convince some philosophers either that the acting person is not part of the natural order open to scientific inquiry or that morally responsible natural agency is an illusion. (Bishop 1989, 15)

Arguably, the conceptual framework presupposed by the ethical perspective arises from the conceptual framework provided by what often and somewhat loosely is identified as common sense. However, Bishop is careful in making sure that, whether or not a commonsensical conceptual framework generates a tension with a reductive strategy espoused by a philosophical theory such as the CTA,[35] the roots of the tension he is reacting to lie in "a genuine philosophical puzzlement" (ibid., 11) related to the effort to understand "how morally responsible agents can be part of the natural order as our natural scientific worldview conceives of it" (ibid., 15).

According to Bishop, what makes the challenge of reconciling the ethical perspective with the natural perspective particularly acute is that actions from the ethical perspective involve essentially a type of agent-causation that reveal the agent's exercise of control. Bishop's proposal is based on the idea that the tension will dissipate if agent-causalism is not fully warranted, and this is what he tries to show. His strategy is to insist that, from a purely metaphysical point of view, "the notion of action that we need for our ethical point of view does not involve ontological commitment to agent-causal relations of a kind foreign to our naturalist ontology" (ibid., 42). Nevertheless, in denying that actions are constituted by agent-causal relations, Bishop does not make claims about what it *means* to perform an action. Although agent-causation may in fact be part of our primitive concepts about agency, a successful CTA shows that agent-causation is not ontologically basic since precisely what the CTA offers are conditions that are "both necessary *and sufficient* for a basic intentional action to occur" (ibid., 178). That is, providing necessary and sufficient conditions for the *occurrence* of a basic intentional action is not the same thing as providing necessary and sufficient conditions for the *concept* of a basic intentional action. If this revisionary response to the problem of the absent agent is correct, drawing out ontological conclusions that are allegedly problematic for CTA based on the *concepts* of "action" and "agency" is controversial at best and confused at worst.[36]

3   Reasons and the Explanation of Action

To its defenders, one of the main theoretical virtues of the CTA consists in the way it captures the motivating contribution of reasons by identifying them as what cause an agent to act. An agent may have lots of reasons *for* acting, but the reason *why* she does it is the one that causes her to do it. This simple idea is at the center of the most serious epistemological debate between causalists and noncausalists about the explanatory role of reasons concerning action. Perhaps the best way to make sense of this debate is in terms of the above-mentioned Davidson's Challenge, that is, the challenge to provide an account of reasons for which someone acts that does not treat such reasons among the causes of the action. Consequently, anticausalists often see it as part of their theoretical job to show that Davidson's Challenge can be effectively answered, thereby seriously undermining theories like the CTA.[37]

One philosopher whose work stands out as a representative of the type of attack on the CTA grounded on an effort to deal with Davidson's Challenge is George Wilson.[38] The following schema articulates Wilson's noncausalist teleological view (Wilson 1989, 172):

An agent S performs some action A with the conscious purpose of satisfying a desire to achieve some goal E, if and only if, S A's because he desired to achieve E and S's A-ing occurred because S thereby intended to satisfy D.[39]

The notable feature of Wilson's account is that it allegedly captures the teleological role of reasons to explain the performance of an action without relying on their causal roles. Regarding Davidson's Challenge, Wilson ends up claiming that it actually "offers no particular support for a causalist account of explanations of intentional action" (ibid., 174). Although we cannot consider here the details of Wilson's positive case for his teleological alternative, it is useful to consider how a causalist may respond to Wilson by appealing to the resources of the CTA. This response is due to Alfred Mele. (In this volume, Mele continues his effort to show the limitations of teleological accounts of reasons-explanations in contrast to the virtues of causalist ones.[40])

Mele (2003) offers the following counterexample to Wilson's teleological approach. Norm has left his hat, tools, and bricks on the roof. He wants to fetch all three but is undecided about which to get when he commences climbing. Halfway up he decides to get the bricks and forms the intention to get the bricks in order to (thereby) satisfy his desire to get the bricks. The question at this point that is central to the debate over reasons-explanations is this: In virtue of what does Norm form the intention to get the bricks? Wilson's answer is that Norm intended thereby to satisfy his desire. Moreover, the role of Norm's desire is irreducibly teleological and, hence, noncausal.

Now imagine that Norm has the intention to get his stuff by climbing the ladder, and (as Wilson would have it) neither the intention nor a desire plays a causal role in the production of Norm's movements up the ladder. At the moment Norm decides to get the bricks, random Q signals from Mars cause his movements. But it seems to Norm that he is moving himself up the ladder. According to Mele:

In that event, it is false that Norm *climbed* the rest of the way up the ladder. Although his body continued to move up the ladder as it had been, and although he *intended of his movements* that they "promote the satisfaction of [his] desire," Norm was no longer the agent of the movements. (Mele 2003, 46)

The problem for Wilson's teleological account is that Norm meets Wilson's conditions for his reasons to explain his movements. Mele argues that "[The thought experiment] lays bare a point that might otherwise be hidden. Our bodily motions might coincide with our desires or intentions, and even result in our getting what we want or what we intend to get . . . , without those motions being *explained* by the desires or intentions" (ibid., 46). Thus, it appears that one can meet all of the conditions Wilson advances for acting for a particular reason and yet the reasons can fail to explain one's action (ibid., 45–51). The upshot, if Mele is correct, is that a noncausal teleological account such as Wilson's cannot meet Davidson's Challenge.

However, the challenges to the CTA with respect to reasons-explanations do not come only from the direction of noncausal teleological theories of reasons-explanations.[41] A more recent challenge, to both causalism and teleological noncausalism, comes from philosophers who argue that reasons and explanations for action are not necessarily mentalistic. The idea is that the reasons that explain and justify an action are not always the internal mental states of an agent. Rather, reasons for action are often "items that objectively favour courses of action" (Mele 2007, 91). A useful way to make sense of this challenge is by considering it as rejecting psychologism, understood as the view that considers the following thesis true:

For every explanation *E* of an action *A* of an agent *S*, *E* is a reasons-explanation of *A* *only if* some hidden, inner mental states of *S*'s constitute *S*'s reasons for action and are included in *E*.

So, for instance, an opponent of psychologism, Jonathan Dancy, asserts that "even the most cursory glance at the sorts of reason we actually give, in explaining our own actions or those of others, reveals that while some certainly seem to be characterized in terms of a psychological state of the agent, others equally certainly do not" (Dancy 2000, 15).[42]

A couple of quick comments are in order regarding the rejection of psychologism as a challenge to the CTA. First, to the extent that antipsychologism alleges to describe the folk practice of explaining actions by reasons, it is not obvious that it gets the folk practice right. In fact, the evidence from current work on attribution theory in social psychology suggests that the folk practice is psychologistic.[43] Second, as Mele (2003, 2007) and Smith (2003b) have separately noted, as a philosophical theory of reasons-explanations, antipsychologism fails to account for cases when agents do not assess whether what they are doing or the ends they are pursuing are *objectively* desirable or favored.

Of course, more needs to be said about why antipsychologism should not be preferred over psychologism, particularly causalist versions of psychologism. Although this task cannot be carried out here, defenders of the CTA will need to do more in the future to address the recent challenges coming from this direction. Like noncausal teleological approaches, antipsychologistic approaches to reasons-explanations are not going away.[44]

We cannot pretend to have provided an exhaustive survey of the present issues surrounding the CTA in this section. But we hope the foregoing gives those who find themselves in new territory a sense of both the history of the CTA and the state of play about core issues related to the CTA. In the remainder of this introductory chapter we will briefly summarize the contents of the other chapters in this volume.

4   A Summary of the Chapters in This Volume

Some of the authors in this volume are defenders of the CTA and others are critics. Some inform their proposals by reaching into the past and drawing from historical sources while others concentrate solely on the present state of the art and its future possibilities. Lastly, some authors rely mainly on the tools of standard analytic philosophy of action to support their claims while others base their conclusions on the latest empirical research on human action. What all the authors of this volume have in common is the recognition that given the centrality of the CTA, this is a theory that for better or for worse one cannot ignore.

The first eleven chapters of the volume focus on metaphysical issues about the CTA. Chapters 12 and 13 address the debate over reasons-explanations of action. The final four chapters focus on assorted new directions for thinking about CTA.

Michael S. Moore's essay, "Renewed Questions about the Causal Theory of Action," starts off the portion of essays that focus on metaphysical issues. Moore not only responds to some challenges to his own formulation of the CTA, but addresses some more general metaphysical challenges for the CTA, including, among other problems, the absent agent problem, how the CTA can account for mental actions and omissions, and the nature of the causal relation between mental items and events that count as actions. Moore goes straight to the heart of many of the debates over the CTA, defending the ontological credentials of the CTA while questioning the tenability of the ontological commitments of some alternatives.

Michael Smith's essay, "The Standard Story of Action: An Exchange (1)," is the first part of an exchange between Smith and Jennifer Hornsby. Hornsby's essay, "The Standard Story of Action: An Exchange (2)," constitutes the second half of the exchange. Smith defends the CTA. His paper is a response to some of the arguments leveled against the CTA by Hornsby (2004), particularly her arguments related to the role of agents in the etiology of action on the CTA. Hornsby responds to Smith and argues that no version of the CTA should be accepted.

John Bishop argues that action theorists must keep their theorizing about action and agency in contact with the motivations for such work. Bishop discusses the motivations for his own work on action, particularly his desire to reconcile the ethical perspective of ourselves as moral agents with the natural perspective according to which intentional action can be the sort of thing open to scientific investigation. Bishop contrasts his own work with that of Donald Davidson by focusing his attention on the problem of causal deviance and addresses recent critical work of David-Hillel Ruben (2003) on the Davidsonian formulation of the CTA.

The problem of basic causal deviance is the focus of the essay by Jesús H. Aguilar. Aguilar discusses sensitivity strategies, focusing on John Bishop's (1989) proposal. Aguilar provides a sympathetic critique of Bishop's work. He finally recommends a way of fixing Bishop's proposal that brings reliability considerations into a working version of the CTA.

Rowland Stout focuses on the causal relation itself that obtains between an agent and her action. Specifically, he takes issue with the view in the ontology of action that takes actions to consist in the causing of events such as bodily movements. It is not the fact that the events are of a certain type to which Stout objects. Rather, he objects to theories of action that take the causing of an *event* to be the source of the problem. Stout explores the metaphysics of causation and gestures toward an account of the etiology of action that affords agents a more intimate causal connection with their actions.

The essays by Carolina Sartorio and Randolph Clarke focus on the challenge of omissions for the CTA. Sartorio argues that the CTA *qua* theory of intentional behavior lacks the resources to account for intentional omissions since omissions are not events and cannot be caused in the way intentional behavior is described as being caused by the CTA. Clarke distinguishes different ways of understanding what occurs in putative cases of intentionally omitting. He argues that the threat to the CTA posed by omissions is a chimera. Sartorio and Clarke directly respond to one another in follow-up essays, extending the dialectic further.

Whether reasons against acting contrary to how one typically acts can be causes is the subject of David-Hillel Ruben's contribution to the present volume. Ruben treats "con-reasons," as he refers to them, as an insuperable problem for causalism about reasons. On the other hand, Alfred R. Mele's essay defends causalism. Mele critiques Scott Sehon's (2005) defense of noncausal teleological accounts of reasons-explanations of action. He focuses on Sehon's response to Mele's (2003) objection to George Wilson's (1989) teleological proposal. Mele additionally assesses Sehon's reply to Davidson's challenge.

In their essay, Josef Perner and Johannes Roessler examine the development of the conception of action and its explanation in children. They consider the implications for how adults think about action and call for a more expansive understanding of intentional action and its explanation that incorporates teleological elements and a wider range of attitudes to account for the perspective of agents toward their actions.

Some regard embodied cognition as a challenge for views of action like the CTA. In his essay, Fred Adams addresses the objections to the features of such theories of action that are the alleged root of the problem. He argues that versions of the CTA are compatible with the demands placed on them by some accounts of embodied cognition.

Alicia Juarrero's essay advances aspects of her project in *Dynamics in Action* (1999). She makes the case that complex dynamical systems have emergent properties that enhance the autonomy of a system (e.g., an agent), making room for the sort of control necessary for moral agency.

Finally, Thomas Nadelhoffer takes up the much-discussed Knobe effect and its implications for the CTA in his contribution. He argues both for the importance of experimental philosophy of action and that the current data pose difficulties for the CTA.

Notes

1. The *locus classicus* for a contemporary presentation and defense of the CTA is Davidson 1963/1980. More recent attempts at defending the CTA have offered a more fine-tuned account of the role of mental items in the causation of intentional behavior. For more recent book-length defenses of versions of the CTA, see Brand 1984; Bishop 1989; Audi 1993; Enç 2003; and Mele 1992, 2003. Prominent alternatives to the CTA include various noncausal theories of action (including versions of volitionism) and agent-causal theories of action. For noncausal theories of action, see Ginet 1990; Goetz 1988; and McCann 1998. For defenses of agent-causal theories of action, see Chisholm 1966; Taylor 1966; and Alvarez and Hyman 1998.

2. Although we believe this schema captures the essential features of the CTA, this is by no means a settled view, particularly with respect to the additional epistemic clause to what otherwise is a metaphysical view on actions. In fact, one of the contributors to this volume has argued precisely against such a formulation, proposing instead that the components of the traditional schema be divided into two different theories: a causal theory of action (CTA) that captures the metaphysical part of the schema and a causal theory of action explanation (CTAE) that captures the epistemological part of the schema. See Ruben 2003, 90.

3. A notable example of this philosophical inclination is found in the work of John Bishop, one of the contributors to this volume. In his book *Natural Agency* (1989) and in chapter 5 of this volume, Bishop emphasizes the crucial role that moral considerations have in our quest for the nature of action and agency.

4. John Ladd's paper, "The Ethical Dimensions of the Concept of Action" (1965), may be the first place where the term "the causal theory of action" is used in the action-theoretic literature. But Ladd does not use "the causal theory of action" just to refer to what we would now identify as the CTA. Rather, any theory of action that "attempts to analyze 'action' in terms of the category of cause and effect" counts as a causal theory of action for Ladd (1965, 640). This differs from current usage since "causal theory of action" is used to refer to an event-causal theory of action. Ladd's usage allows for agent-causal theories of action to be causal theories of action. In the same year, Daniel Bennett identifies "the causal thesis," which is just what we would now call the causal theory of action (Bennett 1965, 90).

5. The claim that Aristotle even had a theory of action is controversial. For instance, John L. Ackrill argued that although Aristotle says much about what interests action theorists (e.g., about the etiology of action and our responsibility for action), "he does not direct his gaze steadily upon the questions 'What *is* an action?' and 'What is *an* action?'" (Ackrill 1978, 601). For a response to Ackrill, see Freeland 1985. For a partial defense of the claim that Aristotle provides a causal theory of action, see Mele 1981.

6. "Under [pro-attitudes] are to be included desires, wanting, urges, promptings, and a great variety of moral views, aesthetic principles, economic prejudices, social conventions, and public and private goals and values in so far as these can be interpreted as attitudes of an agent directed toward actions of a certain kind" (Davidson 1963/1980, 4).

7. The translation is Martha Nussbaum's (Aristotle 1978, 44). Also, in what follows in our discussion of Aristotle, we will simply use "desire" to denote a conative state generally. We will specify what type of desire when relevant.

8. *Boulêsis* is often rendered as "wish." One could just as easily refer to intrinsic conative states aimed at ends. "Wish" is nice shorthand, since wishes are pro-attitudes. But for ease we stick to using "desire." Nothing much hangs on this since Aristotle's story of motivation still has it that conative states are central as the springs of action.

9. Rendering *prohairesis* as "instrumental action-triggering desire" is not uncontroversial. Richard Sorabji translates *prohairesis* as a desire for the means that will lead to one's ends (Sorabji 1979, 57; 2004, 11). H. Rackham in a footnote to the Greek text in the *Loeb Classical Library Edition* of NE suggests that "preference" along with "choice" are suitable translations of *prohairesis* (Aristotle 1934, 128, note *a*). A. W. Price notes that *prohairesis* literally means "taking in preference" (Price 2004, 30). Given the role of *prohairesis* as a pro-attitude directed toward executing the means to achieving one's ends in acting, "instrumental action-triggering desire" seems like a better translation than "decision" or "choice" (which are common translations of *prohairesis*). This is so because "preference" is not very informative, and "choice" may lead one to the mistaken impression that Aristotle was a volitionist about

actions (treating efforts of will as somehow necessary conditions for action). Admittedly, "instrumental action-triggering desire" is infelicitous for reasons we cannot explore here. But such a translation seems warranted given the functional role of *prohairesis* in the execution of the means to satisfy an agent's ends.

10. The translation is based on Irwin's (1999, 87), with some significant changes made based on consulting the Greek text.

11. We thus echo the general understanding of Aristotle's account of intentional action as a causalist account offered by David Charles (1984, chapter 2), and Alfred Mele (1981). Against the understanding of Aristotle as offering a version of the CTA or partial-CTA, see Coope 2004, 2007. Ursula Coope offers a causal powers account of Aristotle's theory of action that is largely based on what Aristotle says about causation in *Physics* III.3 and VIII.5. But it is not obvious that such an approach is incompatible with a CTA. In fact, we think that a complete, ontologically serious version of the CTA should have something to say about the causal powers of agents. But Coope seems to think that any such story we tell cannot be compatible with a CTA (what she labels "the standard story" on which actions are caused by the beliefs and desires of agents). This is not obvious. Rowland Stout in his essay in this volume favorably discusses some of Coope's work in his discussion of the causation of action.

12. In this volume two chapters that explicitly exhibit the influence of Aristotle's ideas are the ones by Stout (chapter 7) and Juarrero (chapter 16).

13. Perhaps the only notable exception is Van Mill's (2001) monograph *Liberty, Rationality, and Agency in Hobbes's "Leviathan,"* who nonetheless avoids drawing the important connection to modern versions of the CTA and Hobbes's theory of action. Other significant discussions of Hobbes's theory of action, though still embedded within a larger account of his philosophy in general, are Peters 1967; Sorell 1986; Tuck 1989; and Martinich 2005.

14. The quotation is taken from Aquinas 1999, 198.

15. See Pink 2004 for a discussion of the relationship of Hobbes's work on action to that of the Scholastics, particularly Suarez.

16. The text is from *Leviathan,* Part I.53. It turns out that all voluntary actions are free actions on his view. He writes in *The Questions Concerning Liberty, Necessity, and Chance* that "I do indeed take all voluntary acts to be free, and all free acts to be voluntary" (1656/1999, 82–83). See *Of Liberty and Necessity* (1654/1999, §28).

17. To give some context, in the sentence in which the definition appears, he writes that "I conceive that in all deliberations, that is to say, in all alternate succession of contrary appetites, the last is that which we call the will, and is immediately next before the doing of the action, or next before the doing of it become impossible" (Hobbes 1654/1999, 37).

18. In the next section of this introduction we discuss the problem of the absent agent.

19. In addressing the problem of basic causal deviance in his later paper, "Problems in the Explanation of Action," Davidson admits that he is "convinced that the concepts of event, cause, and intention are inadequate to account for intentional action" (Davidson 2004, 106). John Bishop, in his essay in this volume, notes that Davidson is here making a conceptual claim. Because Davidson identifies actions with events, Bishop claims that for Davidson the problem of basic causal deviance does not pose a problem for the ontology of action.

20. For a defense of action-triggering intentions as playing a causal role through the completion of an action, see Mele 1992. For a defense of the acquisition of a separate action-guiding intention, see Searle 1983.

21. See Bishop 1989 and Mele 1992, 2003 for explicit statements of the causal role of reasons and intentions that requires that actions be sensitive to the contents of reasons for action and intentions.

22. See Bishop 1989 for extended discussion of this example. In turn, Aguilar's chapter in this volume discusses Bishop's proposal to deal with such cases.

23. There is widespread agreement on the inadequacy of the old ballistic model of mental causation in the etiology of action. The differences can be quite fine-grained at times. Some strategies include, among others, those that emphasize causation by self-referential intentions (Harman 1976/1997; Searle 1983), those that highlight the immediacy of causal relations between action-triggering intentions—taking actions to start in the brain (Brand 1984; Adams and Mele 1992; Mele 1992), and those that afford feedback loops a prominent role in making sense of the guiding function of intentions (Bishop 1989).

24. The most extensive analysis of this version of the absent agent problem and its consequences for the CTA is by Velleman (1992/2000).

25. We can express the core tenets of the ACTA as follows: Any behavioral event A of an agent S is an action if and only if (1) S causes A (either directly or by causing some event); and (2) S's causation of A is not ontologically reducible to causation by some mental event or state of A.

26. Such a view is at least as old as Thomas Reid's (1788/1983) theory of action.

27. In chapter 4 of this volume, Hornsby retakes this line of attack, while Michael Smith in chapter 3 offers a reply. Another recent criticism of the CTA along these lines, although based on a revised understanding of the role of consciousness, is found in Schroeter 2004; for a CTA response, see Aguilar and Buckareff 2009.

28. For an illustration of his misgivings about the CTA, see Frankfurt 1978/1988, 70–72.

29. Most of these are collected in Frankfurt 1988, 1998.

30. "What really produces the bodily movements that you are said to produce, then, is a part of you that performs the characteristic functions of agency. That part, I claim, is your desire to act in accordance with reasons, a desire that produces behavior, in your name, by adding its motivational force to that of whichever motives appear to provide the strongest reasons for acting, just as you are said to throw your weight behind them" Velleman (1992/2000, 141).

31. Precisely for this reason some critics of the CTA argue that the embellishment strategy amounts to a sort of window-dressing, failing to address the source of their concerns; see Hornsby 2004 and Schroeter 2004.

32. So, for instance, where H. A. Prichard proposed that "to act is really to will something" (Prichard 1945, 190), Jennifer Hornsby has defended the view that "every action is an event of *trying* or attempting to act, and every attempt that is an action precedes and causes a contraction of muscles and a movement of the body" (Hornsby 1980, 33). We can express the core tenets of the VTA as follows: Any behavioral event A of an agent S is an action if and only if S's A-ing is either identical with or is the consequence of an instrumental mental action M (a trying, willing, volition).

33. See, e.g., Ginet 1990, 11–14.

34. Velleman's embellished CTA is also seen by him as directly addressing the commonsensical conceptual framework presupposed in ordinary attributions of agency, which goes to show that the two CTA strategies to deal with the problem of the absent agent discussed here are not exclusive but potentially complementary.

35. Writing about the motivation for any theory of action, this is what Bishop has to say about the role of common sense as the basis for generating philosophical theories and distinctions: "For one thing, the fact that common sense draws a distinction does not automatically warrant the need for a philosophical theory of its basis: To provide motivation for such a theory we need to find a source of genuine philosophical puzzlement in the wider context in which the distinction functions" (Bishop 1989, 11).

36. It is worth noting that in this respect Bishop's theory of action is like J. J. C. Smart's (1959) formulation of the identity theory of mind. Smart's identity theory is an ontological theory and not a theory of the meaning of mental terms. Just as the intension of "pain" need not be the same as its extension, so also the intension of "action" need not be the same as its extension. See also Davidson's effort to draw a similar distinction concerning agency: "If we can say, as I am urging, that a person does, as agent, whatever he does intentionally under some description, then, although the criterion of agency is, in the semantic sense, intentional, the expression of agency is itself purely extensional. The relation that holds between a person

and an event, when the event is an action performed by the person, holds regardless of how the terms are described" (Davidson 1971/1980, 46–47).

37. For simplicity we are only focusing on the debate over whether reasons or mental events associated with them are triggering causes of action, explaining action in virtue of their triggering role. Dretske (1988) argues that reasons are structuring causes of action. This is an interesting and provocative theory that is compatible with a standard causalist account of reasons as triggering causes. A fully developed account of the etiology and explanation of human action should have something to say of the different sorts of causal roles played by mental items. Paying close attention to Dretske's work should play a part in such work.

38. In a recent essay, Wilson (2009) indicates that his interest in action theory comes from his bafflement with the widespread acceptance of Davidson's causalism about reasons-explanations of action. This interest led Wilson to offer a full-blown teleological theory of action in his book *The Intentionality of Human Action* (1989), where among other things he tries to take on Davidson's Challenge.

39. For other recent defenses of teleological noncausalism about reasons explanations, see Ginet 1990, 2002; McCann 1998; Schueler 2003; and Sehon 2005.

40. Mele 1992 and 2003 both include responses to significant challenges to causalism and defenses of noncausal accounts of reasons-explanations more generally.

41. Some of what follows is based on Buckareff and Zhu 2009.

42. T. M. Scanlon endorses a similar view. He writes that "A reason is a consideration that counts in favor of some judgment-sensitive attitude, and the content of that attitude must provide some guidance in identifying the kinds of considerations that could count in favor of it" (Scanlon 1998, 67). See also Rudiger Bittner 2001. For a recent critique of Dancy, see Mele 2003, chapter 3, and Mele 2007. For a recent critique of Scanlon, see Mele 2003, 76–79.

43. See, e.g., the experimental work of Bertram Malle (2004) that indicates that the folk practice is more in line with psychologism and also supports causalism. For a discussion of Malle's work in making the case against the antipsychologism of Julia Tanney (2005), see Buckareff and Zhu 2009.

44. E. J. Lowe (2008) defends an antipsychologistic theory in his most recent book on the metaphysics of mind and action.

2 Renewed Questions about the Causal Theory of Action

Michael S. Moore

1 Introduction

The causal theory of action (CTA) has long been the standard account of human action in both philosophy and jurisprudence. The CTA essentially asserts that human actions are particulars of a certain kind, namely, events. Within the genus of events, human actions are differentiated by three essential properties: (1) such actions are (at least partially) identical to movements of the human body; (2) those movements are done in response to certain representational states of belief, desire, intention, volition, willing, choice, decision, deliberation, or the like; and (3) the "doing" in (2) is analyzed in causal terms. Put simply, according to the CTA, human actions are bodily movements caused by representational mental states such as beliefs, desires, and so on.

The CTA is sometimes put as a conceptual thesis—this is what we mean by the verbs of action; sometimes as an ontological thesis—human actions just are certain mental states causing bodily movements; and sometimes as a mere extensional equivalence regardless of any claims of synonymy or identity—wherever there is a human action, there is bodily movement caused by a certain mental state, and vice versa. Sometimes the CTA is advanced as a combination of two or more of these claims. But in any case, these are, broadly speaking, descriptive theses asserted by the CTA.

The CTA also is widely thought to have normative implications. This is because human action is intimately linked to the agency that makes us both morally responsible and legally liable for certain states of affairs. The CTA thus becomes an analysis of the nature of one of the central conditions of responsibility.

In an earlier work I described and defended a version of the CTA (Moore 1993). My theses were recognizable versions of the three theses distinctive of the CTA in general: (1) each human action is partially identical to some bodily movement (and fully identical only to the sequence, volition-causing-bodily movement); (2) the distinctive mental state causing bodily movements that are actions is volition (a kind of intention not reducible to beliefs, desires, or belief–desire sets); and (3) the relationship between volitions and the bodily movements that are their objects is a causal one, in the standard sense of "cause" (no *sui generis* "agent-causation" allowed).

Both the CTA in general and my particular version and use of it have come under scrutiny in the intervening years.[1] It thus seems an opportune moment to reexamine the essential tenets of the CTA in light of those intervening developments. I shall largely organize the discussion of these developments in three clumps, corresponding to the three essential tenets of the CTA. That is, I divide criticisms of the CTA between: (1) those that refuse to identify actions, even in part, with bodily movements; (2) those that refuse to identify the causes of those bodily movements that are actions as mental states of desire, belief, intention, volition, or the like; and (3) those that deny that the relationship between volitions and the bodily movements that are their objects is causal. I thus organize the discussion around the causal relata (1 and 2) and the causal relation (3) asserted to exist between such causal relata by the CTA.

Preliminarily, however, before beginning this three-part discussion, I shall briefly consider a much broader attack on the CTA, an attack that goes to the naturalist impulse behind the CTA more than to any one of the CTA's particular theses. Generally speaking, this is the view that human agency cannot be captured by any kind of causal analysis. Such a blunderbuss objection has been more particularly phrased as the objection: (1) that a bodily movement is the wrong kind of thing to be even a part of human action, because such a movement "is not an agent's doing anything" and that therefore when "bodily movements are identified as actions . . . no-one ever does anything" (Hornsby 2004, 20–21); (2) that mental states like belief, desire, intention, etc., are the wrong kinds of thing to be causes of actions, because the only "event that merits the title 'action' is *a person's* intentionally doing something" (ibid., 19); or (3) that causation is the wrong relationship here, because even persons (as irreducible agents) do not *cause* actions, even if persons can be said to cause the "results in terms of which their actions may be described" (ibid., 18). One can thus phrase the blunderbuss objection in terms of either the relata or the relation posited to exist by the CTA. But the objection should not be force-fit into one of these three pigeonholes. It is much more general. It is that human agency is a kind of primitive that cannot be reduced to causation of anything by anything.

2   The Mysterians of Human Agency

The heart of the blunderbuss objection is that a person's doing something cannot be "equated with" (analyzed as, identified as, held equivalent to) an event or state causing something. "Agents and their irreducible agency get left out of such an analysis," is the objection. I (and others) call this the "mysterian" view of human action. The label comes from the mystery engendered the moment one holds human agency to be special in the sense that it stands outside the normal causal-explanatory matrix of science. Explanations in normal science proceed by citing causal relations (or probabilistic or counterfactual relations, if these are held to be distinct) between states of affairs as well as events; and this is just what the mysterians of human agency deny about human actions and their explanations.

The first thing to do with this objection is to cabin its reach. Surely the "agency is special" view is limited to *human* agency. Surely the claim is implausible about the agency of items like trees, as in the sentence, "the tree shed its leaves."[2] Unlike talk of people doing things like shedding their clothes, talk of trees doing things like shedding their leaves seems easily reducible to ordinary event/states-of-affairs causal talk, as in "The leaves fell off the tree."

The mysterians' objection builds its case by observing that people *shed* their clothes in a sense that trees do not *shed* their leaves. The agency of persons seems different, more robust, than the "agency" of trees. The CTA would capture this difference in terms of mental state causation; the mysterians object that that leaves the agent out.

The CTA of course rejoins that agency and agents are *not* left out by the CTA—for according to the theory, the exercise of human agency that we call a human action just is mental-state causation of a certain sort. Trees lack such mental-state causation of their behavior, which is why trees do not have the sort of agency that persons possess. Agents and their agency are no more left out of CTA analyses than *temperature* is left out in the ideal gas theory (where only mass, velocity, and kinetic energy of molecules is explicitly talked about), or *water* is left out in chemical discussions carried on explicitly only in terms of H_2O. The CTA makes an identity claim about what human actions are, and it roundly begs the question to simply assert that there is no such identity and so agency is left out when one talks of mental-state causation.

The mysterians need to defend a necessity claim here, namely, the claim that necessarily, the agency of trying and acting cannot be identical to events or states of any kind or in any relationship—not to mental states of belief, desires, intention, or volition; and not to the brain states that correlate with these mental states, either. For the mysterians, human agency is what it is, apparently, and not any other thing.

This is an expensive ontology. The mysterians' irreducible agency is about as desperate a maneuver as was Descartes's refuge in dualism, or, closer to our own times, as was Richard Taylor's (1965) "discovery" of a distinct kind of causation, the "agent-causation" supposedly distinctive of persons bringing about changes in the world through their actions. In all cases something is introduced that is inexplicable in the basic terms with which we understand the world. Primitive, irreducible agency fits with the causal-explanatory matrix by which we understand the world no better than did Taylor's distinct kind of causing, or Descartes's distinct kind of mind stuff. In all cases it is mysterious how we are to think about these items and their relations to the world of physical objects, events, states of affairs, and their relations and properties, with which we are familiar.

To be sure, what one finds mysterious depends on what one thinks antecedently to be familiar and unproblematic. Stare at the ordinary causal relationship very long and it too may look a bit mysterious. Analyses of it in terms of primitive causal relations between particulars (Tooley 1987), or primitive causal-law relations between universals (Armstrong 1983), or single-case chance raisings (Mellor 1995), or the *possibilia* of counterfactual dependence (Lewis 1973), or nomically sufficient causal laws (Mackie 1974), or primitive causal powers and dispositional abilities (Mumford 2009), and so on, may not dispel the mystery much. In light of this, one might urge that irreducible agency is no stranger than is the causal relationship with which it is at odds. (As David Armstrong 1999 remarked some years ago, those who live in ontological glass houses should throw few stones.)

Despite these concessions to ontological charity, irreducible agency is too strange to be accepted. We should agree with Michael Bratman (and Davidson before him) when he finds it "difficult to know what it means to say that the agent, as distinct from relevant psychological events, processes, and states, plays . . . a basic role in the aetiology and explanation of action" (Bratman 2000, 39). Causal relationships, or counterfactual or probabilistic dependencies between events and states of affairs, we think we understand, difficult as those notions are. Indeed, those relations and their relata are the bedrock of any naturalistic understanding of our world. Talk of objects standing in these relations may be idiomatic English before our talk grows seriously ontological, but it is always elliptical for events and states of affairs involving such objects.[3] Talk of one such object (human agents) standing in such relationships where the talk is explicitly not elliptical—that is too mysterious to be taken seriously.

3   Are Bodily Movements Essential to Human Actions?

I now wish to examine the first of three more particular skepticisms about the CTA. This is the skepticism denying that bodily movements are necessary for human actions. Initially, we should distinguish the CTA thesis discussed here from a different thesis, namely, the thesis that *when* there are bodily movements involved in some human action, it is to those movements that reference is made when using verbs of action. The latter thesis could well be true while the thesis of interest here—that action essentially involves bodily movements—was false.

My own critics, and those more generally critical of the CTA, often proceed by way of counterexample. Surely, the argument goes, something (*x*) is an action, and yet just as surely *x* involves no bodily movements. It is useful to group the kinds of counterexamples proposed by different values for the "*x*" in this formula. I shall consider four sorts of such counterexamples. First, there are willed stillnesses by some agent. These include the guardsman at Buckingham Palace trying (successfully) to remain perfectly still (Fletcher 1994, 1445), or the bird-watcher prone to twitching who keeps still to avoid alarming the bird she is watching (Duff 2004, 83), or the chocolate lover who is tempted to reach for the chocolates next to her but stays still, resisting the temptation (Hornsby 2004, 5), or the hero standing steadfast on the burning deck of some ship when every fiber of his being urges flight (Annas 1978). These are surely actions, the objection continues, yet they involve no movement of the bodies of the actors involved.

A second set of counterexamples is provided by the very recent construction of "mind–brain interface machines."[4] I imagined one of these in a recent article (Moore 2009b) (before I knew they actually existed): Suppose the American patriot who desires to warn Dawes and Revere whether the British are coming by land or by sea is so wounded that he can't move; yet he is hooked up to a device on his scalp that measures the readiness potential in the supplementary motor area of his brain when he is about to perform a voluntary motor movement, and that device in turn is hooked up to the light in the tower of the Old North Church in Boston. He wills one movement of his finger. This causes not the finger to move, but the device to register his attempt, and the light to shine but once; Revere and

Dawes get the message, alert their fellow rebels, and so on. Surely the paralyzed patriot has performed the action of alerting the rebels even though
he didn't (because he couldn't) move his body.

It is not very plausible to deny that there are actions in each of these
first two sorts of examples. More plausible is to deny that there are no
bodily movements in such cases. Consider, in descending order of obvious-
ness, a series of cases where this might plausibly be asserted.

(a) *Displacement refraining.*[5] We might keep ourselves from twitching one
arm, for example, by holding it still with the other arm. There are obvious
bodily movements here.

(b) *Resistings.*[6] When outside forces threaten to move us, we sometimes
resist them by tensing the appropriate muscles. It is not much of a stretch
to include such muscle tensings as bodily movements.

(c) *Willed but indirectly caused bodily changes.*[7] When we know that having
a certain mental state can cause some bodily change, and we create such
a state in order to effect some further change in the world, there is a bodily
movement in the sense of a change in bodily state. In the Paul Revere
example, this is the change in the scalp picked up by the readiness potential reading device.

Accommodating all three of these as the bodily movements required by
the CTA is to carry out Donald Davidson's early suggestion that the CTA
must "interpret the idea of a bodily movement generously" (Davidson
1980, 49). But the CTA theorist must be careful lest this kind of generosity
give away the theory. Particularly in the third kind of case, one cannot
allow any bodily changes caused by mental states to qualify as actions. An
amputee with phantom limb experience may try to move his phantom
limb, and this may cause a facial tic, yet the tic is no action of his; we thus
need to exclude cases where the bodily change is not adopted by the
subject as the means to causing some further effect in the world.[8] If the
patriot in the Old North Church does not know that his trying to move
will cause changes in his scalp (and that these will set off the brain processes changing his scalp's readiness potential and thereby light the desired
light), setting off the light is no act of his; for he did not intend those
bodily changes, nor did he intend to produce some effect in the world by
those changes.

Nonetheless, as so qualified, these first two kinds of counterexamples
are easily dealt with. There are bodily movements in such cases, so long
as one is generous in one's interpretation of "bodily movements."

A third sort of counterexample is not so easily dealt with. This is the example of mental acts. As Tony Duff has recently observed, "we . . . distinguish within the realm of thought those kinds of thought in which we are actively purposeful from those in which we are passive" (Duff 2004, 81). A memory, for example, can just come to us, or it can be retrieved by conscious effort because it is needed for some purpose. The objection, then, juxtaposes two facts: Mental acts like retrieving a memory are actions too, and yet they involve no movement of the body.

Davidson was inclined to extend his generous interpretation of bodily movements to include mental action. As he said, "the generosity must be openhanded enough to encompass such 'movements' as standing fast, and mental acts like deciding and computing" (Davidson 1980, 49). Yet I have never seen how the CTA theorists can be this generous and still retain any content to the thesis (a part of the CTA) that "mere movements of the body . . . are all the actions there are" (ibid., 59).

One might say that mental actions like computing or deciding do cause changes in bodily states, namely, changes in the brain. Yet for some such changes, the relation is not that of causation but of identity: These mental acts *are* those brain states. And for those brain states not identical to the mental acts in question and that are caused by mental acts, these are not intended by the subject as means to effecting some further end, and thus do not satisfy the restriction I appended to the generosity of interpretation of the CTA.

Mental actions are not of interest to contemporary Anglo-American criminal law, for the law famously does not "punish for thoughts alone."[9] Mental actions are also not of central concern to morality, for one's obligations are not to cause certain states of affairs in the real world. We have few (if any) obligations not to think of (wish for, hope for, etc.) such states of affairs.[10] Still, legal systems and moral theories that do not respect these limitations are not unknown to us. And in any case, the CTA is a descriptive thesis: The claim is that action as such—not just responsibility-enhancing action—essentially involves bodily movements.

The existence of mental actions shows that there is a kind of human agency that exists that does not involve bodily movements. Such agency can be exercised without there being an intended causing of any bodily changes, as when one engages in an act of imagination or computation for the sheer pleasure of doing so. One can of course simply stipulate that we are not very often interested—morally, legally, or otherwise—in such flights of fancy or other instances of such agency. Yet a fourth class of counterexamples shows us that we are often interested in precisely this form of agency, and it is thus to those kinds of examples to which I now turn.

The fourth species of counterexamples (to the CTA's bodily movement thesis) is that of omission. Consider some of Tony Duff's examples: (1) "I can . . . insult someone . . . by not rising from my chair when she enters the room, if politeness or deference requires me to rise; or by not acknowledging an acquaintance when she greets me on the street" (Duff 2004, 81). (2) I can breach a promise by not showing up when promised (ibid.). (3) In the right circumstances I can "vote for a motion by not raising my hand" (ibid.). Duff concludes of these examples both that they are instances of omitting where no bodily movement takes place, and that these are actions the various persons performed. Duff concludes of such cases that "I do something without moving, or by not moving." Duff calls these "commissions by omission" (ibid., 82).

Duff unfortunately equates acting with his idea of doing something, actions with things done. This is an identification to be resisted. Resisting it allows one to say truthfully that there are no *actions* to be found in such cases—in which case, of course, they are not counterexamples to the causal theory of *action*. What is more accurate to say about such cases is this: Sometimes we can insult someone, break a promise, or vote, precisely by *not* acting. Adopting Jennifer Hornsby's (2004) characterization of such cases, in all of these we do something intentionally and yet we perform no action.

My earlier conclusions about omissions are thus secure. One can concede that there are no causally relevant bodily movements in cases of omissions, but since such omissions are not actions they are not counterexamples to the CTA. Yet a critic of the CTA is entitled to reply that the subject of the CTA—actions—loses interest if so construed; rather, the reply continues, the (explanatorily and morally) interesting category is the larger notion of agency illustrated in intentional omissions and in mental actions, captured (along with actions) under the general rubric of "things done."

Conceptual disagreements about how best to carve up the world can rarely be conclusively resolved. There is something to be said for lumping willed omissions, mental actions, and actions together under some general rubric such as "things done," for these items do all express some kind of human agency. Yet cutting the other way are two considerations, one moral and the other metaphysical. Morally, there is an important distinction most of us recognize between the often stringent negative duties of morality, on the one hand, and our less stringent positive duties (plus nonobligatory acts of super- or suberogation), on the other.[11] We have a stringent moral duty not to kill strangers, for example, but only a much less stringent (or nonexistent, depending on the circumstances) duty to prevent their death. A distinction between things done/things not done does not recommend itself as serving to mark these moral differences. For all there would be in the "things not done" category would be noninten-tional omissions; intentional omissions would be on the "things done" side of the conceptual divide, despite these being breaches of less stringent positive duties (if breaches of obligation at all). We need a distinction that tracks the positive/negative duty distinction in morality, which the act/ omission does well and which the things done/things not done distinction does poorly.

Second, there is an important metaphysical distinction between items that can serve as the relata of singular causal relations and items that cannot. Willed bodily movements that are human actions (or on some views of relata,[12] the states of affairs constituted by such actions having a certain property) can serve as such relata; the absence of such actions (i.e., omissions) cannot. The cause/failure to prevent line is not happily marked by the things done/things not done line, for omissions are failures to prevent, no matter whether intentional, negligent, or merely nonnegli-gently inadvertent. Some of the items in the things done category can thus stand in singular causal relations, but others (viz., intentional omissions) cannot.

We thus have two good reasons to prefer an act/omission line to the broader conception of agency implicit in the idea of things done. And by the narrower notion of agency contained in the concept of a human action, omissions and mental acts remain on the nonactional side of the distinction. They thus are not counterexamples to the most desirable concept of human action, that of a willed bodily movement.

4   Are Mental States Eligible to Be Relata in a Causal Relationship with Bodily Movements?

I turn now to the second of the theses constitutive of the CTA. This is the thesis that it is mental states like intention that are the distinctive source of human agency and action. It might well be, though, that the least troublesome subthesis of the CTA is the mental-causation thesis. For the dominant tradition, denying that mental states like intention are the right sort of things to be causes of physical events like bodily movements is the metaphysically dualist tradition; yet non-interactionist-dualist theories of mind are implausible on their face in these denials.

More plausible are recent critiques like that of Helen Steward (1997). Steward attacks the CTA by denying that there are particular mental states that can stand in the requisite causal relation. Steward concedes that facts about persons, such as the fact that a person intends to move his finger, can have "causal relevance" to the fact that his finger moved. But "causal relevance" for Steward is a counterfactual notion, not to be confused with actual causation between particulars. What the CTA holds to be causal relations between particular mental states and particular bodily movements, Steward thinks to be only a counterfactual relation between facts about persons and facts about the movements of their bodies.

Steward joins a lengthening list of metaphysicians who distinguish relations of counterfactual dependence from true causal relations between particulars.[13] She also joins a well-known list of those who take facts to be the relata of some cause-related relation such as her "causal relevance."[14] Peculiar to Steward, however, is her insistence that the facts that are the relata of her relation of causal relevance are just true propositions, not the states of affairs that make true propositions true.[15] Most of us would insist that for the relations of causation or of causal relevance to be in the world, one must at some point abandon propositions for their truthmakers. I (Moore 2009a, 341–348), David Armstrong (1997), and Kit Fine (1982) call such truthmakers "states of affairs"; Peter Menzies (1989) terms them "real situations"; Hugh Mellor (1995) coins the term "facta" for them. But whatever the label, Steward's proposed replacement for the CTA—in terms of counterfactual relations between facts—constitutes its own kind of "linguistic dualism"[16] because of its explicit severance from particulars that exist in the natural world.

However stands Steward's attempt to make sense of seeming causal talk about minds in noncausal terms, her actual critique of states of mind like intentions standing in genuine causal relations rests on her assumption that there is no such thing as an intention-token. Since there are no such things as intention-tokens (or belief-tokens, or desire-tokens), there are no particulars to stand in a genuine (singular) causal relation. So the CTA must be false.

Steward's reasons for skepticism about there being token states of intention are multiple and elusive. She argues that we don't need token states of mind that can figure in causal relations, because we (allegedly—see above) can make do with facts about persons that stand in the relation she calls "causal relevance." She argues that the identity of mental states with brain states depends on there being token mental states, but that such commitments commit us a priori to the view that folk psychology will be borne out by neurophysiology, an a priori commitment she finds "absurd" (Steward 1997, 134). She urges that representational states are (almost) always individuated by their contents and not by the subjects who hold them or the time at which they are held; so we can make do with talk of representational states in the abstract, with no commitment to there being tokens (ibid., 131–133).[17] She argues specifically against there being tropes (or "abstract particulars," or "property instances"), recognizing (correctly enough) that these are distinct from states of affairs (the having of a property by a particular at a time).

These and other arguments raise very broad issues of general ontology, of causal relata, and of mind–brain relations. We are not going to settle such large-scale issues here. My own long-term, naturalistic commitments, argued for elsewhere, are different. Unlike Steward (ibid., 38), I think that there is a right answer, in general, as to what causal relata are, and they do not include whole objects or persons; that there are token states of intention and belief; that these can stand in causal relationships; that such mental states are identical with certain brain states, even if it turns out there are no universal type identities here but only a disjunction of local ones; and that, accordingly, mental states of volition cause the bodily movements that are their objects (i.e., I'm committed to the CTA). Having argued for most of these basic commitments elsewhere,[18] I shall return to more manageable (because more specific) objections to the CTA.

5   Must Mental States of Intention or Volition Cause the Bodily Movements That Are Their Immediate Objects, for Those Movements to Be Human Actions?

The final worry about the CTA focuses on the causal relation between intentions and the bodily movements that are the objects of such intentions. Such worry can concede, *arguendo* at least, that human actions are (at least partially) identical to bodily movements and that there are token mental states of desire, intention, and belief. The worry here specifically is that human action cannot be analyzed in terms of causation.

There is a raft of old worries here that should be mentioned only if to put them aside. These were the worries of the post-Rylean ordinary language philosophers that preceded (and largely motivated) the consensus in contemporary philosophy about the CTA. These included the claims that: analytically, an event could not be a human action if it was caused because such actions had to be the product of free will to be actions at all;[19] reasons are the only appropriate explanation of human actions, and reason-giving explanations are not causal in nature;[20] reasons for action give justificatory warrants for the actions they are cited to explain, not causal explanations;[21] the relation of a reason to its action is logical and thus cannot be causal;[22] actions form the *objects* of reasons, not the *effects* of reasons;[23] actions are meaningful phenomena, not the colorless, dumb events required by mechanistic causal accounts;[24] actions are instances of rule-following behavior, whereas caused bodily movements are only instances of rule-governed behavior; and so on.[25]

The CTA found its present status as the standard philosophical theory by the rejection of these old, linguistically dualist arguments.[26] Yet even among those rejecting these arguments surfaced a new version of the worry about equating action with a *caused* something. This was the "deviant causal chain" worry.[27] This was the worry that "causation of a bodily movement by a mental state" was not a sufficient condition of action—because, for example, I could *desire* my old enemy's demise, *believe* that if I pushed my foot down on the accelerator of the car that was aimed at my old enemy, I would kill him, *intend* to push down my foot, and these beliefs, desires, and intentions could *cause* my foot hitting the accelerator—and yet, my foot moving could be no action of mine. It just slipped *because* I got so excited by my opportunity to satisfy my desire and my intention, for example.

The answer to the deviant causal chain worry that I and others have long accepted is a naturalistic one. It is that not just any causal relation (between intention and bodily movement) is meant by the CTA as a criterion of action. Rather, as Alvin Goldman put it long ago, beliefs/desires/intentions must cause bodily movements "in a certain characteristic way" for these movements to be actions (Goldman 1970, 61). Moreover, although "we are aware, intuitively, of a characteristic manner in which desires and beliefs flow into intentional acts" (ibid., 62), the nature of this "characteristic manner" is not fixed phenomenologically. Rather, the nature of the kind of causal relationship involved in the execution of intentions is a matter for science, specifically, the neuroscience of voluntary motor movement.

This answer may seem to offer comfort to the mysterians of human agency discussed earlier. This, because the answer concedes that not just any old kind of belief-desire-intention (BDI) causation fits human action; only the "agentist" kind of causation does that. This might be thought to be a return to a kind of primitivism about agency and agent-causation. Yet this would be a mistake. There is no second kind of causation being invoked here, nor is there a question-begging reference to irreducible agency. Rather, it is ordinary, garden-variety causation to which agency is to be reduced—only, it is that causal relation as it specifically exists between the supplementary motor area of the brain (and other regions) and the mechanisms that initiate muscle movements that fleshes out the characteristic relation distinctive of human agency. As Goldman said decades ago, this is a matter for scientific discovery, and over the intervening years we have discovered much about the neuroscience of voluntary motor movement.

Ironically, the very neuroscience that has fleshed out the answer to the old "deviant causal chain" worry has also spawned a different worry for the CTA. This worry goes like this. The neuroscience since the mid-1980s has discovered that well prior to a subject's conscious awareness of any intention to move his body, there exist certain brain events that are causally connected to the bodily movements in question.[28] The objection is that the intention to move the body thus comes too late to have the causal role the CTA says it has—the intention is a co-effect of the earlier brain events, along with the bodily movements, but itself without effect on those movements.

I and others have dealt with this worry at some length elsewhere,[29] and there is now an extensive literature. Briefly, and in summary of those longer discussions, there are two sorts of answers to neuroscience's epiphenomenal challenge to the CTA. One is to refuse to identify the intention to move one's finger with the conscious experience of that intention; rather, one identifies such intentions with the brain events that precede such conscious experience.[30] With such an identification, the CTA is secure: for then the intentions to move are not the *effects* of the earlier brain events that are evidenced by the readiness potential, but are identical with such brain events and thus share the causal role of such events in the production of voluntary bodily movements.

There are considerable variations of this kind of defense of the CTA in the literature,[31] but exploring them and choosing between them does not answer my present purposes. Rather, I want here to explore a second kind of reconciliation of responsibility with the facts of contemporary neuroscience. This answer concedes (*arguendo*, to be sure) that intentions do not occur prior to our conscious experience of them, and that therefore, given the evidence from neuroscience, such intentions are indeed epiphenomenal with the bodily movements that they putatively cause. Even so, the argument is that there is both human action and moral responsibility for it, despite the lack of causation of the relevant bodily movements by the intention to do them.

Revert to my earlier imagined patriot trying to alert his fellow rebels that the British are coming by land. Suppose he knows that, because of his wounds, he cannot move his finger. But suppose he also knows enough contemporary neuroscience to know that if he tries to move his finger, 300 milliseconds prior to such effort there will be activated in his brain processes that will cause a "readiness potential" to begin, detectable in his scalp over the supplementary motor area of his brain. Luckily for him, a patriot neuroscientist has hooked him up to a "mind–brain interface" machine, and this machine will read the slow negative shift in his readiness potential, which reading will cause the light to go off in the tower of the Old North Church in Boston. Knowing all this, the patriot tries to move his finger but once, the light goes off but once, Revere and Dawes begin their famous ride to alert the citizens of Lexington and Concord that the British are coming by land, and the rest is history. I take it that the patriot is morally responsible for alerting his fellow rebels and, if caught, is fairly hung for treason by the British. For he has performed the actions of alerting the rebels, sending the signal, lighting the light—even though his intent to do any of these things caused only an intention to try to move his fingers, and that intention, *ex hypothesi*, did not cause any of these things. Rather, the intention to try to move his finger was the co-effect of those brain events that also caused the change in scalp readings, which caused the light to be lit, which caused the rebels to be alerted.

These conclusions are troublesome for the CTA. I put aside two easy responses to them. One is to "outsmart"[32] the argument by denying that there would be either action or responsibility in such cases. As Gideon Yaffe (2009) put it in response to this argument against the CTA, "if I have to choose between the CTA and the conclusions (of action and responsibility) in such cases, I choose to adhere to the CTA." The intuition that the patriot performed the action of alerting the rebels, and that he is responsible for doing so, is too strong for this willing of belief, is it not?

The second response is to rely on the earlier identification of intention with the unconscious brain events measured by the shift in readiness potential. Then in the actual world we live in—as opposed to a merely possible world incompatible with the laws of this world—there are no stories like the one I just told. In the actual world, the imagined patriot would indeed perform the action of alerting the rebels, but he would do so in virtue of his intentions (to alert, to light, to try to move) causing the bodily change that caused the rebels to be alerted. In the actual world, the world in which we live, there is no epiphenomenal problem.

I by and large eschew this response because it is insufficiently ambitious for the CTA. The CTA could not be an *analysis* of human action, on this response, nor could the CTA be giving the essential properties of actions.[33] So I prefer a third response, which is to amend the CTA. What is essential to human actions is that the bodily movements that in part constitute them be the means by which some agent chooses to make changes in the world. Almost always the means–end relationship will be a causal one: usually the states we choose as our means to bring about some state that is our end will be a cause of that end-state. But not always, and not necessarily. If the way I know how to achieve some end-state is by bringing about a means-state that succeeds in time my end-state, the relationship cannot be causal. But I nonetheless do the one *by* doing the other. Two time-honored examples: I may get a square hit on a golf ball *by* getting a good follow-through on the swing; similarly, I may move certain of my muscles *by* moving my arm or leg. In each case what I know how to do—get a good follow-through, move my limb—will involve an earlier state, which is what I am interested in achieving. I may not be able to achieve this earlier state directly, but I can achieve it indirectly, because the doing of what I know how to do will take place only if this earlier state also has taken place—in which case I have performed an action even though my BDI states didn't cause it.

The upshot is that we should amend the CTA with respect to causation (just as we amended it with respect to bodily movements to include any physical changes in the body, whenever those changes were adopted as means to some further end). Epiphenomenal relations between intentions and movements will suffice to make such movements actions so long as such intentions are the means chosen to having such movements occur. In such cases there must still be some kinds of causal relationships, one between certain brain events and such intentions, and the other between those brain events and the bodily movements intended. These are what makes possible the use of the intentions as a means to having had such brain events occur. But there would not need to be, in the limited class of cases imagined, a causal relationship between the intentions and the bodily movements intended.

Notes

1. For criticism of my own version of the CTA, see the twelve articles collected in a symposium on my *Act and Crime* book (Moore 1993). See also Mathis 2003 and Duff 2004.

2. This is Richard Taylor's example; see Taylor 1965, 59.

3. As I (and many before me) have argued. See Moore 2009a 333–334.

4. See the discussion of these in Farahany 2009.

5. See Moore 1993, 87–88. The concept is Bruce Vermazen's; see Vermazen 1985.

6. See Moore 1993, 88.

7. See Moore 1993, 106–108, 263–267.

8. See Moore 1993, 106–108.

9. See the discussion in Moore 1993, 17–19.

10. Morality is not indifferent to how we feel and think, however; the virtues in part concern themselves with such matters. See Williams 1973.

11. See Kamm 1994.

12. See Moore 2009a, chap. 15.

13. See, e.g., Moore 2009a; Dowe 2000; and Hall 2004.

14. See, e.g., Mackie 1974; Mellor 1995; and Bennett 1988.

15. "A fact exists, in my usage, when any proposition is true—there is no more than this to the existence of facts" (Steward 1997, 104).

16. The apt phrase used to describe ordinary language philosophy's attempt to preserve the specialness of the mental without committing to metaphysical dualism. See Landesman 1965.

17. One place Steward might have looked for a commitment to there being intention-tokens is in the law. In contract law, for example, there is no contract unless the contracting parties have "the same intention," i.e., two intention-tokens having the same content but held by different persons. In criminal law, to take another example, when we blame an accused for intentionally hitting one or more persons that he in fact did hit but did so while intending to hit someone else (the "transferred intent doctrine"), we count the intention-tokens held by the accused to see when they are "exhausted" such that no more can be transferred.

18. On functionalism, see Moore 1988; on causal relata, see Moore 2009a, chapters 14–15; on intentions specifically, see Moore 1993, chapter 6, , 1997, and 2010.

19. See, e.g., Moya 1990.

20. See, e.g., Peters 1958.

21. See, e.g., Louch 1966.

22. See, e.g., Melden 1961.

23. See, e.g., Anscombe 1963.

24. See, e.g., Peters 1958.

25. See, e.g., Winch 1958.

26. Most notably in Davidson 1963.

27. Chisholm 1964.

28. This version of the much older epiphenomenal worry surfaced initially in the work of Benjamin Libet. See, Libet et al. 1983 and Libet 1985. Libet's work, and his skeptical conclusions from it, have been carried on by Haggard and Elmer 1999, Wegner 2002, and most recently, Haynes et al. 2007, and Soon et al. 2008.

29. See Moore 2006, forthcoming; and Mele 2006, 2009. There is an extensive early symposium on Libet in 1985 *Behavioral and Brain Sciences* 8 (1985).

30. My main answer is in Moore forthcoming.

31. Mele (2003), for example, identifies these brain events with *urges* to move rather than intentions.

32. The verb defined (out of Jack Smart's name) in Dennett and Lambert 1978.

33. An example of the limited ambitions of this kind of claim is provided by the theory of causation advanced in Dowe 2000.

3 The Standard Story of Action: An Exchange (1)

Michael Smith

Suppose an agent acts in some way. What makes it the case that he acted, as distinct from his having been involved in some mere happening or other? What makes him an agent, rather than a patient? According to the standard story of action that gets told by philosophers, the answer lies in the causal etiology of what happened (Hume 1777/1975; Hempel 1961; Davidson 1963).

We begin by identifying some putative action that the agent performed by tracing its effects back to some bodily movement. This bodily movement has to be one that the agent knows how to perform, and it further has to be the case that his knowledge how to perform it isn't explained by his knowledge how to do something else: in other words, it must be one that could be a basic action (Danto 1963; Davidson 1971). We then establish whether the agent acted by seeing whether this bodily movement was caused and rationalized in the right kind of way by some desire the agent had that things be a certain way and a belief he had that something he can just do, namely, move his body in the relevant way, has some suitable chance of making things the way he desired them to be. If so, then that bodily movement is an action; if not, then it is not.

It is easy to imagine someone objecting to this standard story right from the outset: "If the standard story of action says that I act only if I move my body, then it entails that there are no actions like those performed by children who stand absolutely motionless when given the direction to do so in a game of Freeze, or actions like sitting still in a chair or lying on a bed. In these and a host of similar cases we plainly act, but we do so without moving our bodies." Despite its rhetorical force, however, this objection rests on an uncharitable interpretation of what the standard view has in mind when it talks about bodily movements.

When a defender of the standard view says that actions are bodily movements, this has to be interpreted so that any orientation of the body counts as a bodily movement. Think of sitting in a chair. Sometimes the orientation of your body when you sit in a chair is under your control. Even if you're sitting still, your doing what you're doing is sustained by some desire you have and the belief that you can get what you desire by simply sitting still. It is this feature of the orientation of your body—the fact that it is under your control in the sense of being sensitive to what you desire and believe—that the standard story says makes it an action, whether or not you happen to be actually moving. Sometimes, however, when you're sitting perfectly still the orientation of your body isn't under your control. This is the case when (say) you're sitting in a chair but you're fast asleep. You're sitting perfectly still, but you're not acting. As I understand it, the standard story offers an account of what this difference consists in. In the former case, the orientation of your body is sensitive to what you desire and believe, whereas in the latter it isn't. From here on I will therefore simply assume that any way in which an agent might orient his body counts as a bodily movement.

To see how all of this works in practice, consider a simple example. Suppose that John flicks a switch. What makes it the case that he acted? According to the standard story, we answer this question by first of all identifying what we are imagining to be an action, John's flicking the switch, with some relevant bodily movement of his by tracing back from the imagined action's effects. Let's suppose that the bodily movement we discover when we trace back is John's moving his finger in some way. If John's flicking the switch is to be an action then this bodily movement has to be one that John knows how to perform, and his knowledge how to perform it mustn't be explained by his knowledge how to do something else. It must be the sort of bodily movement that could be a basic action.

Note that this already provides us with grounds on which to disqualify certain doings from being actions. Imagine that John flicked the switch when he brushed against it with his finger, but that this in turn happened because he was hit by a truck and, in the collision, his finger was bent backward. In that case, what we were imagining to be an action, John's flicking the switch, turns out to be no such thing. It is rather a mere happening in which John is involved, albeit not as an agent. For though we can trace the flick of the switch back to a bodily movement, the bodily movement in question—his finger's being bent backward—isn't a bodily movement of a kind that John knows how to perform without performing some other action. Bending a finger backward isn't something that could be a basic action of John's.

Cases like this underscore how very loose the connection is between doings and actions. For though it would be perfectly acceptable to describe John as having done something in this case—he did flick the switch, after all—his doing that isn't an action. Moreover, even though John's finger did indeed bend backward, bending his finger backward isn't something that he did, and nor did his finger bend backward as a result of anything else he did. So, even though John did indeed flick the switch, he didn't act when he did that, and he didn't do it by doing anything else, either. When you dwell on it, it can seem puzzling that we are permitted to describe things in these terms. But I doubt that it is worth dwelling on for too long. Given how loose the connection is between doings and actions, not much in the way of philosophical illumination about action is going to be gained by attending to those occasions on which we do and don't describe people as doing things.

Let's return to our original example. Given that the bodily movement that John performs is one that he knows how to perform without performing some other action—his moving his finger, in our original example—the standard story tells us that we can determine whether it was an action by investigating its causal antecedents. Was that movement caused and rationalized by a desire John had that things be a certain way and a belief he had that his moving his finger had some suitable chance of making things the way he desired them to be? Did he (say) desire the illumination of the room and believe that he could illuminate the room by moving his finger against the switch? If so, did his desire and belief cause his finger movement in the right way? If so, then that finger movement is an action; if not, then we once again have to conclude that John was involved in a mere happening in which he wasn't an agent.

Standard though this story of action is, it is not universally accepted. Jennifer Hornsby, for example, has recently provided several arguments aimed at demonstrating the story's crucial flaws (Hornsby 2004). Defenders of the standard story should welcome such objections, as one of the best ways they have available to them to demonstrate the plausibility of their view is to work through and respond to objections. In what follows I will consider four of the objections Hornsby puts forward. To anticipate, three of her four objections seem to me to be simply misplaced. The fourth objection is more worrying, but it turns out that it isn't so much an objection to the standard story itself as an expression of dissatisfaction with a certain way of developing that story. Once the dust settles, the standard story of action thus seems to me to remain pretty much intact, notwithstanding Hornsby's four objections.

1   First Objection: Actions and Omissions

Hornsby's first objection is that there is a mismatch between a central
concern of the standard story, which is to explain agency quite generally,
and the focus of the standard story on action. This is because, as she puts
it,

> someone can do something intentionally without there being any action that is
> their doing that thing. Consider A who decides she shouldn't take a chocolate, and
> refrains from moving her arm towards the box; or B who doesn't want to be dis-
> turbed by answering calls, and lets the telephone carry on ringing; or C who, being
> irritated by someone, pays that person no attention. Imagining that each of these
> things is intentionally done ensures that we have examples of agency. . . . But since
> in these cases, A, B and C don't move their bodies, we have examples which the
> standard story doesn't speak to. (Hornsby 2004, 5)

But is Hornsby right that the standard story does not speak to what
happens in these cases?

Hornsby is surely right that we ordinarily distinguish between actions
and omissions. The question, however, is whether the standard story of
action is intended to be a story about actions, in the sense of "action" in
which actions are distinct from omissions. Since I agree with her that the
standard story aims to explain agency quite generally, I doubt that this is
so. It seems to me much more plausible to suppose that it is intended to
be a story about actions in a quite general sense in which the distinction
between actions and omissions is invisible. From here on I will assume that
this is so. It might be thought that this just makes Hornsby's criticism even
more acute. For we have already seen that the standard story identifies
actions with bodily movements, so isn't it going to be impossible for it to
be a story about the agency involved in omissions, given that omissions
involve failures of bodily movement? I do not think so.

Focus on the case of A, who decides that she shouldn't take a chocolate
and so refrains from moving her arm toward the chocolate box. Is it true
that A doesn't move her body? Put like that, the question is likely to
mislead. When A refrains from moving her arm toward the chocolate box,
there is no bodily movement of that kind: she does not move her arm
toward the chocolate box. But it hardly follows from the fact that there is
no bodily movement of that kind that A doesn't move her body at all.
Remember what was said earlier. The standard story tells us that whenever
an agent acts, her action can be identified with some bodily movement or
other, a bodily movement that she knows how to perform, where her
knowledge how to perform that bodily movement is not explained by her

knowledge how to do something else. The question is whether these conditions are met in the case of the agent who refrains from moving her arm toward the chocolate box. The mere fact that a certain sort of bodily movement isn't performed leaves that question unanswered.

When A refrains from moving her arm toward the chocolate box, she clearly does exercise control over the way her body moves, because she makes sure that it doesn't move toward the chocolate box. Moreover, she has no alternative but to do that in one of the ways available to her. Perhaps she keeps her arm at her side, or she raises her arm in the air to wave to a friend, or . . . and here follows a list of every possible way that she knows how to control the location of her arm that was available to her at the time she refrained from moving her arm toward the chocolate box, except of course for those movements that result in her arm's being near the chocolate box. The reason she has no alternative but to refrain from moving her arm in one of these ways is, moreover, obvious. For the only way that A can keep her arm from moving toward the chocolate box is by ensuring that it is somewhere else. Applying the tracing back idea, we can therefore identify A's refraining from moving her arm to the chocolate box with whatever it was that she did with her body to ensure that it was somewhere else.

The upshot is that when A refrains from moving her arm toward the chocolate box, even though she does not perform that bodily movement, she has no alternative but to refrain from doing so by moving her body in some other way. The standard story thus applies to the case of omissions after all. Hornsby is just wrong to suppose that there is a mismatch between the standard story's concern with agency quite generally and its concern with action.

2 Second Objection: The Causal Account of Agency

Hornsby's second objection targets the causal account of agency itself:

One may wonder . . . why casual claims like (SS) [Her desire . . . caused an event which was her bodily movement], which are part of the standard story, should ever have been made. For even where there is an event of the agent's doing something, its occurrence is surely not what gets explained. An action-explanation tells one about the agent: one learns something about her that makes it understandable that she should have done what she did. We don't want to know (for example) why there was an event of X's offering aspirins to Y, nor why there was the actual event of X's offering aspirins to Y that there was. What we want to know is why X did the thing she did—offer aspirins to Y, or whatever. When we are told that she did it because she wanted to help in relieving Y's headache, we learn what we wanted to know. (Hornsby 2004, 8)

Hornsby's objection seems to be that the standard story is an answer to a question that never arises when we seek an action-explanation. It is an answer to a question about the occurrence of an event, whereas an action-explanation is never the answer to such a question.

But our requests for an explanation of why someone did something plainly are sometimes requests for the cause of her doing that thing, where her doing of that thing is conceived of as the occurrence of some event, as should be clear from the earlier discussion of the two explanations we might give of someone's sitting in a chair. Let's, however, consider a different example, one that I'm sure will strike a familiar chord with many, just to drive the point home. When we lie in bed at night, I often feel my wife kick me. There are typically three possible explanations: she's asked me to do something that I haven't yet done, so she's reminding me to do it; I'm snoring and she wants me to stop; or she's just fallen asleep and she has kicked me as a result of some sort of bodily spasm. When I feel her kick me, I ask myself why she did what she did. But am I seeking an action-explanation?

The answer is that, in the first instance at any rate, I am asking a question that is neutral with respect to whether or not what my wife did is an action, and here it is irresistible to use the language of actions and events. For though there certainly was an event of my wife's kicking me, what I want to know is whether that event was an action. This is, moreover, a question to which the standard story supplies an answer. It tells us that whether or not what my wife did was an action depends on what the cause was of her doing what she did. She kicked me, but if she was asleep and the cause of her doing what she did was a bodily spasm, then there is no action, merely an event. However, if what prompted her doing what she did was some desire she had, then the event in question is an action. The reason we make claims like (SS) is thus because they allow us to distinguish between these two cases, cases in which my wife's kicking me was an action and cases in which it was not.

Assuming that my wife's kicking me was an action, I then want to know which of the things she typically wants me to do explains why she kicked me on this occasion. Hornsby is surely right that in answering this question I am seeking information about my wife. But that should not now seem inconsistent with the standard story's suggestion that the answer will also tell me about the causal etiology of my wife's doing what she did. For the answer will settle what it was that prompted her doing what she did among a narrower range of options. Was it her desire to remind me of something, or was it her desire to stop my snoring? Once again, we seem to be assuming that claims like (SS) are true.

3 Third Objection: The Irrelevance of History

Hornsby's third objection is that it is a mistake to suppose, as those who accept the standard story must, that the fact that an agent acted could be constituted by facts about the states and events that figure in the causal history of an action:

Bratman and Smith, when they raised questions about what it is for an agent of a certain sort to be at work, turned these into questions about what sort of psychological cause is in operation. Like others who tell the standard story, they suppose that citing states and events that cause a bodily movement carries the explanatory force that might have been carried by mentioning the agent. But unless there is an agent, who causes whatever it is that her action does, questions about action-explanation do not even arise. An agent's place in the story is apparent even before anyone enquires into the history of the occasion. (Hornsby 2004, 19)

But what we just said in response to the third objection shows why Hornsby is wrong to suppose that this is so.

Consider again my wife's kicking me. Her place in this story as doer is of course apparent before we inquire into the history of the occasion. But this doesn't suffice to secure her place in the story as the agent of anything because, depending on how the story gets filled out, what she did may or may not be an action. Moreover, the crucial information that fixes whether or not what my wife did is an action is historical information. What prompted her kicking me? This is a question about causation. If she was asleep and her kicking me was caused by a bodily spasm, then she wasn't the agent of anything: she did something, but she didn't act. But if her kicking me was prompted not by some bodily spasm, but by a suitable desire and belief, then she may well have been an agent. We simply cannot ignore the history of what an agent did in determining whether she was an agent. Her status as an agent is constituted by historical facts.

4 Fourth Objection: Agency as the Exercise of Capacities

Hornsby's fourth objection is that a story about the causal history of an action that mentions only states and events leaves out the crucial causal factor:

[W]hen an account of a causal transaction in the case of agency is given in the claim that a person's believing something and a person's desiring something causes that person's doing something, it is assumed that the whole of the causal story is told in an action-explanation. The fact that the person exercised a capacity to bring something about is then suppressed. It is forgotten that the agent's causal part is taken for granted as soon as she is said to have done something. The species of causality that belongs with the relevant idea of a person's exercising her capacities is concealed. (Hornsby 2004, 22)

Hornsby begins with the charge that the standard story is incomplete, but then ends with the charge that when you add to the standard story what needs to be added to it to make it complete, you discover that the causality required to make sense of agency—the agent's exercise of her capacity to do things—is different from anything that's on offer in the standard story.

Let's begin with the charge of incompleteness. As I understand it, the standard story of action is offered as an account of necessary conditions for agency, not an account of necessary and sufficient conditions. Indeed, it is well known that defenders of the standard story have a very difficult time of it when they attempt to say not just what's necessary, but also what is sufficient for agency (Davidson 1973; Peacocke 1979a,b; Sehon 2005). The following example is typical of those that give rise to the problem. Imagine a piano player who wants to appear extremely nervous when he plays the piano and who believes that he can do so by hitting a C# when he should hit a C at a certain point in a performance. However, when he gets to that part of the performance, the fact that he has that desire and belief so unnerves him that he is overcome and involuntarily hits a C#. In this case the piano player has a suitable desire and belief, and these do indeed cause his hitting a C#, but his doing so is not an action. The piano player is a patient, not an agent.

Defenders of the standard story who wish to provide necessary and sufficient conditions for agency thus need to rule out the possibility of such internal wayward causal chains, and this turns out to be no easy task. But of course, defenders of the standard story aren't obliged to provide necessary and sufficient conditions for agency. They can rest content with the more modest project of providing necessary conditions—or anyway, they can do so provided those necessary conditions illuminate what it is to be an agent. When the standard story is interpreted in this more modest way, the charge of incompleteness as such just doesn't seem to be an objection.

So what is Hornsby's objection? Her view seems to be that, if we are to have any illumination of what it is to be an agent, we have to add to the standard story, so understood, the idea that agents who act exercise their capacity to do things, an idea that cannot be made sense of in the standard story's own terms. There is, however, a certain irony in her offering this as an objection to the standard story, because defenders of the story disagree among themselves about the need to add an agent's exercise of her rational capacities as a distinct causal factor in an action explanation. Hempel thought it is absolutely crucial that we mention the agent's exercise of her capacities; Davidson thought that Hempel was wrong and that it is completely unnecessary (Hempel 1961; Davidson 1976). We must therefore ask which of these two views is correct, and, if the correct view is Hempel's, we must ask whether we can make sense of the idea of an agent's exercise of her capacities within the resources available to a defender of the standard story.

In this connection, it is instructive to consider how defenders of the standard story attempt to rule out internal wayward causal chains. What do they themselves think they need to add to it in order to provide a more complete account of agency (note that they still needn't think that it is sufficient)? Davidson was pessimistic that internal wayward causal chains could be ruled out in anything other than a completely uninformative way. The best that we could say to rule them out, he thought, was that the attitudes in question must cause actions in the right way (Davidson 1973). If this were the best we could say, then I would have sympathy with the view that the standard story doesn't shed too much illumination on what it is to be an agent. For what Davidson thinks of as the right kind of causation is presumably simply whatever it takes to underwrite agency.

On the other hand, others think it is clear what is required. They think that the problem in cases of internal wayward causal chains is that the match between what the agent does and the content of her desires and beliefs is entirely fluky. It is, for example, entirely fluky that the piano player wanted to hit just the note on the piano that his nerves subsequently caused him to hit. For a doing to be an action, they suggest, what the agent does must be differentially sensitive to the contents of his desires and beliefs (Peacocke 1979). The movement of an agent's body is an action only if, in addition to having been caused by a suitable belief-desire pair, if the agent had had a range of desires and beliefs that differed ever so slightly in their content from those he actually has, he would still have acted appropriately.

In order to see how this differential sensitivity condition is supposed to rule out internal wayward causal chains, consider once again the example of the piano player. Suppose he had desired to play the piano as if nervously and believed that he could do so by hitting a B at a certain point in the performance, instead of a C. His actually hitting a C# is an action only if, in this counterfactual scenario, he would have hit a B at that point in the performance. Or suppose that he had desired to play the piano as if nervously and believed that he could do so by maintaining a certain rigidity as he hit the C. His actually hitting a C# is an action only if, in this counterfactual scenario, he would have maintained a certain rigidity while hitting the C. And so we could go on. This further condition of nonflukiness, understood in terms of differential sensitivity, is plainly violated in cases of internal wayward causal chains. For even if the actor had had such ever so slightly different desires and beliefs, his nerves would still have caused him to hit a C#.

But now consider the differential sensitivity requirement itself. What does it guarantee? It guarantees that when an agent acts intentionally, he doesn't just try to realize the desires he actually has, given the means–end beliefs he actually has, but would have tried to realize his desires, given his means–end beliefs, in a range of nearby possible worlds in which he had desires and means–end beliefs with ever so slightly different contents. The requirement thus seems to guarantee nothing less than that someone who acts intentionally does indeed have and exercise the capacity to be instrumentally rational in at least a local domain (Smith forthcoming). The possession and exercise of this capacity is, after all, exactly what's required to underwrite the truth of these counterfactuals.

This casts Hornsby's fourth objection to the standard story in a rather different light. Remember, Hornsby suggests that if we are to have an account of agency at all, we have to add to the standard story the idea that agents who act exercise their capacity to do things, an idea that cannot be made sense of in the standard story's own terms. It turns out that there is a grain of truth in this. For in order to solve the problem of internal wayward causal chains, the modest version of the standard story needs to be supplemented with the differential sensitivity condition, a condition that, when met, guarantees that those who act possess and exercise the capacity to be instrumentally rational in a local domain. Hornsby is thus right that those who act must possess and exercise this capacity, but she is wrong that we are unable to make sense of this within the resources available to a defender of the standard story. For the differential sensitivity condition simply requires a modally rich pattern of regular causation by desire and belief (see also Smith 2003a).

Of course, Hornsby might think that the account of what it is to possess and exercise the capacity for instrumental rationality that we glean from the differential sensitivity condition is mistaken. Or she might think that something over and above the possession and exercise of this sort of capacity is required to be an agent. But if that is her view, she will need to tell us what is mistaken about it, or what else is required. Moreover, she will need to explain why that capacity too can't be made sense of with resources available to a defender of the standard story. I myself am pessimistic about her ability to do this.

Conclusion

Defenders of the standard story should welcome objections, as one of the best ways they have available to them to demonstrate the plausibility of their view is to work through and respond to such misgivings as people have. I have considered four such objections put forward by Jennifer Hornsby.

Three of Hornsby's objections seem to me to be simply misplaced. Contrary to what she suggests, the standard story of action is a fully general story of agency, as it applies equally to actions and omissions; the standard story has a principled reason for talking about events in the context of action-explanation, namely, that we can always raise the question whether something that we do is an action or a mere event; and the standard story therefore has a principled reason for inquiring into the history of our doings, namely, that the status of our doings as actions or mere events turns on facts about their causal history.

Hornsby's fourth objection—that the standard story needs to be enriched with an account of an agent's exercising her capacity to do things—turns out to be not so much an objection to the standard story itself as an expression of dissatisfaction with a modest telling of that story. Some defenders of the standard story, such as Hempel, agree with Hornsby that an agent's exercise of her rational capacities plays a crucial causal role in action. Moreover, that conclusion also seems to be forced on us when a defender of the standard story attempts to solve the vexing problem of internal wayward causal chains. Nothing about the standard story itself thus seems to prevent a defender from agreeing with Hornsby that an agent's exercise of her capacities plays a crucial role in an action explanation.

4 The Standard Story of Action: An Exchange (2)

Jennifer Hornsby

In this second part of this exchange, I respond to Michael Smith by saying why I think that no one should endorse the standard story of action in any of its versions. I hope to show that there is an alternative to it.

In the first part of the exchange, Smith replies to Hornsby 2004. My criticisms there were directed against philosophers (Smith among them) who tell us that deficiencies in the standard story of action are to be remedied by adding states of different sorts from beliefs and desires to the causes of bodily movements (ibid., 2).[1] I said that these philosophers fail to address the question whether their story contains the *causal* notions that belong in an account of human agency (23). Smith now says that I charged the standard story with incompleteness. This strikes me as misleading. True, I maintained that the causal role of *agents* goes missing in an *events*-based conception of the causal order (16). But I never suggested that the story stands in need of completion. I could hardly have suggested this, given that my criticisms were directed against the idea that a correct story could be got by adding to the standard story further conditions, beyond those that it standardly specifies, for a case of agency. Indeed I said that "supplements to the standard story . . . inherit its crucial flaw" (2). The standard story of action is "events-based," I said, and "events-based accounts introduce a conception of the causal order in which agents have no place" (3).

Smith grants me a "grain of truth." In explicating the causal role of agents, I said that in a case of human agency, a human being exercises a capacity to bring something about. And Smith thinks that I am "right that those who act must possess and exercise [such a] capacity." Where I go wrong, Smith says, is in thinking "that we are unable to make sense of this within the resources available to a defender of the standard story." In what follows I hope to show that the game is up for the standard story when it is allowed that a person's acting is a matter of her exercising a capacity she has as agent. I attempt this in section 3. Section 2 will be concerned with the approach to an account of human agency taken by Smith and fellow defenders of the standard story. If I can explain why it seems to me that Smith's understanding of his leading question "What makes it the case that [someone] acted?" is out of place, then I shall have succeeded in showing how one might think that the standard story should be abandoned, not "completed."

1 Responses to Replies to Two Objections

Smith discerns four different objections that I made to the standard story. I'll make brief responses to Smith's replies to the first two of these as a way of introducing the main business. (Sections 2 and 3 are in effect responses to his replies to the third and fourth objections.)

(1) When I said that the standard story fails to accommodate omissions of certain sorts, I was thinking of the story, as Smith thinks of it, as purporting to give an account of what it is for A to do something intentionally by saying what conditions *a movement of A's body* must satisfy if it is to be A's Φ-intentionally doing some particular thing. My point was that someone may do something intentionally although no movement of her body occurs. Now Smith tells us that the standard story makes use of a notion of *moving the body* according to which "any orientation of the body counts as a bodily movement," and "move the body" has application when someone *refrains from moving.* I am sympathetic to an idea of Smith's which is in play here—namely, that there can be an exercise of a piece of bodily agential know-how even when there is no overt movement. So I allow that there can be a rationale for a capacious notion of moving the body, a bit like Smith's. Still, it isn't clear that the know-how that is exercised by an agent who intentionally does something can *always* be brought within the scope of the *bodily,* or that an agent's doing what she does *always* belongs in the category of event. One of the examples I gave was of C, who deliberately paid someone no attention. Suppose that there was a period of an hour during which C paid no attention to X (it might be a period during which X was in the same room as C). Smith, it seems, will have to say that throughout the period, there was an exercise of a piece of bodily agential know-how affecting the way the agent's body was oriented.[2] That doesn't sound quite right to me.

However this may be, I had a particular reason for introducing examples in which an agent's intentionally doing something appears not to be a movement of her body. I wanted to show the impossibility of accommodating agency to the operation of causality as that is conceived by those who tell the standard story. I don't deny that a causal explanation is given when someone does something for a reason and the question why she did it says what she thought and/or wanted. My quarrel was with the idea that such an explanation can always be recorded as the obtaining of a causal relation between states and an event.

(2) My second objection then was to the *general* idea that explanations that reveal a reason why someone did something can be recast simply as causal accounts of why events occurred. I drew attention to the distinctive character of reasons-explanations and the nature of what they convey. I did so in order to weaken the impression, given by those who tell the standard story, that the constituents of reasons-explanations are just those of explanations of other sorts. Smith says that causal explanations of any sort speak to "the causal etiology" of what is explained. I can agree with that. My claim was that when one is told of an agent's reason, that which gets explained is not the occurrence of an event merely, but the fact of an agent's playing a certain causal role. In my own view, an agent's playing such a role should not be assimilated to an event of any old sort, and nor therefore should it be taken to be an event that has the sort of etiology that just any event has.

2   The Approach of Those Who Tell the Standard Story

2.1
On the standard approach, which gives rise to the standard story,[3] actions are taken to be events and treated then as having equal standing with anything else that belongs in the event-causal order, in which causation relates things in the category of events and states. On this approach, the task of a philosophical account of bodily agency is to uncover the conditions that bodily movements satisfy if and only if they are actions. Inasmuch as these conditions are thought to be a matter of how the movements are caused, "what makes it the case that" or "fixes" it that an event is "an action rather than a mere happening in which a person is involved" is treated as "historical information." I think that the standard approach is based in a false assumption. And I hope to make it clear why I think the standard story should be abandoned by locating that assumption now. (Smith points out that some who tell the standard story are content if they can carry out only a more modest task. I shall come to this. The present point is that I reject the assumption that governs the *approach*.)

When Smith says that "the crucial information that fixes whether or not [a bodily movement] is an action is historical information," he is objecting to something I had said. I had said that "unless there is an agent, who causes whatever it is that her action causes, questions about action-explanation do not even arise." What I intended to convey was that historical causal information cannot *fix* whether a movement is an action. When causal information can be given in an action explanation, it is then, as it were, already fixed that there is an action; whereas when a movement of someone's person's body is their involvement in some mere happening, the movement is then not so much as a candidate for an action-explanation, and nothing could fix that it was an action.

Smith's counter to this is his example of his wife's kicking him. The example is meant to show how historical information fixes things. According to Smith, a particular event of his wife's kicking him may, or may not, be an action, depending on its causal history. Smith is surely right in thinking that if he asks why she kicked him, not knowing whether her kick was an action or not, he remains neutral on the question of whether it was. But in order to see why this is not definitive in settling that an event may, or may not, be an action, one can consider a case where Smith assumes that his wife meant to kick him, and gets it wrong. So imagine that Smith asks "Why did you kick me?"—thinking that his wife's answer will give her reason. He expects her to say "I wanted to ——" or "In order to ——." Instead she says "Oh, I didn't mean to kick you: my kick must have been a result of some sort of bodily spasm." In this case, we may think that what Smith was apt to treat as a candidate for an action-explanation wasn't really such a candidate; Smith's mistake was to suppose that the event of kicking was of a different kind from what it was. (It was of the generic kind "bodily movement." But if it was actually not an action, then at least it was of some kind that he assumed it wasn't.) So although there can be an example of the sort Smith describes, in which he fails to know whether or not his wife meant to kick him, this can hardly show that the event about which he is then ignorant might itself equally well be an action or not be an action.[4] If it is not an action, then of course it fails to satisfy such conditions as actions do, and Smith may come to know that it was not an action by learning that such conditions weren't satisfied. But it can still be true that the event could not really satisfy such conditions—that nothing could make *it* an action. And it can also be true that if his wife had meant to kick him—had kicked him for a reason—then the kick that there would then have been could not *itself* have been the product of a spasm. If these things are indeed true, then actions and movements that aren't actions are of *fundamentally* different kinds.[5]

On the standard approach, it is assumed that actions and other bodily movements are of the same fundamental kind, differing from one another in their relational properties. Taking the standard approach, one thinks it possible to find in the event causal order a movement that might or might not be an action, and then, by making use of a notion of causation that relates things in the categories of event and state, to say how the movement differs, in respect of its relational properties, from other things in that order if it is an action. But if actions and other movements are of fundamentally different kinds, then an action in its nature is not an event about which it is genuinely an open question whether it is an action or a movement of some other sort. (Remember that ignorance can ensure that there *seems* to be an open question, even if, in the nature of things, one answer is actually ruled out.)

2.2

We can see now that one may find fault with the standard approach to action even if it leads only to the relatively unambitious account that Davidson gave. Davidson asked "What events in the life of a person reveal agency; what are his deeds and his doings in contrast to mere happenings in his history; what is the mark that distinguishes his action?" (1971/1980, 43). And it is no wonder that the standard story is widely credited to Davidson. He always thought that the key to understanding agency was to take actions to be events, caused by states and other events and states, and described in terms of states and further events that they in turn cause. Although Davidson despaired of giving a set of conditions sufficient for an event's revealing agency, he never doubted that some events are actions only because some of the bodily movements that belong in chains in the event-causal order have a causal history of a certain sort.[6]

What Davidson despaired of doing was solving "the problem of wayward causal chains" (see Smith's chapter in this volume for the details)—a problem that needs to be solved by someone who takes the standard approach and aspires to give sufficient conditions for an event's being an action. Smith for his part thinks that he has a solution to the problem. I shall come to this (section 3). But what I would draw attention to now is an aspect of Smith's own argument which might be thought to suggest that there really need be no problem here in need of a solution. When Smith speaks of the answer to the question of why his wife kicked him as *fixing* whether there was an action, he appears to take susceptibility to a certain sort of *explanation* to guarantee that a movement is an action. At this point in Smith's argument, the idea that there might be wayward causation of his wife's movement (that it might be caused by a belief and desire having the sort of contents that could but actually don't rationalize it) is not in the picture. At this point, Smith would seem to be content to allow that his wife's kicking him is an action if and only if she kicked him for a reason. But then Smith would seem to have helped himself to the idea that actions and action-explanations go hand in hand—that all and only actions are events the facts of whose occurrences can be explained by giving the agent's reasons.[7]

Of course, there can be no harm in helping oneself to this idea. Indeed when *action* is connected with a particular sort of *explanation*, one has an answer to Davidson's question "What is the mark of an action?" For the mark of a kind may be given simply by saying what is distinctive of its members. Thus one might ask, about animals, "Among those that are either stoats or weasels, what is the mark of a stoat?" An acceptable answer could be "Stoats have black tails." One can give this answer, without thinking that stoats might be weasels, or that any animal that is a stoat rather than a weasel is only such because of the blackness of its tail. In a rather similar way, a philosopher can ask, about events, "Among those that are either actions or mere movements, what is the mark of an action?" The answer may be: "Actions are susceptible to a certain sort of explanation." The answer tells of a respect in which actions are distinctive. But in giving this answer, one is not committed to thinking that actions might be movements of some other kind than actions, or that anything that is an action rather than a movement of some other kind is only such because it has certain sort of explanation.

The fact, then, is that one can give a mark of an action (in a sense just roughly indicated) without buying into the assumption of the standard approach. And that means that one can abandon the standard approach without abandoning the idea which seems to inform Smith's treatment of his example, and whose endorsement informs the standard story as it is told in any of its versions. The idea is that when and only when there is an action, an agent does something for a reason he or she has. This was Davidson's idea, and he stuck with it. When he said that a movement is caused by relevant attitudes *in the right way* if it is an action, what he needs to have meant by "caused in the right way" is this: being such that the fact of its occurrence can be causally explained by saying what the agent's reason was for making the movement.[8]

Smith for his part thinks that the standard story in Davidson's version "doesn't shed too much illumination on what it is to be an agent." One can agree with that, and think that further illumination can be shed—that there is more to be said. What we are now in a position to see is that one may have one or another of two very different reasons for thinking that there is more to be said. (A) One may tell the standard story, and think, as Smith does, that it fails of sufficiency because it lacks a specifiable necessary condition of a case of agency. (B) One may reject the standard approach, as I do, but not stop at giving the mark of actions, thinking that there is more to be said about the sorts of causal notions that are in play when there are actions. I suspect that Smith does not countenance alternative (B) because he cannot credit that someone might put the standard approach into question. (This would explain why he should have thought that I must have been charging the standard story with incompleteness when I claimed that something goes missing when it is told.)

3   Exercises of Capacities

Smith's alternative is (A). He wants to improve on Davidson's telling of the standard story: he thinks that the standard story will be complete, and more illuminating, if another ingredient is introduced into it. So I turn now to what Smith takes to be the missing ingredient: I come to agents' capacities.

It was because I spoke myself of agent's capacities as belonging in an account of agency that Smith found a grain of truth in what I said. He writes: "Nothing about the standard story itself . . . seems to prevent a defender from agreeing with Hornsby that an agent's exercise of her capacities plays a crucial role in an action-explanation." But I did not say that agents' exercises of capacities play a crucial role in action-*explanation*. I contested the assumption of the standard story that "the causal story is told in an action-explanation" (Hornsby 2004, 22), maintaining that there is more to a causal story of agency than action-explanations themselves can reveal (20). What I said was that when an agential capacity is exercised, an agent, rather than a state of an agent, plays a causal role; and that "our actions [should] be thought of as exercises of our capacities" (21). In my alternative story, the exercises of capacities have a crucial place because I hold that an agent's doing something that she intentionally does *is* her exercising a capacity she has as a rational agent.

Smith thinks that exercises of capacities, so far from being actions, are among their *causes*. It can seem that Smith and I have different conceptions of a capacity. Certainly I am suspicious of Smith's conception. Smith speaks of a movement "that A knows how to perform, where her knowledge how to perform it is not explained by her knowledge how to do something else." Well, I take it that when one has knowledge how to do something and suffers no relevant impediment, one has the capacity to do it. And a capacity is surely something general: even a simple capacity, such as the capacity to raise one's arm, is something whose exercise might be constituted by movements of various different, specific sorts. But any movement that an agent "performs" is a particular movement, of some utterly specific soft. The problem then is that possession of the capacity to raise one's arm doesn't seem to explain a movement in the way Smith supposes that it does. When knowledge how to raise one's arm belongs in an account of someone's having raised his arm ten inches on some occasion, the knowledge in question could explain his doing something else—raise his arm fourteen inches, as it might be.

However this may be, it is when Smith says that "an agent's exercise of her rational capacities is a distinct causal factor in an action-explanation" that I find I take exception. My own (and I think the ordinary) conception of a capacity of X is a sort of causal power of X, something, then, whose exercise consists in X's bringing something about. Thus, if you have the capacity to raise your arm for a reason, you are so equipped that you can bring it about that your arm is up when you have a reason to raise it. And when, on occasion, you exercise this capacity, you bring it about on that occasion that your arm is up. Your capacity to raise your arm provides for your playing the role of cause, and any exercise of the capacity on any occasion will be your raising your arm, will be your bringing it about that your arm is up. Your *possession* of the capacity is a condition of its exercise, and it might in some circumstances explain an actual exercise. But it is difficult to see how your *exercise* of the capacity to raise your arm could be a "distinct causal factor" in an explanation of your raising it.

It may be, however, that Smith and I disagree not so much about the nature of capacities and their relation to their exercises, as about the kinds of capacities that need to be brought into account. Smith may be concerned exclusively with capacities "to be instrumentally rational in a local domain," which capacities he thinks are sure to be present so long as the differential sensitivity condition is met (again see Smith's chapter for the details). But if we are allowed to think of the differential sensitivity condition as something that is met whenever an agent's doing something is explicable by reference to her reasons, then the condition would seem to be satisfied so long as the agent has rational control over what she is doing.

But then, once again, it would appear to be the sort of capacity whose exercise just *is* her acting intentionally.

Suppose that this is right. And suppose that Smith, persisting with the standard approach, says that the idea of *exercising* a capacity possessed by a rational agent belongs in the standard story. He will be taken round in an evident circle when he tells the story. For if *possession* of a rational capacity is required for there to be an action, then exercises of rational capacities will be the actions of rational beings. But then something's being an exercise of such a capacity will be matter of its being an action. Making use of the idea of such a capacity could not enable one to give a necessary condition that combines with the old standard story's other conditions to say what *else* is causally required for there to be an action.

I hope that this starts to explain why I should think that the game is up for the standard story when capacities are introduced. Just as actions and action-explanations go hand in hand, so it would seem that actions and exercises of certain capacities go hand in hand. An idea of an agential capacity, like the idea of a certain sort of explanation, is presupposed to the idea of an action. Being the exercise of a capacity cannot then be one among a set of conditions of a movement's being an action. It cannot "make" an event that might not have been an action into an action.

4 Summary and Unfinished Business

Those who take the standard approach in philosophy of action seek *conditions* of a movement's being an action. They think that it is proper to ask, about a movement that, according to them, may or may not be an action: "What makes *it* an action?" Being aware that actions are susceptible to a certain sort of explanation, and that this is causal explanation, they treat causation by rationalizing beliefs and desires as one condition of a movement's being an action. But then they face the problem of wayward causal chains. They react either by settling for speaking of such causation as occurring *in the right way* (as Davidson did), or by seeking a further condition of an event's being an action (as Smith does). What I have suggested is that if one disallows their assumption that the question "What *fixes* it that an event an action?" is in good order, then one will say that when there is an action, there is an event the fact of whose occurrence is explicable in a certain way and does not just so happen to be explicable in that way. Actions are not then thought of as movements that count as actions by virtue of having relational characteristics. Actions may be thought to involve intentions essentially.

The question "What makes it the case [or fixes it] that an event is some-one's acting and not her involvement in some mere happening?" has become very familiar. And the fact that it is possible to say what distinguishes actions from other events can help it to seem to be a perfectly good question. (We saw that there is a perfectly good question about what distinguishes actions, which makes use of one idea of a mark.) It can then become hard to believe that the question intended by those who tell the standard story is misguided. But it is not outlandish to suggest that philosophers have sometimes asked the wrong questions.

I'm aware that I have not done much more than quarrel with Smith's interpretation of Hornsby 2004. But my aim in this part of our exchange has been not so much to argue for an alternative to the standard story, as to demonstrate that there can be one. So I have done little here in the way of showing why one should accept an alternative. To persuade someone of an alternative of the sort I favor would require much more work. One needs to demonstrate the counterintuitive character of the conclusions reached if one follows Hume on the subject of causation. (That was a task I did attempt in Hornsby 2004.) One needs also to say something positive about the kind of causation by agents that is irreducible to causation found in the event causal order. Inasmuch as such causation may be causation by agents other than rational agents, one must also say something about what is distinctive of the capacities that rational beings possess. The fact that these tasks can be undertaken helps to show that even if one has no truck with the project set by those who take the standard approach, still one has plenty to do to try to cast light on the phenomenon of human agency.

Acknowledgments

I thank Naomi Goulder for her helpful comments on a draft of this chapter.

Notes

1. Otherwise unattributed page references are to Hornsby 2004. My objections there were directed specifically against philosophers who had said that the standard story needs to be supplemented if it is to include the agency of ethical beings. But I blamed its failure to include ethical agency on its failure to include human agents.

2. Smith might suggest that in the example of C, we find, as well as the bodily actions that the standard story purports to provide an account of, mental actions; and then that there can be intervals during the period when C pays no attention

to X at which even the orientation of C's body is not to the point. My response would be to say that although there may be a recognizable category of mental actions, I doubt that we can plausibly decompose intuitively physical actions into the mental and the bodily in the manner that such a suggestion would seem to require. Consider, say, drinking a cup of coffee, or speaking, which admit of pauses between bits of bodily activity.

3. I don't know who coined the term "standard *story*": perhaps it was David Velleman (who uses it in Velleman 1992). "Standard *approach*" is used in Anscombe 1989/2005 (a paper she wrote in 1974), and I want to mean by it what I think Anscombe meant. At any rate, I think it safe to assume that the standard story, as it is now commonly understood, is a product of the approach that Anscombe called standard (Anscombe 2005, 111), and which she thought was hopeless.

4. I realize that I could seem to have denied the possibility of such examples in Hornsby 2004. Following the sentence above which I've followed Smith in quoting, and whose force I am now attempting to explain, came another sentence, which Smith also quotes: "An agent's place in the story is apparent even before anyone enquires into the history of the occasion." This was careless. I should not have suggested that the agent's place must always be apparent, at least if what is apparent is known. Nevertheless, I take it that the agent's place very often *is* apparent—that very often someone is evidently doing *something* intentionally, even if one knows not exactly what—and then a request for explanation takes for granted what is then apparent.

5. This is the position of someone who endorses a so-called disjunctivism about bodily movements: see Hornsby 1997, and Haddock 2005. Haddock is the better source for present purposes, because he understands bodily movements to be (not effects of actions but) actions themselves; and this understanding is one that I now agree with Smith in endorsing (though didn't in Hornsby 2004). In Hornsby 1997, I distinguished epistemological and metaphysical senses of "could be a mere [i.e., nonactional] movement." Here I have taken "fix" to mean what Smith needs it to mean, and pointed out that one may be ignorant of something that actually is fixed. If "fix" has an epistemic sense, then my point is that something fixed metaphysically may not be fixed epistemically.

6. Davidson is the target of Anscombe's criticism of 'the standard approach' (see note 3 above). She says that Davidson "can do no more than postulate a 'right' [= nonwayward] causal connexion [between causes of actions and actions] in the happy security that none such can be found" (Anscombe 1989/2005, 110). Those who tell the standard story are apt to respond "Does Anscombe not know that Davidson had said that 'the request for an analysis of action goes unanswered,' so that he speaks of 'right' causal connections because he thinks it impossible to give sufficient conditions?" I think that this response to Anscombe fails to take account of the fact that in her view a question based on a false assumption is asked when

an analysis of action is requested (see further note 8). So I think that the critics of Anscombe who take the standard approach interpret her rather as Smith has interpreted me—as if I thought that the standard story were told in response to a good question.

7. I say "facts of whose occurrence can be explained" here because if I were to say simply "can be explained" it might give the impression that the *explanandum* of a reasons-explanation is an event—a false impression, but one that will be welcome to those who take the standard approach (see para. (2) in section 1 above). Still, at various points, I forsake accuracy in order to avoid prolixity, and sometimes speak of actions as being explicable in a certain way. Treat this as a sort of shorthand.

8. When Anscombe speaks of Davidson as able to "do no more than postulate a right [= nonwayward] causal connection" (see note 6 above), we might take her to be saying that insofar as Davidson has found a mark of agency (in the sense roughly explained in the text), the only kind of causal connection that could be present is that which is present when an event has a certain sort of explanation. Hence her saying "Something I do is not *made* into an intentional action by being caused by a belief and desire" (Anscombe 1989/2005, 111; my italics).

5 Skepticism about Natural Agency and the Causal Theory of Action

John Bishop

Action theorists often proceed with little or no motivational prolegomena, as if the question of what it is for something to count as an action is just *there*, most strikingly posed, perhaps, in Wittgenstein's terms: "What is left over if I subtract the fact that my arm goes up from the fact that I raise my arm?" (Wittgenstein 1972, 161).[1] Alfred Mele, for example, in the introduction to his edited Oxford Readings in Philosophy collection in the philosophy of action, begins with the twin questions (a) what are actions? and (b) what is involved in explaining actions? And he says that *"inquiring minds . . . would want to know* what actions are, what it is to act intentionally, what constitutes acting for a reason, whether proper explanations are causal explanations or explanations of some other kind, and how the psychological or mental items (states, events and processes) that are supposed to be explanatory of action are to be understood" (Mele 1997b, 1, my emphasis). Admittedly, Mele does remark that "one hopes that a full-blown philosophy of action will solve part of the mind–body problem and illuminate the issues of free will, moral responsibility, and practical rationality" (ibid.). So it is, of course, clear that inquiring into the nature of actions and action explanation *does* have wider motivation. In my view, however, it is helpful for action theorists to be more explicit about what their wider motivations are, and to keep their theorizing consciously in contact with wider philosophical goals. Debates about action can become unfocused unless they are consciously answerable to some specific motivation or motivations for philosophical interest in action.

1 The Problem of Natural Agency

One such motivation is concern with *the problem of natural agency*. Wittgenstein's question may indeed be a focal one: what is it for behavior to count as action, rather than just "mere" behavior? But this question already deploys a technical notion of action—a technical notion that has its source in our ethical perspective on ourselves. For we hold an agent morally responsible for a given outcome only if it came about or persisted *through that agent's own action.* Even if an agent's *behavior* contributed to a certain outcome, the agent would not be morally responsible for it unless the behavior involved or constituted the agent's own action.[2,3] Now, if our ethical perspective applies to the world (if agents really are sometimes morally responsible for outcomes) then actions must be a feature of the world. But how is it possible for actions in this sense to be part of the natural world as our natural scientific worldview conceives it? Actions either are or necessarily involve physical events—in particular, bodily movements—and those events are open to natural scientific explanation. So there is room for skepticism about how the very same outcome can both result from morally responsible agency and also be in principle explicable scientifically. In previous work, I put the problem of natural agency thus: "We seem committed to two perspectives on human behavior—the ethical and the natural—yet the two can be put in tension with one another—so seriously in tension, in fact, as to convince some philosophers either that the acting person is not part of the natural order open to scientific inquiry or that morally responsible natural agency is an illusion" (Bishop 1989, 15). One important motivation, then, for seeking to understand what it is for something to be an action is to seek to resolve the problem of natural agency. Does the concept of action that we need for our ethical perspective have features that require going beyond the confines of our prevailing natural scientific metaphysics, or may actions be wholly accommodated within a naturalist ontology?

I shall call the claim that actions *can* be fitted into a naturalist ontology *reconciliatory naturalism.* One way to defend reconciliatory naturalism is to advance a causal theory of action. I suspect that this is the only route to reconciliatory naturalism—but will here claim just that a certain sort of causal theory of action, if successful, overcomes skepticism about natural agency. To appreciate why a successful causal theory of action would achieve this, consider how best to state the nature of the tension between our ethical and natural scientific perspectives. That tension has often been expressed as an apparent incompatibility between free will and determinism—but the real problem is not really about determinism, as Gary Watson, for one, makes very clear:

We would lack free will in a deterministic world, incompatibilists think, because there we would not determine our own behaviour—we would lack *self*-determination. But the denial of determinism does not ensure, by itself, that *we* determine anything. So an incompatibilist who affirms freedom—conventionally called a *libertarian*—must say what more is needed besides the absence of causal determination to get "self-determination." The . . . skeptic . . . suspects that the freedom demanded by the [libertarian]—a "self-determination" that could not obtain in a deterministic world—obtains in no possible world. (Watson 1982, 9)

So the real problem is that actions are understood as essentially involving *agent-causation* (where I use that term simply to mean the determination of events or outcomes *by the agent* through the exercise of that agent's own control), yet this is a kind of substance-causation excluded by the fundamental ontology of the naturalist perspective on the world, whether it takes the world to be deterministic or, as is now more plausible, indeterministic.[4]

If a causal theory of action is correct, however, then this problem is resolved, because a causal theory of action (or, to name it more precisely, an *event*-causal theory of action) maintains that episodes of agent-causation can properly be understood *as constituted wholly by events and states of affairs within the natural causal order*, as the prevailing natural scientific metaphysics interprets it. For a causal theory of action (CTA) makes the positive ontological claim that actions consist in behavior caused by mental states and events that constitute the agent's *having his or her reasons* for performing behavior of that very kind. A CTA thus implies that *intentional* explanations (explanations in terms of an agent's reasons for acting), though they are to be given a realist interpretation,[5] do not involve irreducible ontological commitment to agent-causation, but only to event-causation of behavior by the agent's relevant mental states and events. If a CTA is true there can be no mystery about how actions belong to the natural causal order, provided—as I will here simply assume—there is no mystery about how mental states and events may do so.[6] But the CTA will have to be defended against skeptics of the kind Watson mentions, and this will require defeating the arguments of *agent-causationists* who insist that genuine actions must involve an *ontologically irreducible* special kind of causal relation where the cause is a substance, namely, the agent.

Before turning to consider the defense of a CTA, let me say something on the question of motivation. A successful CTA will resolve the problem of natural agency: but why be so concerned to resolve that problem—why should it matter if the presuppositions of our ethical perspective turn out not to fit with the prevailing natural scientific metaphysics? What would be so bad about having to conclude that the commitments of our ethical perspective outrun anything that a naturalist metaphysics contemplates? There is a value judgment here—that, somehow, it would be *"better* for reconciliatory naturalism to be true than for it to turn out either that our belief in [the reality of] agency is mistaken, or that, as agents, we belong mysteriously beyond the natural universe that is open to scientific inquiry" (Bishop 1989, 5). That it would be good for reconciliatory naturalism to be true, while not, of course, counting as any kind of evidence that it *is* true, might nevertheless justify our *taking* it to be true—though only if our best assessment of the relevant arguments and evidence leaves its truth open.[7] But the fact that agency apparently involves a special kind of agent-causation not admissible in fundamental naturalist ontology suggests that its truth is *not* left open—unless a CTA can be successfully defended, that is.

But *why* might one think it good that reconciliatory naturalism be true—and so have a motivation for defending a CTA against agent-causationist skeptics about natural agency? One would need to be committed both to the reality of human agency and to the idea that human existence belongs wholly within the natural order. Such commitment might itself be just intrinsic to a naturalist worldview. It might, however, be derived, as in my own case, from the theistic religious traditions that emphasize human freedom and responsibility but at the same time affirm human creatureliness. We may indeed be creatures in the image of God, but we remain creatures nonetheless. There is thus a tension between our creaturely dependency and our power to act, which I think is properly resolved by reconciliatory naturalism (by contrast with the philosophical libertarianism to which many theists are attracted, under which, it seems to me, it is hard to avoid the view that the human self acts from outside the natural causal order).[8] So I actually have a religious motive for defending a reconciliatory, or "compatibilist," naturalism, and, therefore, a suitably formulated causal theory of action. But such a nonevidential motivation is subject to philosophical correction, and would need to be set aside if a reconciling account of natural agency ran into insuperable difficulty.

2   Davidson's Defense of a Causal Theory of Action

Donald Davidson is the major figure in the defense of a CTA, and he effectively endorses the view that a successful CTA resolves the problem of natural agency. In his essay "Intending," he remarks that "the ontological reduction [implied by CTA], if it succeeds, is enough to answer many puzzles about the relation between the mind and the body, and *to explain the possibility of autonomous action in a world of causality*" (Davidson 1978/1980, 88, my emphasis). Indeed, this ontological reduction is just what Davidson proposed in his most famous article, "Actions, Reasons, and Causes," where he says, in conclusion: "Some causes have no agents. Among these agentless causes are the states and changes of state in persons which, because they are reasons as well as causes, constitute certain events free and intentional actions" (Davidson 1963/1980, 19).

Davidson did, of course, develop his version of CTA in papers following "Actions, Reasons, and Causes." Under his CTA, actions have to be intentional under some description, and to count as such they must have "rational" causes, in the sense of causes that also make reasonable what they cause, at least minimally from the agent's point of view. But, plainly enough, agents sometimes act in ways that are irrational, and that they themselves recognize as irrational, while yet acting intentionally. Akratic, or weak-willed, actions are a major case in point, and Davidson is concerned to defuse this potential counterexample to his CTA. Reading "How Is Weakness of the Will Possible?" (first published in 1970) in the retrospective light of "Intending" (first published in 1978) allows one to see that it is crucial to Davidson's strategy to acknowledge that intention is *sui generis* (rather than syncategorematic, as argued in "Actions, Reasons, and Causes"). An akratic intentional action *is* reasonable with respect to the proximate intention that causes it, but unreasonable in relation to the agent's "all things considered" judgment about how to act.[9] Vulnerability to weakness of will is thus the tendency to be caused to have intentions contrary to one's deliberative conclusions—for example, through "interfering" emotions, or through certain considerations turning out to have more causal power than rational force. This solution to the problem of akrasia does involve a development of the CTA from the account first offered in "Actions, Reasons, and Causes." It allows that the minimally rational cause of an action may be no more than an intention to perform an action of that kind. And that development may also be used to meet other challenges—for example, Rosalind Hursthouse's argument from "arational actions" (Hursthouse 1991). Someone who hurls a recalcitrant tin opener out of the window in frustration is not, of course, acting to serve some further end: but she is acting intentionally, and a CTA can accommodate this by observing that, in such a case, emotion directly causes an intention, which is then carried out. The CTA's ontological reduction is preserved in such cases, as in cases of weakness of will: events are constituted as actions by having mental causes that are rational causes, but the mental causes here are no more than intentions to perform the relevant type of action.

But there is another, potentially serious, threat to the CTA that emerges in Davidson's "Freedom to Act" (first published in 1973): the problem of causal deviance. An agent's behavior can have mental causes that make it reasonable and yet not count as the relevant intentional action—or, indeed, as any kind of intentional action at all. Davidson's nervous climber illustrates the point: "A climber might want to rid himself of the weight and danger of holding another man on a rope, and he might know that by loosening his hold on the rope he could rid himself of the weight and danger. This belief and want might so unnerve him as to cause him to loosen his hold, and yet it might be the case that he never *chose* to loosen his hold, nor did he do it intentionally" (Davidson 1973/1980, 79). For intentional action, behavior has to be caused *in the right sort of way* by mental states and events that make it reasonable, yet, in "Freedom to Act," Davidson reports that he "despair[s] of spelling out" what that right sort of way is (ibid.). But surely, not being able to spell this out will be embarrassing for a CTA defender, if the CTA is to secure the possibility of natural agency. Roderick Chisholm was right, I think, to see in the possibility of deviant counterexamples a major challenge to a CTA-based analysis of action, and hence a potential argument in favor of agent-causationism (Chisholm 1966). No wonder, the agent-causationists will say, that you run into problems in trying to reduce an agent's exercise of control to causation by that agent's mental states. For, arguably, all that can secure "nondeviant" causation is to bring the agent back into the picture: the climber would have acted intentionally only if *he had brought it about* that he relaxed his grip, and that has to be understood as a relation between him, as agent, and the relevant bodily movement.

When he returned to consider problems in the explanation of action in an essay with that title first published in 1987, Davidson had this to say on the problem of deviance, and I know of no evidence that he ever changed his mind: "Several clever philosophers [he mentions Armstrong and Peacocke in a footnote] have tried to show how to eliminate the deviant causal chains, but I remain convinced that the concepts of event, cause and intention are inadequate to account for intentional action" (Davidson 1987/2004, 106).[10] Yet the CTA, surely, is precisely the thesis that "the concepts of event, cause and intention" are *adequate* "to account for intentional action"? Or, at least—and this is a vital point—the CTA is the thesis that the concepts of event, cause, and intention are adequate to provide a suitably naturalistic *ontological* account of *what constitutes* intentional action even if they do not provide a *conceptual* definition of *what it is* to act with an intention. Did Davidson in effect concede, then, that the ontological reduction offered by the CTA could not ultimately be defended against the challenge posed by the argument from the possibility of causal deviance? No. I do not think so. It looks rather as if Davidson thought that the ontological reduction would be secure, even though the deviant cases were enough to put paid to any hope of conceptual, definitional, analysis.[11]

But is that correct? Agent-causationists will, of course, agree that the deviant cases show the impossibility of defining an agent's acting intentionally as her being caused to behave reasonably by her own relevant mental states, but surely they may argue that the deviant cases show further that event-causation by her own mental states could not even *constitute* the agent's intentional action.

So there is something of a puzzle as to why Davidson was not more concerned about resolving the problem of causal deviance and appears to have continued to believe in the CTA's ontological reduction (and its force in resolving the problem of natural agency) even though he himself believed that, despite sophisticated efforts by some philosophers, the deviance problem could not be resolved. It seems as if he thought that this problem was somehow peripheral, and some philosophers have apparently agreed. Berent Enç, for instance, speaks of the "somewhat technical problem" posed by causal deviance (Enç 2003, 3). Enç thinks there is a deeper difficulty with the CTA, namely, the concern that its account of action as constituted wholly by event-causal relations seems to leave *the active agent* out of the picture.[12] While there is indeed such a concern, the problem of excluding deviance is not an independent technical issue but is, rather, *expressive of* that very concern, since the claim that the CTA cannot exclude deviance is a way of drawing attention to its alleged failure to account for the agent's own activity. Any proponent of the CTA who accepts Enç's deeper concern, then, ought to care about resolving the problem of causal deviance.

There is, I think, a simple explanation for Davidson's unconcern over what he thought was the irresolvability of the deviance problem. In "Problems in the Explanation of Action," he says: "Let me begin by answering Wittgenstein's famous question: what must be added to my arm going up to make it my raising my arm? The answer is, I think, nothing. In those cases where I do raise my arm and my arm therefore goes up, nothing has been added to the event of my arm going up that makes it a case of my raising my arm" (Davidson 1987/2004, 101). This is, at first, very surprising. One would expect a proponent of the CTA to say that what must be added to my arm's going up to make it a case of my raising my arm is just the right kind of causal history. Davidson clarifies his answer thus:

When I say nothing has to be added to my arm going up to make it a case of my raising my arm, I don't mean no further conditions have to be satisfied to insure that the rising of my arm is a particular case of my raising my arm. . . . But this addition is an addition to the description we give of the event, not an addition to the event itself. So what my claim comes to is this: of the many individual events that are risings of my arm, some are cases of my raising my arm, and none of the cases of my raising my arm are events that include more than my arm going up. Nothing is added to the event itself that makes it into an action. (Ibid., 101–102)

What Davidson is relying on here is something that was clear from the start in "Actions, Reasons, and Causes": his ontology of actions is an ontology of events. So, on Davidson's view, actions are a subclass of events, so that any particular action is identical with some particular event. Events are happenings, occurrences. So actions, doings, would appear to be a species or subclass of happenings, occurrences. To identify any particular event as an action we do indeed need to satisfy conditions that relate to the event's causal context: but, though that yields a description of the event as an action of a certain type, it does not add anything to the event itself. Given this, the problem of natural agency just reduces to the problem of explaining how mental states and events can belong to the natural causal order. For, if actions are events, to be identified as such by having the right sort of psychological causal history, then, once one has admitted mental states and events to one's ontology, there is no further problem about admitting actions. The problem of causal deviance—even if it proves irresolvable—can have no impact on this: actions are securely within any naturalist ontology that admits psychological states and events, even if we cannot complete in ultimate detail the conditions required for events to count as actions.

3 Ruben on the Ontology of Action

I suggest, however, that Davidson's event ontology of actions begs the question against the agent-causationists, and is thus powerless, by itself, to deal with skepticism about natural agency. The bottom line for Davidson's ontology is that doings are a kind of happening, and that is exactly what the skeptic doubts and the agent-causationist denies. Proponents of the CTA will, I think, have to do better than this if they are to secure reconciliatory naturalism, and show how actions can belong within the ontology of a natural scientific metaphysics. I have thus found very interesting David-Hillel Ruben's recent revisiting of the fundamentals of the ontology of action (Ruben 2003, 2008). I will here focus on the more recent of these works. Although I do not share Ruben's own conclusion—and indeed will argue that accepting it would leave the problem of natural agency quite unresolved—I believe that his canvassing of options for understanding the ontology of action is useful in clarifying what position proponents of a CTA ought to adopt if they are to secure the possibility of natural agency.

Ruben observes that it is widely accepted that whenever someone acts there is an event *intrinsic* to her action, such that there could have been no such action without it, yet an event of just that type could have occurred without any action taking place. To return to Wittgenstein's example: whenever someone raises her arm, there is the event of her arm going up. She could not have raised her arm without her arm going up; but her arm could have gone up without her raising it.[13] How should we understand the relationship between an action and its intrinsic event?

One possibility is that the action *causes*, and is therefore a distinct event from, its intrinsic event. To make sense of this, it seems that actions have to be identified as "internal tryings" or "willings":[14] my raising my arm is my causing my arm to go up, and what could that be other than some antecedent mental event that causes the relevant muscular contractions? On this "volitionist" view, all our actions are really mental actions— which goes contrary to the phenomenology of action under which we experience ourselves as having direct control over bodily movements and are not generally conscious of "internal tryings." Furthermore, on pain of infinite regress, internal tryings or willings cannot *themselves* have intrinsic events, and will have to be accepted as having the status of actions essentially. So, if our ontology of action has to include such items, skepticism about how action can belong in the natural causal order may justifiably persist.

But, if our actions are not the causes of their intrinsic events, does it then follow that they are simply identical with them? The view that it does Ruben takes to be typical of CTAs: "If one holds that actions just are events non-deviantly caused by prior rationalizing mental events, then the action, his bending of his finger, just is the event, the bending of the finger, if the latter is so caused" (Ruben 2008, 232). This is, indeed, Davidson's position—but my present aim is to suggest that this is not the only view tenable for a proponent of a CTA. Ruben has several objections to a Davidsonian CTA. He thinks it leads to a "mental overpopulation" problem when applied to intentional mental actions; and he thinks it fails to deal adequately with habitual and skilled actions (Ruben 2003, chapter 4). But the objection he emphasizes in relation to a CTA's presumed commitment to the identity of an action with its intrinsic event is the very same one that Enç and Velleman press: "the identification of actions with bodily events robs us of the very activity of actions; it is hard to see how action can be constructed from the passivity of what happens" (Ruben 2008, 238). That objection does have some force. But, in any case, as I have argued, identifying an action with its intrinsic event (so that, as Davidson puts it, nothing must be added to my arm's going up to make it my raising my arm) leaves the skeptic about natural agency unsatisfied, and the question begged against the agent-causationist.

If actions are neither causes of, nor identical with, their intrinsic events, how else could they be related to them? Are actions perhaps some kind of complex that includes their intrinsic events as proper parts? Ruben thinks that none of the available possibilities is attractive, and he makes the bold move of denying the widespread assumption that actions have intrinsic events—or, at least, of denying this assumption for the case of basic physical actions such as arm-raisings. So Ruben's answer to Wittgenstein's question—what is left over if I subtract the fact that my arm goes up from the fact that I raise my arm?—must be that typically there can be no such subtraction. On Ruben's view, there is no commonality among the following three cases: (1) the mere event of an arm going up; (2) the event of its going up where it *is* intrinsic to a (nonbasic) action (e.g., where I use a pulley with my right arm in order to raise my immobilized left arm); and (3) the basic action of my raising my arm to which no event is intrinsic. Nevertheless, in a broad generic sense of "event" all these do count as events. But we need a "disjunctive" theory of events in this broad sense, under which there is no essential feature that mere event, intrinsic event, and basic action "event" have in common. (This is to be compared with disjunctive theories of perception, under which veridical perception and hallucination do not have any single kind of "appearing" in common.) This suggestion will strike many as implausible. Judgments of plausibility are hardly decisive, however—besides, what is salient here is that Ruben's account, if correct, contributes nothing toward resolving the problem of natural agency, for it is, in one respect, in the same position as the volitionism he rejects, since it requires including in our ontology a *sui generis* class of items that are essentially actions.

Nevertheless, Ruben has done the signal service of showing that, if we are to avoid his own (perhaps somewhat desperate) move, we have to clean up our account of how actions are related to their intrinsic events. And, if we want to resolve the problem of natural agency—which is not a goal that Ruben takes on, by the way, but it is a goal that provides sound motivation for these inquiries—we will need to give an account of actions and their intrinsic events that shows that it is reasonable to accept that they are realized wholly within an ontology of the kind consistent with prevailing natural scientific metaphysics. This can be done, I think, by defending a CTA, but in a way that avoids identifying actions with their intrinsic events and accepts that Davidson's pessimism about solving the problem of causal deviance will have to be shown to be unfounded.

If actions are not identical with, nor the causes of, their intrinsic events, the only alternative is that they somehow include their intrinsic events as strictly proper parts. The concept of agent-causation explains how this can be: an action is a relation between the agent and the event intrinsic to the action. This relation is the agent's bringing about or making happen the event intrinsic to the action, and this is, at least conceptually, a special relation that is aptly labeled "agent-causation." The agent's agent-causing a certain event (the event intrinsic to the action) is not itself a distinct event that could be the cause of that intrinsic event. But neither is the agent's agent-causing the intrinsic event just identical with that intrinsic event, since it is a relation that has that event as one relatum. Strictly, then, actions are not events—although (inspired by Ruben's disjunctivism) perhaps we can allow that there is a broad generic sense of "event" under which actions count as events, provided we realize that an ultimately disjunctive account must be given of that most inclusive notion of an event.

I see no reason why appeal to agent-causation thus understood should be controversial. Agent-causation*ism*, however, is another matter. For agent-causationists claim that the way we naturally think of actions in terms of the special relation of agent-causation must be the way actions are realized in the world: that is, for actions to be instantiated there need to be ontologically irreducible relations of agent-causation. Since prevailing naturalist metaphysics exclude irreducible agent-causation (and, indeed, irreducible substance-causation of any kind), agent-causationism rejects the possibility of natural agency and so repudiates reconciliatory naturalism. But reconciliatory naturalism may be secured, and doubt about the possibility of natural agency removed, by a CTA that does not simply identify actions with their intrinsic events (under the right causal conditions), but, rather, holds that actions, which are conceptually agent-causal relations, may be wholly realized in event-causal relations of the kind admissible in naturalist ontology. On this account of the matter, what ontologically realizes an action is its intrinsic event *in a causal context of the right kind*. Such a view will be in trouble, though, if it seems that we are unable to specify what that "right kind" of causal context is. And the claim that such a specification cannot be given is, of course, the burden of the argument from the possibility of causal deviance. Without a good reply to that argument, agent-causationism remains persuasive: what is conceptually primitive and irreducible will then seem to be ontologically primitive and irreducible also.

4   Conclusion: Some Desiderata for Defending a Causal Theory of Action

Quite a lot rests, then, on whether or not an ontological CTA-analysis that excludes deviant counterexamples can be provided, and I have previously tried to defend just such an analysis, relying extensively on the work of others, especially Christopher Peacocke and David Lewis.[15] In brief, the view I proposed maintains that, where—as in cases of relatively "basic" action—deviance cannot be excluded by a condition of match with the agent's implicit plan, there are two conditions on the causal link between the agent's intention to A and the agent's A-ing behavior that are necessary and sufficient to ensure that it constitutes a genuine intentional action of A-ing. First, that causal link must be *sensitive* to the content of the intention, in the sense that, over a sufficiently wide range of differences in content, had the agent's intention differed, the resulting behavior would have differed correspondingly. Then, in order to exclude counterexamples where the sensitivity condition is satisfied but the link between intention and behavior passes through another agent's practical reasoning, a further condition is needed. If the causal mechanism linking intention to behavior involves feedback (as typically it does) then the feedback signal must be routed back to the agent's central mental processes, if to anyone's. Now is not the time to consider directly whether an account of this kind can succeed (nor to elaborate it). My present interest has been with the more important and prior question of whether the development and critique of such accounts is of any more than technical philosophical importance. I believe I have shown that it is. I believe I have shown that, if one aims to resolve doubts about how responsible agents could be part of the natural causal order, one may do so by defending a causal theory of action that, though it draws gratefully on most features of Davidson's account, departs from it on two related very significant points: it does not identify actions simply with their intrinsic events, but rather with a complex of related events that constitute the agent's exercise of control; and it remains committed to the project of providing necessary and sufficient conditions that (though they cannot be expected to amount to a real definition of agency) make it reasonable to accept that episodes of agent-causation may be wholly ontologically realized in causal relations of the kind admissible in the prevailing naturalist metaphysics.

Acknowledgments

I am grateful to Folke Tersman and the Swedish Collegium for Advanced Study, Uppsala, for the opportunity to read an earlier draft of this essay at a workshop entitled "Acting for a Reason—Normativity and Mentality in a World of Causality," September 25, 2008, and to Torbjörn Tännsjö for his commentary.

Notes

1. Note that I do not wish to imply that Wittgenstein himself intended to pose this question as the foundational one for the philosophy of action.

2. This is, of course, only a necessary condition for moral responsibility: further conditions are required, relating to behavers' capacities to understand the moral significance of their behavior and to offer explanations of it in terms of their own reasons for acting. Infants and nonhuman animals may arguably perform actions, yet without being morally responsible for related outcomes.

3. Note that agents may sometimes be responsible for an outcome *by failing to act to prevent it.* For example: I sit and do nothing while the kettle boils dry. I may be responsible for the damage—but only if my behavior is genuinely my own (in) action rather than (for example) the result of being paralyzed or in a trance. Not doing something may thus be, in a certain sense, something I do rather than something that merely happens to me. So it is important to recognize two different distinctions: (a) the distinction between active and passive behavior (doing versus omitting, letting happen, refraining, etc.) and (b) the distinction between behavior that is my own doing (through which, *ceteris paribus*, my moral responsibility may be transmitted) and behavior that just happens to me (and blocks my responsibility).

4. This problem would disappear if a scientific revolution took place that presupposed a metaphysics of irreducible substance-causation. I shall argue that the prospects for defending reconciliatory naturalism do not depend on having to expect so apparently unlikely a development.

5. I here set aside Daniel Dennett's "intentional stance" approach to overcoming skepticism about natural agency, since, on such an antirealist view, intentional explanation will obviously involve no ontological commitment that could clash with naturalism. As Dennett explains, "the success of [the intentional stance] is of course a matter to be settled pragmatically, without reference to whether the object *really* has beliefs, intentions and so forth" (Dennett 1979, 238).

6. A CTA can resolve the problem of natural *agency* only if there is a generally satisfactory naturalist solution to the mind–body problem: but that does not make the

CTA otiose, of course, since skepticism about natural agency might coherently persist even if physicalism about mental states and events is accepted.

7. I have attempted a defense of believing on such a "nonevidential" basis—under certain conditions, anyway—in Bishop 2007. My defense is a development of William James's "justification of faith" in his famous, though ill-titled, lecture "The Will to Believe" (James 1956).

8. It is important to note that some libertarians think they can resist this conclusion. Robert Kane (1996) seeks to defend a *naturalist* libertarianism without commitment to agent-causation, and Timothy O'Connor (2002) affirms the ontological irreducibility of agent-causation yet nevertheless hopes to save naturalism by appeal to emergentism. I have discussed these issues more fully in Bishop 2003.

9. An all things considered judgment, as Davidson points out, is still a conditional judgment—i.e., it has the form "given considerations C, the thing to do is φ," where C are all the considerations the agent takes into account. In "How Is Weakness of the Will Possible," Davidson contrasts all things considered judgments with unconditional judgments about how to act. But, in the light of "Intending" it is clear that these "unconditional judgments" are better understood as intentions. Both these papers are included in Davidson 1980.

10. The references are to Armstrong 1973, 1975, and Peacocke 1979a.

11. Here Davidson's discussion in "Intending" is important. Davidson says: "We end up, then, with this incomplete and unsatisfactory account of acting with an intention: an action is performed with a certain intention if it is caused in the right way by attitudes and beliefs that rationalize it" (Davidson 1978/1980, 87). Davidson then adds the following: "This is where Essay 1 ["Actions, Reasons, and Causes"] left things. At the time I wrote it I believed it would be possible to characterize 'the right way' in non-circular terms"(ibid., note 3). And the implicature is clear: by the time he was preparing "Intending" for republication in *Essays on Actions and Events*, he no longer thought that would be possible. His discussion then continues as follows:

If this account [of acting with an intention as caused in the right way by attitudes and beliefs that rationalize it] is correct, then acting with an intention does not require that there be any mysterious act of the will or special attitude or episode of willing. For the account needs only desires (or other pro attitudes), beliefs, and the actions themselves. There is indeed the relation between these, causal or otherwise, to be analysed, but it is not an embarrassing entity that has to be added to the world's furniture. We would not, it is true, have shown how to *define* the concept of acting with an intention: the reduction is not definitional but ontological. But the ontological reduction, if it succeeds, is enough to answer many puzzles about the relation between the mind and the body, and to explain the possibility of autonomous action in a world of causality. (Ibid., 87–88)

12. Enç quotes J. David Velleman's claim that the CTA cannot capture what it is for an agent to be active: "reasons cause an intention, and an intention causes bodily

movements, but [in this picture] nobody—that is no person—does anything" (Velleman 1992, 461; quoted in Enç 2003, 134).

13. It might well be empirically true that arm-risings intrinsic to arm-raisings have distinctive empirical features that distinguish them from all physically feasible "mere" arm-risings (such as might occur in a nervous tic or when a paralyzed arm is lifted, etc.). The possibility that an arm-rising of the very same highly specified type could have occurred without an arm-raising might then be merely logical. Nevertheless, the issues about to be canvassed about how actions are related to their intrinsic events will still need to be dealt with, if we are to be clear about what an action is.

14. Ruben attributes a view of this general kind to H. A. Prichard in "Acting, Willing, and Desiring" in Prichard 1949; to Jennifer Hornsby (1980); and to Paul Pietroski (2002).

15. See Bishop 1989, chapter 5, where I draw on Peacocke 1979b and Lewis 1980. In Lewis's paper the relevant elaboration of causal nondeviance is applied to the case of perception.

6 Agential Systems, Causal Deviance, and Reliability

Jesús H. Aguilar

According to the causal theory of action (CTA) an action is an event caused by a mental state or event that rationalizes its execution. Actions are typically exemplified by bodily movements, and their internal causes by intentions. The CTA has traditionally been saddled with problems emerging from so-called deviant causal chains, namely, chains of events that satisfy the CTA's conditions for the production of an action but whose product is intuitively not an action. A plausible strategy for defending this theory against the possibility of deviant causal chains is grounded on the proposal that the bodily movement corresponding to an action must be sensitive to the content of the mental state that causes it.[1] Let us call this the *sensitivity condition*. Sensitivity here is understood as the specific responsiveness that a bodily movement can have to the particular content of a motivating mental state. However, this strategy faces a serious challenge from cases where bodily movements are produced by means of causal chains of events that involve intermediate actions performed by another agent. These cases are quite challenging because they apparently generate deviant causal chains that satisfy the sensitivity condition.

Consider Christopher Peacocke's (1979b) example of a neurophysiologist who reads an action-triggering intention directly from a subject's brain and then stimulates the corresponding efferent nerves. The stimulation in turn causes a bodily movement that matches the subject's intention. According to Peacocke, although such bodily movement is transitively caused by an intention that rationalizes its execution, and although such bodily movement is sensitive to the specific content of this intention, it is not one of the subject's actions. The reason such bodily movement fails to count as an action is that its production contravenes a fundamental assumption concerning the nature of action and agency, namely, that the agent must be the originator of her own actions.[2] Given the strange causal path involved in these type of scenarios, they are usually considered deviant and presented as counterexamples to the CTA.

If indeed such scenarios involving what we may call "prosthetic agents" generate causal deviance, we are facing a serious challenge to the CTA's best effort to avoid causal deviance based on the appeal to sensitivity. Oddly enough, if one believes that Peacocke's neurophysiologist scenario is deviant, then one also needs to explain in what sense this particular case is different from other scenarios involving prosthetic agents that share with it all their salient features without themselves being obviously problematic. Consider a similar fictional scenario where an assistant's job is simply to hold some wires that connect the efferent nerves of a subject, allowing the production of the subject's bodily movements.[3] This case of prosthetic agency is analogous to the neurophysiologist's since in both cases there is an intermediate agent who intervenes in the causal chain that ends with the subject's bodily movement. And yet, in contrast to the neurophysiologist's case, it is hard to say that the subject's ensuing bodily movement is not an action performed by the subject. If anything, the causal role of the assistant is very similar to the causal role played by the subject's own efferent nerves, namely, that of a causal bridge connecting the subject's intentions to the subject's bodily movements.

Peacocke's answer to the challenge arising from deviant cases involving prosthetic agents consists in requiring that intentional behavior explicitly exclude the possibility of two agents interacting in this prosthetic way. He believes that by stipulating that a causal chain leading to intentional behavior "should not run through the intentions of another person" (Peacocke 1979b, 88), one can safely rely on the sensitivity condition to take care of deviance. If by definition no cases involving two agents interacting in this way are possible, then the puzzling resemblance between the cases of the neurophysiologist and the assistant is not an issue.

But this is hardly a satisfactory reply if one is a supporter of the CTA. Not only is it an arbitrary exclusion of cases that are clearly conceivable like the assistant's, but this reply is also in tension with the CTA's general approach to action. In particular, Peacocke's stipulation is in tension with the CTA's acceptance of transitive causal relations involving actions as much as wires and nerves.[4] Moreover, if there is a promising line of attack open to the defender of the CTA to deal with general cases of deviance, it is one based on sensitivity. But the sensitivity condition is useless in prosthetic cases since they all involve outcomes that are sensitive to their causal antecedents. Thus, it is important to know exactly what is wrong or unacceptable about a causal chain of events that goes through someone else's action, produces an event that satisfies the conditions to count as an action, and yet fails to be an action.[5] At stake is nothing less than the viability of the CTA.

Similar considerations have motivated defenders of the CTA to confront the challenge arising from prosthetic agency and in doing so reap the benefits of a plausible answer in the form of extra conditions that identify an intentional action. The most ambitious and promising of all these efforts by defenders of the CTA is due to John Bishop. Not only does Bishop offer a causalist answer to the challenge arising from prosthetic agency, but contained in his answer he also offers a set of necessary and sufficient causal conditions for a basic intentional action. Not surprisingly he calls this a "final breakthrough" in the search for the elusive and much-sought-for causal conditions for an intentional action.[6] Furthermore, Bishop's necessary and sufficient conditions are the result of an analysis of intentional action that comes from a rich systemic perspective in which the agent and her contributions to the world of events are at the center of attention. All these reasons justify our taking a careful look at Bishop's proposal and assessing his claim to have found the necessary and sufficient conditions for a basic intentional action. In the rest of this chapter I first examine Bishop's proposal, stressing the way in which he uses the notion of agential control to deal with deviance arising from prosthetic deviance. Then, I raise some problems for the specific way in which feedback is supposed to enter in this systemic picture, and I end up by suggesting a move in the direction of reliability to complement Bishop's otherwise attractive strategy to tackle basic deviance.

1   Bishop's "Final Breakthrough"

Bishop's version of the CTA belongs to a family of causal theories that consider agents as functional systems capable of producing intentional behavior by entering into internal states that besides causing such behavior also rationalize it.[7] A crucial aspect of this way of understanding agency is that it sees the relevant agential systems as dynamic centers of behavioral control extending their agential reach by functional mechanisms. In turn, an action is seen as the causal product of agential systems involving antecedents such as intentions and/or belief-desire sets of internal states. In this way, the set of causal conditions that give rise to an event legitimately identified as an action is framed within an agential systemic setting.

Correspondingly, the efforts to deal with the challenge posed by causal deviance involve the offering of systemic conditions that would prevent such cases.

Bishop's strategy to establish the systemic conditions that would identify an action and thereby prevent causal deviance is grounded on the most fundamental attribute that an agential system must satisfy, namely, control over the actions generated by such a system. In particular, this is the strategy that he offers to account for the deviant cases involving prosthetic agency. Take the puzzling different ways in which we tend to react to the prosthetic case involving the neurophysiologist and the prosthetic case involving the assistant. According to Bishop, it is possible to make sense of these two different reactions by looking into the corresponding ways in which each of the two prosthetic agents carries out his or her interventions:

Sometimes the second agent's [i.e., the neurophysiologist's] involvement in the causal chain *preempts or blocks the agent's exercise of direct control* over his or her bodily movements. Then the second agent is no mere cog in the mechanisms that realize the first agent's direct control. Rather, the second agent is part of a system that provides the first agent with, at best, only *indirect* control over the movements of his or her own body. (Bishop 1989, 159)

Hence, cases (e.g., the neurophysiologist's) where the intervention of the prosthetic agent disrupts the first agent's direct control over her bodily movements are deviant, whereas cases that do not disrupt her control are nondeviant. Consequently, to distinguish deviant from nondeviant cases it is necessary to identify the specific features of the prosthetic agent's intervention capable of undermining the first agent's control over her bodily movements. Bishop identifies these disruptive features by focusing on the "sustained" nature of most actions.[8]

An action is sustained when it involves a process whereby its agent regulates its execution by monitoring whether the ensuing behavior has been completed or whether it has satisfied the intended goal. This process necessarily involves feedback information arising from the behavior under execution. Bishop proposes that under normal conditions the information is fed to the brain of the subject who triggers the chain of events leading to the behavior. However, under abnormal conditions the information may never reach the subject's brain. Bishop contends that this last thing is exactly what happens in deviant cases when the prosthetic agent disrupts the control of the main agent over her bodily movements, for in such cases:

There is a servo-system functioning to match the agent's intention all right; but given its detailed architecture, it can hardly count as realizing *the agent's* controlled regulation of his or her bodily movements since the feedback information about orientation and muscular states does not get carried back to the agent's central processing system. (Bishop 1989, 170)

To illustrate Bishop's proposal let us try it on Peacocke's neurophysiologist case. If indeed the neurophysiologist is capable of reading the action triggering intentions from a subject's brain in order to produce behavior that exactly matches their content, then the feedback information involved in the execution of this behavior will miss the subject's brain. That is, if anyone is getting this feedback information, it would be the neurophysiologist. This results in the subject's lack of behavioral control, revealing its deviant nature. In contrast, when the assistant simply holds the wire, nothing prevents the feedback information from reaching the subject's brain, allowing her to control her bodily movement. This would explain why the assistant's case is not deviant.

Presumably this imaginary scenario does not involve the possibility of obtaining feedback information through some external way, say, checking whether indeed the neurophysiologist is satisfying the action-triggering intention by watching the presence or absence of the corresponding bodily movement. Bishop is only concerned with the internal feedback information that is normally involved in the production and control of an intentional bodily movement. However, the possibility of external feedback does raise interesting questions concerning Bishop's proposal to deal with deviant cases involving prosthetic agents. For instance, one can imagine a perceptually deviant scenario where the external feedback information is obtained through a deployment of mirrors and fake images that produce some data capable of being used by the subject to control one of her bodily movements. We can then imagine that the subject's body moves exactly as she "sees" it moving. So she has a true belief concerning her bodily movement that in fact is influencing and partly rationalizing her actual bodily movement, and yet, she does not seem to be producing an intentional bodily movement. This appears to be a case in which the subject makes her body move without moving it. This type of case suggests that Bishop is always assuming that the relevant scenarios for his proposal do not involve external feedback.[9]

Thus, Bishop proposes the inclusion of feedback as a necessary condition to identify an event as a basic action. In fact, he believes that the addition of this condition leads to the "final breakthrough" in the CTA's traditional effort to provide necessary and sufficient conditions to identify an action. Hence, according to Bishop:

M performs the basic intentional action of a-ing if and only if,

(1) M has a basic intention to do a; and,
(2) M's having this basic intention causes M to produce behavior, b, which instantiates the types of state or event intrinsic to the action of a-ing; where the causal mechanism from M's basic intention to b satisfies the sensitivity condition; and if this causal mechanism involves feedback, then the feedback signal is routed back to M's central mental processes if to anyone's. (Bishop 1989, 172)[10]

Thus, besides sensitivity, which Bishop requires to preclude deviance in typical causal chains, his proposal adds the feedback condition to deal with the peculiar deviance that emerges in some cases involving prosthetic agents. This move involves the recognition of a feedback signal as a constitutive element of many actions. That is, the relevant causal chain of events producing an action involves in most cases a two-way causal sequence of events: one that goes from the agent's mental processes of control to the bodily movement, and a second one that sends back information about the bodily movement that is performed to the agent's mental processes of control.

2 The Problem with Bishop's Move

Unfortunately, Bishop's reply is insufficient to deal with deviant cases involving prosthetic agents like Peacocke's neurophysiologist. Even the addition of the feedback condition to the sensitivity condition does not eliminate the possibility of having cases where these conditions are met and yet deviance seems to occur. The source of difficulties comes from the systemic approach favored by Bishop's version of the CTA, together with this theory's commitment to causal transitivity and the way in which Bishop himself conceives the role of the prosthetic agent.

Let us remember that in nondeviant prosthetic cases Bishop is willing to grant that a prosthetic agent's action can be placed between the mental states of the main agent and her bodily movements without this undermining the main agent's control. Thus, Bishop accepts that cases involving prosthetic agents by themselves are not the source of deviance. Rather, he proposes that deviance occurs only when the prosthetic agent blocks the control of the main agent by stopping the feedback information from reaching the main agent. However, let us note that in order for this proposal to even start making sense the causal chain going from the main agent to the movement of her body needs to go through the prosthetic agent's action. This in itself does not yet distinguish this causal chain from a nondeviant one, for it is only in the process of receiving information from the bodily movement that the desired distinction supposedly arises. Bishop then asks whose brain is getting the feedback information: if it is the prosthetic agent, then we are dealing with a deviant case; if it is the main agent, then this is not a deviant case.

The problem with this suggestion is that nothing prevents enriching the neurophysiologist scenario with the possibility of a further link going this time from the neurophysiologist back to the subject's brain—in other words, an extra link that sends the information received from the subject's bodily movement back to the subject's brain with the help of the neurophysiologist. If causal transitivity is sufficient to go in one direction, causal transitivity should be sufficient to permit the flow of information to go in the other direction. If this occurs, then both brains receive feedback information, and hence this sole feature cannot be what distinguishes cases that are deviant from cases that are not deviant.

There are different ways in which Bishop could reply to this objection. One way is to stipulate that it is unacceptable to have a second agent who sends back the information to the first agent in the way suggested, much like Peacocke's stipulation rejecting the possibility of prosthetic agency. But this answer is clearly at odds with Bishop's acceptance of nondeviant cases like that of the assistant. If with Bishop we can conceive that the assistant is capable of bridging the subject's brain with the subject's behavior, then we can enrich this thought experiment and conceive that the assistant is capable of bridging the subject's behavior with the subject's brain. This of course will not pose a problem for Bishop's proposal. However, if with Bishop we can also conceive that the neurophysiologist is capable of bridging the subject's brain with the subject's behavior, then nothing stops us from similarly enriching this thought experiment and conceiving that the neurophysiologist is capable of bridging the subject's behavior with the subject's brain. This does create a serious problem for Bishop's proposal.

Alternatively, Bishop can answer this objection by accepting that if the feedback information that allows the first agent to exercise his control reaches his brain in the suggested way, then strictly speaking we do not have a case of deviance. The enriched neurophysiologist scenario would involve a rather strange and circuitous causal path, but nonetheless a nondeviant one insofar as the relevant information is reaching the subject. In fact, this alternative possibility, where the neurophysiologist acts as a functional bridge of feedback information, is consistent with a systemic approach to agency. For what seems to emerge in this enriched neuro-physiologist scenario is a larger agential system that makes use of two subsystems in the form of two cooperative agents.

As attractive as this option may seem, it also faces substantial difficulties. Even if on the surface we are apparently dealing with a larger agential system composed of two subsystems made up of two agents working in coordination, as soon as we analyze the details of such an arrangement, problems emerge for this picture, particularly with the key notion of agential control. To continue with our thought experiment, let us note that although the subject's action-triggering intentions are apparently guiding the enlarged agential system, the reality is quite different. The functional role played by the subject's action-triggering intentions is completely parasitic on the active functional participation of the neurophysiologist's own intentions, whose functional role is among other things to produce the relevant bodily movements and send back the relevant information about their execution. Moreover, whereas it is up to the neurophysiologist to satisfy the subject's action-triggering intentions and provide the corresponding feedback information, it is not up to the subject to satisfy his own action-triggering intentions or those of the neurophysiologist. This asymmetry is crucial to establish things like agential control and attribution of responsibility for the outcome of this enlarged agential system. For once it is clear who is doing what in this agential system, then it is incorrect to attribute any significant agential control to the subject. His role resembles more the one played by a subject who advises another about what to do than an agent who collectively participates in the execution of the proposed action.

If this analysis of the very limited participation of the subject inside the enlarged agential system is correct, then it appears that strictly speaking we are dealing with only a single agent in the form of a neurophysiologist who uses someone else's intentions as guidance and someone else's body as means to produce actions. Notice that no amount of feedback information reaching the subject is going to change this situation. This interpretation of the case at hand effectively undermines the causal efficacy of the subject's action-triggering intentions. So, under this interpretation of the enlarged agential system, Bishop's feedback condition can be satisfied and still the performance of a basic intentional action by the subject does not occur.

Nevertheless, if one insists that given the subject's admittedly very limited participation in the overall system there is a sense in which he is causally contributing to the behavioral outcome, then we are back to a more traditional case of causal deviance: The subject's action-triggering intentions cause a matching behavior that is not under his control. So, under this second interpretation of the enlarged agential system, Bishop's feedback condition can be satisfied and still the performance of a basic intentional action by the subject does not occur.

What emerges from this enlarged systemic picture is that in terms of agential control the subject's contribution to the whole system is completely parasitic on the contribution of the neurophysiologist. It is ultimately with this second agent that the decision to fulfill the relevant action-triggering intention and/or inform via feedback about its execution takes place. Let us also note that it is this crucial part in the exercise of agential control that is absent in the case of the assistant since he is not even aware of the action-triggering intentions that by holding some wires he is helping to realize. Correspondingly, were we to imagine that not only is he holding some wires but also fully aware of the action-triggering intentions that he is helping realize, then we would treat his intervention in much the same way as the neurophysiologist's, that is, as giving rise to prosthetic deviance. It is thus unclear how the satisfaction of Bishop's feedback condition can make any difference in terms of the agential control that needs to be in place if the subject is going to produce intentional behavior in this way as part of a larger agential system. And, if it is unclear how the feedback condition is going to give weight to the required agential control, it is also unclear how the satisfaction of such condition is going to deal with the challenge coming from causally deviant cases involving prosthetic agency.

3   Reliability and Differential Explanation

Despite Bishop's failure in dealing with deviant cases involving a prosthetic agent via the feedback condition, and hence his failing to produce the "final breakthrough" by offering the necessary and sufficient conditions for a basic intentional action, important points arise directly from his effort. Indeed, they suggest a plausible answer to this unique type of deviance essentially grounded in reliability and in Peacocke's account of the sensitivity condition. Moreover, this answer is fully consistent with Bishop's systemic approach to agency.

I propose that what gives rise to problems concerning deviance in cases involving a prosthetic agent like that of the neurophysiologist is basically the *unreliability* accompanying the prosthetic agent's intervention. So, as correctly diagnosed by Bishop, in cases of deviance the prosthetic agent's intrusion is seen as undermining the control of the first agent over the movements of his body. However, against Bishop's diagnosis, the lack of control arises not because some feedback information is misdirected or unavailable to the first agent, but rather because typically the intervention of an agent involves the breaking of the relevant causal chain, bringing with it causal unreliability.

In fact, this is the type of scenario that essentially troubles Peacocke with respect to cases involving a prosthetic agent. For instance, in the case of the neurophysiologist, he suggests that:

When we say that an event is, under a given description, intentional of a person, we normally imply that that person was the originator of that event. It is not clear whether there is such a person as *the* originator of the bodily movement in our example, but if there is, it is certainly not the person whose brain the neurophysiologist is inspecting. (Peacocke 1979b, 88)

Nevertheless, Peacocke incorrectly locates the precise source of deviance. For we have seen how there can be cases involving a prosthetic agent where the intervention by a second agent does not undermine our attribution of control to the first agent. These nondeviant cases involving a prosthetic agent effectively mimic what normally occurs when nerves connect brain states with bodily movements. So, the mere intervention of a prosthetic agent in these cases is not what is creating the problem alluded to by Peacocke's qualms about the originator.

Rather, and as suggested by Bishop, the source of deviance is linked to the undermining of agential control. More precisely, the actual source of deviance is the way in which the prosthetic agent is thought to be intervening, namely, a way that strongly diminishes our confidence that his intervention leaves intact the reliability of the causal connection leading to the first agent's bodily movement. Hence, it is because interventions like the neurophysiologist's turn out to be far less reliable than, say, wire holders, real wires, or nerves, that deviance occurs. Correspondingly, if somehow the connection were to be reliable, for instance, if the neurophysiologist turns out to be a compulsive satisfier of the subject's intentions, then it is no longer clear that we are dealing with a deviant case. For then the situation would be very similar to the reliable and nondeviant intervention of the wire holder.[11]

Moreover, despite Peacocke's stipulative reaction to cases involving prosthetic external agents, he has also provided a conceptual tool that effectively identifies the presence of reliable causal chains, and that can help us in dealing with deviance in such cases, namely, through the sensitivity condition understood in terms of his differential explanation.[12] This is how Peacocke roughly defines this type of explanation:

x's being φ differentially explains y's being ψ iff x's being φ is a non-redundant part of the explanation of y's being ψ, and according to the principles of explanation (laws) invoked in this explanation, there are functions . . . specified in these laws such that y's being ψ is fixed by these functions from x's being φ. (Peacocke 1979b, 66)

Although differential explanation strictly speaking deals with sentences, the laws that appear in a differential explanation refer to regularities in the world where items having certain properties functionally fix the properties of other items. Peacocke also stresses that the functions specified in the laws invoked in a differential explanation "may be defined not only over numbers but also over colours, chemical elements, compounds, shapes, and so forth" (ibid., 67), and, of course, over behavior.

For our purposes of articulating a way to distinguish reliable causal connections, two general features of differential explanation are worth noting. The first feature is that the covering laws appearing in a differential explanation are nonredundant statistical causal laws, as befits an account that is linked to reliability. Even when these causal laws capture relationships among properties where some of them functionally "fix" the presence of others, the laws are still statistical.[13] So, only the continuous occurrence of these relationships ensures that indeed we are facing a reliable connection, which incidentally is something that we should also expect when dealing with a connection that normally comes in degrees.[14] The second feature is that "differentially explains" is a transitive relation. Thus, if there are intermediate stages of a causal chain that can be differentially explained, every one of them is differentially explained by properties of the event initiating the chain. This means that properties of the first event functionally fix the causally relevant properties of all the members in the chain. When this occurs, according to Peacocke, "we may say that the chain is *sensitive*, relative to an initial object's being in a certain state" (ibid., 69).

Coming back to deviant cases involving prosthetic agents, we can make the following two points that emerge from the proposal linking reliability to differential explanation. The first point is that it should be clear why cases like that of the neurophysiologist are considered deviant, namely, because they involve nonreliable causal chains. The neurophysiologist is usually portrayed as someone whose intervention starts a new causal chain that breaks the one initiated by the subject, hence allegedly making it impossible for this last chain to ensue in a true intentional behavior. But we know that this cannot be the reason for considering this case deviant, as the assistant case shows. Rather, what is crucial is the level of reliability accompanying the intervention of the neurophysiologist. In particular, what is crucial is the role played in this intervention by that central agential feature which can easily increase the unreliability of any system possessing it, namely, the "up-to-ness" implicit in autonomous agency. Thus, if the neurophysiologist intervenes in such a way that it is up to her to decide to materialize the subject's intention, then the chances that this involves a reliable connection diminish and the chances of its being deviant increase, for it is easy to imagine all sorts of considerations that may lead her not to satisfy the subject's intention. However, if her intervention is very similar to the assistant's, namely, essentially blind to the content of the subject's action triggering intention, then the chances that this involves a reliable connection increase and the chances it involves deviance diminish.

Furthermore, a second point concerning deviant cases involving prosthetic agents is that making use of reliability shows that there is an inevitable misleading oversimplification in the neurophysiologist case as it is normally presented in the literature. For if indeed this case can be differentially explained then this is the best proof that it is reliable, and hence, that it is not deviant. What is misleading, of course, is that we are asked to consider a single successful case obviating the statistical evidence that would show it to be a reliable one. Presumably, this is a fair move when trying to pull the intuitions associated with the obstacle of an originator. But as soon as we recognize that there are nondeviant cases involving prosthetic agents this move loses much ground. Thus, as it stands, we strictly speaking lack the relevant information that would settle the issue as to whether indeed the neurophysiologist case is deviant or not. However, this does not amount to a proof that cases involving prosthetic agents are a real source of deviance. All it shows is that one can, with a little imagination, construct cases where the reliability of a normal causal connection diminishes, and, hence, where the presence of deviance proportionally increases. But that is all.

Nevertheless, it is important to note that although appealing to reliability seems to take care of the sources of deviance involving prosthetic agents, the larger question remains as to whether indeed reliability is an objective feature of causal chains of events that separates those that are not deviant from those that are. My view on this is that reliability together with sensitivity and perhaps some condition involving feedback à la Bishop provides the CTA with the conditions to identify a basic action, and hence to eliminate the possibility of causal deviance. Although a full development of these ideas would take us away from the main objective of this essay, let me conclude with a sketch of the way in which reliability plays a constitutive role in our understanding of action and agency.

4   The Constitutive Role of Reliability

Even assuming that it is possible to deal with deviance in cases that involve prosthetic agents by appealing to the presence or absence of reliable causal chains, we still need to know why an unreliable causal chain undermines agential control and provides the basis for deviance. This question is even more pressing when it is not hard to imagine cases where an agent performs an intentional bodily movement despite the unreliability of the causal chain involved in the production of such movement. For this seems to show that agential control can be preserved even when the relevant causal chain is not reliable.

For example, it is conceivable that after trying many times a subject whose arm is paralyzed succeeds only once in moving her arm. Although generated through an unreliable causal chain, there is no obvious reason why in this case the relevant movement is not intentional. It appears, then, that the reliability or unreliability of the relevant causal chain is independent of the intentional status of a bodily movement. But, if this is the case, then it is unclear how reliability can be seen as a necessary element in the production of an action.

Nevertheless, a more careful analysis of, say, the case of the single action performed by the paralyzed subject reveals that reliability does play a constitutive role in the recognition of this subject as an agent and the acceptance of her single fortuitous arm movement as an action. Mutatis mutandis, the same considerations apply to every case involving an intentional action that result from an apparently unreliable causal chain.

As has been suggested earlier, the paralyzed subject would count as an agential system insofar as she is capable of producing specific types of bodily movements that correspond to the content of some specific type of internal states capable of causing such bodily movements. However, in order to make sense of these different types of events and states into which an agential system can enter, more than a causal relationship among particular events and states is required. This extra requirement is that the relevant causal connections among the particular events and states of the system are reliable enough to establish a distinctive type of event or state that is exclusively related to another distinctive type of event or state. That is, the particular events and states of the agential system are grouped into relevant types of events and states insofar as they are captured by reliable connections. Only then do we have the required types of events and states presupposed in our description of an agential system and its functions.

If this is correct, then the very types of bodily movements available to an agential system turn out to be a function of the reliable connections that link such types of intended events with their corresponding internal types of states, typically, with types of intentions. In fact, the production of such types of intentions is grounded on some further cognitive state of the system that conveys the information that indeed the intended type of bodily movement is potentially executable, again, because a reliable connection is assumed to exist between the state of having a specific type of intention and the production of a specific type of bodily movement.[15]

Therefore and despite appearances, the single successful movement of the paralyzed subject is an action insofar as it is an instantiation of a type of behavior that is reliably connected to a specific type of intention. Her agential effort is to be understood as producing an intention to move her arm, hoping that it will in turn give rise to what it normally produces, namely, the movement of her arm. It just happens that in her abnormal situation the reliable connection will not likely be instantiated because of her physiological problem. But her intention remains and it is the rational one to have if indeed she wants to move her arm, since under normal conditions this is the most reliable way to give rise to such movement. Note how the very basis of our rationalizing not just her single bodily movement but her forming the intention to produce it against all odds is precisely the assumption that under normal conditions that is what it takes to move one's arm. The main point here is that normalcy can only be cashed out in terms of reliability.

Acknowledgments

I am very grateful to Andrei Buckareff, John Bishop, Fred Adams, Paul Pietroski, David Davies, Sarah Stroud, and Mary Clayton Coleman for helpful discussions on these issues.

Notes

1. Peacocke 1979b, Lewis 1980, and Bishop 1989, although differing with respect to the details of their respective accounts of the sensitivity condition (in the case

of Lewis, actually dealing with perception), are the key sources for an analysis of this condition.

2. Here is Myles Brand articulating a very similar assumption: "A person must perform his own action: no one can perform someone else's action. A person can be guided, cajoled, commanded, coerced, even hypnotized, into acting; but nevertheless, if he acts, it is *his* action" (Brand 1984, 22).

3. John Bishop presents this example in Bishop 1989, 159.

4. The most common cases where an agent transitively causes another agent's action are so-called interpersonal interactions (Hart and Honoré 1959). They involve a first agent causing a second agent's action and hence producing a causal chain of events that, as in the present cases, also goes through an agent's mental events. However, the main difference between the present cases involving prosthetic agents and those of interpersonal interaction is that in cases involving prosthetic agents the relevant chain produces a basic action with the help of someone else's action, whereas in interpersonal interactions a causal chain starts with an agent's basic action and ends with another agent's basic action. Nonetheless, these two cases exhibit the versatility of the CTA with respect to its use of causal transitivity. I have explored some of the features of such interpersonal interactions in relation to the exercise and attribution of agency in Aguilar 2007.

5. At this juncture one may be willing to bite the bullet and propose that cases like the neurophysiologist's are not deviant. That is, one might propose that the causal chain satisfies in the relevant way the content of the motivating internal events of the first agent and that despite its going through a second agent's action and deliberation it nonetheless counts as one of the first agent's actions. An enriched version of this move will be considered later and shown to be a rather unappealing strategy.

6. See Bishop 1989, 171.

7. Other versions inspired on similar systemic approaches to action and agency include: Enç and Adams 1992; Jeannerod 1997; Clark 1997; Juarrero 1999; and Enç 2003.

8. The inclusion of such sustained character in the production of an action goes back at least to Irving Thalberg (1984), who in turn was inspired by a critic of the CTA, namely, Harry Frankfurt (1978/1988). The extensive literature on guiding intentions directly captures some features of such sustained aspect of many actions. See, e.g., Searle 1983 and Mele 1992.

9. However, as we will shortly see, internal feedback is problematic. Note also that feedback is essentially a cognitive feature of a system. Hence, this opens the door to an epistemic analysis of deviance and reliability that apparently has an impact on this type of issue in action theory.

10. An interesting question here has to do with the specific mental states associated with the "mental processes" that Bishop speaks about that are fed by the bodily movement. Are they the same mental states that started the causing of the bodily movement, or are they different? If they are the same mental states, then Bishop needs to defend the idea that such mental states are sustained. If they are not the same mental states, then he needs to defend the idea that there is some way in which different mental states (say, different intentions) are able to work in tandem and respond to feedback information. It seems that the most plausible proposal is the first one. However, let us note that the questions arise as to how a state is capable of having the required sustaining nature to count as "the same" intention and how this intention is supposed to monitor the ensuing behavior. These questions need to be answered if one is to have a complete account of the elements involved in the production of a basic intentional action.

11. Note that this move effectively undermines the agential control that the neurophysiologist has, for now she is seen as a neutral satisfier of whatever is intended by the patient, that is, the "up-to-ness" of her intervention has been reduced to a bare minimum.

12. Peacocke himself disagrees with this connection between differential explanation and reliability, thinking that reliability is not a way to complement differential explanation but rather is a rival theory. See, e.g., Peacocke 1979b, 91–95.

13. Hence, Peacocke, when clarifying the nature of the "fixing" relationship involved in differential explanation, states that "'fixed' adverts only to the uniqueness of determination by the function (as a matter of mathematics in numerical cases): it does not imply that the laws are not statistical" (Peacocke 1979b, 67). The laws that Peacocke has in mind are of this general form: $(\forall x)(\forall n)(\forall t)((\text{F}xt \ \& \ \text{G}xnt) \supset \text{H}xk \ (n)(t + \delta t))$, where n ranges over numbers, t over times, and k is a numerical functor. This does seem to take care of the main concern raised by Sehon (1997), who concentrates his criticism of Peacocke's proposal on the possibility of satisfying particular causal chains of events as opposed to statistical types of causal chains of events.

14. Here is Peacocke again alluding to this feature: "There need to be many cases in which conditions producing sensitive chains actually obtain and produce a bodily movement believed to be a φ-ing . . . in order for us to be able to discern an underlying pattern of beliefs and desires" (Peacocke 1979b, 109).

15. This picture does not preclude accepting that agential systems can be much more complex than this simple view, which seems correct for most intentional bodily movements like walking, eating, or moving an arm. Things get more complicated when the type of intended action and hence the accompanying intention require from the agential system things like guidance or wholehearted commitment.

7 What Are You Causing in Acting?

Rowland Stout

My target for attack in this essay is the fairly widespread view in the philosophy of action that what an agent is doing in acting in a certain kind of way is causing an event of some corresponding type. On this view agency is characterized by the agent's causing of events. To pick one of many manifestations of this view, here are Maria Alvarez and John Hyman:

We can describe an agent as something or someone that makes things happen. And we can add that to make something happen is to cause an event of some kind. (Alvarez and Hyman 1998, 221)

And a particular instance of this view might be the following:

In raising your arm you are causing the event of your arm's rising.

Such claims about the causal nature of action are sometimes presented as conceptual claims: claims about when it is correct to describe someone as performing such an action. But I am interested here in the possibility of making a constitutive claim: a claim about what such an action *is*. Actions seem to be *causings* in some sense yet to be worked out. The causal theories that I am questioning take someone's action of raising their arm to *consist in* that person (or perhaps some of his or her mental states or events) causing the event of his or her arm's rising.

Despite its widespread philosophical currency, there is something puzzling about the idea of causing an event. The relation of causing, like the property of acting, is not a timeless relation. By this I mean that when we attribute this relation or property to things we must specify or presume a time for the attribution. Gavrilo Princip was assassinating the Archduke Ferdinand at one time but not a year earlier or a year later. But events are things that are usually predicated timelessly in that sense; standardly, when philosophers of causation talk about a causal relation between events, they take it to be a timeless relation. Saying that the assassination of the Archduke Ferdinand caused the First World War, even though we employ the past tense of the verb "to cause," is to attribute a relation timelessly. It is not that it caused it then and continues to cause it now. Rather, we can attribute this relation between the events without having to specify a time for that attribution.

So a standard approach to the philosophy of causation focuses on the timeless relation of causality holding between events. And that is why it seems appropriate to think of this in terms of the relation of counterfactual dependence, for example, which holds timelessly in the same way. But when we address the constitutive question about actions we are concerned with processes that happen at one time and not at others. And if what Princip was doing was causing something, then he was doing it then but not at other times.

Given this, how are we to understand the claim that he was causing at some particular time an *event*—the event of the death of the Archduke or perhaps the event of the First World War? One way to understand his causing these events is in terms of his initiating processes, the completion of which constituted these events.[1] We can say that as Princip was squeezing the trigger he was initiating a process in the gun, giving momentum to the bullet. This process in turn initiated the process of the bullet moving under its own momentum, which initiated a process of the bullet causing a perforation of the jugular vein of the Archduke, and then the process of the Archduke dying as a result of this damage. Perhaps this initiated an international relations process leading to war being declared and pursued. Princip set the ball rolling, as it were, by squeezing his finger. Once he had done this, various mechanisms outside of him took over one after the other, resulting eventually in the Archduke's being dead. In this way we can say that in squeezing the trigger he was causing the event that was the death of the Archduke. He was initiating these things at one time and not at others. And his initiating the dying of the Archduke was his action of killing the Archduke.

The idea under attack in this essay is that all actions are like this. The target idea is that in acting I am causing an event by initiating (or perhaps sustaining) a process whose completion is that event. Given this idea, my role as agent is separate from the process that is initiated. Even if we start off by identifying my action with me and some event in a causal relation, the bit that is really associated with my agency does not include that event itself. We are forced to accept the model of action in which I do my stuff and then as a result the world does its—a model that forces agency inward.

But the example of killing someone, which leads to this idea, may have peculiarities that mean that its treatment cannot be generalized to all actions. Philosophy of action has an unhealthy obsession with murder. It also needs to have something to say about phoning someone up, saying something, going for a walk, eating a healthy lunch, writing a paper, buying a train ticket, and so on. It is not at all clear that what we should say about killing people will generalize to these other cases. In particular, it is a peculiarity of Princip's action of killing the Archduke that it is an initiation of a series of processes.

On the face of it, this aspect of doing something and then waiting to let nature take its course is not shared by all actions. My writing a paper, buying a train ticket, going for a walk, or saying something are not obviously cases of initiating processes; in these cases I do not do my bit and then sit back and let nature take its course. In none of these cases is there a plausible candidate for being the event that is caused by me as I act. For example, the event of the paper being written is not the completion of some process initiated by me as I exercise my agency. It *is* the completion of the process of my exercising my agency. It is my action, not some further event caused as I act. Indeed, even in the assassination case, Princip did not sit back and let nature take its course. For in reality he did not just *take a shot* at the Archduke. If he had missed he would have shot at him again. Seeing that he had hit him, he went on to shoot the Archduke's wife instead.

So on the face of it, many actions are not causings of events. But this initial rejection of the target idea would be too quick if you thought that every action is really a moving of parts of one's body and that every such moving is a causing of the event of those parts of one's body moving. Although there is no plausible candidate for being the event caused in writing a paper, there seems to be a plausible candidate for being the event caused when I move my body—namely, the event of my body moving.

Donald Davidson famously argued for the conclusion that "we never do more than move our bodies: the rest is up to nature" (Davidson 1980, 59). His argument has two premises. The first premise is that whatever we do, we do by moving our bodies. The second premise (following Anscombe 1963) identifies our actions with the things by which we do them. So, if the Queen killed the King by emptying the vial into his ear, her action of killing the King is the same event as her action of emptying the vial into his ear. And if she did that by moving her hand in a particular way, then it is the same event as that movement of her hand.

One might deny either premise. In particular, it is not clear that whatever we do, we do by moving our body. Think of the action of checking
whether the baby is asleep. There may be some moving of bodies involved
in this. But there is also plenty of watching and listening. And watching
and listening are not done by moving your body. Arguably all action
involves some perceptual feedback of this sort. Or think of the action of
walking. Only when you are relearning to walk after a major injury do you
do it by moving your legs in certain ways. And even then what you do is
more than just change the relative positions of bits of your body; you have
to employ the friction of the surface you are walking on to propel the
weight of your body forward. This is not just putting one foot in front of
the other. Equally, it seems to be the wrong answer to the question, "How
do you write a philosophy paper?" to say "You do it by moving your fingers
in a certain very complicated way."

But even if we accepted that every action is a moving of parts of one's
body, to get to the target idea under attack in this essay we would also
have to accept the claim that moving part of one's body is causing the
event of that body part's moving. And I want to reject that too. In particular I want to reject the following claim:

In raising your arm you are causing the event of your arm's rising.

If such a claim is to stand a chance, the event of your arm's rising better
be distinct from your action of raising your arm. An action cannot be
identical with the causing of itself. In the final section of this essay I will
challenge the idea that the event of your arm's rising is usually distinct
from that of your raising your arm. Although there may be odd examples
where we can identify a distinct event of your arm's rising that is caused
by you as you raise your arm, I will argue that this is not the normal case.
But first I want to question the approach to causality and processes that
drives one to this sort of theory.

It does seem clear that in raising your arm you do cause your arm to
rise. But we can resist the further step to saying that in raising your arm
you cause the *event* of your arm's rising. The phrase "your arm to rise" is
not really a noun phrase at all and certainly does not encode some implicit
reference to an entity that is the event of your arm's rising.

To echo Zeno Vendler's useful treatment of results and effects, results
are fact-like rather than event-like. Vendler gives the example of a prolonged frost in which the water under the pavement turned to ice, which
caused the ground to swell, which caused the pavement to crack (Vendler
1962, 13). The phrase "the ground to swell" can be nominalized to "the

swelling of the ground." And once nominalized in this way we can describe it as a result of the water turning to ice. But here we can talk interchangeably of the result of the water turning to ice being the *fact* that the ground swelled and its being the swelling of the ground. Other ways of understanding the phrase "the swelling of the ground" are more event-like, however. For example, if we say that the swelling of the ground was gradual, it is clearly the event, or perhaps process, rather than the fact that is being described as gradual. With this distinction in mind, the result of your raising your arm looks like it must be taken to be the fact that your arm rises, not a particular event or process of rising.

The need to locate an event as the result of a causal process characterizes what we might think of as a Humean approach to the relationship between causation and particular happenings in nature. According to this approach, causation is not to be found *in* real things but *between* them. The cause and effect are taken to be real things, and are usually described as *events* in modern Humeanism. But the *causing* is not taken to be another thing.

In the Humean model, a basic happening is usually understood very simply as something being in one state at one time and then in a different state at a subsequent time—so-called Cambridge change. Happenings are sequences of states. This model perhaps reached its classic formulation in Russell's conception of motion. Russell wrote: "Motion is the occupation by one entity of a continuous series of places at a continuous series of times" (Russell 1903, section 442). This claim can be extended to processes generally, so that we have the claim that a process is a series of states of affairs. For each kind of process there is a characteristic type of series of states. The obtaining of a succession of such states is the Russellian conception of a process.

In this model causality is a relation *external* to happenings—not itself something that happens but lying instead between those things that do happen. Causality can only be part of a happening in this Humean model if the happening consists of a sequence of lesser happenings linked by the causal relation. But on this model, if what happens is taken to be the sum of the component happenings, then causality is not really part of what happens; hence Humean skepticism about causation.

Opposed to the Humean model of causality as a relation between real things is an Aristotelian approach, which allows causings to *be* real things. Causings—or causal processes—are basic constituents of our dynamic world; causality is *internal* to happenings. And unlike the Humean model, since this model takes the *causing* itself to be an identifiable particular in the world, there is no need to take the result to be one as well.

Applying this to the case of human agency, the answer to the question of what you cause when you act need not be that you cause some constituent of the dynamic world—some event or process. What you cause when you raise your arm is not the process or event of your arm's rising. What you cause is your arm to rise, and that need not be taken to be an entity itself.

If causings or causal processes are identifiable elements of nature, then they are things that we can identify at one time but which have implications, conditional on nothing interfering, for what will happen at a later time. So these things incorporate natural necessity of a sort; when the causal process is happening, what is present is the conditional necessity for certain results. This means that there are two aspects to its nature: what makes it identifiable at the time, and what its existence at that time requires to be the case afterward.

If you identify one of these dual natures in an object, O, you can see that O has the property that results, R, will follow if nothing interferes. You are identifying a conditional necessity in O for R. To put it another way, you are identifying the actualization of a potentiality in O for R. The reason for calling it the *actualization* of a potentiality is that there is often a need to distinguish between more or less stable intrinsic properties of the object that contribute to this dual nature and those features that can be introduced from outside but which also contribute to this dual nature. We can call O's having these relatively stable intrinsic features O's having a potentiality for R, and O's having all these features the actualization of O's potentiality for R. A car has the potentiality to accelerate under pressure to the gas pedal, even when the engine is not switched on. That potentiality is actualized only if the engine is also running, the gears are engaged, and so on. But since I am not concerned here with unactualized potentialities I do not need to pursue this distinction now.

We do not have to limit results to single end-points of causal processes. A causal process typically has a characteristic sequence of stages as its result. For example, we might identify the process of an object moving in a straight line at a certain velocity with the process of that object's momentum causing it to continue traveling in that line at that velocity. It would not make sense to identify what is caused here with the process of the object traveling under its own momentum, since that is the causal process itself and so cannot also be its result. But nor should we just identify what is caused with the state of the object being at a certain end-point. The result is that it continues traveling in a certain direction at a certain velocity, and this requires that it be not just at the end-point at a later time but also that it be at intermediate points at intermediate times according to the standard equations for motion. In other words, the result of the process of an object traveling under its own momentum is precisely the Russellian conception of what its motion consists in. So Russell has described not what motion is but the results of motion—what must obtain for motion to have happened.

This is why the whole issue can seem so confusing. The object's *traveling* under its own momentum results in its *traveling* in a certain direction at a certain velocity. The first instance of the word "traveling" in this sentence picks out a causal process—an identifiable particular. The second picks out the sequence of stages that characterizes this process. These stages are not the process itself but the results it necessitates—what must be the case for the process to have happened.

Aristotle's definition of motion in the *Physics*, Book 3, has seemed confusing to some commentators in just this way: "Motion is the actualisation of what exists potentially, as such" (1983, 201a10–11). So the process of building is the actualization of the buildable as buildable. Here I take the actualization of a potentiality to be nothing more than the complete realization of the conditions that constitute that potentiality. To say that something is buildable is to say that it has the potentiality for something. What something? Could it be the process of building itself? This would be at the cost of making the definition very thin. It would be equivalent to saying that the process of building was the actuality of something that when actual was the process of building. Should it then be taken to be the end-point of the process of building—the state of a house existing, or perhaps the house itself? No, because the characteristic results of the process of building are not limited to this. Building a house is more than just bringing a house into existence. The intermediate stages also belong to the process.

So we get the claim that a particular process of building is the complete actualization of the conditions that constitute the potentiality for that structure of stages that characterizes the result of building. An Aristotelian process of *F*-ing is the presence of the potential for the Russellian conception of the process of *F*-ing.

To summarize, a process is the realization of a potentiality for certain results in certain circumstances. You have to describe a structure of stages to specify the potentiality. These are its characteristic results; they correspond to the Russellian conception of the process itself. But calling this a process is misleading; it is just the set of things that must obtain for the process to have happened. What is required for the Aristotelian process to be happening is not just that that structure of stages obtains, but that there is present a potentiality for such a structure. When a potentiality is fully present (or actualized), the Russellian process that it is a potentiality for is not yet complete. The Aristotelian process is fully present; the conditions for the potentiality are fully realized. But what it is a potentiality for is still incomplete.[2]

So a potentiality has two sets of conditions. It has underlying conditions whose satisfaction means that the potentiality is actualized. And it has the conditions that characterize its results, whose satisfaction follows from its being actualized. This essentially dual nature of Aristotelian processes can be easily missed with certain readings of the idea of the actualization of a potentiality. If we take a potentiality to be merely a possibility and its actualization to be nothing more than the thing the possibility is a possibility of, then this dual nature is lost. The possibility of there being a cup on the table in front of me is now actualized; there is a cup on the table in front of me. But nothing is happening.

In the same way if we think of the actualization of a potentiality as the exercise of a power, then the notion is trivialized. My power to be frightening is exercised as I reveal my most hideous facial expression; but again nothing is happening. My exercising my power to be frightening is not separate from my being frightening. There is nothing gained by describing my acting as my exercising my power to act. What is crucial for the Aristotelian idea to yield a proper notion of a process is that the actualization of the potentiality be distinct from whatever that potentiality is a potentiality for.

Why has the Aristotelian conception of processes been so unpopular? Empiricists like Hume assumed that one could not experience potentialities. The perceivable qualities that were the building blocks of experience for these early modern empiricists were supposed to be present in individual flashes of experience. Potentialities, if they are perceivable at all, can only be perceived through a process of engagement with the thing that has the potentialities. A purely passive model of perception, in which a quality in an object transfers itself to the mind of the perceiver and *imprints* itself on that mind, can make no sense of the perception of potentialities. And if it follows that we can have no idea of a potentiality, then we can have no more idea of the realization of a potentiality.

But if that is the objection to the Aristotelian model it should be dropped, since the passive model of perception as a kind of imprinting from world to mind no longer has any currency. You perceive the world by engaging with it, exploring, interrogating, experimenting, tracking.

There is no reason for doubting that potentialities and their realizations can be discerned in these ways.

Davidson was opposed to introducing realizations of potentialities into his metaphysics. The real things for him were the bits at either end of the causal relation, not the causing itself. He argued that an action like my raising my arm was an identifiable particular—an event—and he identified it with the event of my arm rising.[3] This was not to identify the raising of my arm with the causing of the raising of my arm, since Davidson was not trying for a *constitutive* causal account of action. For Davidson, the causal history of an arm's rising is what makes it correctly describable as an (intentional) action of raising an arm, but that causal history is not somehow contained in the action of raising an arm.

But since Jennifer Hornsby's *Actions* (1980), we have learned to distinguish between arm raisings and arm risings. Hornsby argued that actions are transitive movements of the body, events distinct from the events that are intransitive movements of the body. In moving one's body one causes one's body to move, and in doing so one causes the event that is the intransitive movement of one's body.

It is a necessary condition of the truth of "a $\phi_T s$ b" that a cause b to ϕ_I. In that case movements$_T$ of the body are *events that cause body movements$_I$*. (Hornsby 1980, 13)

Alvarez and Hyman (1998) argue that I am the cause of the event of my arm's rising. Since my action of raising my arm is identified with my causing that event, it cannot be identified with that event itself. They go on to say that it is not an event at all. In this respect they hold on to part of the Humean conception of causal processes: events are the effects of causal processes and sometimes the causes, but they are not the bits in the middle—the causings. If causings are not allowed any metaphysical identity, we are faced with the choice of denying that actions are causings and denying that actions have any metaphysical identity.

If the event of my arm's rising is distinct from the event of my raising of my arm, then it might appear to be a good candidate for being the thing that is caused when I raise my arm. But as Ursula Coope (2007) has recently argued, my arm rising, if it is taken to be an Aristotelian process, should be taken to be the very same process as the process of my raising my arm. And although this claim may seem to fly in the face of Hornsby's account of action, we can see that it is very close to something she has been arguing for too. For Hornsby rejects the idea that the event of an arm rising is something we could describe as physical rather than as mental. The event of the arm rising is, then, to be identified not with a series of changes in position of the arm, but as something that may essentially involve the agent.

This is expressed clearly in the postscript to "Bodily Movements, Actions, and Epistemology" (Hornsby 1997, 102 ff.), where she considers a disjunctive approach to bodily movements. She raises the question of whether a bodily movement that is just a reflex or the result of some external manipulation could have been the sort of movement that is associated with action, and she answers that it is fairly evident that it could not (ibid., 103). Despite the fact that one might be ignorant as to whether a movement is or is not associated with the action of an agent, whether it is or is not associated with an action is essential to its identity.

Hornsby cannot here be identifying an arm rising with a series of positions of the arm through the air. She is not thinking of the Russellian conception of a process of arm-rising. For there is nothing essential to the series of states that an arm is in when it rises that links the rising with an action. The natural alternative is that an arm rising is being considered as an Aristotelian process; it is the realization of an arm-rising potentiality. It is a different potentiality that is realized when an arm rises as a result of the agency of the owner of that arm from the potentiality that is realized when an arm rises as a reflex or because of external manipulation. And it seems reasonable to say that the realizations of these different potentialities are also different.

It does not follow that there is no process in common between these processes. There might be a highest common factor between an arm rising as a result of external manipulation and an arm rising as a result of the arm owner's agency. If there were, then this might count as a neutral arm-rising. Where might this potentiality be? Do one's muscles have the potentiality to raise one's arm? No. They have the potentiality to shorten the distance between the points at each end of the muscles, but that is something else.

One might try to argue that the system of muscles in the arm and shoulder has the potentiality to raise the arm inasmuch as under certain circumstances of electronic nerve inputs to these muscles the arm will rise. But in fact this is not the case. Those nerve inputs only result in the arm going up if the arm is oriented in exactly one way at the start of the process—both with respect to the body and with respect to gravity—and has the precise weight it has, the muscles have precisely the responsiveness they have, and so on. If any of these factors is different then that set of nerve inputs applied to the muscle mechanism will result in something quite different from the arm going up.

What makes the arm go up is a mechanism that guides that movement in response to feedback from proprioception. It is a control mechanism. So might there be a "subpersonal" control mechanism for arm raising? When my arm rises, might there be something less than me that is controlling its rise?

I think it would be very difficult to defend the idea that there was such a subpersonal mechanism raising my arm when I raise my arm. What would my relationship with that mechanism be? Would I be giving it instructions? But in that case we would say that my action was to instruct my arm-raising mechanism to go into action. And this does not seem right. This is not to deny that the process of raising one's arm involves other automatic or subpersonal processes. For example, it seems that there are stages in my arm's rising in which my arm just continues with a certain trajectory with no active involvement by me. The point is that the feedback required for the overall process to be properly guided happens at the level of the person (whether he or she is thinking about it or not). It is me who adjusts the movements in accordance with this feedback, rather than anything less than me.[4]

So, we should accept Hornsby's disjunctive conception of a bodily movement. My arm's rising, at least in normal cases, might be *either* an arm-rising of an agent *or* be a movement that is not associated with action, and there is no process in common between them. Hornsby, however, rejects a way that the disjunctive conception of bodily movement might be more strictly analogous with the disjunctive conception of perceptual appearance that John McDowell is associated with. For McDowell, "an appearance that such-and-such is the case can be *either* a mere appearance or the fact that such-and-such is the case making itself perceptually manifest to someone" (McDowell 1982, 472). So a strictly analogous disjunctive approach to bodily movements would say that a bodily movement can be either a mere bodily movement or the agent doing something—an action. For Hornsby the second disjunct is not the bodily movement being an action but the bodily movement being an action-associated movement; hence the disanalogy.

Coope (2007) has argued for the stronger claim—that the event of an arm's rising can itself be the event of an agent raising their arm. She endorses what she takes to be Aristotle's view that the process of raising my arm is the very same process as that of my arm rising. If we accept, with Hornsby, that the agent may be essentially involved in the process of his or her arm rising, then at least one objection to Coope's identification is lost. The process of my arm rising is for neither of these writers a series of stages of my arm's position in space. So, why not identify it with my action of raising my arm?[5]

It might be thought that the process of my arm rising must be different from the process of my raising my arm since they have different agents. One is the process of me doing something; the other is a process of my arm doing something. But my arm is the patient rather than the agent in this process. It is not raising itself; it is being raised by me. My arm rising under my agency is the same process as my raising my arm, just as the butter melting under the sun's agency is the same process as the sun melting the butter. This appears to be Aristotle's view (*Physics*, Book 3, chapter 3; and see Coope 2007, 123–124). So the process of my arm rising is the process of my arm rising under some agency. There are not two processes occurring here; there are not two potentialities being realized or two mechanisms working.

If this is right then what is caused when I raise my arm is not normally the process of my arm's rising. Although I cause my arm to rise I do not normally cause the process of my arm's rising. And if my raising my arm is correctly construed as the realization of some potentiality in me, then this potentiality is not the potentiality for the process of my arm rising, also construed as the realization of some potentiality.

So, what is the potentiality whose realization is my raising my arm (or my arm rising) a potentiality for? Coope (2007, 114) argues that it is not the potentiality for another process, but the potentiality for a state to obtain. In particular, it is the potentiality for my arm to be up. But this is too simple. For it is essential to my raising my arm that my arm pass through all the appropriate stages of a rising. The complete realization of the potentiality cannot be characterized just by an end-state. Suppose that I get my arm to be up by pulling it in close to my body and then shooting it out again at a higher angle. I haven't in this case raised my arm though I have done something that results in it being up.

What seems to be the natural candidate for the job of being the thing that my arm-raising potentiality is a potentiality for is the Russellian conception of the process of my arm rising. It is not just the end-state of my arm being up but a particular kind of structure of stages between my arm being down and my arm being up. There is a structure of stages characteristic of an arm-rising, and my raising my arm is the realization of a potentiality for a series of states that match that characteristic structure.

So I propose to extend Coope's account by saying that the process of my raising my arm or my arm rising is the realization of a potentiality for the arm to be in a series of states characteristic of arm-rising, rather than just being the realization of a potentiality for the arm to be up. In raising my arm and realizing that potentiality, I am causing my arm to be in that characteristic series of stages. But I am not initiating a separate process of my arm's rising, nor am I causing the event of my arm's rising.

Notes

1. Another way to understand this might be in terms of *sustaining* processes—by removing obstacles to these processes or by ensuring that the necessary underlying conditions of the processes are in place. What I have to say about initiating processes would by and large transfer to sustaining processes.

2. This might make sense of Aristotle's claim that processes are incomplete actualizations of potentialities (1983, 201b31–33). What is incomplete is not the degree to which the potentiality is actualized but the structure of stages that characterizes what the potentiality is for.

3. In "Agency" (Davidson 1980, chapter 3), he makes no distinction between my raising my arm and my arm rising. And, in "Problems in the Explanation of Action" (Davidson 2004, chapter 7), he explicitly identifies them: "If I raise my arm, then my raising my arm and my arm rising are one and the same event" (Davidson 2004, 103).

4. Even if there are deliberate bodily movements that do just consist in instructing subpersonal mechanisms to do their stuff, it would be absurd to generalize this to all bodily movements, including controlled movements like raising one's arm. I may be able to make my arm move, though not in a very controlled way, by initiating some process of arm-moving. But this, like the example of Princip's assassination of the Archduke, would be a rather special case.

5. Adrian Haddock (2005) also argues in this way and recommends that Hornsby adopt the stronger disjunctive approach to body movements.

8 Omissions and Causalism

Carolina Sartorio

1 Introduction

Omissions are puzzling—so puzzling that people tend to say puzzling things about them and give up otherwise attractive philosophical theories in order to accommodate them.[1] In this essay I suggest that omissions make trouble—serious trouble, and trouble of a new, *sui generis* kind—for "causalism," the standard view or family of views of agency. In particular, I am interested in causalism as an attempt to explain what it is for an agent to behave intentionally. I will argue that causalism cannot accommodate intentional omissions—or, at least, it cannot account for them in the same way it accounts for (positive) actions. As a result, causalism is incomplete—or, at best, highly disjunctive—as a theory of what it is to behave intentionally.

I will bypass the question whether omissions can be, properly speaking, actions—"negative actions" or "active nondoings," as they have been called (see, e.g., Kleinig 1976). For some people (notably, Thomson 1977), actions are a subclass of events, where events are particulars with specific spatiotemporal locations, intrinsic properties, and so on. On this kind of view, it's hard to count omissions as actions, for omissions don't appear to have specific spatiotemporal locations, intrinsic properties, and so on. Nevertheless, even if omissions aren't actions, it seems that agents can still fail to do things intentionally, and it makes sense to ask under what conditions an agent's not doing something is intentional (see, e.g., Ginet 2004). Thus, even if omissions aren't actions, a theory of what it is to behave intentionally should be able to accommodate omissions. (Note that, if omissions aren't actions, a theory of what it is to behave intentionally is not the same thing as a theory of what it is to perform an intentional *action*, and it might not even be the same thing as a theory of what it is to *act* intentionally.)[2]

Causalism, as a theory of what it is to behave intentionally, is the view that an agent behaves intentionally when certain events/states involving the agent's body (such as the agent's moving in a certain way) are appropriately caused (nondeviantly caused, or caused in the "normal" way) by certain mental events or states of the agent, in particular, the agent's intentions, belief-desire pairs, decisions, and so on. The causal link between those mental events or states and the bodily events or states singles out the specific reasons for which the agent behaves in the relevant way from the possibly more inclusive set of reasons that he had for behaving in that way. Causalism is traditionally attributed to Davidson (Davidson 1963/1980), and it is the most commonly held view of agency nowadays. Among the mental items that cause the relevant bodily movements/states, causalists seem to agree, intentions are special in that they play the most central role. For intentions are those mental states by which the agent settles on a particular course of action: they initiate and guide behavior.[3] Hence my focus will be on intentions as the relevant mental items: I will take causalism to be the view that, when an agent behaves intentionally, the agent's intending to behave in a certain way, or the agent's forming an intention to behave in a certain way, appropriately causes the relevant bodily movement/state.

As noted, just as agents can do things intentionally (these are the agents' "positive" intentional actions), they can also *fail* to do things intentionally (these are the agents' intentional omissions). In fact, it seems that there are many things that we fail to do intentionally. This is so even though, as Ginet (2004, 95) points out, there seems to be an important asymmetry between actions and omissions in that, whereas most things we do are things we do intentionally, most things we don't do are not things we don't do intentionally (this is, presumably, because, for anything we do, there are several things we don't do). As a paradigm example of intentionally omitting to do something, consider the following case:

Drowning Child   A child is drowning in a nearby pond. I could jump in and save him. However, after deliberating about it for a bit, I choose not to jump in and to eat an ice cream instead.

In this case, I intentionally omit to jump into the water to save the drowning child. Hence causalism should tell us in virtue of what this is so. In general, causalism should tell us what makes an agent's omission intentional, when it is intentional.

Surprisingly, very little has been said about omissions in connection with causalism.[4] Davidson, in particular, confesses to have omitted addressing this issue (presumably, intentionally!) in a reply to Vermazen—which I discuss briefly below (Davidson 1985, 217).[5] It is particularly surprising that so little has been said about omissions and causalism, for the causal status of omissions and other absences is a highly debated issue in the metaphysics of causation. As I have pointed out, on a natural view of events, omissions (and absences in general) are not events, but absences thereof. However, on a familiar view of causation, only events can be causes and effects.[6] If so, it seems that causalism cannot account for intentional omissions, in particular, it cannot account for my omission in Drowning Child.

How can a causalist try to address this problem? Even if omissions aren't events, there at least three different things the causalist could say.

First, the causalist can say that other things besides events can be causes and effects—notably, *facts*—and that, moreover, causal talk involving facts is the most "primitive" kind of causal talk: any other kind of causal talk, such as causal talk involving events, is made true by causal talk involving facts.[7] For example, an event can be said to cause another event because the fact that the first event occurred caused the fact that the second event occurred. On the basis of this view, a causalist could say that my failure to jump into the water in Drowning Child is an intentional omission because the fact that I formed the intention not to jump in appropriately caused the fact that I didn't jump in. More generally, a causalist could say that an agent intentionally omits to do something just in case the fact that he formed an intention with the relevant content appropriately caused the fact that his body didn't move in a certain way.

Second, a causalist could claim that other things besides events can be causes and effects but causal talk involving events is still the most basic kind of causal talk. In particular, causal talk involving omissions and other absences can be true, but it is made true, ultimately, by causal talk involving events. This is Vermazen's suggestion (Vermazen 1985), which Davidson explicitly embraces in his reply to Vermazen (Davidson 1985). How can a causalist do this? Roughly, Vermazen's idea is the following. Imagine that I am tempted to eat some fattening morsels, but I refrain. Then my passing on the morsels is an intentional omission because the relevant mental states/events (pro-attitudes, intentions, etc.) cause my not eating the morsels, and this is, in turn, because, had those mental states been absent, then some other mental states/events (competing pro-attitudes, intentions, etc.) *would have caused* my eating the morsels. In other words, actual causal talk involving omissions is made true by counterfactual causal talk involving positive occurrences or events.

Third, a causalist can claim that there are two (or maybe more) concepts of causation, and that omissions and other absences can only be causes and effects in the sense captured by only one (or some) of those concepts. For example, it could be argued that there is a "productive" concept of cause and a "counterfactual" concept of cause (as in Hall 2004), and that omissions can be causes and effects in the counterfactual sense but not in the productive sense. Still, to the extent that both concepts are genuine concepts of *causation*, it is open to the causalist to say that an agent behaves intentionally when his moving in a certain way, or his not moving in a certain way, is caused by the agent's intentions in the normal way.

On any of these views, then, what makes an omission intentional is similar to what makes an action (a "positive" action) intentional: the fact that a relevant piece of behavior (positive or negative) is caused by the agent's intentions in the normal way. For example, my failure to jump into the water in Drowning Child is an intentional omission because I formed the relevant intention not to jump in and such intention caused my not jumping in, in the normal way. This is parallel to the way in which, if I *had* intentionally jumped into the water to save the child, my forming the opposite intention (the intention to jump in) would have caused the bodily movement consisting in my jumping in, in the normal way. As we have seen, there are different ways in which a causalist can resolve the issue of how omissions can be causes and effects. But, to the extent that omissions *can* be causes and effects, it might seem that causalism has the resources to account for intentional omissions in basically the same way it accounts for intentional (positive) actions.[8]

In what follows I argue that omissions pose a *recalcitrant* problem for causalism, that is to say, a problem that persists even under the assumption that omissions can be causes and effects in any of the ways outlined above. Interestingly, it is a problem that bears some similarities to what can be construed as a different challenge to the view: the challenge of the causal exclusion of the mental by the physical (Kim 1993). This is because the recalcitrant problem of omissions can be seen as an *exclusion* problem.[9] Briefly, the exclusion problem for the mental and the physical is this. According to nonreductive physicalism, a widely held view in the philosophy of mind, mental states are realized by, but not identical to, physical states. For any piece of behavior that a mental state allegedly causes, there is an alternative explanation that appeals only to the underlying physical state. We want to say that the physical world is "causally closed," and thus that the physical state is a cause of the behavior. Hence, it is tempting to conclude that the mental states don't really do any causal work. And, if so, causalism doesn't seem to get off the ground. Many people think that this problem is not intractable.[10] But what I will suggest is that the problem that omissions pose for causalism is an exclusion problem of its own: one that threatens not to show that mental states in general are causally inefficacious, but only that, in the specific case of omissions, the relevant mental states (in particular, intentions) cannot do the causal work that the causalist would want them to do. For there is an alternative, and arguably better, explanation that doesn't appeal to those mental states, even if mental states in general are causally efficacious, and even if omissions in general are causes and effects.

2 The Exclusion Problem for Omissions

As we have seen, in Drowning Child, the causalist seems to be committed to (roughly) the truth of the following claim:

(Claim 1)   My forming the intention not to jump in causes my failure to jump in.

I say "roughly" because many causalists would reject the idea that intentionally ϕ-ing requires forming an intention *to* ϕ. Still, the consensus is that a closely related intention is required.[11] For simplicity, I will assume that the intention in question is the intention not to jump in.

At first sight (again, assuming that there is no problem with absences being causes and effects, or with mental events and states in general being causes and effects), Claim 1 seems very plausible: it seems natural to say that I didn't jump into the water because I formed the intention not to do so. On the face of it, intentions (and other mental events or states) can cause people not to do things just as they can cause them to do things. For instance, it seems that my abstaining from voting in an election can be the result of a careful process of deliberation ending in my forming the intention not to vote, just like my voting for a certain candidate can be the result of a careful process of deliberation ending in my forming the intention to vote for that particular candidate. Thus it might seem that, once we resolve the issue of how omissions can be causes and effects, and the issue of how mental events and states can be causes and effects, the claim that causalism can account for intentional omissions in the same way it accounts for (positive) actions is very plausible. I will argue, however, that this view is misguided and that Claim 1 should be rejected.

I said that I would bypass the question of whether omissions should be regarded as actions in their own right, on a par with "positive" actions. By this I meant the question of whether we should take nondoings of certain sorts to be actions ("negative" actions). But what I *have* been assuming so far is that omissions are not just *identical to* positive actions. In other words, I have been assuming that, even if omissions were actions, they wouldn't be actions because nondoings just are doings of certain kinds (rather, because certain kinds of nondoings are *also* actions). Of course, if omissions were simply identical with positive actions, then the question of whether omissions can be causes and effects wouldn't arise: it would be uncontroversially true that they can, for positive actions are positive occurrences and positive occurrences can clearly be causes and effects. In what follows, I reserve the word "action" for *positive* actions.

The assumption that omissions are not identical to actions requires, in particular, that we distinguish an agent's omission from anything that the agent might have done instead of the action omitted. For instance, in Drowning Child, my failing to jump in should be distinguished from my eating ice cream on the shore at the time when I could have been jumping in to save the child. On the face of it, this is a reasonable assumption: at least generally, my failing to do something doesn't seem to be identical to my doing something. In particular, although I failed to jump in *by* eating ice cream, my failure to jump in *isn't* my eating ice cream.[12] In support of this idea, note that it seems that I could have failed to jump in by doing something other than eating ice cream on the shore, for example, by reading a book. This is a reason not to identify the omission with the action. Another reason not to identify them is that they seem to have different causal powers. For instance, it seems that my failure to jump in didn't cause my stomachache later that day, but my eating ice cream did. Finally, sometimes there seems to be no action with which to identify the omission—or, in general, no positive occurrence with which to identify an absence that appears to be causally efficacious. In those cases it seems that the causal story would be incomplete without reference to an omission, or an absence of some sort. Imagine that the zookeeper promised to get an elephant for the local zoo but he failed. This made Jimmy sad. It seems that there isn't anything that the zookeeper did or anything that actually happened that made Jimmy sad. We don't want to say, for instance, that, when Jimmy visited the zoo, the presence of a rhinoceros made him sad. The presence of a rhinoceros didn't make him sad; the absence of an elephant did.[13] At any rate, this will be an assumption of this essay: that omissions aren't identical with actions, or at least not generally. In particular, my omitting to jump in is not identical with my action of eating ice cream on the shore in Drowning Child.[14]

Now, it seems that, if we should distinguish between my eating ice cream and my omitting to jump in, then we should also distinguish between *my forming the intention not to jump in* and *my omitting to form the opposite intention (the intention to jump in)*. In other words, just as there is something I did and something I didn't do at the level of overt or bodily acts (I ate ice cream, and I omitted to jump in), there is also something I did and something I didn't do mentally (I formed the intention not to jump in, and I omitted to form the intention to jump in). Call my forming the intention not to jump in "A1," my omitting to form the intention to jump in "O1," and my omitting to jump in "O2." As we have seen, the causalist would want to suggest that A1 causes O2 (this was Claim 1). But consider, as an alternative:

(Claim 2)   O1 causes O2.

Whereas Claim 1 says that the cause of O2 is what I did (mentally), Claim 2 says that it is what I omitted to do (mentally). Which one is more likely to be true? Or can both of them be true simultaneously? In the next section I argue for the truth of Claim 2 and for the idea that Claim 2's truth threatens to undermine Claim 1's truth. I will call this thesis the thesis of "causal exclusion for omissions" (CEO).

3   Argument for CEO

Start by focusing on bodily actions and omissions. As I have pointed out, it is natural to draw a distinction between O2 (my omitting to jump into the water, a bodily omission) and what I did instead of jumping in, for example, my eating ice cream on the shore (a bodily action, call it "A2"). But then consider the question: What caused *the child's death*? Did O2 cause it? Did A2 cause it? On the assumption that omissions can be causes and effects, it seems clear that O2 was a cause of the child's death: the child died because I omitted to jump into the water to save him. Should we think that A2 also caused it? Presumably not. For, intuitively, the child died because of what I didn't do, not because of what I did in its place. It seems, in fact, irrelevant that I was eating ice cream on the shore (as opposed to, say, reading a book, or doing anything else but jumping in): all that matters is that I failed to jump in to save him.

In other words, consider the following claims:

(Claim 3)   A2 caused the child's death.

(Claim 4)   O2 caused the child's death.

The first premise of the argument reads:

(P1) Claim 4 is true and its truth undermines the truth of Claim 3.

Now, the argument continues, if the truth of Claim 4 is enough to cast doubt on Claim 3, then, by the same token, the truth of Claim 2 should be enough to cast doubt on Claim 1. For, again, on the assumption that omissions can be causes, Claim 2 seems clearly true: O1 caused O2. I omitted to jump in because I omitted to intend to jump in. And it seems that we shouldn't say that A1 (my forming the intention not to jump in) also caused O2. For, again, I failed to jump in because of what I omitted to intend to do, not because of what I intended to do. It seems, in fact, irrelevant that I actually formed the opposite intention: all that seems relevant is that I omitted to form the intention to jump in.[15]

Thus the second premise of the argument reads:

(P2) If P1 is true, then Claim 2 is true and its truth undermines the truth of Claim 1.

From which the conclusion follows:

(C) CEO is true.

In other words, the argument suggests that the best way of conceiving my relationship to the outcome of the child's death is as a negative relationship *throughout* the causal chain. This includes my mental behavior: the child died because of what I omitted to do, including what I omitted to *intend* to do. Even if I also formed a positive intention not to be involved in certain ways, the fact that I formed that intention seems causally irrelevant; all that was causally relevant is the fact that I omitted to intend to be involved in certain ways. The argument relies heavily on an analogy between bodily acts and mental acts. The main claim is that, if what accounts for the outcome of the child's death is what I didn't do "extramentally," then what accounts for what I didn't do extramentally is, in turn, what I didn't do—this time, mentally.

An important clarification is in order. I don't mean to suggest that omissions can only have other omissions as causes—or, in general, that absences can only be caused by other absences. All I want to suggest is that this is true of the type of situation that is our focus here. It is certainly possible for omissions—and for absences in general—to have positive occurrences as causes. Imagine that, besides not jumping in myself, I talked the lifeguard into thinking that it is not worth risking one's own life to save other people's lives, and, as a result, the lifeguard also failed to jump in. In this case my talking to the lifeguard (an action) caused his omission. Or imagine that yesterday I wrote a note to myself reminding me how much I hate water. Had I not seen the note today, I would have decided to jump in to save the child, but seeing the note today stopped me from doing that. In this case my writing the note (an action) caused my omission.

Why is it that in these versions of the drowning child case, but not in the original version, an omission is caused by a positive occurrence or an action? The answer is that in these versions of the case a positive intervention is needed to "counteract" the current train of events. In the lifeguard version, the lifeguard would not have intentionally omitted to save the child had it not been for what I said to him: what I failed to do isn't sufficient to account for his failure to jump in. And, in the self-addressed note version, I would not have intentionally omitted to jump in had it not been for the note: again, what I failed to do isn't sufficient to account for my failure to jump in. By contrast, in the original version of Drowning Child (and, more generally, in paradigmatic or "ordinary" omission cases) the agent's omission simply seems to "flow from" other things the agent omits to do—in a similar way, I take it, that the absence of elephants from a room at a given time is accounted for by the absence of elephants from the room an instant earlier. So it is certainly possible for an omission to be caused by something other than an omission; all I am claiming is that this is not true of, for example, Drowning Child and other paradigmatic cases of intentional omission.[16]

If the argument is sound, then the causalist faces an exclusion problem for omissions. An enlightening way to put the problem is the following. Whereas, in Drowning Child, the causalist would want to say that my omitting to jump in stems from my forming certain *malevolent* (or otherwise morally deficient) intentions, I have argued that we should regard it as flowing from my omitting to form certain *benevolent* (or otherwise morally virtuous) intentions. Importantly, there is no similar problem for actions, on the face of it. Whereas my forming the malevolent intention and my omitting to form the benevolent intention seem to compete for their causal role in the case of my omission, there is no such competition in the case of an ordinary action. Suppose I form the intention to shoot my enemy and this leads me to pulling the trigger. Here, clearly, my forming the malevolent intention plays a key role: what I do extramentally flows from what I do mentally.

In what sense is the problem for omissions an *exclusion* problem? In the sense that, once one recognizes the distinction between actions and omissions and everything that it entails, the mental items singled out by the causalist as causes of the relevant bodily states (i.e., the relevant intentions) are excluded by other items. Those other items are better suited to play the relevant causal role than the candidates identified by the causalist. Crucially, the problem for omissions doesn't rest on a general "exclusion principle" according to which no phenomenon can have more than one sufficient cause, or on the claim that there is no widespread overdetermination, or on any other claim in the vicinity. In this sense the exclusion problem for omissions is very much unlike the traditional exclusion problem for the mental and the physical, as it is typically laid out in the literature.[17]

What does the argument for CEO rely on, if not a general exclusion principle? As I pointed out, it relies on an important *analogy* between bodily and mental items. The claim is that, given what we want to say about the causal powers of the bodily items, we should say something similar about the causal powers of the mental items. In particular, given that my eating ice cream isn't a cause of the death (my failing to jump in is), my intending not to jump in also isn't a cause of my omitting to jump in (my omitting to intend to jump in is). This is so even if, at first sight, the claim that the intention had those causal powers seemed plausible.

What justifies the claim about the causal powers of the *bodily* items, to begin with? That is, what justifies the claim that my eating ice cream didn't cause the child's death, but, instead, my failure to jump in did? There are several things one could say to answer this question. But, on the face of it, it seems enough to point out that, on the assumption that omissions can be causes, the view that my failure to jump in is a cause of the death and my eating ice cream isn't is very intuitively plausible (as suggested above). Again, on the face of it, there are certain things that I cause in virtue of eating ice cream and there are other things that I cause in virtue of not jumping into the water. Perhaps there are also other things that I cause in virtue of *both* eating ice cream and failing to jump in (maybe my remaining above my ideal weight, if I would have weighed less by dieting *or* exercising?). But certainly not everything I cause in virtue of eating ice cream is something that I cause in virtue of failing to jump in, or vice versa. In particular, just as it seems that I cause myself to feel sick to my stomach by eating ice cream, and not by failing to jump in, conversely, it seems that I cause the child to die by failing to jump in, and not by eating ice cream. Again, this is not motivated by a general exclusion principle of any sort: it's just a claim that seems very plausible on its own.[18] (More on the causal powers of bodily actions and omissions in section 5.)

This concludes my discussion of the argument for CEO. How could the causalist try to respond to the argument? In the following sections I discuss two possible responses by the causalist. The first response is an attempt to disarm the analogy between bodily and mental acts; the second response is an attack on the claim about bodily acts.

4   First Response: Cause Essentialism

First, the causalist might want to reply in the following way. An event consisting in my arm moving is not an action if it was the result of someone else's grabbing my arm and making it move in a certain way; in that case it is a "nonactional" event, a mere bodily movement (something that merely "happens" to the agent, as opposed to something that the agent does). To borrow an analogy by Mele,[19] an intrinsic duplicate of a US dollar bill fails to be a genuine bill if it is not the output of a certain causal process involving the US Treasury Department (e.g., if it is counterfeit); similarly, an event fails to be an action if it is not the output of a causal process involving mental items of a particular kind. In particular, the causalist would want to say, it is not an action unless it is the output of a causal process involving *intentions* of the relevant kind. And the same goes for (intentional) omissions, the causalist might claim: my failing to jump into the water in Drowning Child would not be intentional unless it were caused by a relevant intention in the relevant way. Imagine that I didn't jump in because someone restrained me when I was about to do so. In that case, the causalist would say, I didn't intentionally fail to jump in. Although it is true that I didn't jump in, my not jumping in isn't an intentional omission but a nonactional state (a mere "bodily state," something that "happens" to me, but not something I intentionally omit to do).

In other words, the objection is that the analogy on which the argument for CEO rests breaks down: although we don't have reason to believe that my eating ice cream causes the child's death (all the work is plausibly done by my failing to jump in), we *do* have reason to believe that an intention with a relevant content causes my failure to jump in. For this failure is not any failure: it is an intentional failure, and it would not have been intentional unless it was caused by a relevant intention in the relevant way.

However, this objection fails. I agree that my not jumping in wouldn't have been intentional if someone had been restraining me the whole time, just like I wouldn't have intentionally raised my arm if someone had forced my arm upward. But this isn't enough to show that I wouldn't have intentionally failed to jump in unless A1 (my forming the intention not to jump in), or my forming a similar intention, had caused it. Why not? Because it is very plausible to think that my failure to jump *would* be intentional if *O1* (my omitting to intend to jump in) caused it. For O1 is *itself* an intentional omission: I voluntarily failed to form that intention, after deliberating about whether to do so, after considering reasons for and against doing so, and so on. And if I fail to jump in as a result of my *intentionally* omitting to intend to jump in, then, presumably, my failing to jump in is intentional too. In other words, if I am right and O1 causes my failure to jump in, then this *by itself* helps explain why that failure was intentional; we don't need to say, *in addition*, that my intention not to jump in caused it.

The causalist could protest that this isn't a satisfying answer. For he could say that the same question arises in connection with O1: what makes *it* intentional, if not the presence of an intention?

In response, note that there are two different claims that the causalist wants to make in the case of intentional omissions. First, the causalist wants to say that some intention has to exist in order for an agent to omit to do something intentionally (call this the *existential* claim). Second, the causalist wants to say that such an intention has to cause the relevant bodily nonmovement (call this the *causal* claim). Clearly, unless the existential claim is true, the causal claim cannot be true. But the existential claim can be true and the causal claim still fail to be true. The argument for CEO from the last section is an argument against the causal claim only. For all the argument says, it might be that the existential claim is true: perhaps some intention needs to *exist* in order for my omission to jump in to be intentional.[20] Imagine, for instance, that my failure to intend to jump in would not be intentional unless I actually formed the opposite intention, the intention not to jump in. If that were so, then I would claim that, although the relevant intention needs to exist for my omission to be intentional, the argument still shows that it doesn't do the causal work that the causalist says it does. There might still be a sense in which it would be true to say, in that case, that the relevant intention is part of what "makes" my omission to jump in intentional. But this wouldn't be because the intention *causes* the nonmovement, as the causalist claims; it would only be because the nonmovement wouldn't have been intentional in the absence of such an intention.[21]

I conclude that the objection fails to establish that an omission is intentional unless it is caused by an intention. It seems, in fact, plausible that an omission could be intentional even if it were not caused by an intention. The question of whether an intention with the relevant content needs to *exist* in order for an omission to be intentional is a separate question, which we may set aside here. Naturally, if no such intention were even needed, then this would be an independent problem for causalism. But, even if an intention of that type had to exist, it still wouldn't follow that it causes the nonmovement, as the causalist claims.[22]

5   Second Response: Happy Coexistence

Alternatively, the causalist might want to object to the claim about bodily acts on which the argument for CEO rests: the claim that my eating ice cream (A2) isn't a cause of the child's death. One way in which the causalist could try to make this reply is this. As I have suggested, the child died because I didn't jump in to save him. However, I didn't jump in to save him, in turn, because I was eating ice cream on the shore (since, given that I was eating ice cream on the shore, I couldn't have been jumping in). Therefore, by transitivity, the child died because I was eating ice cream on the shore.

The main problem with this suggestion is that, even if all of this were right, it still wouldn't follow that A2 caused the child's death. For consider the claim that I didn't jump in to save the child (at t) because I was eating ice cream on the shore (at t). If this claim is true, there is an explanatory connection between A2 and O2.[23] But this explanatory connection is non-causal. (For one thing, A2 and O2 obtain simultaneously, whereas it is generally thought that causes precede their effects.) So, even if it were true that the child died because I was eating ice cream on the shore, it still wouldn't follow that A2 caused the child's death.

Alternatively, the causalist might want to suggest that A2 caused the child's death, although it did so "directly" (i.e., not by way of causing O2). However, I find this reply unmotivated. Anscombe dismissed a similar view in a two-sentence paper.[24] But I am going to try to do (a bit) more to convince you that this view is not very plausible.

Why would anyone be tempted by this view? One might think that there is some intuitive support for it. Imagine that Jim spent the night previous to the exam partying instead of studying, and then he flunked the exam on the following day. We are tempted to say: "*Jim's partying the night before the exam* caused him to flunk it" (instead of, in my view, the more appropriate claim: "*His failing to study the night before the exam* caused him to flunk it"). But, should we take this literally? Should we think, on this basis, that Jim's partying was also a cause of his flunking the exam? Or should we think that we are speaking loosely in claiming that it was?

Here is an argument that we should think the latter. As I am imagining the example, to the extent that we judge that Jim's partying caused his flunking the exam, it's because he was parting instead of studying (not because, say, too much partying impaired his writing or thinking capacities, which were a necessary requirement for doing well on the exam). But then, by the same token, anything else that he could have done instead of studying would be a cause too, in the corresponding scenario. In particular, had Jim been caring for convalescent Grandma all night long instead of partying, his caring for Grandma would have caused him to flunk the exam. Also, had he been reading a book on how to pass exams, his reading such a book would have caused him to flunk the exam. And so on. But these results are implausible (again, unless the book's advice was really bad!). Instead, it seems preferable to hold that it wasn't really Jim's partying, but what that *entailed* (namely, the fact that he didn't touch the books) that caused him to flunk the exam.

Why does it seem so appealing, then, to mention Jim's partying in connection with his flunking the exam? Presumably, because it's a vivid way of implicating that he didn't study for the exam, when he should have been studying for the exam. We mention his partying because it is a more colorful way to describe what happened, not because the partying is a cause of the flunking of the exam per se. Again, unless there was something about the partying itself that accounts for Jim's doing badly on the exam, it seems that he flunked because he didn't study, not because of what he did instead of studying.[25]

Finally, the causalist might want to argue that, although O2 was the "main" cause of the child's death in Drowning Child, A2 still played a causal role in some "secondary" or "derivative" sense. Consider an example by Yablo (1992): a pigeon, Sophie, is conditioned to peck at (all and only) red objects; one day she is presented with a scarlet triangle and she pecks. According to Yablo, although the triangle's being red plays the major causal role (it plays the role of being the *cause* of Sophie's pecking, in Yablo's terminology), the triangle's being scarlet (a determinate of the determinable red) is still causally *relevant* to Sophie's pecking. The idea, I take it, is this: something's being scarlet is *a way* of being red; thus the triangle is red, on this occasion, *by* being scarlet. So on this occasion the triangle has the causal powers that it has, in some sense, thanks to its being scarlet. This role is "derivative" or "secondary" in that being scarlet only gets to play that role in virtue of the causal powers that being *red* has; however, one might argue that it still is an important role. Similarly, the causalist could say, although O2 plays the major causal role in the drowning child case, A2 is still causally relevant to the child's death. For my eating ice cream on the shore is, also, *a way* of failing to jump in (I fail to jump in, on this occasion, *by* eating ice cream).

Now, imagine that this were right, that is, imagine that it were right to say that A2 played a derivative causal role with respect to the child's death. Then the causalist could say that A1 plays a similar derivative role: one that depends on the role played by O1. Would this help the causalist? I don't think so. For presumably, the causalist wants to say that mental items like intentions play a *primary* role in giving rise to intentional acts, not one that is parasitic on the role that something else plays. At least, this is what the causalist wants to say about intentional actions. So, if intentions played a primary role in the case of actions but not omissions, this would still make for an important asymmetry between actions and omissions, and thus it would present a problem for causalism as a general theory of intentional behavior.[26]

6 Conclusion

I conclude that omissions pose a serious problem for causalism. Briefly, the problem is that, whereas omissions can be intentional, causalism cannot account for them in the same way that it accounts for intentional actions. This is not so because omissions cannot be causes and effects, for it is quite plausible to think that they can. The problem is, rather, that omissions are not caused (at least ordinarily) by those mental items that the causalist identifies as causes in the case of actions. As a result, causalism, conceived as a theory of what it is for agents to behave intentionally, threatens to be an either incomplete or highly disjunctive theory.

Acknowledgments

Special thanks to Randolph Clarke, Juan Comesaña, Michael Fara, John Gibbons, Christopher Hitchcock, Richard Holton, Rebekah Rice, Daniel Speak, and a referee for *Noûs*. Thanks also to audiences at the University of Nebraska-Lincoln, the 2006 Inland Northwest Philosophy Conference, the 2007 Arizona Ontology Conference, the 2007 MITing of the Minds, and the 2007 Pacific APA.

Notes

1. For example, omissions were responsible for Lewis's claiming that causation is not a relation (Lewis 2004), and for Thomson's and McGrath's claiming that it is a normative notion (Thomson 2003; McGrath 2005). My focus here is also omissions and causation, in particular, on the question of whether omissions can be accommodated by causal theories of agency.

2. On this point, see Vermazen 1985, 104, and also Mele 2003, 151.

3. Different philosophers have different views of intentions: some believe that they are reducible to belief-desire pairs, others believe that they are irreducible mental states. But causalists seem to agree about the key role that intentions play in the etiology of intentional action.

4. Alvarez notes this in Alvarez 2005.

5. In Davidson's original work, there are only two brief references to omissions: Davidson 1963, n. 2, and Davidson ,1971, 49,. In those places Davidson seems to want to make room for omissions, but he is not very explicit about how.

6. See, e.g., Dowe 2000 and Beebee 2004. Davidson's own view of causation in Davidson 1967 appears to be of this kind (although he seems to take it back in his discussion of Vermazen's proposal, which I discuss below).

7. See, e.g., Bennett 1988 and Mellor 1995.

8. There are several questions that I'll bypass here. For example, if we think that there are two concepts of causation, what makes them both concepts of *causation*, as opposed to concepts of something else? The two-concepts proposal only helps the causalist to the extent that the nonproductive concept is genuinely a concept of causation. Also, about Vermazen's proposal: it's unclear that the proposal explains why my failure in Drowning Child is intentional. Imagine that, had I not formed the intention not to jump in, I would have remained undecided. In that case it's not true that, had I not formed the intention not to jump in, I would have formed the opposite intention, which would have caused my jumping into the water. So, then, in what sense did my forming the intention not to jump in cause my not jumping in?

9. However, as I will note in due course, there are also very important differences between the two challenges. Notably, the strongest formulation of the problem of omissions doesn't appeal to a general exclusion principle. To my mind, this makes the problem of omissions much more powerful than the traditional exclusion problem (more on this later).

10. There are two main options: to insist that mental states are still causally effica-cious, or to restate causalism as the claim that the physical realizers of mental states are the causes of actions.

11. See Mele 1992 and Mele and Moser 1994. For arguments that intentionally ϕ-ing doesn't require an intention to ϕ, see Harman 1976 and Bratman 1984.

12. Davidson famously embraced a coarse-grained conception of events according to which some "by statements" involving events are identity statements. For example, if I flip the switch by moving my finger in a certain way, then my flipping the switch is my moving my finger (Davidson 1971). On this view, the only actions

that exist are "primitive" or "basic" actions, or mere bodily movements (the actions that take place "inside the agent's skin"). Now, the sense in which I flip the switch *by* moving my finger is not the same sense in which I fail to jump in *by* eating ice cream. I flip the switch by moving my finger because the moving of my finger *causes* the switch to be flipped; by contrast, I don't fail to jump in by eating ice cream in this sense: the eating of my ice cream doesn't *cause* my not being in the water (more on this later). The class of omissions that is of interest to us is that of primitive bodily *non*movements (see Vermazen 1985, 102–103). Davidson acknowledges this in his reply to Vermazen (Davidson 1985).

13. Or consider Ginet's example (in Ginet 2004, 105): *S* intentionally did not mow the grass in her backyard this summer because she wanted it to revert to a wild state. As Ginet claims, it would be very implausible to suggest that there is something *S* intended to *do* this summer in virtue of which she intentionally not mowed the grass. For related arguments, see Weinryb 1980, Higginbotham 2000, and Vihvelin and Tomkow 2005.

14. Note that this assumption is consistent with different views of omissions. In particular, it's consistent with views according to which some, but not all, omissions are identical with actions.

15. Note that my omission to intend to jump in is also an intentional omission (this will play a key role in my response to an objection in section 4 below). I argued for a similar claim, although in a different context, in Sartorio 2005, 464–465. However, I then (unintentionally) failed to draw attention to the significance of the fact that my failure to form the relevant intention was also intentional.

16. By calling these cases "ordinary" and "paradigmatic" I do not mean to suggest that there aren't many cases of intentional omission of a different sort, say, cases where the agent has to take active measures to counteract an existing trend or habit. All I mean to imply is that the cases that are my focus here are the ones with the simplest structure, given that the nonmovement simply flows from another omission. Thanks to Richard Holton for discussion of this point.

17. Kim famously grounded his exclusion argument in a general exclusion principle. For discussion of this principle, see Kim 1989.

18. In particular, note that this claim is consistent with the existence of cases where both an agent's action and an omission by the same agent are sufficient causes of an outcome. Imagine that a sick patient will die at *t* unless his doctor gives him a certain drug before that time. Imagine that, besides not giving him the drug, he injects him with a poisonous drug that takes effect at *t*. In that case, arguably, both the doctor's failure to inject the patient with the medicine and his poisoning him cause the patient's death. Now, I think it is clear that the Drowning Child case doesn't have a relevantly similar structure: whereas here there is a good reason to think that both the action and the omission are causes, there isn't such

a reason in Drowning Child. Thanks to an anonymous referee for discussion of this point.

19. Mele 1997b, 3–4.

20. Zimmerman (1981), Ginet (2004), and Clarke (forthcoming) believe this. But what if I had remained undecided about what to do until the child died? In that case, you'd still want to blame me for not jumping in; I was aware of the presence of the child in the water, I knew that I could save him, etc. Could one argue that my omission is still intentional in this case, even if I don't form an intention one way or the other? I think that the causalist can plausibly argue that my omission isn't intentional in this case. Maybe it's not *un*intentional either. But even if it's not unintentional, some philosophers see a middle ground between intentional and unintentional behavior (see, e.g., Mele and Moser 1994), and it is plausible to suggest that my omission in this case falls in that middle ground. Another potential counterexample to the claim that intentionally failing to jump in requires an intention with the relevant content is this: a neuroscientist has been closely monitoring my brain; he lets me fail to intend to jump in (which I do intentionally), but he prevents me from forming the intention not to jump in (or any other intention with a similar content). Is this scenario possible? I don't know; fortunately, we don't need to decide this issue here.

21. The following objection might be raised: if I couldn't intentionally omit to intend to jump in without forming the intention not to jump in, then it is plausible to think that the following counterfactual holds: had A1 not occurred, O2 wouldn't have occurred. But counterfactual dependence is sufficient for causation. Therefore, it follows that A1 causes O2. In response, I think that counterfactual dependence *isn't* sufficient for causation, and it is illuminating to see why. Change the Drowning Child case slightly: imagine that the two things I most love in the world are eating ice cream and swimming. In that case, we may suppose, had I not eaten ice cream, I would have jumped into the water and I would have rescued the child. So the child's death would counterfactually depend on my eating ice cream. Still, my eating ice cream would not cause the child's death. For, again, the child dies because of what I don't do, not because of what I do; this is so even if, if I hadn't done what I did, the child would have lived. By the same token, it seems to me that A1 still wouldn't cause O2, even if O2 counterfactually depended on A1.

22. Another potential challenge that I have chosen to set aside is the challenge that negative intentions are impossible. According to some views of intentions, forming an intention requires settling on a plan of action (Bratman 1984; Mele 1992; Enç 2003). This view creates some pressure to reject negative intentions. For it's hard to say what the plan might be in the case of omissions (for an argument that omissions don't involve "plans," or "methods," see Thomson 1996).

23. Although, is it really true that I didn't jump in because I was eating ice cream? Let's assume that, if I was eating ice cream on the shore, then I couldn't have been

jumping into the water at the same time, maybe in the sense that it was physically impossible for me to do both at once. Does this mean that A2 *explains* O2? Compare: I couldn't have been a professional philosopher *and* a professional basketball player. Does my being a philosopher explain my not being a basketball player? Or is this explained by my lacking the relevant qualities for being a basketball player?

24. That's right: a *two-sentence paper* (in *Analysis*). Here is the full text of the paper: "The nerve of Mr. Bennett's argument is that if A results from your not doing B, then A results from whatever you do instead of B. While there may be much to be said for this view, still it does not seem right on the face of it" (Anscombe 1966).

25. It might be argued that our judgments whether Jim's partying caused his flunking the exam depend on the contrast class with respect to which we are making the assertion: whereas it's not the case that his partying rather than his caring for Grandma caused him to flunk, his parting rather than studying did cause him to flunk. (For a recent defense of a contrastive view of causation, see Schaffer 2005.) If causation were a contrastive relation instead of a two-place relation, maybe the causalist could make a similar claim about the intention not to jump in: whereas it's not the case that my intending not to jump in rather than my merely omitting to intend to jump in caused my omitting to jump in, my intending not to jump in rather than my intending to jump in did cause my omitting to jump in. I cannot do full justice to this view here. But let me just note two things. First, causalism would have to be revised accordingly, as the claim that intentions of a certain type *rather than intentions of another type* cause the relevant bodily states in the relevant way. Second, whereas the claim that explanation is not a two-place relation (but a three-place relation, or even a four-place relation) bears some initial plausibility, the corresponding claim about causation is very counterintuitive.

26. On similar grounds, Kim argues that the nonreductive physicalist shouldn't settle for the claim that the mental is causally efficacious but the causal powers of the mental are parasitic on the causal powers of the physical (Kim 1998, 45).

9 Intentional Omissions

Randolph Clarke

Often when one omits to do a certain thing, one's omission is due to one's simply not having considered, or one's having forgotten, to do that thing. When this is so, one does not intentionally omit to do that thing. But sometimes one intentionally omits to do something. For example, Ann was asked by Bob to pick him up at the airport at 2:30 AM, after his arrival at 2:00. Feeling tired and knowing that Bob can take a taxi, Ann decides at midnight not to pick him up at 2:30, and she intentionally omits to do so. Other examples of intentional omissions include instances of abstaining, boycotting, and fasting.[1]

Intentional omissions would seem to have much in common with intentional actions. But the extent of the similarity is not immediately obvious. Intentional omission has been recognized as a problem for theories of agency, but it is one on which, especially lately, little effort has been expended. My aim here is to advance a conception of intentional omission, address a number of claims that have been made about it, and examine the extent to which an account of it should parallel an account of intentional action. I'll argue that although there might indeed be interesting differences, there are nevertheless important similarities, and similarities that support a causal approach to agency.

Although much of our interest in omissions concerns responsibility for omitting, my focus is on the metaphysical and mental dimensions of intentional omission. What sort of thing (if it is a thing at all) is an omission? What, if any, mental states or events must figure in cases of intentional omission, and how must they figure? Answers to these questions have some bearing on the moral issue, but the questions are interesting in their own right. And they stand in some degree of mutual independence from the moral issue, as there can be intentional omissions for which no one is responsible, and (on the assumption that we can be responsible for anything at all) we can be responsible for omissions that aren't intentional.[2]

A preliminary distinction might help clarify the object of my attention. My focus is on cases about which it is correct to say that someone intentionally omits to do something. There are cases of another sort in which we might say that it is intentional of some individual that she doesn't do a certain thing, but she doesn't intentionally omit to do it. For example, wanting to ensure that he wouldn't leap into the sea when he heard the Siren song, Ulysses had himself bound to the mast of his ship. As planned, he didn't jump into the sea; but he nevertheless didn't intentionally omit to leap in, for while he could hear the song, he tried his best to free himself and jump into the water.[3] Intentionally omitting to A at t would seem to require, at least, that one is not at t trying to A.[4]

1   Omissions and Actions

Let us call actions of a familiar sort, such as raising one's arm, walking, or speaking, "positive actions." It is on positive actions that action theory has, understandably, largely focused. How are omissions related to positive actions? For one thing, when one intentionally omits to A, is one's omission identical with some intentional positive action that one then performs?

Perhaps sometimes it is. Imagine a child crouching behind a chair and holding still for several minutes while playing hide and seek.[5] The child's holding still is arguably an intentional action; it requires the sending of a pattern of motor signals to certain muscles, perhaps the inhibition of other motor signals, the maintenance of balance, with fine adjustments made in response to feedback, at least much of which arguably results from the child's intending to hold still. The child's not moving is an intentional omission. And perhaps the child's not moving in this case is just her holding still.[6]

It might be objected that the child might have not moved even if she hadn't intentionally held still—she could have been frozen stiff. But we may grant this possibility without accepting that the child's holding still (that particular event) is distinct from her not moving, just as we may grant that on some occasion when I walked slowly, I might have walked without walking slowing, without thereby committing ourselves to the implausible view that I performed two acts of walking when I walked slowly.

On a minimizing view of act individuation, when one flips the switch, turns on the light, illuminates the room, and startles the burglar, one might perform only one action, which might be intentional under some of these descriptions and unintentional under others (Davidson 1980, 4–5; Anscombe 1963, 46). Having flipped the switch, it might be said, there is nothing further that one must do to turn on the light, and so on.

One competing view takes actions to be instantiations of act-properties, and holds that actions are nonidentical if they are instantiations of different act-properties (Goldman 1970, 10). Such an account will take one's turning on the light and one's startling the burglar to be different actions. But even this second view may count the walking and the walking slowly as one action, for an instantiation of a given act-property can be designated by each of several different expressions (cf. Bennett 1988, 93). And, similarly, either of these two views may count the child's holding still as identical with her not moving.

An extreme maximizing view combines the second account of what an action is with the claim that we have the same act-property only when we have the same act-description. On such an extreme view, it will be the case that no omission (nothing described as an omission) is identical with any positive action. Setting aside such a view, we may allow that in some cases there is such an identity.

A further consideration favors this allowance. One might for a time plan not to A, but then change one's mind and decide to A. An agent in such a case who realizes that she has a tendency to absent-mindedly revert to abandoned plans might form an intention not to omit to A as well as the intention to A. She might then not just intentionally A but also intentionally omit to omit to A. In such a case, her omission would seem to be just her action of A-ing.[7]

But in many cases—perhaps in most—one's intentionally omitting to A at a certain time isn't identical with any positive action that one then performs. Ann intentionally omits to pick up Bob at 2:30. Suppose that, though feeling too tired to go out, Ann is at home playing piano from 2:00 to 3:00. Her playing piano, let's imagine, keeps her neighbor awake. It isn't Ann's omitting to pick up Bob that keeps the neighbor awake (cf. Lewis 2004, 282; Sartorio 2009, 518). Her omitting to pick up Bob isn't her playing piano, nor does it seem to be any other positive action that Ann performs. And there are similar reasons in many cases of intentional omission for denying the identity of the omission with any positive action that one then intentionally performs.

In a case in which one's intentional omission isn't itself some positive action that one performs, must one intentionally perform some other positive action during some relevant time period? Suppose that it is A-ing during the interval t that one intentionally omits. Must one have intentionally performed during t some positive action other than A-ing?

We are almost always, during our waking lives, intentionally doing something. Besides performing overt bodily actions, we attend to things, concentrate, try to think of or remember something, and so on. So it might come close to a trivial truth that when one intentionally omits to A at t, one is, at t, intentionally doing something else. But it isn't a truth. Ann intentionally doesn't pick up Bob at 2:30. This might be so even if she went to bed at 1:00, is sound asleep at 2:30, and isn't intentionally performing any positive actions at that later time.

A related claim is that refraining from A-ing requires performing some other action to prevent oneself from A-ing (Brand 1971, 49). One might take refraining to be something different from intentionally omitting, though I doubt that ordinary language precludes an overlap. In any case, the claim is mistaken about refraining. I might comply with instructions to refrain from touching a freshly painted object until it's dry. There might be several things I do *while* refraining, but there need be nothing that I do in order to prevent myself from touching the object (cf. Vermazen 1985, 103; Walton 1980, 322).

If no positive action is required at t, and none need be performed in order to prevent oneself from A-ing, does intentionally omitting to A at t nevertheless require that one intentionally perform some positive action at t or earlier, such that one believes one can't both intentionally do that then and A at t (as Zimmerman 1981, 547 claims)? When I comply with the instructions not to touch the painted object, I might remain standing where I am—within easy reach of the object—my arms hanging freely at my sides, whistling a tune. I needn't believe that my standing there whistling is incompatible with my touching the object (obviously it isn't). And having my arms at my sides during this period need not be any more an intentional action than it was before I read the instructions and came to intend not to touch the object. I might have no temptation that needs to be resisted, and I need not intentionally hold my arms at my sides.

If intentional omissions are not always identical with positive actions, and if one need not, at any relevant time, perform any other positive action when one intentionally omits to A, are intentional omissions nevertheless themselves acts, even if "negative acts"? One might take them to be such because, one holds, they fulfill intentions and forming an intention is an act (McIntyre 1985, 93). But intentions can be nonactively acquired as well as actively formed in making decisions. (See, e.g., Audi 1993, 64, and Mele 2003, 200–201.) One might wish to call even nonactively coming to have an intention a "mental act," but we should not lose sight of the difference between such an occurrence and an intentional action.

We might decide to call intentional omissions "acts of omission" simply because they're intentional, or on the grounds that (we think) they express intentions. (Whether intentionally omitting requires having a pertinent intention is a question I'll address below.) There is warrant for this choice of terminology, as what is done intentionally is, in some sense, a manifestation of agency. (I'll return to this point in section 6.)

Still, we ought not assume that intentional positive actions and such negative acts are thoroughly alike. The question of whether there are in fact significant differences arises at several points in the discussion to follow. Since it will be convenient to have an economic way to refer specifically to positive actions, henceforth when I use "action" or "act" without qualification, I intend positive action. Using the terms this way is, of course, meant to be consistent with what I observed in the preceding paragraph.

2 Absences

When an omission isn't itself an action, what is it? It would seem to be an absence, an absence of an action. Ann's intentional omission is the absence of an action by her of picking up Bob at the airport at 2:30.

What is such an absence? One might take it to be a negative event, or a negative state of affairs, or the instantiation of a negative property. Any such view is problematic, for there are good reasons to deny the existence of such negative entities. (See, e.g., Armstrong 1978, 23–29.)

One alternative view holds that when one omits to do a certain thing, one stands in the not-causing relation to a certain (positive) event. For example, "when I refrain from shooting a child, it might be appropriate to say that I stand in the 'not-causing' relation to the event, 'the child's being shot *by me*'" (Fischer 1985–1986, 265). Aside from quarrels about a relation of not-causing, the suggestion is objectionable on the grounds that no one stands in any genuine relation to any nonexistent thing; relations require relata (Lewis 2004, 283).[8] Typically, if one refrains from shooting a child, there is no event that is the child's being shot by oneself.

Omissions aren't, of course, the only sort of absence. The world is missing certain events, states of affairs, objects, and properties. Arguably, the absences of these things aren't queer sorts of entities; they aren't beings or things at all, simply absences of things (Kukso 2006, 29; Lewis 2004, 282). The view is available, and with much to recommend it, that when

Ann doesn't pick up Bob, her omission is such an absence, and nothing more, even if more is required for it to be an intentional omission.

It can seem puzzling just when and where omissions occur. Does Ann omit to pick up Bob at midnight, when she decides not to pick him up, or at 2:30, when she isn't at the airport to pick him up, or during some portion, or all, of the interval from that earlier time to the later one? Does her omission take place at her house, where Ann is located throughout that interval, or at the airport, or along the route that Ann would have taken had she gone to pick up Bob? If omissions (those that aren't actions) are absences, and absences aren't things, then (these) omissions don't occur anytime or anywhere. There isn't an action by Ann at 2:30 of picking up Bob at the airport. The time and place in question are some pertinent time and place at which there isn't such an action. That there isn't such an action at that time and place is what it is for there to be such an absence.

Which absences of actions are omissions? Some philosophers (e.g., Fischer 1985–1986, 264–265) take it that there is an omission anytime an agent does not perform a certain action. Somewhat less generously, others (e.g., Zimmerman 1981, 545) hold that there is an omission whenever (and only when) an agent is able to perform some action A and does not A.[9]

Whether omitting to A requires that one be able to A is a complicated matter, for there are several different sorts of thing each of which may fairly be called an ability to act. Arguably, some type of ability to do other than what one actually does is ruled out if determinism is true. Some other types of unmanifested abilities, such as talents or skills, general capacities, or powers to do certain things, are plainly compatible with determinism. Similarly, it seems that in cases of preemptive overdetermination, in which an agent does a certain thing on her own, but would have been made to do it anyway had she not done it on her own, some type of ability to do otherwise is precluded, while the agent might nonetheless retain a capacity or power to act that, it is ensured, she won't exercise.[10]

It hardly seems to follow from the truth of determinism that no one ever omits to send holiday greetings, wear their seat belts, and so forth, or that we never abstain, boycott, or fast. It doesn't seem credible that omitting to A, or that intentionally omitting to A, requires that one have any sort of ability to A that would be ruled out by determinism. And agents in cases of preemptive overdetermination might omit to do things that, in some sense, they're unable to do.[11]

On the other hand, lacking an ability of another sort *can* seem to preclude one's intentionally omitting to do a certain thing. We might plausibly judge that an agent who intended not to get out of bed, and who didn't so act, didn't intentionally omit to get out of bed if, unbeknownst to her, she was paralyzed and wouldn't have risen from bed even if she had tried (Ginet 2004, 108).[12] I suspect that it would be a delicate matter to say exactly what type of ability to act is required for omission, or for intentional omission, and I'll not attempt that project here.

Although for some purposes we might wish to say that there is an omission whenever an agent doesn't perform a certain action that she is, in a relevant sense, able to perform, we don't commonly use the term so broadly. Setting aside cases of intentional omission and those in which it is intentional of some agent that she doesn't do a certain thing, in ordinary contexts we tend to take "omission" to be applicable only when an action isn't performed despite being recommended or required by some norm (not necessarily a moral norm; cf. Feinberg 1984, 161; Smith 1990; Williams 1995, 337). We may sensibly count as omissions only those absences of actions that satisfy some such restriction (as well as whatever ability requirement is appropriate).

In any case, since the focus here is on intentional omissions, the absences that count will be restricted in a different way. Only absences of actions in cases in which the agents have certain mental states are intentional omissions.

3   Intentions

At least generally, in cases of intentional action, the agent has some intention with relevant content. Typically, when I intentionally walk, I intend to walk. However, arguably, even if intentionally A-ing requires having an intention, it doesn't require intending to A (or having an intention to A). While walking, I might intentionally take a certain step, without intending specifically to take that step. It might suffice that while taking that step I intend to walk then, I'm a competent walker fully capable at the moment of exercising that competence, there's no obstacle requiring any special adjustment of my walking, and my taking that step results in a normal way from my intending to walk then. (On this type of case, see Mele 1997a, 242–243; I'll describe below some further cases in which, apparently, one can intentionally A without intending to A.)

Does intentionally omitting to A require having some intention with relevant content? If so, what content must the intention have? And when must one have the intention?

Suppose that one intentionally omits to A during t. Must one (as Ginet 2004 maintains) intend throughout the interval t not to A?[13]

No. Some actions require preparation, and preparatory steps must some-times be taken by a certain time prior to the action in question. If I am to attend a meeting in a distant city on Monday afternoon, I must earlier book a flight, get to the airport, and so forth. Suppose that having decided not to attend, I intentionally don't perform such preparatory actions. Having forgone the preparations, I have no further need of the intention not to attend, and with other things on my mind, I may dispense with it. (The claim isn't that the intention *couldn't* be retained, only that it need not be.) Nevertheless, when I don't show up at the meeting, I might inten-tionally omit to do so.[14]

Does intentionally omitting to A during t require having, at some rel-evant time, an intention not to A? Several writers (e.g., Ginet 2004 and Zimmerman 1981) have claimed that it does, but again the claim appears mistaken. An intention with some other content might do.

Suppose that Charles wants to abstain from smoking for a week, but he thinks it unlikely that he'll succeed. Cautious fellow that he is, Charles forms only an intention to try not to smoke. He plans to spend time with friends who don't smoke, to chew gum to diminish his desire to smoke, and so forth, which he hopes will enable him to resist the temptation. Suppose that Charles then makes the effort and succeeds, and there's nothing magical or fluky about his success: his plan works just as he hoped it would. Charles omits to smoke because he tries not to smoke. He inten-tionally omits to smoke for a week, even though he didn't have an inten-tion not to smoke for a week.[15]

The case parallels one of action in which, though thinking success unlikely, one intends to try to A, one makes the effort, and one unexpect-edly succeeds. If the success isn't a fluke, one might then have intention-ally A-ed without having intended to A (cf. Mele 1992, 131–133).

It might be objected that Charles has it as his aim or goal that he not smoke, and to take something as an aim or goal is to intend that thing.[16] But one can have something as a hoped-for goal without intending that thing. Arguably, there is a negative belief constraint on rationally intend-ing, such that it isn't rational to intend to A while believing that one probably won't succeed.[17] Given his expectations, Charles might take abstaining from smoking for a week only as a hoped-for goal, intending no more than to try his best.

Some different cases also suggest that one might intentionally omit to A without intending to omit to A. Suppose that while walking in the countryside you come to a fork in the path. You're aware that the path on the left is more pleasant, and you realize that should you take the path on the right your walk will be less enjoyable. Suppose that you nevertheless decide to take the path on the right (perhaps believing that path shorter), and you then do so, aware that in so doing you aren't taking the left path. It seems that you needn't intend not to take the left path in order for it to be the case that you intentionally don't take (omit to take) that path.

As several theorists see it, one can carry out an intention to A and be aware that by A-ing one will do something B, without then intending to B, and yet intentionally B. This might be so when one is aware of a reason not to B and one decides to A despite that consideration. For example, I might intentionally start my car in the morning despite being aware that (since my car is very noisy) by so doing I'll disturb my neighbors' sleep. I might then intentionally disturb them without having intended to do so (Ginet 1990, 76; cf. Harman 1976/1997, 151–152).[18] Examples such as that in the preceding paragraph make an equally strong case for the view that one can carry out an intention to A and be aware that, in intentionally A-ing, one will not do something B, without then intending not to B, and yet intentionally omit to B.[19]

Must any intention with relevant content figure in the history of an intentional omission? Suppose that I see a child struggling in a pond but intentionally omit to jump into the water to save the child. I don't intend to jump in. Might it suffice for my omitting to jump in to be intentional that this omission results from my intentionally omitting to intend to jump in (as Sartorio 2009, 523 suggests)?[20]

What would make it the case that my not intending to jump in is itself an intentional omission? One might say: "I voluntarily failed to form that intention, after deliberating about whether to do so, after considering reasons for and against doing so, etc." (Sartorio 2009, 523). But the claim that my failure to intend was voluntary seems to presuppose that, rather than explain how, it was intentional. And that my not intending to jump in comes after deliberation about whether to do so, and after consideration of reasons for and against jumping in, does not suffice to make my not so intending intentional. I might have simply failed to make up my mind.

Suppose the case unfolds this way. I deliberate about whether to jump in or not, never making up my mind. As I continue deliberating, I realize that the child is drowning and I'm doing nothing to save her. In this version of the case, do I intentionally omit to jump in to save the child despite having no intention with pertinent content?

Deliberating is itself activity, and typically it is intentional activity. (We can intentionally try to think of relevant considerations, intentionally turn attention to one thing or another, intentionally try to make up our minds.)

I am engaged in that activity as I stand on the shore. Presumably, I intend to deliberate, or something of that sort, and as I watch the child drowning, I carry out an intention to continue deliberating, all the while aware that in doing so I am failing to rescue the child. My mental state includes an intention that is relevant to my omission. Just as, in the earlier case of the forking paths, your not taking the left path might be intentional even though you don't intend not to take that path, so here my not jumping in might be intentional even though I don't form an intention not to jump in. In both cases, one's mental state includes some relevant intention, together with an awareness that, in acting as one intends, one won't perform a certain other action that one has reason to perform.

Might some combination of wanting not to A and awareness that one is not A-ing suffice, as far as having the required attitudes goes, for intentionally omitting to A? Just as one can desire to A without being committed to A-ing, so one can desire not to A without being committed to not A-ing. And just as desiring to A, together with an awareness that one is A-ing, does not suffice, as far as having the required attitudes goes, for intentionally A-ing, so it seems having the desire and the awareness is not enough for one's omission to be intentional. Someone who sees the child in trouble might want not to jump in to help, and she might be aware that she's not jumping in, but she might nevertheless not intentionally omit to jump in. She might not be committed to not jumping in, or to anything else at that moment.

If, as appears to be the case, intentionally omitting requires having an intention with relevant content, what content counts as relevant? The concept of intentional omission, like that of intentional action, is vague. There are cases in which the agent clearly has a relevant intention, cases in which the agent clearly does not, and cases in which it is unclear whether the content of any intention possessed by the agent is suitably relevant. In the last of these cases, it might be unclear whether the agent intentionally omits to act. Besides saying that, for intentionally omitting to A, intentions other than one not to A can have relevant content, I doubt that there is much more to say on this point.

Several further observations can be made about intentions in cases of intentional omission. On a widely held view, the representational content of an intention to act is an action plan, and the attitudinal mode is that of being settled or committed: intending to perform an action of A-ing is being settled on or committed to A-ing (see, e.g., Mele 1992, chs. 8 and 9). When one intends not to A, the content of one's plan is not-to-A. There is no need to see the attitudinal mode as any different from that of intending to act.

Sometimes, in intentionally omitting something, one performs some action as a means to that omission (e.g., chewing gum so that one won't smoke). An intention to omit to A can include a more or less elaborate plan for so omitting. But there are cases in which one's intention not to A need not include any plan at all about *how* not to A. One need not always, in order to intentionally omit to A, perform or intend to perform any action at all as a means to not A-ing.[21]

Moreover (contrary to Wilson 1989, 137–142), no intention that one has in a case of intentional omission need refer to anything that the agent in fact does; the agent need not intend of some positive behavior in which she engages that it not be (or not include, or be done instead of, or be allowed not to be, or not allow her to perform) the omitted action (cf. Ginet 2004, 104–106). Ann intends not to pick up Bob at the airport. She need not also intend of her piano playing, or of her going to bed, or of anything else, any of the suggested things. (I might boycott veal for the remainder of my life, without intending of any particular thing I do—and certainly without intending of all of it—that it not be the purchasing of veal.)

At least generally, when one intentionally omits to A, for some relevant time period, one does not intend to A. Certainly one might have earlier intended to A and have since changed one's mind. And one might cease to intend to A and come to intend not to A without ever revoking one's earlier intention. One might forget that one so intends, cease to so intend because one so forgets, and not remember the earlier intention when one later acquires the intention not to A. Finally, just as one can have a nonoccurrent intention to act of which one is unaware and intentionally do something contrary to that intention, so one can have a nonoccurrent intention to A and yet intentionally omit to A. Intentionally omitting to A does not strictly require (for any time period) not intending to A.

4 Causes

On a widely held view of intentional action, mental states or events (or their neural realizers)[22] play a significant causal role in each case of intentional action. It might seem that if many intentional omissions are absences, then such omissions aren't caused by the agents' mental states (or by events involving those agents).

The conditional might be affirmed on the grounds that absences can't be causes or effects.[23] The issue is a contentious one, with many writers on causation holding that absences can indeed cause and be caused. Even some (e.g., Kukso 2006 and Lewis 2004) who take absences not to be entities at all hold that there can be causation of and by absences.

However, it has been argued (by Sartorio 2009) that even if absences can be causes and effects, in a case of intentional omission, it isn't the agent's intending something that causes her omission; it is, rather, her not intending something that causes the omission.

Suppose that Diana is standing by a pond eating ice cream when she sees a child struggling in the water. Diana decides not to jump in to save the child, she intentionally omits to jump in, and the child drowns. One might think that if absences can be caused, then Diana's intending not to jump in is a cause of her not jumping in. However, the argument goes, it is instead her not intending to jump in that causes her omission.

The argument appeals to an analogy between what causes the child's death and what causes Diana's omitting to jump into the water. Suppose that, instead of jumping in, Diana remains on the shore and continues eating ice cream. Consider the following two candidates for causes of the child's death: Diana's eating ice cream on the shore, and her not jumping into the water. Assuming that absences can be causes, clearly the latter causes the death; the child dies because Diana doesn't jump in to save her. Moreover, Diana's eating ice cream isn't an additional cause of the death. The child dies because of what Diana doesn't do, and not because of what she does instead. In fact, it's irrelevant that Diana goes on eating ice cream; all that matters is that she fails to jump in to save the child.

Now, the argument continues, the question of what causes Diana's not jumping in should be answered in an analogous way. Consider these two candidates: her intending not to jump in, and her not intending to jump in. Again, assuming that absences can be causes, the latter clearly causes Diana's not jumping into the water; she omits to jump in because she doesn't intend to jump in. And again, we shouldn't say that her intending not to jump in also causes her omitting to jump in. She omits to jump in because of what she doesn't intend, and not because of what she does intend. In fact, it's irrelevant that she intends not to jump in; all that matters is that she doesn't intend to jump in.

I don't know whether absences can be causes or effects, and although I find the argument just presented less than fully convincing,[24] I'm far from sure that it's mistaken. I'll suppose, for the sake of argument, that (many or all) intentional omissions that are absences aren't caused by the agents' mental states (or by mental events involving those agents), either because absences can't be caused, or because absences of mental states or events cause these omissions. Still, I contend, the agents' mental states (or mental events involving those agents) play a causal role in such cases, one that parallels, in interesting respects, the role they are required by causal theories of action to play in cases of intentional action. Relevant mental states (or events) must cause the agent's subsequent thought or action, even if they needn't cause the absence of some action.

If Diana's omission to jump into the water is caused by her not intending to jump in, the omission's being so-caused evidently isn't what renders it an intentional omission.[25] There might be other folks on the shore who also don't intend to jump in, who also don't jump in, whose not intending to jump in is as good a candidate for a cause of their omission as Diana's is of hers, but who nevertheless don't intentionally omit to jump in. Perhaps the lifeguard fails to notice that the child is in trouble; perhaps someone else, though noticing the trouble, doesn't think of jumping in to help.

We've seen reason to think that in order to intentionally omit to *A*, one must have an intention with relevant content. As the story goes, Diana has such an intention: in deciding not to jump into the water, she forms an intention not to jump in.

Is it enough for Diana's omission to be intentional simply that she have this intention? Need the intention do anything at all? Suppose that, upon deciding not to jump in, Diana immediately wonders what to do instead, forms an intention to walk over to get a better view of the impending tragedy, and then does so (eating her ice cream all the while). In the normal case, we would take it that the intention not to jump in is among the causes of this subsequent sequence of thought and action.[26] Moreover, this causal role seems more than incidental; if we suppose that the intention causes no such things, then it no longer seems that we have a case of intentional omission.

Suppose that Diana's intention not to jump in, whatever it is—some distributed state of her brain, perhaps—comes to exist with the usual causal powers of such a state but is from its start prevented from causally influencing anything—prevented, that is, from manifesting its powers. Just after deciding not to jump in, Diana happens to wonder what to do instead, decides to walk over for a better view, then does so. Something causes this stream of thought and action—perhaps a chip implanted earlier in Diana's brain by a team of neuroscientists, who just happen to have picked the present moment to test their device—but her intention not to jump in isn't a cause of any of what Diana does. In this case, does she intentionally omit to jump into the water?

It seems clear that she does not. Her not jumping in is intended—and she's guilty of so intending—but she doesn't intentionally omit to jump in, because her intention doesn't in any way influence her subsequent thought or action. It's pure happenstance that what she does accords in any way with her intention. For all her intention has to do with things, what she was caused to do might just as well have been to jump into the water and save the child.

The case is analogous to one in which an agent intends to perform a certain action, the appropriate bodily movement occurs, but the agent doesn't perform the intended action, because his intention is ineffective. Unaware that my arm has become paralyzed, I might intend to raise it now. Unaware that I currently so intend, my doctor might test the new motor-control device that she implanted in me during recent surgery. It's sheer coincidence that the movement caused by the doctor accords with my intention, and I don't intentionally raise my arm.

Lest one think that Diana's not jumping in fails to be intentional because, it might now seem, her omission doesn't counterfactually depend on her not intending to jump in,[27] suppose that the implanted chip has an unforeseen flaw: it will remain inert if, when the activation signal is sent to it, the agent in whose brain it's implanted has just decided to jump into water. In any case, an omission's being intentional doesn't require that the omission depend counterfactually on the absence of an intention to perform the action in question. Diana might intentionally omit to jump into the water even if, had she acquired an intention to jump in, she might have changed her mind.

In some cases, the role played by an intention not to act might be less pronounced. Suppose that having decided not to jump in to help, Diana simply stays where she is and continues eating her ice cream. Arguably, an intention she already had—to eat the ice cream—causes her continuing activity. Nevertheless, there would seem also to be a causal role played by her newly formed intention not to jump in. That intention might play a sustaining role, contributing to her continuing to intend to stand there eating the ice cream, and thus to her continuing activity. As intentions usually do, this one could be expected to inhibit further consideration of the question that it settles—the question of whether to help the child. It thereby causally influences Diana's flow of thought. And it might play a causal role that isn't just a matter of what it in fact causes, that of standing ready to cause behavior in accord with its content, should that be necessary.

Generally, there is much less that an intention not to act must do in order to succeed than is required of an intention to act. Where A-ing is performing some positive action, A-ing generally requires that one's behavior fall within some fairly narrow range of possible behaviors, while not A-ing generally requires only that one's behavior remain outside—anywhere outside—some quite narrow range.[28] Hence, the work demands on intentions not to act are usually comparatively light. They can generally succeed by doing relatively little. But if they had no work to do at all—or if in fact they typically did no work at all—it would be a wonder that we ever bother to form such intentions.

The similarity between intentional action and intentional omission appears to go further. In both cases, if one's intention causes what it causes in some peculiar way, so that one has no control over what follows it, then we don't have a case in which something is done intentionally. It's a common observation in action theory that an intention might cause the intended behavior and yet that behavior not constitute intentional action, if the causal pathway is wayward or deviant.[29] Something similar would seem to be so in the case of intentional omissions. Ann might intentionally omit to pick up Bob at the airport at 2:30 even if she's asleep at 2:30, but we won't have a case of intentional omission if her falling asleep happens this way: her forming the intention not to pick up Bob immediately (and unexpectedly) triggers a prolonged episode of narcolepsy.[30]

If, in a case of intentional omission, an intention with relevant content must indeed play a causal role in the course of what does occur, then, in many cases at least, there is an important sense in which intentional omissions result from intentions not to act, even if such intentions don't cause the omissions. Suppose that Diana's standing on the shore eating ice cream at time t is caused by (among other things) her intention (formed prior to t) not to jump in. It can't be that at t she's standing on the shore and at t she's jumping into the water; the one precludes the other. Her not jumping in is a consequence of (it results from) her intending not to jump in, even if it isn't a causal consequence. (Note that this holds as well if the omission, because it is an absence, can't be caused by anything.)[31]

A standard causal theory of action holds that, in a case of intentional action, an intention with relevant content must appropriately cause certain agent-involving events. It seems that in a case of intentional omission, likewise, an intention with relevant content must play an appropriate causal role with respect to what happens.

In the latter case, no specific intention is required, at no particular time, and what intention there is need not cause anything in particular—it need not, for example, directly cause any action. Still, there are imaginable cases in which no intention with relevant content is present at any pertinent time, or in which, though present, such an intention causes nothing, or causes what it does in such a way that control is lost. And in such cases, it does not seem that the omission is intentional. The apparent need for the appropriate causal effectiveness of a pertinent intention is nontrivial, and it constitutes an interesting and important similarity between intentional action and intentional omission.

5   Omitting for Reasons

Generally, intentional actions are actions performed for reasons. Likewise, typically when one intentionally omits to A, one omits for a reason. Ann omits to pick up Bob at the airport because she's tired and (she knows) he can take a taxi. What, if anything, is the causal role of the reasons for which one intentionally omits?

According to causal theories of action, when one acts for reasons, the reasons for which one acts (or mental states with those reasons as their objects—for brevity I'll henceforth ignore this alternative) are causes of one's action. On the supposition that causal theories are correct about the role of reasons in cases of intentional action, in cases of intentional omission in which the omission is itself an action, the role of reasons is the same. On that same supposition, in cases of intentional omission in which the omission is not an action, reasons still seem to play a causal role.

Intentionally omitting to A, it appears, requires having at some pertinent time an intention with relevant content. Reasons for which one intentionally omits to A would play the same role in causing such an intention as do reasons in causing the intention to act that one has when one intentionally As. (This is so in Diana's case as well as in cases like that of the forking paths.)

I've argued, further, that if in fact an intention with relevant content is required, then when one intentionally omits to A, such an intention is a cause of one's subsequent thought and action—it plays a causal role with respect to events that do occur. Reasons for which one omits to A would, on our supposition, play a similar role, by way of causing one's intention. Even if one's intention not to A (or other relevant intention) doesn't cause one's omission, there is causal work for the reasons for which one omits to *A*.

6 Agency, Actions, and Omissions

Still, if for either of the reasons identified at the start of section 4, intentional omissions that are absences aren't caused by the agents' intentions, does this fact constitute trouble for "causalism as an attempt to explain what it is for an agent to behave intentionally" (Sartorio 2009, 513)? It presents no problem for causal theories of *action*. Such theories are not theories of omissions that aren't actions, and they strictly imply nothing about such things.

We might sensibly construe agency more broadly as encompassing all that is done intentionally, and so as including intentional omissions. At least typically, things done intentionally fulfill intentions and are done for reasons. Such things may fairly be said to be manifestations of our agency. We might then wonder about the prospects for a causal theory of this broader phenomenon.

But with agency so construed, it should not be expected that it must be possible to construct a uniform theory of it, for the phenomenon itself lacks uniformity, including, as it does, actions as well as things that aren't actions. It will be no fault of any theory of intentional action if it does not apply, in a straightforward way, to all of what is then counted as intentional agency. And a comprehensive theory of agency (if any such thing is possible) might play out one way in the case of action and another in the case of omission. If such an account has to have a disjunctive character, that need might accurately reflect the diversity of its subject matter.

We might nevertheless expect that the right account of intentional omission will resemble in important respects the right account of intentional action. If what I've said here is correct, the resemblance to causal theories of action is significant. But to the extent that omissions that aren't actions are unlike actions, it should not be surprising that the similarity is imperfect.

Acknowledgments

For helpful comments on earlier versions of this essay, I wish to thank Carl Ginet, Alison McIntyre, Al Mele, Carolina Sartorio, Kadri Vihvelin, Michael Zimmerman, and an anonymous referee for *Noûs*.

Notes

1. The last two of these, and more, are mentioned by McIntyre (1985).

2. Some theorists (e.g., Bennett 2008, 49) hold that one is responsible for something only if one is either blameworthy or praiseworthy for that thing. Plainly on this view there can be intentional omissions—those that are morally neutral or indifferent—for which no one is responsible. But there can be such omissions even if there can be moral responsibility for morally neutral things. Some agents (e.g., young children, or people suffering from certain mental illnesses) lacking some of the capacities required for responsibility nevertheless engage in intentional action and intentionally omit to do certain things. And while many theorists hold that responsibility for unintentional omissions must stem from something done intentionally, others (e.g., Smith 2005) deny this claim. In sum, the relation between responsibility and what is done intentionally is both complex and contested. This fact constitutes one reason for taking a direct approach to the topic of intentional omission.

3. Cf. Mele 2003, 152, and McIntyre 1985, 47–48. McIntyre draws the distinction as one between intentionally omitting and its being intentional on one's part that one omits. Note that we might say that Ulysses intentionally prevented himself from jumping into the sea. We should then recognize that one can intentionally prevent oneself from doing a certain thing and yet not intentionally omit to do that thing. Finally, one might take this case to support the view that intentionally omitting to A requires that one be able to A. I briefly discuss such a requirement in section 2 below.

4. "To A" is used throughout as a stand-in for expressions indicating types of positive action, such as to raise one's arm or to speak.

5. The example is from Mele (1997a, 232), though he employs it for a different purpose.

6. Note that the child doesn't simply prevent herself from moving; she both intentionally holds still and intentionally omits to move. Unlike Ulysses, at the time in question she isn't trying to do what she does not do.

7. This kind of case was suggested in conversation by Al Mele. Note that one can omit to intentionally omit to A, and yet not A. I might plan not to A, forget my plan, but also not think to A (and thus not A).

8. But can't we think about nonexistent things? Sure, but the intentionality or directedness of a thought isn't a genuine relation (Brentano 1995, 271–274; cf. Molnar 2003, 62).

9. Fischer and Zimmerman make these claims with respect to a "broad" conception of omission; both recognize that there are narrower conceptions.

10. Cases of this sort are offered by Frankfurt (1969) to rebut the thesis that one can be responsible for what one has done only if one could have done otherwise.

11. There is a sizable literature addressing the question of whether agents in Frankfurt-type cases might be responsible for omitting to do certain things even though they're unable to do those things. See, e.g., Byrd 2007; Clarke 1994; Fischer 1985–1986; Fischer and Ravizza 1998, ch. 5; McIntyre 1994; and Sartorio 2005. Participants in this debate evidently take there to be some type of ability to *A* that isn't required for omitting to *A*.

12. Ginet (2004) takes the case to support his claim that intentionally not *A*-ing at *t* requires that one could have *A*-ed at *t* (or at least could have done something by which one might have *A*-ed at *t*). I've suggested that whether the requirement holds depends on which type of ability to act is being invoked.

13. To be precise, it is "intentionally not doing" that is the target of Ginet's analysis. However, his examples are cases of what I'm calling intentional omissions.

14. McIntryre (1985, 79–80) discusses a similar case, though for a different purpose.

15. Al Mele suggested this case in conversation.

16. The objection was raised by a referee for *Noûs*.

17. For discussion of such a requirement, see Mele 1992, ch. 8. Bratman's video-game case (1987, 113–115) supports a different line of argument for the claim that one can take something as a hoped-for goal, and try to achieve it, without intending it. The case also supports the view that one can intentionally *A* without intending to *A*.

18. Some writers distinguish between "direct intention" and "oblique intention," holding that although one might lack a direct intention to bring about certain consequences, one has an oblique intention to bring them about if one's so doing is foreseen (or considered likely or certain). (The distinction stems from Bentham 1996, 86.) An oblique intention is said to be "a kind of knowledge or realisation" (Williams 1987, 421).

Such a state differs importantly from what action theorists commonly call intention. The latter is typically distinguished by its characteristic functional role. Having an intention to perform a certain action at some point in the nonimmediate future (a future-directed intention) tends to inhibit subsequent deliberation about whether to do that thing (though having such an intention doesn't altogether preclude reconsideration); it tends to inhibit consideration of actions obviously incompatible with what is intended; and it tends to promote further reasoning about means to what is intended. When one becomes aware that the time for action has arrived, a future-directed intention to act tends to cause (or become) an intention to act straightaway. Such a present-directed intention tends to cause an attempt to perform the intended action. When carried out, a present-directed intention typically triggers, sustains, and guides action, often in response to feedback. (Bratman 1987 and Mele 1992, part 2, develop this conception of intention.) So-called oblique intentions don't play such a role in practical reasoning or action.

One might suggest that actions that are only obliquely intended can only be obliquely intentional. It is hard to see more to the claim than an acknowledgment that an action can be intentional even though the agent lacked an intention (of the sort just characterized) to perform it.

19. I've described several cases (that of an individual step taken while walking, that of trying to do something when one expects not to succeed, and that of foreseen consequences that one has reason to avoid) that have been taken to undermine a certain thesis about intentional action, viz., that intentionally A-ing requires intending to A. As a referee for *Noûs* observed, one might seek to defend that thesis by appealing to a distinction between an action's being intentional (under some description or other) and its being intentional under a certain specified description. One might claim, for example, that while what I do when I take the step is intentional under some description (such as "walking"), it isn't intentional under the description "taking that step." I don't myself find this claim convincing. However, it isn't my aim here to refute the indicated thesis. What I've aimed to do is present some forceful considerations that have been brought against it and show that there is an equally strong, largely parallel case to be made against the view that intentionally omitting to A requires intending not to A.

20. Sartorio is mainly concerned to argue that no intention need cause an intentional omission. Though she seems doubtful that any relevant intention need even be possessed, she doesn't commit herself on this latter question.

21. Sartorio (2009, 528, n. 22) suggests that "negative intentions" might have to be rejected, for "it's hard to say what the plan might be in the case of omissions." In some cases, one's plan for not A-ing might be just not-to-A.

22. Some causalists (e.g., Mele 1992, ch. 2), in response to the problem of mental causation, hold that (roughly) it is enough for intentional action if the neural realizers of the agent's mental states play the appropriate causal role, provided that what the agent does counterfactually depends, in a certain way, on her mental states. I'll henceforth simplify the causalist view by omitting this variation.

23. Weinryb (1980) argues that omissions have no causal effects. Beebee (2004) argues that absences aren't causes or effects.

24. For one thing, the argument relies heavily on explanatory claims. But true explanatory claims don't always cite causes, even when the explanations are causal. On this point, see Beebee 2004.

25. As discussed earlier, Sartorio takes the omission to be intentional because, she says, it is caused by the agent's *intentionally* omitting to intend to jump into the

water. I've raised questions about how it can be made out that the agent's not so intending is itself intentional.

26. Might an argument like the one sketched earlier in this section show that, in the normal case, it would be the absence of an intention to jump in, and not the intention not to jump in, that causes not just the omission but also the subsequent thought and action? Diana's decision and her subsequent thinking might be brain occurrences, and (in our original version of the case) the production of the latter by the former might consist in just the sort of transfer of energy that we have in standard cases of direct causal production. Moreover, her decision seems as plainly a cause of her positive behavior in this version of the case as our intentions to act seem to be causes of our intentional actions. One might try pushing a standard argument against mental causation at this juncture, but the special argument focused on omissions seems inapplicable.

27. One might take a lack of counterfactual dependence as at least a defeasible reason for denying a causal relation. Then, if like Sartorio, one thinks that an intentional omission to A must be caused by the absence of a certain intention, one might take a lack of counterfactual dependence to count against the claim that the omission is intentional.

28. Bennett (1995, ch. 6) makes a similar point, albeit about what I take to be a different distinction, that between making happen and allowing to happen.

29. For discussion of the problem of causal deviance, and for some proposed solutions, see Bishop 1989, ch. 5; Brand 1984, 17–30; Davidson 1980, 79; Enç 2003, ch. 4; Goldman 1970, 61–63; and Mele 2003, 51–63.

30. It's an interesting question, and one that I can't answer here, whether the required nondeviance in the case of intentional omission is susceptible to conceptual analysis. Given how little causal work might be required of one's intention in such a case, there's reason to doubt that causation "in the right way" is analyzable here in the same way that it is in the case of intentional action. Whether the impossibility of conceptual analysis would be fatal to a causal theory of intentional omission depends on what is to be expected of such a theory. (I'm grateful to a referee for raising this issue.)

31. One might (as a referee suggested) take Diana's not jumping in to be a causal consequence of her intending not to jump in on the following grounds: her so intending causes her standing on the shore, and (one might hold) her not jumping in is a logical consequence of her standing on the shore. It would seem that, barring time travel, Diana's jumping into the water at t is logically incompossible with her standing on the shore at t. However, it is far from obvious that an event causes the absence of whatever is logically incompossible with what that event causes.

10 Comments on Clarke's "Intentional Omissions"

Carolina Sartorio

Clarke argues for two main claims in his essay. The first is:

(i) In order for an agent's omitting to A to be intentional, some intention with the appropriate content (e.g., the intention not to A or a related intention) must play a causal role in the situation.

This is the main source of disagreement between Clarke's proposal and my proposal. I argued that, at least ordinarily, the agent's *omitting to intend* to A (which is itself an intentional omission) causes his omitting to A, and that this is enough to explain why the agent's omitting to A is intentional. There is no further need to say that the agent's having formed a certain intention also plays a causal role (in particular, by causing his omitting to A).

Clarke also argues for:

(ii) The causal role the relevant intention plays in each case is that (or includes the fact that) it causes the agent's subsequent thought and action.

I'll briefly comment on each of these claims.

1 Clarke's Argument for (i)

This comment is partly a request for clarification, since I'm not sure I understand exactly what Clarke's argument for (i) is. Clarke doesn't seem to have objections to my claim that, when an agent intentionally omits to A, the agent's omission to intend to A causes his omitting to A. But, presumably, he thinks that this isn't enough to explain why the agent's omitting to A is intentional. For, he seems to think, such a fact would only explain why the omission to A is intentional if it were clear that the omission to intend to A is *also* intentional; however, it is hard to say what it is for an agent's omitting to intend to act to be intentional (Clarke, this vol., chap. 9, 143–144 and n. 24).[1]

I agree that it might be hard to specify precisely the conditions under which an omission to intend to *A* is intentional. But, surely, we can make sense of the concept of intentionally omitting to intend to act, and there seem to be some clear applications of such a concept. I will consider a couple. Take, first, an agent who is unaware of the presence of the child in the water. According to a broad conception of omissions that Clarke thinks is theoretically fruitful (one on which "there is an omission when-ever an agent doesn't perform a certain action that she is, in a relevant sense, able to perform," 141), one of the things that the agent omits to do in this case is to form the intention to jump in (since she didn't form the intention to jump in and, arguably, she was, in the relevant sense, able to do so). But, surely, her omitting to intend to jump in isn't intentional (jumping in didn't even cross her mind). By contrast, take one of Clarke's characters, Diana. Diana is fully aware of the presence of the child but still, after deliberating about it for a while, decides not to save him and to con-tinue to eat her ice cream on the shore. Again, according to the extant conception of omissions, Diana omits to intend to jump in. Is this omis-sion intentional? Surely, it is: one of the differences between the two cases is that, although both agents omit to form the intention to jump in, Diana does so intentionally, unlike the agent in the first case.[2]

But, if Diana's omitting to form the intention to jump in is intentional, and if her omitting to form the intention to jump in causes her omitting to jump in, then why is it that some intention of hers must *also* play a causal role in the situation, in order for her omitting to jump in to be intentional?

2   Clarke's Argument for (ii)

Clarke argues that, when Diana decides not to save the drowning child and to continue to eat her ice cream on the shore, her intention not to jump in causes her subsequent action of continuing to eat ice cream on the shore. This is an interesting proposal that would (if true) preserve the causal efficacy of negative intentions, and would also bring actions and omissions a bit closer together, as Clarke points out. I will argue, however, that some plausible assumptions (including assumptions that Clarke explicitly accepts) suggest that Diana's negative intention doesn't actually play such a causal role.

For Clarke, a main reason not to identify omissions with actions (at least generally) is that actions and omissions tend to have different causal powers. As an example of this, he gives the following case (137). Ann promised to pick up Bob at the airport late at night. Feeling lazy, and thinking that he can take a cab, she decides to stay home playing piano instead. This keeps her neighbor awake. Clarke believes that, whereas Ann's playing piano causes her neighbor to stay awake, her omitting to pick up Bob doesn't. Again, this is a reason not to identify Ann's omission to pick up Bob with her action of playing piano. I agree.

Now consider the intentions that Ann forms in this case. Presumably, Clarke would say that we should distinguish a "positive" intention—the intention to play piano—from a "negative" intention—the intention not to pick up Bob at the airport. Which of these intentions causes her to play piano? Surely, her intention to play piano causes her to play piano. But, does her intention not to pick up Bob *also* cause her to play piano? Given what Clarke wants to say about the Diana case, it seems that he would have to say that it does: given that Ann's omitting to pick up Bob was intentional, her intention not to pick up Bob must have caused her subsequent thought and action, including her playing piano. But this is an odd result, given Clarke's initial assumption about the causal powers of actions and omissions. Why think that bodily positive and negative acts have different causal powers but their mental counterparts (positive and negative intentions) don't? If there is good reason to think that Ann's omitting to pick up Bob doesn't cause what her playing piano causes, isn't there also good reason to think that her intending to omit to pick up Bob doesn't cause what her intending to play piano causes?

I believe that there is, in fact, good reason to think this. Presumably, the reason to think that Ann's omitting to pick up Bob doesn't cause her neighbor to stay awake is that her neighbor stays awake, intuitively, not because of what she *doesn't* do that night, but because of what she *does*. Similarly, it also seems that Ann plays piano that night, not because of what she intends *not* to do that night, but because of what she intends to *do*.

One could try to object to this by saying: there is a sense in which she plays piano because of what she intends not to do. Namely: in the circumstances, were it not for the fact that she intended not to pick up Bob, she couldn't have intended to stay at home playing piano, and then she wouldn't have played piano. But the same is true of her omitting to pick up Bob and the outcome of her neighbor's staying awake: were it not for the fact that she omitted to pick up Bob, she couldn't have stayed at home playing piano, and then her neighbor wouldn't have stayed awake. So it seems that whatever reasons we have for thinking that Ann's omitting to pick up Bob doesn't cause her neighbor to stay awake are also reasons for thinking that her intending not to pick up Bob doesn't cause her playing piano.

In support of his claim that the agent's negative intention must cause the subsequent positive behavior in order for his omission to be intentional, Clarke imagines a case where the agent (Diana) forms a negative intention but then the intention gets to play no causal role at all (it is preempted by a chip implanted by neuroscientists, which causes Diana to continue eating her ice cream on the shore). In this case, Clarke argues that Diana's omitting to jump in isn't intentional. But, even if this is true, this doesn't show that, for Diana's omission to be intentional, her intending not to jump in must cause her continuing to eat ice cream. Perhaps she must intentionally omit to intend to jump in and such omission must cause her omitting to jump in (as I propose). Or perhaps I am wrong and her intending not to jump in must cause her omitting to jump in. Or, finally, perhaps three things have to happen: (i) she must intend not to jump in; (ii) she must intend to perform a different act incompatible with jumping in (e.g., eating ice cream on the shore at the time); and (iii) such an intention must cause that action. There could be other possibilities. Presumably, none of these sets of conditions is met in the neuroscientist scenario. The chip, and only the chip, accounts for Diana's subsequent behavior in that case. Hence the neuroscientist case doesn't support Clarke's claim that, for an agent's omission to be intentional, the agent's negative intention must cause her subsequent thought and action.

Acknowledgment

I am grateful to Andrei Buckareff and Randolph Clarke for helpful discussion.

Notes

1. All page numbers refer to Clarke's chapter 9 of this volume.

2. A natural thing to say, at least in this case, is that what makes Diana's omission to intend to jump in intentional is the fact that she considered possible reasons to jump in but she took those reasons to be outweighed by reasons to continue eating her ice cream on the shore.

11 Reply to Sartorio

Randolph Clarke

After drinking with his buddies one evening, Tom was tired. While they vowed to carry on all night—and did—he went home and slept. Tom intentionally omitted to join them in toasting the sunrise. Was he engaged in some kind of behavior at dawn? Something dormitive, perhaps, but nothing of the kind that action theory aims to characterize.

We can perfectly well use the term "behavior" in a broader sense, to cover all things done intentionally, including Tom's omitting to drink till dawn. But if we do, we should see that "behavior" is a disparate category, including actions and things that aren't actions. And we should then not expect a highly uniform theory of this broader phenomenon.

If, then, the right account of intentional omission doesn't precisely parallel a causal theory of action, does this fact make trouble for "causalism as an attempt to explain what it is for an agent to behave intentionally" (as Sartorio, this vol., chap. 8, 115, claims)?[1] That depends on just how the correct account goes and to what exactly "causalism" is committed.

Sartorio alleges that a proponent of causalism will hold that when one intentionally omits to A, one's omission is caused by one's forming an intention not to A (or an intention with some other relevant content). But a causal theory of action doesn't commit one to this view, since it isn't a theory of things that aren't actions; and one can be a causalist about intentional behavior, broadly construed, without holding this view. Indeed, Sartorio's account of intentional omission is causalist while rejecting the indicated view, for she holds that a paradigmatic intentional omission is caused by one's omission to intend.

Still, as her account is spelled out, something that a standard causal theory requires for intentional action—an important causal role for mental states or events—is not said to be required for intentional omission. If there is no such requirement, that is an important fact, even if it doesn't force the rejection altogether of a causal approach to intentional behavior.

However, I'm not convinced that no such requirement falls on intentional omission. Consider, first, what Sartorio says suffices for intentionally omitting to A: that the omission is caused by one's intentionally omitting to intend to A (or to have some other pertinent intention). It strikes me as a misstep to try to account for one omission's being intentional by appealing to yet another omission's being intentional. Further, the notion of intentionally omitting to intend is rather obscure, and I don't see that Sartorio provides much clarification of it.

One does not intentionally omit to intend to A, she holds, if A-ing does not even cross one's mind; that much seems right. One intentionally omitted to intend to A, she says, if one "voluntarily failed to form that intention, after deliberating about whether to do so, after considering reasons for and against doing so, and so on" (126). As I observed in my essay (chapter 9 of this vol.), the claim that the omission to intend was voluntary seems to presuppose that, rather than explain how, it was intentional. And the fact that one had deliberated and considered relevant reasons and still not formed the intention doesn't suffice to make the omission to intend intentional, for one might have simply failed to make up one's mind.

It's not just that Sartorio hasn't specified "precisely the conditions under which an omission to intend to A is intentional" (chap. 10, 158). There are few philosophically interesting phenomena for which we can do this. Rather, the notion appealed to here is left quite unclear, and the appeal seems both unnecessary and unhelpful. We are not told, for example, whether intentionally omitting to intend to A requires that the omission to intend to A be caused by something in particular (some further omission, or the individual's mental states), or whether in order for that omission to be intentional, there must be some further intentional omission to intend. The latter requirement, of course, would threaten an endless regress; but if the regress can be stopped at this point, why can't it be avoided altogether?

Although Sartorio doesn't claim that intentionally omitting to intend to A (or to have some other pertinent intention) is *necessary* for intentionally omitting to A, it is perhaps worth observing that it doesn't seem to be. One might intentionally omit to A without having deliberated about whether to A, and without having made a decision on the matter. One might spontaneously—and nonactively—acquire an intention not to A without having raised the question of whether to A, just as one can so acquire an intention to act. (Audi 1993, 64 provides a nice example of the latter. As for the former: I see a snake crossing the path ahead, and I immediately intend not to take another step forward. I refrain from walking further.) If one's omitting to intend to *A* (e.g., to continue walking) might nevertheless be intentional, it remains to be explained how this can be so.

Indeed, strictly speaking, lacking an intention to *A* isn't necessary for intentionally omitting to *A*. One can have intentions of which one is unaware, just as one can have beliefs and desires of which one is unaware. Unaware that one intends not to *A*, one might *A*, and do so intentionally—meaning then to *A* (and *A*-ing attentively, carefully, expertly). Similarly, unaware that one intends to *A*, one might refrain from *A*-ing, meaning then not to *A*.

Just how far Sartorio's view of intentional omission diverges from what causal theorists require for intentional action depends on what she thinks about omitting for reasons, something that she doesn't discuss. Things done intentionally are typically done for reasons. If one's omitting to intend on some occasion is intentional, and done for reasons, we might ask in virtue of what the latter is so. Must certain of one's reason-states—one's beliefs, desires, affections, aversions, and the like—be causes of one's omitting to intend? If Sartorio accepts such a requirement, that will render her account more thoroughly causalist, even if it still denies intentions any necessary causal role. If she denies the requirement, then we might fairly request a sketch of some alternative view.

I claimed in my essay that in order to intentionally omit to *A*, one's intention not to *A* (or some other pertinent intention) must cause some of one's subsequent thought and action. It must play a causal role with respect to what does happen, even if it need not cause any absences. Sartorio asks what my argument for this claim is. I observed that in standard cases of intentional omission, such an intention does in fact cause such things. And when I considered a case in which this was not so, it seemed to me that the omission was then not intentional, and that it failed to be intentional because the intention in question didn't play the indicated causal role.

In the imagined case (this vol., chap. 9, 147–148), Diana decided not to jump into a pond to save a drowning child. She then wondered what to do instead, formed an intention to walk over to get a better view of the impending tragedy, and did so. But her intention not to jump in caused none of these things; they were all caused by a chip that had been implanted in Diana's brain earlier by a team of neuroscientists, who (unaware of Diana's decision) just happened to have picked this moment to test their device. They got lucky, for the chip, I noted, had an unforeseen flaw: it would have remained inert if, when the activation signal was sent, the agent in whose brain it was implanted had just decided to jump into water.

Sartorio finds no support here for the causal requirement I proposed. There are, she says, other possible explanations of why Diana's not jumping in isn't intentional. She suggests, first, that Diana's omission might fail to be intentional because her omitting to intend to jump in doesn't cause her not jumping in. But is that so? The chip causes Diana's thought and action, but, as Sartorio recognizes, it's a further question what causes Diana's omitting to jump in. As the case is imagined, if Diana had intended to jump in, she would have; her not so intending made a difference to what she did. If omissions to intend ever cause omissions to act, it isn't clear why this one doesn't.

Second, Sartorio suggests that Diana's omitting to jump in might fail to be intentional because her intending not to jump in doesn't cause that omission. But if that is correct, it suggests that intentions not to act must play an even more robust causal role in intentional omissions than what I argued, and the right account of intentional omission will, after all, closely parallel a causal theory of intentional action.

Finally, Sartorio suggests that in order for Diana to have intentionally omitted to jump in, she must have intended to perform some act incompatible with her jumping in, and that intention must have caused that action. But, as I think the paint case from my essay (this vol., 138) shows, intentionally omitting to A doesn't require performing any action that one takes to be incompatible with A-ing; it doesn't require, either, intending to perform any such action.

There might, in fact, be more than one correct explanation of why Diana's omitting to jump in isn't intentional, as there will be if several necessary conditions are unsatisfied. Though the case seems to me supportive, perhaps no single example will decisively show my proposal correct. The proposal can, however, be undermined if there is a case in which someone intentionally omits something and yet no relevant intention plays the indicated causal role.

I said that in standard cases of intentional omission, one's intention not to act (or other relevant intention) is in fact a cause of one's subsequent thought and action. Sartorio disputes this claim. In my case involving Ann (135), she maintains, it is Ann's intention to play piano, not her intention not to pick up Bob, that causes her piano playing. But the two intentions aren't competitors; they are, respectively, later and earlier members of a causal sequence leading to Ann's playing piano. The intention not to pick up Bob causes Ann to consider what to do instead, which causes her to decide to play piano, which causes her piano playing. One need not hold that causation is necessarily transitive to find plausible the claim that Ann's intention not to pick up Bob indirectly causes her piano playing.

Comparing Ann's intention not to pick up Bob with her omitting to pick him up, Sartorio asks, "Why think that bodily positive and negative acts have different causal powers but their mental counterparts (positive and negative intentions) don't?" (chap. 10, 159). But Ann's intention not to pick up Bob is an intention, whereas her omitting to pick him up is not an action. Were the case real, the former would be an actually existing being, negative only in its content (just as is my belief that Santa Claus doesn't exist). In contrast, the latter (I'm inclined to think) would be an absence of being—the absence of an act by Ann of picking up Bob at the airport. A causal impotence of the latter is no reflection on the former.

Although I don't, in my essay, dispute Sartorio's claim that omissions to intend cause intentional omissions, I'm in fact doubtful about this. At bottom, I find it doubtful that an absence of being can cause something. Sartorio writes of omissions having causal powers; but I don't see how nonbeings can have any such powers.

I've advanced considerations favoring an account of intentional omission that makes no appeal to causation by absences. The proffered view accords a causal role to mental states, including intentions, and sees intentional omissions as resulting—even if noncausally—from such states. If an account along these lines is correct, omissions make trouble neither for causal theories of action nor for causal approaches to intentional behavior, broadly construed.

Note

1. Unless otherwise noted, all page numbers refer to Sartorio's chapters in this volume.

12 Causal and Deliberative Strength of Reasons for Action: The Case of Con-Reasons

David-Hillel Ruben

An agent's having of a reason for an action (hereafter, simply "a reason") is often said to be among the causes or causal conditions of the action for which it is a reason (in this wide sense, "action" includes many cases of inaction).[1] Hereafter, this view is referred to as *causalism*, or (1). Causalism as here understood is a thesis about causation, not about causal explanation.

Causation and causal explanation might come apart in both directions, as it were. There might be causal explanations that do not cite any or only causes, under any description. In any case, it is clear that there can be true causal statements such that the cause is not explanatory of its effect because of the description of the cause in that statement, but there might even be causes such that, under no description of the cause, does the cause explain its effect. In this essay, I remain agnostic about all such possibilities.

An agent can, of course, have a reason for an action without its being a cause of that action, but in the case in which the agent performs the action because of that reason, the reason is said, according to causalism, to cause the action. If we conflate just for the moment questions about causation and causal explanation, Donald Davidson's well-known argument attempts to demonstrate just this: "If . . . causal explanations are 'wholly irrelevant to the understanding we seek' of human actions then we are without an analysis of the 'because' in 'He did it because . . .,' where we go on to name a reason" (Davidson 2001a, 86–87). The reasons Davidson focuses on, in this argument and elsewhere, are reasons which function as "pro-reasons," in two closely connected senses: (a) these are reasons that are relevant to, or bear upon, the action the agent does in fact take; (b) they are reasons that favor that action. Davidson's reasons consist of a belief and a pro-attitude toward the kind of action the agent does. Other views might identify intentions or some other mental items as these reasons, but precisely which mental items count, on a causalist view, as reasons will not concern me here (von Wright 1978, 46–62). I also take no view here about the nature of such mental items; they might or might not be token-identical to brain or other physiological states.

The reasons that (1) is about are sometimes called "explanatory" reasons in contradistinction to "justifying" reasons, or "motivating" reasons in contradistinction to "normative" reasons, or "internal" reasons in contradistinction to "external" reasons. These are three different distinctions, related to one another in complicated ways. The reasons required by (1) are surely at least motivating: these are the reasons that have actual psychological "purchase" on the agent, and are not *just* there and merely in principle available to the agent in some wholly objective sense. A well-known view, which is also adopted by the position I am considering, asserts that the only reasons that could play the causal role required by the idea of motivation, and hence explain why the agent did what he did, are the agent's internal psychological states. So the reasons required by (1), as I construe it, are internal, explanatory, and motivating, although these reasons, just insofar as they are *reasons* for action, are being asked to play something of a weakly normative role as well.

The literature in action theory has tended to overlook the fact that reasons function in another way too.[2] (a) One can have reasons for an action that one does not take; (b) one can have reasons that disfavor an action taken (a "con-attitude," to parallel Davidson's "pro-attitude"). Sometimes a person has conflicting reasons for acting, one set of which is a set on which he does *not* act, and both sets of conflicting reasons can be rationally or deliberatively relevant to, or bear upon, the same choice situation and rationally or deliberatively relevant to the same action finally chosen. The con-reason is relevant to the action taken, in the sense that that it is the action it disfavors. Both the pro- and the con-reason, as I shall continue to say, are "rationally or deliberatively relevant" to, or "bear upon," the same eventual choice made or action taken. The pro-reason is relevant to the action taken because it favors it; the con-reason is relevant to the action taken because it disfavors it. Each set of reasons justifies or supports a different proposed action on the agent's part, and the agent is not able to perform both actions, because it is impossible to act in both ways at the same time.

The reasons might strongly conflict, in the way in which a reason to do some token act of type *A* (or, as I sometimes elliptically say, a reason to *A*) and a reason not to do any token act of type *A* conflict; or the reasons might weakly conflict, in the way in which a reason to do some token act

of type A and a reason to do some act of type B (or, as I sometimes elliptically say, a reason to B) conflict on any occasion on which one cannot as
a matter of fact do both. On an occasion on which one cannot do both,
a reason to do an act of type B must also be a reason not to do an act of
type A, but only modulo the additional information that one cannot do
both acts in the circumstances. In the case of strong conflict, no additional
information is similarly required.

Suppose that X has a reason to do a token action of type A and a reason
to do a token action of type B, where the two reasons weakly conflict on
the particular occasion. Suppose further that X chooses to perform a token
action of type A. The first reason, which favored doing A, was rationally
or deliberatively weightier (in the circumstances, of course) than the
second, which favored doing B; the first counted for more, as far as X was
concerned. As we say, all things considered, X chose to perform a token
action of type A. (I write as if choice precedes every action, but my argument would be unaltered if choice were not ubiquitous in this way.) The
single final choice made or action taken is made or taken *because* of the
pro-reason and *in spite of* the con-reason. Indeed, that is what "all things
considered" must mean: because of the one set of reasons and in spite of
the other.[3] As Dancy (2004, 4) says about these con-reasons: "But still I
was influenced by them [the con-reasons] and they do figure in my motivational economy."

We use the language of reasons, weights, and strength, in describing
our deliberations. Such language is metaphorical, but, metaphorical or not,
it certainly seems irreplaceable. We can order reasons for action by their
comparative strengths: one reason for action can be stronger than another,
weaker than a third. Whether or not there are nonrelational truths about
the deliberative strength of reasons, on which the relational truths about
them supervene, it is relational information about reasons that is crucial
for understanding the deliberative story.[4] (Note that if there is such supervenience, the same relational story can supervene on different nonrelational stories. What supervenience rules out is the possibility of different
relational stories supervening on the same nonrelational or intrinsic story.)
If we have both pro- and con-reasons, we want to know which reason wins
the deliberative contest. It is only the relational information about the
rational strength of reasons for action that interests us in cases of choices
between actions.

The notion that reasons are causes, causalism, ties rationality and causality, in some way yet to be discerned. This would allow us to distinguish
two kinds of strengths for reasons: rational or deliberative strength (as

above) and causal strength. Deliberative or rational strength is a measure of the extent to which a reason for action supports that action. Rational strength is an epistemologically normative idea, sometimes called "weak normativity." There is an analogy between this idea and the idea of the degree of support given by evidence to a conclusion in an inductive argument. A reason's comparative or relational rational strength compares it to the support competing reasons give to the alternative actions they support.

The problem of weakness of the will arises for the causalist as an issue because it challenges the natural tie, on the causalist program, between rational and causal strength of reasons for action. For the causalist, weakness of the will appears to force a wedge between the normative/rational and the causal/motivational ideas of a reason. Davidson himself says that

(2) "if reasons are causes, it is natural to suppose that the strongest reasons are the strongest causes" (Davidson 2001a, xvi).

Any causal view is going to have to address the question: how are rational and causal strength related? It is this question that gives rise to the problem that the causalist faces with weakness of the will. In a case of weakness of will, the rationally stronger reason is not the reason that causes or motivates the agent to act, if reasons do in fact cause actions. The agent acts on a rationally weaker reason, but one that is causally strong enough, where the rationally stronger reason is not causally strong enough. "Causally strong enough or not so" just means: the rationally weaker reason causes the action it supports, and the rationally stronger reason does not cause the action it supports.

I do not know whether the causalist can really successfully deal with the phenomenon of weakness of the will. But I want, in this essay, to address a different issue, unconnected to weakness of the will. Let's start by trying to trace out the causal chains that lead from the con-reasons, for on the causalist view con-reasons must have some effects, whatever they might be. The thought that there are events, con-reasons, which have no effects at all, is not one likely to appeal to the causalist. To be part of the causal order is surely to have both causes and effects.[5]

There are two importantly different cases that I want to distinguish (from the causalist point of view). In cases of Type I, the pro-reason and the con-reason jointly cause the same effect; in cases of Type II, they have separate and causally independent effects.

Type I: These cases are the ones that will most naturally spring to mind on a causalist view, but I believe that such cases are more limited than one might unreflectively assume. Let's start with an analogy from natural science. In circumstances c, a ball falls toward the Earth because of gravitational attraction and despite the presence of an upward wind. One could say: the cause of the ball falling to Earth is jointly both the gravitational attraction and the relative weakness of the wind's counteracting force. The two causal factors jointly contribute to the same result, the ball's final trajectory. The relative weakness of the wind is a causal factor in the ball's actual fall to Earth. If there had been no, or even less, weak counteracting force of the wind, the ball would have fallen to Earth faster, somehow differently, or some such. Perhaps the difference is temporal: if there had been no or less a counteracting force of the wind, the ball would have fallen to Earth sooner, earlier. Both factors were parts of the full cause; had either been absent, the result would have been (or probably would have been) different, or at least differently placed temporally.

A Type I example in the case of action would also not be hard to find, and, as I said above, it is these cases that spring most readily to mind: suppose Buridan's ass is drawn to hay pile A because it is more attractive, hay pile B is less attractive. (In a real Buridan's ass case, the piles are equally attractive, but not so in the case I am now imagining.) No starving ass here. Both the attractiveness of A and the relative unattractiveness of B result in the ass's choosing hay pile A. We are all such asses much of the time; many cases are of this type. Again, the same causal factors jointly contribute to the same result, the ass's final choice. The relative unattractiveness of B is a causal factor in the ass's actual choice of A over B. If pile B, although unattractive, had not even been available, or had been even less attractive, but pile A had remained the same, the ass would have chosen hay pile A more quickly, earlier, more determinedly, with less hesitation, or some such. Since both factors, the degree of attractiveness that pile A had and the degree of unattractiveness that pile B had, were both parts of the full cause of the ass's token choice of A, had either been absent, the result would have been (or probably would have been) different, either in character or in time. For example, absent pile B, the ass would have still chosen pile A, but the token choosing would have been different in some significant way from the actual choosing, as a result of the difference in its cause.

In examples of cases of Type I, it is assumed that both causal factors jointly influence the same outcome, so the outcome would have been different, or probably would have been different, if either of the causal factors had been different. Both causal factors matter to the same outcome. Although something like this might be true, and indeed no doubt is true in many cases, it need not be. That is, on the causalist program, there could be other cases (Type II) in which the presence of the con-reason has some effect, but has no effect of any sort on the actual action taken, but instead has some effect on something else. I do not know how to prove that there must be such cases for the causalist, but it seems to me intuitively clear that there could be.

What would the causalist have to hold, in order to deny this claim that I have just made? Since in cases of joint causation of a single effect by multiple part causes, it follows that the effect would have been different, or probably would have been different, had any one of the part causes been different (or altogether absent), the causalist who wishes to deny the possibility of cases of Type II would have to say that:

(3) In every case of action for which the agent has both pro- and con-reasons that figure into his deliberations, had the agent not had such a con-reason, the action he took would have been different or altered, or probably would have been different or altered in some way, or occurred at a different time.[6]

I just don't think that (3) could be true. I can envisage many cases in which, were the con-reason absent, the action taken could be qualitatively the same (in all nontrivial respects) as the action that was actually taken. We can say of such cases: "the agent had, and acknowledged that he had, a less weighty reason not to do something, which figured into his deliberative activity, but that less weighty reason did not at all causally influence his eventual choice to do what he did, in any way." Perhaps such a case might be one in which the agent has, and acknowledges that he has, a weak moral reason that he does consider in his deliberations, but the weak moral reason has in the end no actual effect on his eventual choice or behavior. Or a case in which the ass considers both hay piles in its deliberation but is so determined to get to hay pile A that he would make exactly the same choice regardless of what he acknowledges to be the lesser but not negligible attractiveness of hay pile B, and so the ass would make the identical choice—a choice qualitatively identical in character, timing, and so on—had hay pile B not been available at all. That is, had the agent not have had the con-reason, his actual choice would have been (or probably would have been) qualitatively the same in all relevant respects. Cases of Type II already presume that reasons and causation even on the causalist program can part company to this extent: a con-reason must cause something, but the con-reason might not be a part-cause of the same effect that the pro-reason causes or part-causes.

The case of temporal location might merit special consideration. Perhaps the action chosen in the face of both pro- and con-reasons could be intrinsically qualitatively the same as the action the agent would have chosen had he only had the pro-reason. But at least won't the time of the actions be different? If the agent had had no con-reason, he could not have deliberated and weighed up pro- and con-reason, and however short a time that deliberation might have taken, had he had no con-reason, the action would have occurred just that much sooner.

It might be so, but then again, it might not be so. Consider cases in which the con-reason, although it remains a con-reason, is so obviously (to the agent) weaker than the pro-reason that the agent has no need to go through some actual deliberative process. The con-reason is not strong enough to act as the countervailing wind did in my earlier example, as a force dragging and delaying the decision to act. So the action taken and the action the agent would have taken had he had no con-reason would display no difference in time of occurrence.

I don't think these cases are at all far-fetched. If we focus on cases in which decisions are difficult, in which pro- and con-reasons are finely balanced, it will seem that the con-reason, if causalism is to be believed, must exert some sort of causal influence on the action taken, even if only a difference in temporal placement. But we are not normally so conflicted in our choice of action. Think instead of cases, and I suggest that these will be the vast majority of cases, in which, although the agent has a con-reason, or con-reasons, that in some sense "weigh" with him, the relative weighting of the pro- and the con- is clear and obvious. Deliberation is not necessary. In those sorts of cases, I can see no reason to believe that the con-reason, if it has causal influence, must display that causal influence by affecting the character or time of the action actually taken.

So, let it just be stipulated that we are considering a case of Type II, in which the agent does something in the circumstances in which he does have conflicting pro- and con-reasons, but that he would have also done that action in an intrinsically qualitatively identical manner, and at the same time, had he only had the one set of pro-reasons. His "opposing" con-reason does not make him hesitate, or dither, in doing whatever it is that he does, in any way. There must, therefore, be cases in which the con-reason is not causally necessary for the actual action taken, if it is, as the causalist insists it is, a cause at all.

But if causalism is true, the con-reason must be a cause or part-cause or causal factor of something else other than the choice or action actually taken. In such cases, if causalism is true, the pro-reason will initiate a causal chain leading to the action taken, and the con-reason must initiate a different, independent causal chain that leads to something else. One thing that the con-reason can certainly not cause is the action it favors, since that action never happened and therefore nothing could cause *it*. To be sure, *that* something does not occur can have a cause, but what does not occur can have no cause since it does not exist.

If we assume that the con-reason does not also contribute to the causation of the action it disfavors, but rather would have to cause something else, there is any number of possible candidates for the effects of such con-reasons available to the causalist. Perhaps a person's con-reason *directly* causes regret (Williams 1981, 27ff.), or causes some other change in his mental landscape (his dispositions to act, for example), or causes some psychological illness in him. He does the action favored by the pro-reason, but since he had reasons against it, his con-reason ends in him regretting what he did, or some such. Or perhaps the effect of the con-reason is not even at the personal level at all. Might its effect not be some physiological or brain event of which the actor is perhaps ignorant or unaware?[7] (Or, "some further physiological or brain event," if the having of a con-reason is such a physical event too.)

The important feature of all these candidate effects for cases of Type II is that they require a second causal chain, in addition to the one that goes from the stronger pro-reason to the action taken. If so, there would be one causal chain leading from his having a pro-reason to his subsequent action. There would be another quite independent causal chain leading from his con-reason to his subsequent regret, or illness, or to some (further) physiological or similar event. The causal chains would not converge causally on the final choice or action, as they would if both pro- and con-reasons causally contributed to the same action taken, as we sketched above in cases of Type I.

On this rather simple picture, the pro-reason initiates a causal chain leading to the action; the con-reason initiates a wholly independent, second causal chain, leading to the regret or brain state or whatever. One thing to note about this view is that it might not permit us to capture causally the idea that both pro- and con-reason are rationally or deliberatively relevant to the same token final choice or action. The con-reason might not be a reason against acting in a certain way in virtue of whatever causal role it plays. A con-reason could not be the con-reason it is (a reason not to do what was done) in virtue of its causing something else other than that action. At the level of reasons for choice and action, the two reasons bear differently on (one favors and the other disfavors) the same choice or action, but the causal story might not mirror this in any way. There would be just two distinct causal chains, each of which leads to a different result; one leads to an action, the other to some psychological or neurophysiological or dispositional state. But perhaps a causal model of how pro- and con-reasons work in choice situations need not capture within the causal model this fact about the rational significance that both types of reasons have to the same action or choice, one in favor of it and one against it, so I don't take this as a decisive objection to the suggestion under discussion.

My argument now focuses only on cases of Type II, such that pro- and con-reason initiate independent causal chains. I do not deny that there can be many cases of Type I, but these are not the ones I wish to consider. In the cases on which I now focus, the pro-reason initiates one causal chain and the con-reason initiates another, whatever it might be and to wherever it leads.

In Type II examples, consider the actual situation, c. In c, the pro-reason to A is rationally weightier for the agent than the con-reason to B. Causally, assuming (2), if there is no weakness of will, it is the pro-reason that causes the agent to A, rather than the con-reason causing the agent to B (so the con-reason causes something else, whatever that might be). But now consider a counterfactual situation, c^*.

c^* is just like c, save in one feature, and whatever is a causal consequence of that one feature: in c^*, although the pro-reason retains the same deliberative weight that it has in c, the con-reason becomes much weightier. This sort of scenario is very common. At a later time, an agent can assess a reason as having more "gravitas" than he earlier imagined it had. It might weigh more with him than it did before. So in c^*, the con-reason counts more for the agent. The agent does not judge that the reason to A has become less strong than it was; it is just that the reason to B has become deliberatively stronger, and so stronger than the reason to A.

The reason to B now rationally outweighs the reason to A in the agent's deliberations, so the agent now Bs rather than As. In c^*, the reason to B has become the pro-reason and the reason to A has become the con-reason. Something about the reason to B has changed, and consequently the ordinal information about relative strength of reasons has changed. But nothing about the reason to A need have changed, other than certain relational, ordinal truths about its deliberative strength.

At the level of decision, choice, and reason, this is all straightforward. But how should we represent the allegedly underlying causal facts of the matter in c^* (in order to obtain a coherent causalist story)? In c^*, the reason to B is rationally weightier than the reason to A, so assuming that (2) is true and that there is no weakness of will, the reason to B will cause the agent to B instead of causing whatever it did cause in c. In c^*, there will now be a causal chain leading from the reason to B all the way to the agent's B-ing. But what does the reason to A now cause in c^*?

Before we try to answer that question, let's return for a moment to the question about the relational and intrinsic strengths of reasons for action that we briefly mentioned earlier on. Aside from the requirements of causalism, I do not know whether there are intrinsic truths about the deliberative strengths of reasons for action, on which their relational deliberative ordering supervenes. I would prefer to remain agnostic on that issue too. But it seems clear that causalism is committed to there being an intrinsic reality to the causal strength of reasons. On causalism, reasons are also causes (to put it succinctly), and there certainly must be an intrinsic reality to causal strength. The whole truth about causes and their relative strengths cannot be exhausted by only relational information. If c_1 is causally stronger than c_2, there must be something intrinsic about c_1 and c_2 that makes this relational fact true. One of the consequences of causalism's tying together rational and causal strength is that reasons must have strength both in a rational/normative and a causal/motivational sense, as I claimed earlier, and, as a result of that, reasons must also have causal strength in an intrinsic sense.

Now revert to our two circumstances, c (the actual situation in which the reason to A outweighs the reason to B) and c^* (the counterfactual situation in which the reason to B outweighs the reason to A). In c, the reason to A, the deliberatively strongest reason, caused the agent to A. Remember that we are supposing that the only difference between c and c^* is the fact that the reason to B in c^* rationally outweighs the reason to A and hence causes the agent to B. In c^*, the reason to A also undergoes a deliberative relational change, since in c^* it is outweighed by the reason to B but was not so outweighed before in c. But there is no reason to think that there must be some intrinsic causal change to the reason to A, simply in virtue of the deliberative and causal changes to the reason to B, remembering that in cases of Type II the causal chains initiated by the pro- and con-reasons are independent. Whatever changes the relational deliberative change to the reason to do A supervenes on, in the case described, they may not include any intrinsic causal change in the reason to A. The deliberative relational change to the reason to A (for it is now outweighed in c^*) may supervene only on changes, deliberative and causal, to the reason to B.

If so, then the reason to A should have the same causal strength in c^* as it had in c (even though it is now rationally outweighed by the reason to B), and since the reason to A caused the agent to A in c, then the reason to A should cause the agent to A in c^* as well (with one possible exception, described below). If the reason to A in c was strong enough to cause the agent to A, then it should still have the same causal strength in c^*, and therefore should be strong enough to cause in c^* whatever it caused in c, given that there are no causal nonrelational differences between c and c^* as far as the reason to A is concerned. If the reason to A has the same causal strength or power in both, then its effects should be the same in both circumstances. What it is strong enough to cause in one, it should be strong enough to cause in the other. The relational difference that in c^* the agent's reason to A is outweighed rationally by his reason to B can't make a difference to what the former is causally strong enough to do, since its causal strength is intrinsic.

So why doesn't the agent do A in c^*, just as he did in c? If the reason to A is able in c to cause the agent to A, and if it has the same causal properties in c^* that it had in c, then it should still cause the agent to A in c^*. True, the reason to B gains in deliberative strength in c^* (and so the relational facts about the relative strength of both reasons will change from c to c^*). Given the causalist's (2), what the reason to B causes, what its causal strength is, must have changed from c to c^*, a causal change on which its new deliberative strength supervenes. So the reason to B should also cause the agent to B in c^*. There should be, in c^*, as far as we can tell, a standoff: the agent should be caused both to do A and to do B.

To be sure, the agent can't do both A and B; by assumption, the agent is not able to do both on a single occasion. But in the counterfactual situation c^*, causally speaking, there should be no grounds for thinking that the con-reason will now win out "over" the pro-reason. The con-reason is now rationally and hence causally strong enough to cause the agent to B, but the pro-reason remains at the same intrinsic causal strength and hence, on the causalist view, should still be strong enough to cause the agent to A. So why should we expect the agent to do one or the other? Why doesn't the agent do A rather than B, even in the counterfactual situation, since his reason to do A remained in principle strong enough to cause him to do A, or why doesn't he do nothing at all, as in a true Buridan's ass example, since the two causes might cancel themselves out?

I mentioned one possible exception, above, to the claim that "since the reason to A was strong enough to cause A in c, then the reason to A should be strong enough to cause the agent to A in c^* as well." We need to take note of this qualification. Perhaps the causal chains initiated by the reason to A and the reason to B are independent in the actual circumstances, c (they are not joint causes of a single effect or joint effects of a single cause), but they might not remain independent in the counterfactual situation c^*. If the reason to B gains deliberative strength in c^*, this relational change might supervene on some changed intrinsic causal fact about it. Suppose that in c^* the reason to B, in addition to causing the agent to B, is now able to interrupt the causal chain that would otherwise lead from the reason to A to the agent's A-ing, and that explains why the agent does not, after all, do A in c^*. Let's consider this possible rejoinder to the difficulty we have detected.

There would be some flexibility in deciding just where, in c^*, the requisite inhibitor blocked or stopped the chain commencing with the reason to A from leading to its "natural" conclusion, A, as long as the chain did not get all the way to that action. For the sake of argumentative simplicity, let us suppose that the reason to B inhibited the very next link on the chain. On such a chain, let m be the node that would have followed immediately after the reason to A. So let us say that, in the counterfactual situation, what happened is that the reason to B inhibited or prevented m from occurring, prevented or inhibited the reason to A from causing m, and hence prevented the action A. That is why the agent does B instead of A in the counterfactual situation, and why his reason to A does not lead to his A-ing in c^*, an explanation entirely consistent with the causalist position.[8] (In fact, the same result would be achieved if something else other than his reason to B was the blocker or inhibitor, but the reason to B is going to prove the most likely candidate for that role.)

The problem with this solution is simply that it is not true to the phenomenological facts of the case. What this purported solution does is to try and construe an agent's not acting on a causally strong enough reason that he has as a case of having that reason blocked or impeded by a conflicting reason that he also has. The identification doesn't succeed.

Even apart from cases of weakness of the will, there is an indefinitely large number of ways in which an agent's wishes, wants, desires, and so on can be thwarted. Bad luck affects us all. A typical sign of this happening is agent frustration. In weak-willed cases, according to causalism, the agent's rationally strongest reason does not commence a causal chain leading to an action because it is not causally strong enough; a rationally weaker but causally strong enough reason does.

On the other hand, in the rather different case we are now considering, the causalist rejoinder has it that the agent's otherwise-causally-strong-enough reason commences a causal chain that simply gets blocked. If an agent's causally strong-enough reason does not lead to action only because the causal chain leading from it to action is blocked in some way, the agent will be and feel thwarted. Something that he is causally driven to do, as much as he is causally driven to do what he does do, gets closed off to him.

Recall that on this view, since the reason to A is meant to retain in c^* whatever causal properties it had in c, it should therefore cause the agent to act in c^* as well as in c. If the agent failed to A in c^*, only because the causal efficacy of his reason to A had been blocked, even if by another reason, the agent would feel this as some sort of failure. In one kind of frustration or failure, an agent might feel frustrated because he did not do what he thought was rationally the best thing to do. This kind of frustration is more properly, perhaps, thought of as a kind of defeat. It is the kind of frustration that an agent experiences in cases of weakness of the will. The agent knew that he had a stronger reason to do A, but did B instead. Alas, his reason to B produced more psychic turbulence than did his reason to A, in spite of the fact that rational or deliberative strength should have inclined him otherwise. This is a case in which the agent acts on the rationally less weighty, but the causally more effective, reason.

On the other hand, the case we would need to envisage if the solution being proposed worked is different but would also give rise to a kind of frustration. It is a case in which the agent would fail to act on the reason (albeit the less weighty reason, rationally speaking) that otherwise is (equally) causally strong enough to drive him to act. In the case we are considering, the agent has a rationally stronger reason to do B, and a rationally weaker reason to do A. But (according to my argument) both his reason to B and his reason to A should cause him to act, since each is causally strong enough to lead to the action it supports.

But of course he does B in c^*, not A, and we asked why this should be so. We asked: in c^*, why doesn't his reason to A lead him to act too? The suggested reply is that it does not lead him to act only because something blocks the path leading from this otherwise causally strong enough reason to the action for which he has that reason, thereby preventing him from so acting. Here too, the agent would experience a kind of frustration. It is not defeat or rational frustration, as in the case of weakness of the will. It is the inability to act on a reason that would otherwise be causally strong enough for an action, whatever its relational rational weight might be. It is more like being unable to scratch an itch severe enough to drive you to scratch (but, to be sure, when you have a rationally overriding reason not to do so), because the frustration arises from the causal failure, not from a rational failure. At a rational level, the agent would be happy that the reason to *A* did not lead to his *A*-ing, since he had more reason to *B* than to *A*. But at a causal level, he was primed to do *A* just as much as to do *B*. But if he does not do what he is causally primed to do, he would feel frustrated. It would indeed be like not being able to scratch an itch, when the desire to scratch was as causally strong as any reason not to do so was.

How much weight should we put on these sorts of phenomenological facts in deciding metaphysical matters? It is, I think, too easy to be a skeptic about this. What we are deciding are not just metaphysical matters generally, but specifically issues in action theory. If some view in action theory attributes to agents various kinds of mental states, or has the consequence that they have those states, what better check is there than introspection? I think that many views in action theory can be judged in this way, for example, ones that attribute various second-order mental states to agents, or ones that require of the agent almost a limitless stock of beliefs (Ruben 2003, chap. 4). One might dispute my argument that the causalist view does imply that the agent would experience the kind of frustration that I claim. But if the argument about this implication is sound, then introspection is the only way I know to test the claim.

What the causalist was trying to do was to give a causal model for the case in which the agent *B*s, because his reason to *B* has become deliberatively weightier than his reason to *A*, even though his reason to *A* has retained its original nonrelational, causal strength. In this case, surely the truth of the matter is that nothing needs to be thwarted and the agent need feel no frustration. He gladly "surrenders" his reason to *A*, at least in the circumstances, to his now-superior-because-weightier reason to *B*. It is not true that his reason to *B* prevents or blocks him from acting on his otherwise causally strong enough reason to *A*. In the case at hand, he chooses not to do *A*, because he takes his reason to do *A* as relatively of less importance or weight than his reason to do *B*, and in the case as we have constructed it, I do not see how this fact can be modeled causally. There is a perfectly clear deliberative story about what goes on in this case, but it is a story for which the causalist can provide no convincing causal counterpart.

There is, I submit, no fully convincing way causally to model decision making that includes con-reasons, at least for cases of Type II. It is the element of relational deliberative weight, comparative strength, which cannot be captured causally, at least in those cases in which the con-reason does not contribute causally to the action taken. What matters in deliberation is the comparative or relative strength of reasons. If reasons were causes, there would be nonrelational truths about the causal strength of reasons. Because of these nonrelational causal truths, the two scenarios, the causal/motivational and the rational/normative, won't mesh. As long as one thinks only about pro-reasons for action causing the actions they favor, the point is not salient. But once con-reasons are introduced, it becomes clearer that there is no plausible causal modeling for all the ways in which con-reasons work in our deliberation scheme.

Acknowledgments

An earlier version of this essay appeared as "Con-Reasons as Causes" in *New Essays on the Explanation of Action*, ed. C. Sandis (Basingstoke: Palgrave Macmillan, 2009), 62–74. Richard Bradley, LSE, has helped in improving this essay from what it otherwise would have been.

Notes

1. (1) is understood here to speak of causation, not necessarily only of deterministic causation. The causation in question might be probabilistic or stochastic. I frequently add "or probably" to cover cases of probabilistic or stochastic causation. My discussion should apply equally whether the causation in question is deterministic causation or stochastic causation.

What are causes? No essay can do everything and, with that, I intend to beg off any responsibility for explicating the idea of causation. I am presupposing a fairly standard account of causation, on which causes are token events or token states, and that a causal chain is a series of such.

2. Although Jonathan Dancy (2000, 4) notes their existence: "but still I will normally speak as if all the reasons that do motivate all pull in the same direction."

3. A con-reason is also a pro-reason in its own right for the action not taken, and is a con-reason only in the sense that it counts against the action that was taken. Similarly, a pro-reason is only a pro-reason for the action taken and is itself also a con-reason for the action not taken. In what follows, to simplify terminology, I will only use the idea of a pro-reason to be the reason that counts for the action one takes, and the con-reason to be the reason that counts for the action one does not take, the reason that gets outweighed. In the light of this, it would be wrong to think of pro-reasons and con-reasons as two different sorts of reasons. I was careful above only to say that reasons can function in these two different ways, depending on context.

4. Instead of "relational" versus "intrinsic" (or, "nonrelational"), I would have spoken of "ordinal" versus "cardinal," but there seem to be presuppositions built into the latter contrast that do not necessarily exist in the former contrast. Even apart from the demands of causation that I discuss below, I doubt whether the whole truth about reasons is exhausted by merely relational information, although nothing in this essay requires that to be true. In a theoretical syllogism, a set of premises can confer a nonrelational probability on a conclusion, making the conclusion rational to believe to some degree; similarly, reasons for action can confer nonrelational support on an action, making it a rational action to perform to some degree. Reasons have an intrinsic strength as well as a comparative strength relative to other reasons one has, if indeed one has any others.

5. I have often wondered why the principle "Every event has an effect" does not have quite the same intuitive appeal as "Every event has a cause." It might seem obvious that they should stand or fall together.

6. Of course, the choice to A that he would have made or the A-ing he would have performed had he not had a reason to B must differ from the choice to A that he did actually make or the A-ing he actually did do in at least one way, simply in virtue of the fact that it would have been a choice made in the absence of having a conflicting reason to B. The qualification "in some intrinsic way" is meant to exclude such trivial differences.

7. I do not think that one should underestimate the importance of the shift from the personal to the subpersonal level, in order to maintain (1) and (2), broadened to include con-reasons. It is a major concession on the part of the causalist. I do not intend to develop the point here, but certainly the hope that lay behind the causalist program for reasons for action was that reasons could be construed as causes, yet doing so was compatible with understanding reasons and actions in their own terms, sometimes called "the space of reasons." This program was not necessarily committed to construing reasons and actions as "really" about brain states and gross behavior (even if they turn out to be identical to brain states and gross behavior). The language of psychology and action was meant to have an internal coherence and integrity all its own. To that extent, this option can easily take the causalist program somewhere it had not intended to go.

8. Note that this example is not one of preemption, as some have suggested to me. If it were a case of preemption, one would have two reasons both favoring the *same* line of action, the first of which causes the action and the other of which did not cause the action but would have caused the same action, had one not had the first reason. In causal preemption, the inhibition or prevention is by the preempting cause of some node on the chain that would have led from the preempted cause to the effect. This is certainly not the case we are considering. But, arguably, all cases of preemption involve some sort of causal inhibition or prevention, as does the case we are considering.

13 Teleological Explanations of Actions: Anticausalism versus Causalism

Alfred R. Mele

Teleological explanations of human actions are explanations in terms of aims, goals, or purposes of human agents. According to one familiar *causal* approach to analyzing human action and to explaining instances thereof, human actions are, essentially, events that have appropriate mental items (or neural realizations of those items) among their causes.[1] Many causalists appeal, in part, to such goal-representing states as desires and intentions (or their neural realizers) in their explanations of human actions, and they take acceptable teleological explanations of human actions to be causal explanations. Some proponents of the view that human actions are explained teleologically regard all causal accounts of action explanation as *rivals*.[2] I dubbed this position "anticausalist teleologism" (AT for short; Mele 2003, 38) and argued against it (ibid., ch. 2).

I revisit AT in this essay. In section 1, after providing some background, I rehearse an objection raised in Mele 2003 to a proposal George Wilson (1989) makes in developing his version of AT. In section 2, I assess Scott Sehon's (2005, 167–171) recent reply to that objection. In section 3, I articulate a version of Donald Davidson's (1963/1980) challenge to anti-causalists about action explanation and assess Sehon's (2005, 156–160) reply to Davidson's challenge.

1 Wilson's Proposal and My Objection

Are there informative, conceptually sufficient conditions for such things as a human being's acting in pursuit of a particular goal that do not invoke causation? In chapter 2 of Mele 2003, I argued that attempts to identify such conditions by leading anticausalists about action explanation— Carl Ginet, Scott Sehon, R. Jay Wallace, and George Wilson—are unsuccessful. In the present section, I review Wilson's proposal and my objection to it.

Regarding a particular case, Wilson claims that facts of the following kind "about the context of the action, about the agent's perception of that context, and about the agent's sentient relations to his own movements . . . make it true that he intended of those movements that they promote his getting back his hat [read: make it true that those movements were *sentiently directed* by him at promoting his getting back his hat]":[3]

[1] The man, wondering where his hat is, sees it on the roof, fetches the ladder, and immediately begins his climb. [2] Moreover, the man is aware of performing these movements up the ladder and knows, at least roughly, at each stage what he is about to do next. [3] Also, in performing these movements, he is prepared to adjust or modulate his behavior were it to appear to him that the location of his hat has changed. [4] Again, at each stage of his activity, were the question to arise, the man would judge that he was performing those movements as a means of retrieving his hat. (Wilson 1989, 290)

Here Wilson apparently offers what he takes to be conceptually sufficient conditions for its being true that the man sentiently directed certain movements of his at promoting his getting back his hat. Are these conditions in fact sufficient for this?[4]

Two points need to be made before answering this question. The first concerns the second sentence of the passage just quoted. What knowledge is attributed to the man there? Not the knowledge that he is about to perform a sentiently directed movement of a certain kind, if sentient direction is a notion that this passage is supposed to explicate. However, this does not block the supposition that the man knows, in some sense, that he is about to perform a movement of his left hand onto the next rung, for example, in Wilson's broad sense of "perform a movement" (according to which "A man performs a convulsive and spasmodic movement when he clutches and cannot loose a live electric wire, and someone undergoing an epileptic seizure may perform a series of wild and wholly uncontrollable movements" [Wilson 1989, 49]).

Second, Wilson claims that "to try to [A] is (roughly and for the pertinent range of cases) to perform an action that is intended to [A]" (ibid., 270). Brief attention to trying will prove useful. Suppressing Wilson's qualification for a moment, his claim amounts, for him, to the assertion that to try to A is to perform an action that is sentiently directed by the agent at A-ing. Regarding the following plausible proposition, there is no need to worry about limiting the range of cases: (T1) if one is doing something that one is sentiently directing at A-ing, then one is trying to A, in an utterly familiar, unexacting sense of "trying." Although people may often reserve attributions of trying for instances in which an agent makes a considerable or special effort, this is a matter of conversational implicature and does not mark a conceptual truth about trying.[5] A blindfolded, anesthetized man who reports that he has raised his arm as requested quite properly responds to the information that his arm is strapped to his side by observing that, in any case, he *tried* to raise it—even though, encountering no felt resistance, he made no *special* effort to raise it.[6] And when, just now, I typed the word "now," I tried to do that even though I easily typed the word. Now, T1 entails (T2) that one who is not trying to *A*, even in the unexacting sense of "trying" identified, is not sentiently directing one's bodily motions at *A*-ing. T2 is very plausible, as is the following, related proposition: (T3) one who is not trying to do anything at all, even in the unexacting sense of "trying," is not sentiently directing one's bodily motions at anything.[7]

In the following case, as I will explain, although Norm is not, during a certain time, trying to do anything, even in the unexacting sense of "trying" that I identified, he satisfies all four of the conditions in the quotation at issue during that time. The moral is that these conditions are not sufficient for a person's sentiently directing "movements" of his at the time. Their insufficiency follows from the details of the case and the platitude that an agent who is not trying (even in the unexacting sense) to do anything is not sentiently directing his bodily motions at anything.

Norm has learned that, on rare occasions, after he embarks on a routine activity (e.g., tying his shoes, climbing a ladder), Martians take control of his body and initiate and sustain the next several movements in the chain while making it seem to him that he is acting normally. He is unsure how they do this, but he has excellent reason to believe that they are even more skilled at this than he is at moving his own body, as, in fact, they are. (The Martians have given Norm numerous demonstrations with other people.) The Martians have made a thorough study of Norm's patterns of peripheral bodily motion when he engages in various routine activities. Their aim was to make it seem to him that he is acting while preventing him from even *trying* to act by selectively shutting down portions of his brain. To move his body, they zap him in the belly with M-rays that control the relevant muscles and joints. When they intervene, they wait for Norm to begin a routine activity, read his mind to make sure that he plans to do what they think he is doing (e.g., tie his shoes or climb to the top of a ladder), and then zap him for a while—unless the mind-reading team sees him abandon or modify his plan. When the team notices something of this sort, the Martians stop interfering and control immediately reverts to Norm.

A while ago, Norm started climbing a ladder to fetch his hat. After he climbed a few rungs, the Martians took over. Although they controlled Norm's next several movements while preventing him from trying to do anything, they would have relinquished control to him if his plan had changed (e.g., in light of a belief that the location of his hat had changed).

Return to facts 1 through 4. Fact 1 obtains in this case. What about fact 2? It is no less true that Norm performs his next several movements than that the man who clutches the live electric wire performs convulsive movements. And the *awareness* of performing movements mentioned in fact 2 is no problem. The wire clutcher can be aware of bodily "performances" of his that are caused by the electrical current, and Norm can be aware of bodily "performances" of his that are caused by M-rays. Norm also satisfies a "knowledge" condition of the sort I identified. If Wilson is right in thinking that an ordinary ladder climber knows, in some sense, that he is about to perform a movement of his left hand onto the next rung, Norm can know this too. What he does not know is whether he will perform the movement on his own or in the alternative way. But that gives him no weaker grounds for knowledge than the ordinary agent has, given that the subject matter is the performance of movements in Wilson's broad sense and given what Norm knows about the Martians' expertise. Fact 3 also obtains. Norm is prepared to adjust or modulate his behavior, and one may even suppose that he is *able* to do so. Although the Martians in fact initiated and controlled Norm's next several movements up the ladder while preventing him from trying to do anything, they would not have done so if his plans had changed. Fact 4 obtains too. In Wilson's sense of "perform a movement," Norm believes that he is performing his movements "as a means of retrieving his hat." (He does not believe that the Martians are controlling his behavior; after all, he realizes that they very rarely do so.)

Even though these facts obtain, Norm does not sentiently direct his next several movements up the ladder at getting his hat because he is not sentiently directing these movements at all. Wilson maintains that sentiently directing a bodily movement that one performs entails exercising one's "mechanisms of . . . bodily control" in performing that movement (Wilson 1989, 146). However, Norm did not exercise these mechanisms in his performance of the movements at issue. Indeed, he did not make even a minimal effort to perform these movements; owing to the Martian intervention, he made no effort at all—that is, did not try—to do anything at the time. And it is a platitude that one who did not try to do anything at all during a time t did not sentiently direct his bodily motions during t.

It might be suggested that although Norm did not directly move his body during the time at issue, he sentiently directed his bodily motions in something like the way his sister Norma sentiently directed motions of her body when she vocally guided blindfolded colleagues who were carrying her across an obstacle-filled room as part of a race staged by her law firm to promote teamwork. If Norma succeeded, she may be said to have brought it about that she got across the room, and her bringing this about is an action.[8] Notice, however, that there is something that she was trying to do at the time. For example, she was trying to guide her teammates. By hypothesis, there is nothing that Norm was trying to do at the relevant time, for the Martians blocked brain activity required for trying. And this is a crucial difference between the two cases. The claim that Norma sentiently directed motions of her body at some goal at the time is consistent with T3; the comparable claim about Norm is not.[9]

Wilson proposed sufficient conditions for its being true that a person's movements were sentiently directed by him at promoting his getting back his hat. Norm satisfies those conditions even though it is false that the "movements" at issue were sentiently directed by him. So those conditions are not in fact sufficient.

Can Wilson's proposal be rescued simply by augmenting it with an anti-intervention condition? No. If the addition of such a condition does contribute to conceptually sufficient conditions for a person's sentiently directing his movements at a goal, it may do so because the excluded kinds of intervention prevent, for example, the obtaining of normal causal connections between mental items or their neural realizers and bodily motions. An anticausalist who augments Wilson's proposal with an anti-intervention condition also needs to produce an argument that the condition does not do its work in this way.

2   Sehon on Norm

In a book defending AT, Scott Sehon (2005, 167–171) replies to my objection to Wilson's proposal. The present section is an assessment of his reply.

Sehon contends that it "is not obvious that Norm's behavior fails to be an action" (ibid., 168). In support of this claim, he sketches a version of my story in which Norm is about to shoot someone when "the Martians take over his body and make it carry out the dirty deed." Sehon asks, "Does this completely absolve Norm of responsibility for shooting his professor?" He reports that it is not obvious to him how to answer this question.

"Accordingly," he writes, "even in the routine case of going up the ladder, I take it not to be obvious that Norm failed to act."

Things are not nearly as murky as Sehon thinks. I start with an obvious point. Norm is responsible for shooting his professor only if Norm shoots his professor. This is an instance of the truism that a person P is responsible for doing A only if P did A. But notice that P may have some responsibility for *the shooting of X* even if, because P did not shoot X, P has no responsibility for *shooting X*. For example, if P hires—or forces—someone to shoot X, then, other things being equal, P has some responsibility for the shooting of X. In Sehon's story, the Martians "make it seem to Norm as if he is acting, and if Norm had changed his mind and decided to put the gun down [they] would have immediately relinquished control" to Norm (ibid.). (Here Sehon is following my lead, of course.) So readers may be strongly inclined to see Norm as responsible for more than, in Sehon's words, merely "having a plan to commit murder." In light of the distinction I have drawn between P's having some responsibility for shooting X and P's having some responsibility for the shooting of X, those who, like me, are convinced that Norm did not shoot the professor can maintain that, even so, he has some responsibility for the shooting of the professor.

Imagine that Sehon's story remains basically the same, except that a Martian makes himself invisible and then, with his slim but powerful tentacle, pulls Norm's paralyzed finger down on the trigger. (The Martian also makes it seem to Norm as though Norm is pulling the trigger, and "if Norm had changed his mind and decided to put the gun down, the [Martian] would have immediately relinquished control" to Norm.) Obviously, Norm did not pull the trigger. So Norm did not shoot the professor. That entails that Norm is not responsible for shooting the professor. Even so, he may have some responsibility for the shooting of the professor. After all, the Martian would not have pulled the trigger with Norm's finger if Norm had not been bent upon shooting the professor, and the professor's life would have been spared if Norm had changed his mind. Sehon's uncertainty about whether Norm shot the professor seems to derive from his failure to distinguish having some responsibility for shooting the professor from having some responsibility for the shooting of the professor.

Some readers may wonder why my story about Norm in Mele 2003 portrays the Martians as using M-rays rather than moving Norm with their tentacles. Recall that Wilson's conditions include the man's "performing movements"; and although he is happy to say that a wire clutcher whose body is being jerked about by the wire's electrical discharge is performing movements in his thin sense, I doubt that he would count a man whose limb motions are caused by Martians pulling and pushing on his limbs as performing movements with those limbs. Naturally, I thought the M-rays were just fine for my purposes, but instead I could have portrayed the Martians as moving Norm's paralyzed body with just the right sorts of electrical jolts to muscles and joints. Call this *E-manipulation.*

Sehon wonders why my Martians interfere with Norm. "What's in it for the Martians?" he asks (Sehon 2005, 168). In Mele 2003, I neglected to mention that the Martians had read page 290 of Wilson's (1989) book and wanted to provide a living counterexample to his proposal. In any case, Sehon's reflection on his question leads him to the following claim:

> Mele stipulates that the Martians are going to make Norm's body do exactly what Norm planned to do anyway. If this were an ironclad promise from the Martians, or better yet, something that followed necessarily from their good nature, then . . . I have little problem saying that Norm is still acting, despite the fact that the causal chain involved is an unusual one. If he commits a murder under these circumstances, we will definitely not let him off. (Sehon 2005, 169)

Yes, if Norm commits a murder, he should be blamed for that. But if he is not acting, he commits no murder. Is Norm acting in Sehon's scenario? Presumably, for the purposes of his thought experiment, Sehon means to retain as much as he can from my story about Norm while turning the Martians into beings whose good nature entails that they always make "Norm's body do exactly what Norm" plans to do. Evidently, Sehon is not impressed by the following details of my story: the Martians prevent Norm "from even *trying* to act by selectively shutting down portions of his brain," and they move his body by zapping "him in the belly with M-rays that control the relevant muscles and joints" (Mele 2003, 49). I am not sure why. Possibly, he rejects T3 (the thesis that one who is not trying to do anything at all, even in the unexacting sense of "trying," is not sentiently directing one's bodily motions at anything). And possibly, he accepts T3 and believes that Norm counts as trying to do things when his Martians replace mine.

Consider a scenario in which, instead of using M-rays, Sehon's good Martians paralyze Norm's body and then move it by E-manipulation while making it seem to Norm that he is acting normally. When, for example, Norm intends to climb a ladder to get his hat, the Martians paralyze him and E-manipulate his body up the ladder. (They do all this while making it seem to Norm that he is acting normally, and if Norm were to change his mind his paralysis would immediately cease and control would revert to him.) I do not see how the claim that, in this scenario, Norm is climbing the ladder can be regarded as anything but utterly preposterous. Yet, unless Sehon can identify a crucial difference between the use of M-rays and this alternative mode of Martian body manipulation, he is committed to having "little problem saying" that Norm is climbing it.

Sehon is willing to grant that when my Martians are at work rather than his, Norm is not acting (Sehon 2005, 168). He contends that, in my story, "since Norm fails . . . to satisfy" the following condition, "his behavior does not count as goal directed" on his "account of the epistemology of teleology" (ibid., 169): (R1) "Agents act in ways that are appropriate for achieving their goals, given the agent's circumstances, epistemic situation, and intentional states" (ibid., 155). If I am right, Norm is not acting at all, in which case invoking R1 is overkill. And if Norm is not acting, as Sehon is willing to grant, then Wilson's proposal about sufficient conditions for its being true that a person's movements were sentiently directed by him at promoting his getting back his hat is false, which is what I set out to show with the Martian example in Mele 2003.

Some readers may feel that they have lost the plot. The following observation will help. One thing that Sehon would like to show is that a proponent of AT can "accommodate our intuition that Norm is not acting" in my story (Sehon 2005, 170). He argues that "Norm's motion is not that of an agent, because in a range of nearby counterfactual situations his behavior is not appropriate to his goals. Specifically, in all those situations in which the Martians simply change their mind about what they want to have Norm's body do, Norm's body will do something quite different" (ibid.).

Sehon's explanation of why Norm is not acting is seriously problematic. Imagine a case in which the Martians consider interfering with Norm but decide against doing that. Norm walks to the kitchen for a beer without any interference from the Martians. There are indefinitely many variants of this case in which the Martians change their minds about not interfering and make Norm's body do something else entirely. So "in a range of nearby counterfactual situations his behavior is not appropriate to his goals" (ibid.). But this certainly does not warrant the judgment that Norm is not acting in the actual scenario. Obviously, he *is* acting in that scenario: he is walking to the kitchen for a beer. If Sehon is thinking that his counterfactual test for whether an agent is acting is to be applied in scenarios in which the Martians interfere with Norm but not in scenarios in which they do not interfere with him, he does not say why this should be so.

The problems with Sehon's explanation of why it is that Norm is not acting in my case do not end here. He considers a woman, Sally, who "has an odd neurological disorder" (ibid.). When she tries to move her finger in way W, her finger often becomes paralyzed and "her body goes through any number of other random motions." In a particular case, Sally successfully tries to move her finger in way W when pulling a trigger and murdering a professor. Sehon contends that because Sally's "behavior is generally very sensitive to her goals"—after all, it is "subject to these flukes only when it involves a finger pulling"—she, "unlike Norm, satisfies the condition imposed by ($R1$) well enough to make her an agent at the time in question" (ibid., 171).

This will not do. Imagine a variant of Norm's story in which a rogue Martian interferes with Norm only on one occasion. (The Martian is imprisoned for life by the Martian authorities immediately afterward and no one else ever interferes with Norm.) He moves Norm's paralyzed body up the ladder by E-manipulation while making it seem to Norm that he is acting normally. Sally's behavior is "generally very sensitive to her goals," and I stipulate that Norm's behavior is generally even more sensitive to his goals. Even so, he is not acting as his body moves up the ladder. That Sally is acting whereas Norm is not is not explained by a difference in the general sensitivity of their behavior to their goals.[10]

Sehon concludes his discussion of my objection to Wilson's proposal with the following report:

One could alter the example by making Sally's neurological disorder much more general, such that she rarely does what she intends; but with that revision, my own intuitions about the case grow flimsy. I'm not sure what to say about her agency in such a case, and I'm not too troubled by the conclusion that she is not exhibiting genuine goal-directed behavior at any particular moment. (Ibid.)

Imagine that you read in a medical journal a study of a sixty-year-old patient, Pat, who for the past ten years has suffered from a horrible illness that has the consequence that in about 99 percent of the cases in which he tries to do something, his "body goes through any number of other random motions" and his attempt fails. About 1 percent of the time, he succeeds in doing what he tries to do. Sometimes, for example, he makes a successful attempt to signal his nurse by pressing a button. Apparently, Sehon would not be "too troubled by the conclusion" that Pat *never* exhibits "genuine goal-directed behavior." But if unwarranted conclusions are troublesome, Sehon should be troubled by this. Pat's story clearly is conceptually possible. In it, some of his behavior is genuinely goal directed.

Two conclusions may now be drawn. First, Sehon has not shown that my objection to Wilson's proposal is unsuccessful. In fact, insofar as he concedes that Norm is not acting in my story, he apparently concedes that the objection is successful. (He nowhere claims that Norm does not satisfy Wilson's proposed conditions.) It is perhaps worth mentioning in this connection that Sehon might have misled not only his readers but also himself by treating my objection to Wilson's proposal as though it were an argument for the claim that no version of AT can "accommodate our intuition that Norm is not acting" in my story (ibid., 170). Other anticausalists about action explanation—for example, Carl Ginet (1990) and R. Jay Wallace (1999)—have proposed other sufficient conditions for a human being's performing an action or acting in pursuit of a particular goal, and my objections to Ginet's and Wallace's proposals in Mele 2003 were very different from my objection to Wilson's proposal.[11] Naturally, the objections I offered were designed to apply to the details of the specific proposals. Second, Sehon's attempt to produce a version of AT that distinguishes cases of action from cases like Norm's is unsuccessful.

3   Causalism versus AT: Davidson's Challenge Revisited

What can causalists about action-explanation and proponents of AT reasonably challenge one another to do? Distinguishing the project of producing a *conceptually sufficient condition* for a human being's acting in pursuit of a particular goal from the project of producing an *analysis* of this is useful in answering this question. The latter project obviously is more challenging than the former: producing conditions that are individually conceptually necessary and jointly conceptually sufficient for X is more challenging than producing a conceptually sufficient condition for X. And if it were demonstrated, for example, that having a mental state or event of a certain kind among its causes is a *necessary* condition for an event's being an action performed in pursuit of a goal G and that no attempted explanation of an action that did not appeal either explicitly or implicitly to such a cause is an adequate explanation, that demonstration alone would show that AT is false. A causalist does not need to generate an acceptable analysis of an action's being performed in pursuit of a goal G in order to show that AT is false.[12]

Similarly, a proponent of AT does not need to generate an acceptable analysis of an action's being performed in pursuit of G in order to show that causalism about acting in pursuit of a goal is false. I have never challenged proponents of AT to produce an *analysis* of this. (To ask for an analysis of any contested philosophical concept that will be widely accepted is to ask for a great deal.) My challenge to proponents of AT concerns a much more modest task: producing an informative conceptually sufficient noncausal condition for an action's being performed in pursuit of a goal G. Teleologists contend that "teleological explanations explain by specifying an action's goal or purpose; for example, when we say that Jackie went to the kitchen in order to get a glass of wine, we thereby specify the state of affairs at which her action was directed" (Sehon 1997, 195). But in virtue of what is it true that a person acted in pursuit of a particular goal? Wilson and Sehon have failed to answer this question successfully, as I have argued here. (So have Ginet and Wallace, as I argued in Mele 2003, ch. 2.)

Can causalists do any better? Elsewhere, I have argued that they can. In chapter 2 of Mele 2003, I offered, from a particular causalist perspective, what I argued to be an informative, conceptually sufficient condition for a being's acting in pursuit of a particular goal. And I observed that if the condition I offered is indeed conceptually sufficient for this, causalists are in much better shape in this connection than proponents of AT, none of whom have succeeded in offering noncausal conceptually sufficient conditions for this (ibid., 59). Interested readers are encouraged to consult chapter 2 of Mele 2003. The present section is concerned with some related business.

If I had ever thought I knew of a convincing *direct* argument for the thesis that an agent's acting in pursuit of a particular goal requires the satisfaction of a specific causal condition, I would have gone public with it. My way of defending causalism has been indirect. I have challenged proponents of AT to produce informative, conceptually sufficient noncausal conditions for acting in pursuit of a particular goal, argued against their proposals, and developed a causalist view of what actions are, how they are explained, and how they are produced (Mele 1992, 2003). If readers who compare my causalist view with anticausalist alternatives in light of the arguments I offered for the former and against the latter are justified in judging that my view is considerably closer to the truth, I am satisfied.

It is possible that some opponents of some causal views of action or action explanation oppose these views partly because they misunderstand them. For example, significant differences between how some causalists and some of their opponents understand causation may help to explain some of the opposition. In the literature defending or attacking causal theories of action or action-explanation, not much is said about what causation is. This is understandable: both sides may be thinking that, whatever the best account of causation is, their view about what actions are or how they are to be explained is the correct one to take, and they may want to avoid hitching their wagon to a specific theory of causation. The same goes for causal explanation.

David Lewis defends the thesis that "to explain an event is to provide some information about its causal history" (Lewis 1986, 217). Presumably, any anticausalist about action explanation who takes even some actions to be events would reject this thesis. But suppose it were agreed on all sides that a sufficient condition for an explanation of an event being a *causal* explanation is that the explanation explains the event at least partly by providing some information about its causal history. With this agreement in place, one can ask, for example, whether every acceptable teleological explanation of an action is a causal explanation of the action. Are there acceptable teleological explanations of actions that do not explain the actions even partly by providing some information about their causal history? (Teleological explanations of actions, again, are explanations in terms of aims, goals, or purposes of the agents of those actions.)

Sehon asserts that "Teleological explanations simply do not purport to be identifying the cause of a behavior" (Sehon 2005, 218). But, as Lewis observes, speaking in terms of "the cause of something" can easily generate confusion (Lewis 1986, 215). Lewis adds: "If someone says that the bald tire was the cause of the crash, another says that the driver's drunkenness was the cause, and still another says that the cause was the bad upbringing which made him so reckless, I do not think any of them disagree with me when I say that the causal history includes all three" (ibid.). In any case, causalists like me do not purport to be identifying *the cause* of an action when we offer causal explanations of actions in terms of agents' aims, goals, or purposes. The basic idea—oversimplifying a bit—is that a putative teleological explanation of an action in terms of a goal, aim, or purpose G does not explain the action unless the agent's wanting or intending to (try to) achieve G has a relevant *effect* on what he does. Obviously, the notion of *having an effect* is a causal notion; and the assertion, for example, that an agent's intending to achieve G had an effect on what he did places his intending to do that in the causal history of what he did.

At this point, some causalists part company with others. Some causalists posit token mental states such as intentions, desires, and beliefs and attribute causal roles to these states or to their neural realizers in the production of actions.[13] Other causalists are wary of postulating such token states of mind.[14] I take no stand on this issue here.

Over four decades ago, Donald Davidson posed a much-discussed challenge to philosophers who oppose causalism about action-explanation (Davidson 1963/1980, 9, 11). I set the stage for a version of his challenge with a story. Al has a pair of reasons for mowing his lawn this morning. One reason has to do with schedule-related convenience and the other with vengeance. Al wants to mow his lawn this week and he believes that this morning is a convenient time, given his schedule for the week. But he also wants to repay his neighbor for the rude awakening he suffered recently when she turned on her mower at the crack of dawn, and he believes that mowing his lawn this morning would constitute suitable repayment. As it happens, Al mows his lawn this morning only for one of the two reasons mentioned.

Suppose that Al's wanting to mow his lawn this week and his believing what he does about convenience have no effect at all on what Al does with his lawnmower this morning. Might it be the case, even so, that he mows his lawn for the reason having to do with convenience rather than for the reason having to do with vengeance? A philosopher who answers in the affirmative faces the challenge of producing an informative, conceptually sufficient condition for "Al mows his lawn this morning for the reason having to do with convenience" that is consistent with this answer and the details of the story.[15]

Sehon seemingly intends to tackle Davidson's challenge head on. He writes: "Briefly put, teleological explanations support certain counterfactual conditionals, and this will allow us to distinguish the reason for which an agent acted from other nonmotivating reasons" (Sehon 2005, 157). He contends that "when we are determining which of" two alternative teleological explanations "is true, we can look at a variety of counterfactual situations" (ibid., 158). "Basically speaking, we look at the agent's behavior in the counterfactual situations and determine the goal or goals for which her behavior would have been appropriate. . . . The general point," Sehon reports, "is that we are looking at counterfactual situations to see what account of the agent's behavior makes the most rational sense. Thus, the sort of case that Davidson proposes is not enough to undermine the teleological alternative to causalism" (ibid.).

A fatal flaw in Sehon's reply to the challenge is easily identified. Suppose you know Al pretty well and you know that he mowed his lawn this morning. Al's friend Ann tells you that he had the two reasons for doing this that I mentioned, and she voices her confidence that he did it for only one of these reasons. She promises to give you ten dollars if you figure out for which of the two reasons he mowed his lawn this morning and tell her how you figured it out. You decide to follow Sehon's lead and to consider various counterfactual scenarios. You know that Al dislikes mowing his lawn in even a light rain, and you start by asking yourself what he would have done this morning if there had been a light rain. You think that if he would have mowed his lawn anyway, "that is good evidence that in the actual circumstances [he] was directing [his] behavior" (Sehon 2005, 158) at getting revenge, because the rain, for Al, would outweigh schedule-related convenience. "Would he have mowed it anyway?" you ask yourself. And you find that you are stumped. You realize that if you had substantial grounds for believing that Al mowed his lawn to get revenge, you could use those grounds to support the claim that he would have mowed it even in a light rain; and you realize that if you had substantial grounds for believing that Al mowed his lawn only for reasons of convenience, you could use them to support the claim that he would not have mowed it if it had been raining. It dawns on you that the strategy of trying to identify the reason for which Al actually acted by trying to figure out what he would have done in the counterfactual scenario I mentioned and other such scenarios puts the cart before the horse. Asking your counterfactual question about the rain scenario is nothing more than a heuristic device— and not a very useful one. The truth about what Al would have done in a light rain is grounded partly in the truth about the reason for which he actually acted.

As I pointed out in Mele 2003, 51, in response to an earlier proposal by Sehon that featured counterfactuals, the truth of true counterfactuals is grounded in facts about the actual world; and if, for example, relevant counterfactuals about Al are true for the reasons one expects them to be, their truth is grounded partly in Al's acting for the reason for which he acted. As far as Davidson's challenge is concerned, we are back to square one. Certain counterfactuals about Al are true partly because he acted for a certain reason. But in virtue of what is it true that he acted for that reason? Sehon's proposal about counterfactuals leaves this question unanswered.

For a critical examination of several leading anticausalist treatments of action-explanation, see chapter 2 of Mele 2003. In the present essay I have focused on some elements of Sehon's recent defense of AT. If I am right, Sehon has not undermined my objection to Wilson's proposal, has not produced a version of AT that distinguishes cases of action from cases like Norm's, and has not offered an adequate reply to Davidson's challenge. This is bad news for at least one version of AT.

Acknowledgments

This essay was completed during my tenure of a 2007–2008 NEH Fellowship. (Any views, findings, conclusions, or recommendations expressed in this essay do not necessarily reflect those of the National Endowment for the Humanities.) I am grateful to Andrei Buckareff and Randy Clarke for comments on a draft of this essay.

Notes

1. See Bishop 1989; Brand 1984; Davidson 1980; Goldman 1970; Mele 1992, 2003; Thalberg 1977; and Thomson 1977.

2. See, e.g., Sehon 1994, 1997, 2005; Taylor 1966; and Wilson 1989, 1997.

3. For a justification of the instruction in brackets, see Mele 2003, 47.

4. This paragraph and the next eight are borrowed, with some minor modifications, from Mele 2003, 48–50.

5. See Adams and Mele 1992, 325; Armstrong 1980, 71; McCann 1975, 425–427; and McGinn 1982, 86–87.

6. See James 1981, 1101–1103. For discussion of a case of this kind, see Adams and Mele 1992, 324–331.

7. How readers interpret my action-variable "A" should depend on their preferred theory of action individuation. Davidson writes: "I flip the switch, turn on the light, and illuminate the room. Unbeknownst to me I also alert a prowler to the fact that I am home" (1963/1980, 4). How many actions does the agent, Don, perform? Davidson's *coarse-grained* answer is one action "of which four descriptions have been given" (ibid.). A *fine-grained* alternative treats A and B as different actions if, in performing them, the agent exemplifies different act-properties (Goldman 1970). On this view, Don performs at least four actions, because the act-properties at issue are distinct. An agent may exemplify any of these act-properties without exemplifying any of the others. (One may even turn on a light in a room without illuminating the room: the light may be painted black.) *Componential* views represent Don's illuminating the room as an action having various components, including his moving his arm (an action), his flipping the switch (an action), and the light's going on (Ginet 1990). Where proponents of the coarse-grained and fine-grained theories find, respectively, a single action under different descriptions and a collection of intimately related actions, advocates of the various componential views locate a "larger" action having "smaller" actions among its parts. Readers should understand the variable "A" as a variable for actions themselves (construed componentially or otherwise) or actions under descriptions, depending on their preferred theory of

action-individuation. The same goes for the expressions that take the place of "*A*" in concrete examples.

8. Readers who regard the claim that Norma brought it about that she got across the room as an exaggeration may be happy to grant that she helped to bring that about. Her helping to do that is an action.

9. On a case that may seem to be problematic for T3, see Mele 2003, 64–65, n. 22.

10. In my original story, the Martians interfere with Norm only "on rare occasions" (Mele 2003, 49). So, seemingly, they may interfere with him much less often than Sally has her finger problem. The variant of Norm's case just sketched renders speculation about this comparative issue otiose.

11. For my discussion of Ginet 1990 and Wallace 1999, see Mele 2003, 39–45.

12. Incidentally, I have never offered an analysis of action nor of acting in pursuit of a particular goal, although I have defended causalism in both connections (Mele 1992, 2003). Paul Moser and I (Mele and Moser 1994) have offered an analysis of what it is for an action to be an intentional action.

13. See, e.g., Brand 1984; Davidson 1980, ch. 1; and Mele 1992, 2003.

14. See, e.g., Child 1994; Hornsby 1993.

15. There is considerable disagreement about what reasons for action are, and I have spun my story in a way that is neutral on this issue. For example, the story does not identify the reasons mentioned in it with belief-desire pairs, as Davidson (1980, ch. 1) does; nor does it deny that this identity holds.

14 Teleology and Causal Understanding in Children's Theory of Mind

Josef Perner and Johannes Roessler

In "The Emergence of Thought," Donald Davidson argues that while we have no difficulty in describing, on the one hand, mindless nature and, on the other, mature adult psychology, "what we lack is a way of describing what is in between." He claims that there is a deep and "perhaps insuperable problem in giving a full description of the emergence of thought"; and he expresses relief at not working "in the field of developmental psychology" (Davidson 2001, 128). In this chapter we argue that Davidson was right about the depth and difficulty of the problems involved in describing the emergence of thought. But we think Davidson was unduly pessimistic about the prospect of making progress, empirical and philosophical, with these problems. Indeed we hope to show that describing the emergence of thought may help to shed light on the *nature* of thought.

We should make it clear immediately that our concern here will not be with Davidson's completely general problem, the "conceptual difficulty" he sees with the very idea of attributing beliefs and other propositional attitudes to immature thinkers. For the purposes of this chapter, we simply assume that such attributions can be literally correct. We will be concerned with a much more specific issue: the question of how young children understand intentional action. The problem is akin to Davidson's, though, in that it involves a "conceptual difficulty." According to current philosophical orthodoxy, to understand what it is to act intentionally one has to be able to find actions intelligible in terms of the agent's reason *for* acting, the agent's *purpose* in doing what he or she does. Call this the Reason claim, or R. Current orthodoxy also holds that reasons for action are provided, or constituted, by suitable pairs of beliefs and desires. Call this the Belief-Desire claim, or BD. (The classical source for both R and BD is Davidson's [1963] paper "Actions, Reasons, and Causes.") Put together, R and BD suggest that to see people as acting intentionally you have to think of them as acting on the basis of what they believe: understanding intentional action requires a grasp of the explanatory role of beliefs. There is a large body of evidence to suggest that 2- and 3-year-olds do not satisfy this condition. On the other hand, there is also convincing evidence that 2- and 3-year-olds do have some grasp of what it is to act intentionally. Hence the "conceptual difficulty": the hypothesis that children have some understanding of intentional action enjoys empirical support, yet it is hard to see how it can be sustained, given that children apparently lack a basic conceptual prerequisite for such understanding.

In what follows we develop and defend the following diagnosis. What is to blame for our "conceptual difficulty" is a dogma of contemporary philosophy of mind, that reason-giving explanations of actions are explanations in terms of beliefs and desires. The suggestion we will pursue is that young children find actions intelligible in terms of reasons that are not conceived as mental states at all—but that can nevertheless intelligibly be taken to provide causal explanations. We'll call this the teleological account of children's conception of intentional action. We argue that the teleological account is of more than developmental interest. Its genealogy of commonsense psychology has an important bearing on the nature of the adult conception of intentional action. For, as Wittgenstein remarked: "the thing about progress is, it tends to look more momentous than it really is."[1]

1 The Puzzle

What evidence is there to suggest that young children have some under-standing of intentional action? Some psychologists maintain that even toward the end of the first year, as infants begin to engage in joint atten-tion interactions with others, they perceive and understand others' actions as goal-directed (Tomasello 1999). Others have argued that such under-standing manifests itself in 18-month-olds' more sophisticated capacities for imitation of intended actions (Meltzoff 1995). Here we will focus on evidence provided by (slightly older) children's performance on classical false-belief tasks. The question put to children in such tasks is what the protagonist in some story will *do* next. For example: Suppose Maxi's mother transferred the chocolate Maxi put into the green kitchen cupboard to the blue cupboard while he is out playing. Maxi, feeling peckish, returns to the house. *Where will he look for the chocolate*? Three-year-olds' performance on this task is poor, but far from random. They reliably predict that Maxi will look in the blue cupboard. They don't suggest that he will look under the kitchen table or in the playground or in the loft. What explains this general pattern in 3-year-olds' performance? The natural, and standard, interpretation is that they tend to predict what Maxi will do on the basis of *what it makes sense for Maxi to do*, given the actual location of the chocolate. If you want to find the chocolate, looking in the blue cupboard is precisely what you should be doing—what you have a good reason to do. Thus, on the natural interpretation, children do think of Maxi as an intentional agent. They assume that Maxi acts in a purposive manner; that he will do what, given his purpose, he has good reason to do.

The puzzle, then, is this. Young children's performance on false-belief tasks simultaneously provides evidence that they think of others as intentional agents and that they have a systematic deficit in understanding the explanatory role of beliefs.[2] Yet, if recent philosophical orthodoxy is right, failure to grasp the explanatory role of beliefs should make it impossible to understand what it is to act intentionally. For (to repeat) recent orthodoxy holds that

R: Understanding what it is to act intentionally requires finding actions intelligible in terms of agents' reasons for acting

and

BD: Reasons for action are provided, or constituted, by suitable pairs of beliefs and desires.

2   Desire Psychology

There is, in the developmental literature, an influential view that may seem to offer a simple solution to our puzzle. The basic idea is that while thinking of someone as acting intentionally certainly requires understanding something about the mental states causally responsible for intentional actions, such understanding may be more or less comprehensive. A fully developed conception of intentional action will require a large and complex set of psychological notions, including, of course, the notion of belief. But, the claim is, children may have a rudimentary grasp of intentional action in virtue of understanding something about the explanatory role of *desires*, without yet appreciating how desires tend to interact with other states, such as beliefs (Bartsch and Wellman 1995).

Straight off, though, it is not obvious how this suggestion speaks to our puzzle. To understand Maxi's behavior as intentional, you have to *put two things together*: the purpose of the action and the means by which Maxi seeks to accomplish his purpose. A simple "desire psychology" may enable you to identify Maxi's purpose (his purpose is to get hold of his chocolate), but it is silent on what he might be expected to do to accomplish his purpose. So, on the face of it, the proposal has nothing to say on how children understand the intentional, purposive nature of the instrumental action they expect Maxi to perform (his opening the blue cupboard). Of course, you might say that the desire to locate his chocolate is at least part of what gives Maxi a reason to act. But understanding part of what gives someone a reason for acting intentionally is not the same as a partial understanding of intentional action.

Perhaps one reason the problem tends to go unnoticed is this. It is common practice in developmental psychology to equate goals with desires (Gopnik and Meltzoff 1997;[3] Tomasello et al. 2005). On this way of thinking, the ability to explain bodily movements in terms of desires may be redescribed as the ability to explain actions in terms of goals. The latter ability, in turn, is naturally equated with an understanding of *goal-directed action*. This can make it look as if a grasp of the explanatory role of desire just is a grasp of goal-directed action. But that appearance is deceptive. To ascribe to children a conception of goal-directed action is to say that they have mastered a distinctive way of explaining actions. They understand what it means for someone to do one thing *in order to* achieve another. This mode of explanation essentially involves putting together someone's purpose in acting with a particular way of pursuing the purpose. Put differently, it involves an understanding of instrumental reasons for action. In contrast, explaining a bodily movement in terms of some mental cause, even if that cause is a desire, does not necessarily involve any such "putting together" of end and means.[4] A "desire psychologist" might correctly explain someone's salivating in terms of a desire for chocolate. This does not mean that she thinks of the activity as an intentional action. The ability to explain bodily movements as the effects of desires is not sufficient for even a rudimentary understanding of what it is to act intentionally.

3 Objective Reasons

The conception of practical reasons articulated by BD (practical reasons are constituted or provided by suitable pairs of beliefs and desires) is arguably not the only conception familiar to commonsense psychology. We often think of practical reasons not as mental states but as worldly facts. When deliberating about what to do—say, where to look for some prized object—we tend to be more interested in the facts than in our beliefs about the facts. We think of the *fact* that looking in a certain location will enable us to retrieve the object as giving us a reason to look there. From the perspective of deliberation, only true propositions—facts—can provide genuine reasons. This point is not inconsistent with BD. The claim is not that BD is false. It is only that BD does not exhaust the commonsense psychology of practical reasons. In this observation, we suggest, lies the solution to our "conceptual difficulty." Young children find intentional actions intelligible in terms of "objective" practical reasons.

Let's clarify the basic idea with the help of a relatively uncontroversial example from Bernard Williams. Suppose you believe of the content of a certain bottle that "this stuff is gin," when in fact the bottle contains petrol. You feel like a gin and tonic. Should we say that you have a reason to mix the stuff with tonic and drink it? Williams suggests that you do not have such a reason, although you think you do, and although it would certainly be rational for you to drink the stuff (Williams 1981b, 102). One might object that to say that it would be rational for you to drink the stuff just is to say that you have a reason to drink it—a reason that might be appealed to, for example, in offering a "reason-giving" explanation of your action. But Williams is surely right in drawing our attention to the fact that you are *mistaken* in thinking you have a reason to drink the stuff. Your putative reason can be set out as follows: "I need a gin and tonic. This stuff is gin. So I should mix it with tonic and drink it." Certainly the inference reveals your action to be rational from your point of view. Correlatively, appeal to the inference may figure in a reason-giving explanation of your action. But the fact remains that the inference is unsound. Given that the second premise is incorrect, the inference fails to establish the truth of its conclusion: you are mistaken in taking the premises to establish that you should drink the stuff. In this sense, you are mistaken in thinking you have a reason for drinking it. This is perfectly consistent with acknowledging that there is a sense in which you do have such a reason. The point is sometimes put by saying that you lack a *justifying* or *guiding* reason, but have an *explanatory* reason to drink the stuff (Raz 1978). But this can be misleading, given that an explanatory reason too may be said to justify, at least in the "anaemic" sense (Davidson 1963/1980) of revealing the action to be justified or rational *from your perspective*. Marking the distinction as one between justifying and explanatory reasons would, in the current context, be awkward in another way. For the suggestion we want to pursue would now (confusingly) have to be put by saying that young children *explain* intentional actions in terms of *justifying* (rather than explanatory) reasons. So we'll simply distinguish between *subjective* and *objective* reasons: you have a subjective reason to drink the stuff, but you lack an objective reason to do so. Note that by itself the distinction does not imply that we are talking about different sorts of *things* here. Subjective reasons need not be taken to *be* mental states. Instead they might be taken to be propositions forming the contents of mental states. The distinction turns on whether or not a reason statement is to be understood as relativized to the agent's current perspective. To say that you have a subjective reason to drink the stuff is to say that, from your perspective, it looks as if you have an (objective) reason to do so.

It might be said that even objective reasons have to be relativized in one respect: they must be relativized to the agent's set of desires or objectives or projects. But on reflection it is not clear that this is so. As is often pointed out by critics of the Humean theory of motivation[5] (and as is acknowledged by some of its defenders[6]), practical deliberation does not always or even typically start from reflection about one's current desires. Practical inferences are often premised on evaluative propositions, to the effect that some action or some state of affairs is important or desirable; or, more specifically, on propositions involving "thick" evaluative concepts (e.g., promise, treachery, brutality, courage), apparently embodying "a union of fact and value" (Williams 1985, 129); or again, as in the example above, on propositions to the effect that someone needs, or needs to do, a certain thing, where claims of need are also best understood as a species of evaluative propositions, not to be confused with, or reduced to, ascriptions of desire (Wiggins 1987).[7] This suggests that there may after all be such a thing as a fully objective reason, relativized neither to the subject's instrumental beliefs nor to her set of desires and projects. A possible illustration might be the suggestion that the subject in Williams's example not only lacks an (objective) reason to drink the stuff, but actually has an (objective) reason *not* to drink it—a reason provided by the fact that drinking petrol is bad for your health.[8]

4 Teleology and the Hybrid Account

We are now in a position to formulate two possible solutions to our puzzle. One proposal might be that young children find actions intelligible in terms of partially objective reasons: reasons that are relativized to the agent's desires but not to her instrumental beliefs. For example, children might take it that given Maxi's desire to eat some chocolate, he has a good reason to look in the blue cupboard (for doing so will as a matter of fact enable him to satisfy his desire). Put differently, they conceive of Maxi's reason as a combination of a desire and an objective instrumental fact.

Children predict and explain intentional actions by "putting together" a mental state, defining the objective of the action, and an objective fact, determining the means to achieve the objective. We will call this the *hybrid account* of children's conception of intentional action. (The hybrid account is one way of developing the idea that young children are "desire psychologists."[9]) The second solution agrees with the hybrid account that understanding the way young children think about intentional actions requires going beyond BD. But it gives a more radical twist to that strategy. It maintains that children find actions intelligible in terms of fully objective reasons, relativized neither to the agent's instrumental beliefs nor to her pro-attitudes.[10] They conceive of Maxi's reason in terms such as these: "Maxi needs his chocolate. (Or: It is important, or desirable, that Maxi obtain his chocolate.) The way to get it is to look in the blue cupboard. So he should look in the blue cupboard." We call this the *teleological account*.[11]

How might we tell which of the two explanatory schemes young children go in for? We can spell out the key difference between them as follows. Finding actions intelligible in terms of objective reasons implies a certain lack of detachment. It involves commitments we do not normally associate with reason-giving explanations (accustomed as we are to taking such explanations to be a matter of citing subjective reasons). The two explanatory schemes differ in the kinds of commitments they entail. An explanation following the hybrid scheme carries with it a commitment concerning the effectiveness of some means for achieving the agent's purpose. The teleological scheme in addition commits the interpreter to some evaluative proposition. Both schemes share a crucial limitation: they break down when it comes to actions informed by false instrumental beliefs. But the teleological scheme is more limited still. It also breaks down in relation to actions informed by values the interpreter does not share. (Thus the teleological account might be said to involve an unusually strong version of the principle of charity.) There are two obvious sorts of cases where this extra limitation makes itself felt. One is the case of interpreting actions informed by objectionable values (e.g., hurting someone because it's fun to do so). The other is the case of interpreting the activities of two agents pursuing conflicting goals. Consider a competitive game. If you understand A's activities in terms of the fact that it's desirable that A win the game you will be hard pressed simultaneously to understand B's reasons for his contributions to the game, on pain of finding yourself committed to inconsistent evaluative propositions: It's desirable that A should win (by beating B), and it's desirable that B should win (by beating A).[12] Thus the teleological account would predict that young children have difficulties in understanding competitive games; more precisely, that they have difficulties in understanding the reasons informing the activities of participants in such games. By contrast, if young children subscribe to the hybrid scheme, they should find it easy to understand each of the competing activities, viz. in terms of the desires of each of the protagonists. (That A wants to win is plainly consistent with B's wanting to win also.) In general, for a teleologist, cooperation is utterly natural; practical reasons are subject to a kind of preestablished harmony. As conceived by the teleologist, reasons are essentially intersubjective. If we explain Maxi's action in terms of the fact that he needs his chocolate, reference to that very fact may also help to understand the actions of other agents. For example, the fact may explain why someone else is doing something that will assist Maxi in retrieving his chocolate.

How should we understand the issue between the hybrid view and the teleological account? And what, if anything, is there of *philosophical* significance in this debate? Well, it certainly looks initially as if the issue were a straightforwardly empirical one. And there is some suggestive initial evidence in favor of the teleological account: young children do seem to have difficulties in understanding both wicked behavior and competitive games. On the other hand, some will be inclined to doubt whether the teleological scheme is even intelligible. If this were right, it would be implausible to attribute the scheme to any rational thinker (even to very young thinkers). Thus the teleological account might be rejected on *a priori* grounds. One philosophical issue, then, is whether an objection of this sort can be sustained. As will become clear later, there is also much of philosophical interest in interpreting the empirical evidence. But there is a further way in which the debate bears on the philosophy of action. Suppose the teleological account is intelligible and enjoys a measure of empirical support— as we will argue it is and does. Suppose, in other words, that at least a rudimentary conception of intentional action is available prior to, and independently of, grasping concepts of propositional attitudes such as belief or various kinds of pro-attitudes. This would raise the question of how to understand the relation between the teleological conception and the mature adult conception of intentional action. We return to this question in section 7.

5   Teleology and Causal Understanding

We begin with the issue of intelligibility. A preliminary point to make about the idea of objective practical reasons is that it amounts to nothing very grand or eccentric, metaphysically speaking. It is not the idea that values belong to the fabric of the world as it is in itself, or that we have, or need, a special faculty for detecting values. It is merely the idea that there are true evaluative propositions. While this commits one to the view that evaluative statements can be true or false, such a commitment need not be seen as a particularly contentious matter. For it may be argued that, as Williams put it, "truth *in itself* isn't much" (Williams 1996, 19). The central point here is that evaluative statements show the sorts of "surface phenomena" (e.g., possible embedding in conditionals) that make it plausible to think of them as bearers of truth-values. There is no commitment to any substantive account of what it is in virtue of which such statements are true (nor even to the possibility of any such account).

If there is a serious worry about the intelligibility of teleology, it is surely over the claim that objective reasons can intelligibly be regarded as *explanatory*. One version of the challenge may be summarized as follows: "The teleological scheme purports to explain actions in terms of facts that are taken to constitute justifying reasons for it. Now, as Davidson has taught us, it is one thing for someone to have a reason to perform a certain action; it is another for that reason to explain her action—to be the reason *for which* the agent acts. (For one thing, the agent may simply fail to do what she has a reason to do. For another, even if she does it, and does it intentionally, she may do it for some other reason.) There are well-known and powerful considerations that suggest the notion of causation holds the key to a proper understanding of the difference: reason-giving explanations have to be conceived as a species of *causal* explanations (Davidson 1963/1980). But of course, causal explanations have to appeal to causes. Yet causes are conspicuous by their absence in the teleological scheme."

One might wonder whether the hybrid view fares any better than the teleological account vis-à-vis the Davidsonian challenge. After all, the hybrid account, too, envisages action explanations in terms of external facts rather than just in terms of mental states. But it might be said, quite plausibly, that there is a key difference. Suppose the upshot of the Davidsonian challenge is that, as one recent commentator put it, intentional actions are to be explained "in terms of mental *items*—such as beliefs, desires, intentions, and associated events . . . or their physical realizers" (Mele 2003, 51, our emphasis). The idea is that for reason explanation to be intelligible it has to make reference to *particulars*—events or, perhaps, states—that stand in a causal relation to someone's doing something intentionally. The teleological account does not provide for that requirement. Values are not events. It would be fanciful to think of Maxi's need for chocolate, or the importance of his getting his chocolate, as an "item" that stands in a causal relation to the event of his opening the green cupboard. In contrast, the hybrid view may seem to provide for causes, conceived as particulars. True, even on the hybrid view, the explanatory force of early reason explanations cannot be exhaustively explained in terms of causal relations between "mental items" and actions. External facts also play a vital explanatory role. But defenders of the hybrid view might argue that such facts should be seen as "standing conditions," whose explanatory role essentially depends on that of causally efficacious "items." Their role may be not unlike that of the dryness of the ground in an explanation of a forest fire caused by someone's dropping a cigarette. In brief, the Davidsonian challenge might seem to provide materials for an *a priori* argument in favor of the hybrid view.

We want to suggest that this argument rests on an implausible premise. The Davidsonian challenge consists of two central claims. One is that action-explanation must be a species of causal explanation. This is usually motivated by arguing, convincingly, that action-explanations are explanations of the occurrence of events, and that it's hard to see how the occurrence of an event can be made intelligible other than in causal terms. The second claim is that causal explanation has to appeal to causes, conceived as particulars. The correct teleological response to the a priori argument for the hybrid view, we suggest, is to accept the first but reject the second claim. The key question here is: What does it mean for an explanation to be causal? Adapting Bernard Williams's remark about truth, perhaps the right thing to say here is that causal explanation *in itself* isn't much. It's not explanation in terms of laws of nature; it's not explanation in terms of event causation; it's not explanation in terms of causal processes or causal mechanisms. The basic idea of a more minimalist account is that causal explanations advert to facts that "make a difference," where this is to be spelled out in terms of patterns of counterfactual dependence.[13] Our suggestion, then, is that teleological explanation is a species of causal explanation. So we agree with the idea underpinning the Davidsonian challenge to teleology, that the development of the commonsense conception of intentional action is inextricably entwined with the development of causal understanding. But we deny that causal understanding in this area takes the form of understanding causal relations between "mental items" and actions.

Specifically, the version of the difference-making approach we propose to draw on is the so-called interventionist approach to causation and causal explanation (Woodward 2003). The central idea of interventionism is this. To say that there is a causal relation between two variables X and Y is to say that if there were to be an intervention changing the value of X, there would also be a change in the value of Y. To say that taking aspirin causes relief from headache is to say that if there were an intervention on the amount of aspirin ingested by someone suffering from headache, there would also be a change in the intensity of her headache. The notion of an intervention is itself a causal notion. Crudely, an intervention on X is a causal relation between some variable I and X such that I causes a change in the value of X in an "exogenous" way—I takes complete control of X without affecting Y in any other way than through X.[14] This sort of account aims to elucidate the meaning of causal claims in terms of interventionist counterfactuals—in terms of how the value of Y would change under interventions on X—without, of course, undertaking to offer a reductive analysis.

Now on an interventionist approach there is, on the face of it, nothing *a priori* objectionable about the idea that objective reasons may causally explain intentional actions. The idea comes to this: were there to be an intervention on the evaluative or instrumental facts that give someone a practical reason, there would be a corresponding change in her action. The suggestion that young children think about intentional actions in this way is not at all implausible, especially in light of the sorts of social interaction characteristic of early childhood. Consider games of mutual imitation. The simple rule defining such games is that one participant has to imitate the actions of the other. In the context of this game, I can reliably manipulate your actions by intervening on your reasons. For example, my banging my toy gives you a reason to bang yours. (Only by banging yours can you achieve the defining purpose of the game, viz., to imitate my action.) So the fact that I am banging my toy offers a good causal-teleological explanation of your action, a causal explanation in terms of reason-giving facts.[15] To grasp such explanations it is not enough to understand that you have a reason to perform the action. Children also have to understand the reason as explanatory of the action. This they do, in virtue of their developing understanding of interventionist counterfactuals.[16] On this view, the causal understanding that goes into children's conception of intentional action does not require, or consist in, a conception of unobservable entities—"mental items"—conceived as causes of bodily movements. Rather, it is a matter of understanding what will, or would, happen under interventions on someone's practical reasons.

Note that the teleological account is concerned exclusively with the core element of children's understanding of intentional action, their capacity for reason-giving explanation. The account does not imply that the capacity operates in isolation. Nor does it imply that psychological properties play no role in such explanations. One way in which teleology may be enriched is by adding the idea, which may be in place quite early in development, that people's responsiveness to their practical reasons is subject to certain enabling (and disabling) conditions. For example, the agent has to be awake, not too tired or distracted, she may have to be able to perceive some critical object, and so on. Of particular interest here is the notion of attention: even young children may have some understanding of someone's attention or "engagement,"[17] as something that has to be suitably focused if the person is to respond to the reasons afforded by a situation. Children's understanding of the causal relevance of this condition may manifest itself in their practical interventions on others' focus of attention; for example, their attempts at attracting someone's attention by pointing or shouting. The point is important since it helps to allay the worry that the resources of teleology are simply too limited to offer a credible picture of early social understanding. Pure teleology admittedly leaves many things unexplained. A teleologist who thinks it's time for a game of mutual imitation should be baffled if his chosen partner shows herself to be unresponsive. Of course, being unable to make rational sense of an action need not prevent a teleologist from registering that the action (or inaction) is taking place. (Much of the time, mature commonsense psychologists are in the same position.) Still, the limitation may seem crippling. But there are two ways in which teleologists may overcome this limitation. An initially inscrutable action may become intelligible once the teleologist comes to understand, and share, the value informing it.[18] Alternatively, someone's (in-)action may remain rationally unintelligible, but the agent's failure to respond to her reasons may itself be unsurprising given the satisfaction of some disabling condition. (She may be asleep.) Teleologists need not be at sea in the social world.

What we suggest would be a *non sequitur* is to move from the involvement of psychological material in young children's understanding of intentional agency to the conclusion that they must be finding actions intelligible in terms of subjective reasons—reasons relativized to the agent's cognitive/evaluative perspective. There may be important roles for the psychological material to play other than to delineate what, relative to the agent's subjective perspective, it is rational for her to do. (The same is true in the case of mature commonsense psychology.) It is no trivial task to decide whether a particular example of early mentalism manifests an understanding of subjective reasons—as becomes clear when we turn to the experimental evidence.

6   The Evidence

It is sometimes said that children appreciate the subjectivity of desires many years before they grasp the subjectivity of belief (e.g., Repacholi and Gopnik 1997; Rakoczy, Warneken, and Tomasello 2007). There is more than one way to understand this claim. On one reading, it amounts to an endorsement of the hybrid view: children are able to understand the relativity of practical reasons to the agent's desires before they are able to relativize practical reasons to the agent's beliefs. We want to suggest that, on this reading, the claim lacks empirical support. There is a rough distinction we can make between two sorts of evidence that are relevant here. On the one hand, there is evidence that might be appealed to in support of the hybrid view. We discuss two such findings: concerning infants' understanding of subjective preferences, and concerning verbal references to desires in action-explanation. On the other hand, there are findings that appear to support the teleological account. As will become apparent, our empirical defense of the teleological account is somewhat qualified. While there is some suggestive evidence in its favor, and no persuasive evidence against it, we believe that more tightly controlled experimental work is needed to make further empirical progress with these matters.

6.1   Subjective Preferences
Even 18-month-olds seem to be aware of the subjectivity of desire in the following sense: they are sensitive to individual preferences. Evidence for this comes from a study where infants were presented with two kinds of food (yummy crackers and yucky broccoli). In a control condition, when another person asked them for something to eat, they almost always gave that person a cracker rather than a piece of broccoli. However, in the discrepant desire condition the other person first demonstrated deviant preferences. Taking the crackers she exclaimed "Yuck, that's awful!," underlined by the appropriate facial expression. When she tasted broccoli she looked pleased and also said so: "Mmm, that's good!" Now when this person later asked the infant for something to eat, most children younger than 18 months still handed her the crackers, but most children over 18 months handed her the broccoli (Repacholi and Gopnik 1997). A similar finding is that 2-year-old children freely verbalize subjective preferences: "Daddy likes shaving cream. I hate shaving cream" (Bartsch and Wellman 1995).

One sort of question raised by these findings is how we should characterize children's conception of subjective preferences. Questions under this heading include the following: Do children think of "liking" as a mental state, something like a desire or an emotion—associated perhaps with a distinctive experience—or rather as something like a character trait (on the lines of "he likes to be in charge")? Another question raised by the findings is: what sort of explanatory role do subjective preferences occupy in children's theory of mind? Do children think of subjective preferences as desires in the sense of BD—as part of what makes it rational for the subject of the desire (but for no one else, unless he or she has a desire to cooperate) to use suitable means to satisfy the desire? Or do they think of subjective preferences in some other way, giving them a different sort of explanatory role?

Note that these are quite different issues. Suppose children do think of subjective preferences as involving conscious mental states, say, desires for objects. This should not automatically lead us to assume that they conceive of such desires as states that provide agents with subjective reasons. That would be to ignore the possibility that children think of "likings" as being essentially linked to *objective* purposes. Thus children's conception of subjective preferences may be part of their conception of objective needs. Subjective preferences may be taken to determine what is good for different sorts of people or creatures. Broccoli is good for A, but not for B. Eating grass is good for cattle but not for humans. This is a relatively sophisticated (perhaps in one sense, nonegocentric) conception of needs. But it does not require any understanding of subjective reasons. On this conception, the import of A's and B's differential preferences is that it is objectively desirable that A, but not B, should obtain some broccoli (Perner, Zauner, and Sprung 2005). Correlatively, there is no privileged explanatory relation between A's preference and A's action: A's preference makes it as reasonable, and as intelligible, for B to pass A a piece of broccoli as for A to set off for the greengrocer. The findings concerning subjective preferences are consistent with this interpretation, and hence with the teleological account.

6.2 Talk about Desires

We mentioned two potential instances of early psychological understanding: children's grasp of attention (and perhaps perceptual experience), and their understanding of subjective preferences. Neither of them has any tendency to suggest that children appeal to mental states as providers of subjective reasons; both are naturally incorporated into the teleological scheme of explanation. But there is another sort of connection between teleology and psychology. There is a sense in which teleology *provides for* certain psychological notions. If the teleological account is right, finding someone's actions (causally) intelligible in terms of reason-giving worldly facts provides for a primitive notion of intentional action—arguably, a psychological phenomenon. Now setting out a teleological explanation in full would require reconstructing the practical inference that articulates the reason for which the agent performed the action, with an evaluative and instrumental premise and a conclusion to the effect that, say, the agent should open a particular cupboard. A more minimalist way of explaining the action would be merely to identify its goal. Rather than saying Maxi opened the cupboard because he needs his chocolate etc., a teleologist may simply tell us that it was in order to get his chocolate that Maxi opened the cupboard. Or: Maxi opened the cupboard with the intention of taking out his chocolate. In this way, the teleological scheme of explanation can be seen to provide for a simple notion of intention (the intention with which someone acts). This is arguably a psychological notion in good standing, but it is not one that helps to explain actions on the model of BD. The intention with which someone acts, as it is understood by a teleologist, may be classified as a (kind of) desire, but a teleologist does not conceive of it as a state that provides the agent with a subjective reason—a desire that, together with a belief, helps to rationalize intentional actions. Rather, that an agent has this intention *follows* from the fact that his action is open to a reason-giving, teleological explanation.

The point is significant given that it may help to interpret some interesting data concerning early verbalizations. Children talk about desires substantially earlier than about beliefs (see Bartsch and Wellman 1995). Much of this talk is a matter of expressing their own requests and wishes. Some of it is a matter of reflecting on sometimes contrasting subjective preferences (see above). Least frequently, but perhaps most interestingly, some examples have been recorded of early appeals to desires in action-explanations. A striking illustration is the following (Bartsch and Wellman 1995, 118):

Ross (2;10):   Look, there's a car up in the air. [on a hoist]
Adult: Oh. Why is it up there?
Ross: Man put it up there.
Adult: Why did he put it up there?
Ross: He want to fix it.

On one reading, "want to fix it" is to be construed as an ascription of a mental state distinct from, and causally responsible for, the intentional action in question—a desire that both gives the man a subjective reason to put the car up in the air and causally explains his doing so. But there is an alternative reading. The child may make the man's action intelligible by stating the intention with which it was performed: his intention in putting the car up was to fix it. The example reveals the child's understanding that people act on the basis of good reasons, and provides a partial reconstruction of the reason operative in this case, identifying the purpose informing the action. Note that on this reading, it's possible that Ross takes the reason to be provided by the objective desirability of the man's fixing the car, rather than by the man's desire to fix it. Thus, the example provides no evidence against the teleological account.

6.3 Competitive Games

When introducing teleology we mentioned the importance of two sorts of cases: actions informed by (to the interpreter) unacceptable goals (e.g., throwing a ball at someone because one finds it desirable to hurt her); and competitive actions. If children make sense of intentional actions via the teleological scheme, they should find these sorts of cases unintelligible. If they use the hybrid scheme, these cases shouldn't pose any special challenge. As we indicated, there is some evidence to suggest that young children do find these cases challenging. Now the evidence relating to unacceptable goals (Yuill 1984) relies on an experimental paradigm that, at least in the current context, is to be treated with some caution (as we argue in appendix 2). So we will focus here on the second kind of case.

A good test case between teleology and the hybrid view arises when it comes to understanding competitive behavior as intentional actions, done for a reason. In a competitive (zero-sum) game (as are most simple strategic or probabilistic games) one player's win means the other player's defeat. So their respective contributions to the game cannot be understood as attempts to attain some objectively desirable end, valid for both. The teleological account therefore predicts that competition involving reasoned actions can only be appreciated by children who understand differences of perspective, including the case of false beliefs. In contrast, on the hybrid theory, understanding competitive behavior should pose no particular challenge: children should be able to appreciate that relative to their respective objectives (to win the game), both A's and B's behavior makes rational sense. The question is where to find relevant developmental evidence. The only directly relevant evidence that we are aware of is based on the hand-guessing (commonly also known as "penny hiding") game used in a study by Gratch (1964).

The penny-hiding game is a two-person game in which the subject is actively involved either as a guesser or as a hider. Both try to win. The hider hides the penny in one hand or the other, and then invites a guess. This is repeated over a row of trials, after which the participants change roles. In the role of hider "the child was judged to be *competitive* if he expressed displeasure on any of the trials in which E found the marble, or if any of the following events occurred: 1. when E selected the marble-holding hand, S refused to show the marble or made an attempt to transfer it to his other hand; 2. S extended an empty hand for E to guess from. A child was judged to be *non-competitive* if none of the above events occurred. The non-competitive children frequently told E where the marble would be hidden, after a trial in which E had failed to guess correctly; and many of them extended the marble in an open hand on all trials" (Gratch 1964, 53–54).

The proportion of children who displayed competitive spirit increased steadily from 5 percent below the age of 3 years to 58 percent at 4.5 years to practically 95 percent at around 6 years. This fits very well the typical developmental trend on false-belief tests (see Perner, Zauner, and Sprung 2005, figure 4, for a graphic display). Gratch's study is particularly helpful insofar as he analyzed indicators of competitive spirit separately from indicators of the ability to deceive, fool, or conceal information from the opponent. Since deception requires an understanding of false belief, a developmental link between understanding the deceptive aspects of the game and understanding false belief would not be terribly interesting and no support for the teleological theory developed here. The shortcoming of Gratch's data for present purposes is, of course, that there is no direct comparison of how many of the children in his sample would have passed the false-belief test. Ideally one would also see the use of a control task with similar cognitive demands except for the competitiveness and in which children of all ages can succeed.

The good news is that more recently several studies included the penny-guessing game and the false-belief tasks (Baron-Cohen 1992; Chasiotis et al. 2006; Hughes and Dunn 1997, 1998). The bad news is that, without exception, these studies only analyzed the hand-guessing behavior for indicators of deceptive abilities (or a mix of combative spirit and decep-tion). Hence the reported correlations with false belief understanding provide no convincing evidence against the hybrid theory and, therefore, also no support for teleology.

We should also mention two other pieces of evidence that go well with teleology. Although children seem to have problems understanding the point of competition, they are quite concerned about obeying the rules of a game (Rakoczy, Warneken, and Tomasello 2008) even at the age of 2 years when they just start to use "desire" terms for other people (Bartsch and Wellman 1995; Imbens-Bailey, Prost, and Fabricius 1997). At 3 years (36 months) this concern becomes almost obsessive. Clearly they expect people to act a certain way because it is the right, conventional way, and they seem to have little understanding for idiosyncratic deviation.

Following the pioneering work by Shultz and Shamash (1981), several studies reported that children have difficulty distinguishing intentions from desires (see reviews by Astington 1999, 2001). The latest study by Schult (2002) included children as young as 3 years. They had to toss bean bags into three different colored buckets, some of which contained a ticket for a prize. For each toss they had to indicate which bucket they intended to hit. On some trials they hit the intended bucket, on others they missed it; on some they won a prize, on others they didn't, resulting in four different combinations. The 4- and 5-year-olds were remarkably accurate in answering all types of questions. The 3-year-olds, on the other hand, had serious problems with questions about their intentions, in particular when satisfaction of their intention contrasted with satisfaction of their desire, as shown in table 14.1.

This pattern of results follows from our assumption that children remain basic teleologists until about 4 years, when they can understand differences of perspective. They have no problem knowing what they want, i.e. the desirable goal of the action (winning the prize), and whether they got it or not. They also understand intentions to hit a particular bucket, though only insofar as there are *objective* reasons for such intentions. Consider now a case of fortuitous success, where children accidentally get the prize after hitting a bucket they didn't intend to hit. To understand that they didn't intentionally hit the bucket, children have to understand that they had

Table 14.1

Data from Schult (2002): number of children giving correct answers to the satisfaction questions, "Did you do what you were trying to do?" (intention), and "Did you get what you wanted?" (desire).

Condition (correct answer)	3-Year-Olds	4-Year-Olds	5-Year-Olds
Miss target/get prize: *fortuitous success*			
Intention ("no")	4/15	8/8	8/8
Desire ("yes")	12/15	8/8	8/8
Hit target/no prize: *bad luck*			
Intention ("yes")	8/15	8/8	8/8
Desire ("no")	13/15	8/8	8/8

no reason for hitting that particular bucket, despite the fact that doing so turned out to be conducive to reaching their goal. Or consider a case of bad luck, where they hit a certain bucket without getting a prize. To understand that they hit the bucket intentionally, children have to understand that they did have a reason for hitting that bucket, despite the fact that doing so turned out *not* to be conducive to reaching their goal. Under the teleological interpretation, it is unsurprising that young children have problems under these kinds of circumstances. Correct judgment of these cases only becomes possible when one understands that one acted on the assumption that the prize might be in the bucket one was aiming for. Since in the critical cases this assumption turns out to be false, the intentionality of the intended action can only be understood if one can understand it in terms of the perspective of that assumption.

In sum, there is some suggestive evidence against the hybrid theory and some support for the teleological account in Gratch's finding that children show little competitive spirit before the age at which they are able to understand false belief as a motivating reason. More importantly (for the developmental psychologists), our account also provides us with a clearer analysis of what young children should find difficult about competition and incompatibility of goals. In appendix 2, we discuss further evidence that is prima facie relevant to the debate between teleology and the hybrid view (evidence concerning children's understanding of emotional reactions to the satisfaction or frustration of desires). In appendix 3, we present an outline of a new experimental paradigm to test for children's ability to understand competitive actions.

7   Teleology in Perspective

We conclude with a brief suggestion as to how the teleological account bears on our understanding of adult commonsense psychology. Suppose young children find intentional actions intelligible in terms of reason-providing facts, rather than mental states. We can distinguish two different ways in which this initial understanding subsequently gets refined and enriched, corresponding to two distinct elements of the mature adult conception of intentional action. Both involve giving explanatory relevance to an agent's perspective, though in quite different ways.

First, a central element of a more sophisticated conception of practical reasons is an appreciation of the role of knowledge and ignorance. We may think of this as a more subtle application of the possibly earlier developing idea, that agents' responsiveness to reasons is subject to enabling and disabling conditions. In its subtler (adult) form, the idea is this: if someone doesn't know that action x causes event y, it's unsurprising that she won't perform x, despite having reason to cause y—for she lacks a *subjective* reason to perform x. Correlatively, her performing x can be intelligible in terms of her knowledge that x causes y. Note that explanations in terms of knowledge are simultaneously teleological (they accord an explanatory role to reason-giving facts, knowledge being a factive state) and psychological (knowledge being a psychological state).

Second, mature interpreters are also able to explain actions in terms of considerations the agent takes to provide her with a reason, without endorsing the consideration or the claim that they constitute reasons. It is this dimension of the "adult theory" that enables us to figure out why someone is adding petrol to her tonic or to understand competition. And it is here that we find the rationale for BD: adopting a detached, relatively noncommittal stance toward others' intentional activities requires finding them intelligible in terms of reasons provided by their propositional attitudes.

The teleological genealogy of the adult theory has important implications for the sorts of psychological properties invoked in the mature conception of intentional action. It should lead us to question the relentless focus on just two kinds of mental states, beliefs and desires, encouraged by the "belief-desire model" of action-explanation. The teleological genealogy highlights the explanatory role given in the adult theory to *knowledge*.[19] It also suggests that the notion of desire in BD should be interpreted not in the narrow Humean sense but along the lines of Davidson's "pro-attitudes,"[20] as subsuming the immense variety of attitudes that constitute agents' perspectives on the purposes for which they act. Reflection on the teleological origin of commonsense psychology also helps to shed light on the sort of explanation required for understanding intentional action. It is not enough to think of certain mental states as the causes of bodily movements. What matters is the ability to see how some of the agent's psychological properties provide her with considerations that from her point of view can be seen to amount to a practical reason. Understanding the subjective reason informing someone's intentional action requires delineating what, from her perspective, presents itself as an objective reason.

Appendix 1: Direct and Indirect Tests

The recent investigations of children's understanding of rational action and belief have made it necessary to distinguish two sources of evidence. The "traditional" evidence is based on what is called in the consciousness litera-ture (Reingold and Merikle 1993; Richardson-Klavehn and Bjork 1988) a *direct test of knowledge*: Children are asked a question (or set a task) that refers (directly) to an actor's action in question. For instance, in the false-belief task children are told a story or made to observe a scene in which a protago-nist puts an object in one of two locations, which is unexpectedly trans-ferred to the other location in the protagonist's absence. When he returns children are asked: "Where does the protagonist think the object is?" or "Where will the protagonist go to get the object (he desires)?" On these measures a large amount of data shows that children start to give correct answers between the ages of 3 to 5 years. (See the meta-analysis by Wellman, Cross, and Watson 2001.) The younger children's difficulty stands in stark contrast to their ability to predict with conviction where someone will go for the object when the protagonist has witnessed the transfer and no false belief is involved (e.g., Clements and Perner 1994; Ruffman et al. 2001). Indeed, children not only fail to take belief into account in their predictions of the protagonist's actions but also fail to use it in explanations of the erroneous actions. For instance, when shown that the protagonist in the false-belief story goes to the empty location and they are asked why he went there, many of them answer (not incorrectly but uninformatively) "because he wants to get the object." When asked to specify why he then went to the empty location, they admit their ignorance: "Don't know" (Wimmer and Mayringer 1998; Perner, Lang, and Kloo 2002).

The fact that children feel comfortable talking about desires (want) before they address beliefs is also apparent in Bartsch and Wellman's (1995) study of naturally occurring speech. The authors tried, as best as they could, to identify genuine references to beliefs and desires from the limited context of the transcribed utterances (their figure 5.1). Reference to desire started with the first words as early as 18 months, peaking just before 3 years (33–36 months) to level off at about 3 percent of all utter-ances. In contrast, references to beliefs started at 3 years, reaching a con-stant level of about 2 percent of all utterances at 4 years. A similar picture also emerged from induced utterances in a study by Imbens-Bailey, Prost, and Fabricius (1997), conveniently displayed in our figure 14.1. Also, by using a method for eliciting extensive explanations, Bartsch, Campbell, and Troseth (2007) were able to get half the 3- to 4-year-olds to give belief-explanations of erroneous actions, but emotion- and desire-explanations were still much more frequent. However, when relying on nonverbal indi-cators of understanding belief and desire, recent research has complicated this seemingly clear picture.

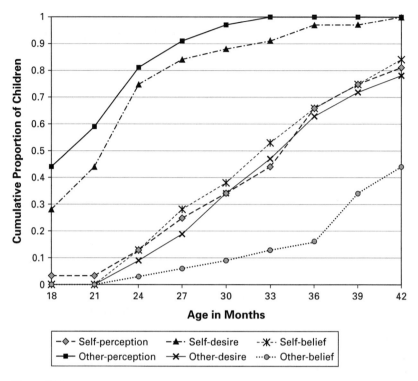

Figure 14.1
Proportion of children who use different categories of mental verbs.

Starting with Clements and Perner (1994), research has recently focused on using *indirect tests of knowledge*: Children are not asked any question about the protagonist's belief or action, but one of three other measures is used. (1) Looking time: The duration of looking at an erroneous action is compared to looking at a successful action. Longer looking at the successful action than at the erroneous action in cases of false belief is interpreted as children being surprised about a successful action when the actor has a false belief. These data indicate sensitivity to the protagonist's belief as early as 14 or 15 months (e.g., Onishi and Baillargeon 2005; Surian, Caldi, and Sperber 2007). One problem with these data is that the looking-time differences are multiply interpretable and not a clear indicator of expectation (Perner and Ruffman 2005; Sirois and Jackson 2007). (2) Looking in expectation: A better measure in this respect is children's direction of eye gaze as an indication of where they expect the protagonist to reappear (Clements and Perner 1994). This method has recently indicated that children understand belief-based action as early as 2 years (Southgate, Senju, and Csibra 2007) or even earlier (Southgate 2008). (3) Interpretation of referential gestures: Southgate (2008) used a paradigm developed by Carpenter, Call, and Tomasello (2002) and Happé and Loth (2002) on children as young as 17 months. These infants observed a confederate putting object A into container X and object B into container Y. In her absence the infants watched the experimenter switch the objects (A now in Y and B in X). When the confederate returned she pointed to, say, box X and said, "I want this one." Then the covers of the boxes on the child's side were opened so that the child, but not the confederate, could see inside and the confederate asked the child to give the object to her. Children above chance handed her the object in box Y, which contained the object that the confederate had put inside box X but was no longer in there when the confederate expressed her desire for the object in box X.

We concentrate in our discussion on the evidence from direct tests. Answers to questions more clearly express a reasoned commitment, that is, an understanding that the protagonist will act the indicated way because he has good reason to do so. Indirect measures contain no commitment. I can look to a location because of a vague, unreasoned hunch even when to my proper reasoning he will appear somewhere else. Indeed, that is what the looking-in-expectation data seem to indicate: Children look (in expectation) to where the protagonist thinks the object is, but steadfastly and with conviction (Ruffman et al. 2001) they claim that he will appear at the location where the object actually is. Perner, Rendl, and Garnham (2007) proposed that the false-belief data from infancy (see also, e.g., Moll and Tomasello 2007; Tomasello and Haberl 2003; Southgate, Senju, and Csibra 2007) show an unexpectedly strong preoccupation with what other people can and cannot see, and keep an "experiential record" for the other person, using this record to compute likely actions and referential gestures but without clear understanding that these records constitute beliefs that direct action in the real world.

Investigations of children's understanding of knowledge presents a similar picture. In line with the evidence of early sensitivity to beliefs, children as young as 14 or 18 months keep track of what another person has or has not yet encountered (Moll and Tomasello 2007; Tomasello and Haberl 2003; Southgate, Senju, and Csibra 2007) and make their communicative behavior dependent on it by preferring to show the person objects that the person has not yet encountered over encountered objects (regardless of the child's own familiarity with the object). In all these cases, the use of this experiential record (Perner, Rendl, and Garnham 2007;

"registration of encounters," Apperly and Butterfill 2008) is limited to a single purpose, namely, to bring the other person into informational contact with yet unencountered objects. In the only other experimental paradigm used, children are asked to decide whom to ask for information, the one who has seen the hiding of the object or the one who was not able to see it. Here children seem oblivious to the other person's informational access until 4 years (Povinelli and deBlois 1992), or, with improved methodology, not before 3 years (Sodian, Thoermer, and Dietrich 2006).

Appendix 2: Action versus Emotion

As we mentioned in the text, there is more than one way to interpret the claim that children understand the "subjectivity of desires." One reading is: they understand subjective preferences. A second reading is: they understand that a desire provides an agent with a subjective reason, a reason that makes it rational for the agent (but for no one else—unless they wish to cooperate) to act in a certain way. We argued that evidence regarding subjective preference provides no support for the claim that children understand subjective reasons. Some of the experimental work in this area, however, is concerned with a third claim. This is the claim that young children are able to understand and predict someone's emotional reaction to the satisfaction or frustration of some desire even when they don't *share* the desire. For example, Yuill (1984) addressed the question of whether children can predict that an agent will take pleasure in the satisfaction of a *wicked* desire (such as a desire to hit someone). Similarly, Perner, Zauner, and Sprung (2005) investigated children's ability to attribute emotional reaction to the satisfaction/frustration of desires in the case of two protagonists with mutually *incompatible* desires.

Does evidence from these paradigms help to settle the issue between teleology and the hybrid view? There are two reasons for skepticism. One is simply that the experimental state of play regarding the third claim is currently inconclusive. Crudely: Yuill's (1984) and Perner, Zauner, and Sprung's (2005) findings suggest that until they pass the false-belief task, children have great difficulty attributing emotional reactions to the satisfaction of goals they don't take to be objectively desirable. But more recently, Rakoczy, Warneken, and Tomasello (2007) and Rakoczy, Warneken, and Tomasello (2008) reported some evidence that children can attribute appropriate emotions in competitive situations before they pass the false-belief test.

A second, weightier reason for skepticism is this. It is not clear that explaining emotional reactions to the satisfaction/frustration of desires is a case of reason-giving explanation. It is not clear, for example, that to understand and predict that A will feel sad about the frustration of his desire, children have to appreciate that A has a *reason for* feeling sad. Emotional reactions *happen* to us: they are caused, for example, by perceived events, not formed for reasons. Correlatively, understanding such reactions is not a matter of reconstructing the agent's reason for undergoing it. To understand A's sadness you merely have to know that the frustration of a desire tends to lead to sadness, not that it makes it *rational* to feel sad. Admittedly, this crude contrast doesn't do justice to the subtleties of adult commonsense psychology in this area. (See Goldie 2000, ch. 2, for some helpful distinctions.) But it is enough to suggest that it would be a non sequitur to move from evidence (if there were such evidence) that children are able to understand emotional reactions to desires they don't share to the conclusion that they grasp subjective reasons—that they think of A's desires as making certain actions (or emotions) rational *from A's perspective*.

Appendix 3: Sabotage

The empirically pressing question now is how to derive testable predictions from the assumption that young children use teleology before they are able to understand perspective differences. We need a task for which simple teleology is insufficient, i.e. which requires understanding the protagonists' intentional actions in terms of their perspectives on what's desirable. We need another, control task, identical to the experimental task except that teleology can provide the correct answer without need for understanding perspective differences. The predictions then are that the experimental task should be mastered after the control task and not before (within a margin of error) other typical perspective tasks (involving perspective differences, e.g., false-belief task) are mastered. Here is a suggestion involving sabotage.

Children can engage in sabotage before understanding false belief (Sodian 1991)—in seeming contradiction to our claim. In Sodian's tasks the children were asked to think of a way to prevent a robber from getting to the treasure. They correctly locked the treasure box when the robber approached but not when the good prince came to look for treasure. Critically for us, correct responding may not require children to *interpret* the

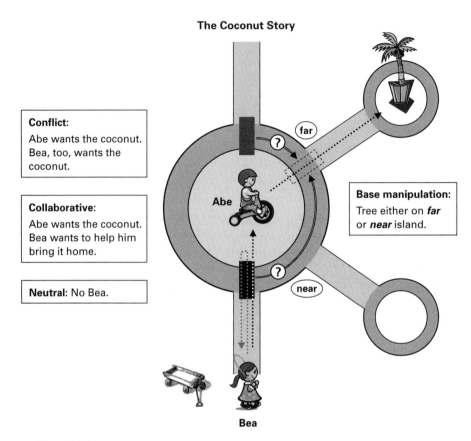

Figure 14.2
Test question: Which board will Abe use to get to the coconut?

robber's behavior—to find it intelligible in terms of his reasons. The child's task is only to find a means to prevent something bad. A new paradigm must ensure that prediction of the saboteur's act must be based on understanding what the sabotee will do for (his) good reasons.

In the experimental conflict story of the coconut scenario in figure 14.2 the girl, Bea, wants to get the one coconut left on the tree on the island. She crosses over the black board to the center island. Then she remembers that she needs her cart. She goes back to get the cart. Meanwhile, the boy, Abe, has arrived also with the intention to get the last coconut. To get to the tree he needs another board. He has the choice between the black and the brown board. Test question: Which board will he take to cross the moat, the brown or the black one? Correct answer: the black board.

In a collaborative condition, Bea indicates that she wants to help Abe pick the coconut. The correct answer to the test question in this condition is: the brown board. In a neutral condition, without Bea, we can get an estimate of children's preference for the "near" board (brown) over the "far" board (black). Presumably most children will make him use the nearer one. By counterbalancing the competitive and collaborative conditions with whether the palm tree is on the *near* (to Bea's approach) or the *far* island, we can check whether the understanding of the collaborative and the competitive aspects, respectively, can overrule the natural tendency to predict use of the most convenient nearer board.

We expect young children who fail false-belief tasks (as a measure of their ability to understand conflicting perspectives) to be able to predict correctly what Abe will do in the cooperative condition (use the brown board), but to fail to see that he will act differently in the competitive condition (he will use the black board). Children who pass the false-belief test, we expect, will make correct predictions in both conditions.

Notes

1. Or rather Johann Nestroy, as quoted in the motto of Wittgenstein (1958).

2. It is tempting to think the solution to our puzzle may be provided by some recent experimental findings, widely taken to show that under certain conditions even very young children have some grasp of the causal role of false beliefs. In Appendix 1 we explain why we think the temptation should be resisted.

3. Compare Gopnik and Meltzoff's claim that 18-month-olds who participated in a study of imitation of failed attempts were able to treat different kinds of movements "as the causal consequence of the same underlying mental state, the same goal" (1997, 151).

4. See Schueler 2009 for illuminating discussion of the importance, and the theoretical implications, of the "putting-together" point.

5. See e.g., Parfit 1997; Scanlon 1998; Schueler 2003, 2009; Hornsby 2008.

6. "[T]ypically, in deliberation what I do pay attention to are the relevant *features* of the external world [rather than one's own desires or impulses]: the cost of the alternatives, the quality of the food, the durability of the cloth, the fact that I made a promise" (Blackburn 1998, 253).

7. Crudely, claims of need have implications to do with matters such as harm and flourishing, but they have no immediate implications regarding the agent's desires. (That you need some vitally important medicine does not imply that you want to take it.)

8. Are fully objective reasons *external* reasons in Williams's (1981a) sense—reasons that cannot be derived by practical deliberation from the agent's "subjective motivational set"? The question raises complex interpretative and substantive issues we cannot pursue here. Two brief comments will have to suffice.

One comment is that objective reasons in our sense are not necessarily external in Williams's. At least in some of his later writings on external reasons, Williams (1995b) allows that the application of "thick ethical concepts" can provide us with practical reasons. Of course, Williams insists that whether a certain application of a "thick" concept provides an agent A with a reason essentially depends on whether A uses the concept ("*chastity* is an example that focuses the mind"; ibid., 37). The idea here is that the reason-giving role of "thick" facts turns on the presence in A's subjective motivational set of the sorts of dispositions tied up with mastery of the relevant thick concept. Still, it is significant that this version of internalism is not committed to the view that only certain kinds of mental states (passions or desires) can constitute the noninstrumental element of practical reasons. Suppose someone is tempted to make a remark that, unbeknownst to him, would be a very tactless remark to make in the circumstances. Williams's "liberal" internalism allows us to say that—provided only that *tactless* is one of the person's concepts—he has a reason not to make the remark, even though from his current perspective the remark seems unobjectionable. In our terminology, this would be an objective reason; but the reason would still count as internal by Williams's lights.

Our second comment is that nevertheless, the developmental suggestion we will be pursuing may be put by saying that we all started life as external reasons theorists. For the suggestion is that young children are familiar with objective reasons before even *understanding* subjective reasons—before they grasp that there are two sorts of perspectives from which to consider what someone has reason to do. It is not clear, though, that there is anything in Williams's account that would be inconsistent with this suggestion. (The "liberal" internalism Williams espouses in this later writings does not imply that external reasons statements are *meaningless*; it merely says they are false.) In fact our developmental account may shed some light on what is going on when people make what appear to be external reasons statements. It is significant that Williams's most convincing example of an external reasons statement (his gloss on James's story of Owen Wingrave) turns on a conflict among members of a family. (Despite Owen's loathing for the military, "[h]is family might have expressed themselves by saying that *there was a reason for Owen to join the army*"; Williams 1981, 106.) Our developmental suggestion would make it unsurprising if the family were a context in which the idea of external reasons could sometimes be seen to linger.

9. Although this is not the way Bartsch and Wellman put things, some of their suggestions fit well with the hybrid account; they stress the importance of desire psychologists' drawing on their *own* knowledge of the world in predicting how someone will go about satisfying his or her desires (see Bartsch and Wellman 1995, 155).

10. We use the term "pro-attitude" in Davidson's sense, as subsuming "desires, wantings, urges, promptings, and a great variety of moral views, aesthetic principles, economic prejudices, social conventions, and public and private goals and values" (Davidson 1963/1980, 4).

11. Compare Aristotle's conception of teleological explanation: "the fourth cause is the goal: i.e., the good" (quoted in Charles 1984, 198). More recently, Csibra and Gergely (1998) have used the notion of a "teleological stance" in their theory of infants' expectations concerning rational actions. Their account differs from ours (and Aristotle's) in that it does not appeal to evaluative facts as the source of goals, but takes the notion of a goal as primitive. Another difference is that their account is concerned with children's *expectations* as to the movement of certain kinds of agents under certain circumstances, not with children's ability to *explain* intentional actions in terms of agents' reasons.

12. Of course, there is a (to adults, natural) way of taking these latter propositions that would make them conflicting without being inconsistent, along the lines of "there is something to be said for A's winning, and there is something to be said for B's winning." But construed in this way, the propositions could not do the work a teleologist expects them to do. To provide teleological explanations, the relevant evaluative propositions have to license conclusions as to what the agent should do or has most reason to do; *prima facie* reasons, on their own, do not license such conclusions. That there is something to be said for A's winning, and that A can win by doing x, only gives A a reason to do x if there are no other more important considerations in favor, e.g., of letting B win. In brief, teleology, as we conceive it here, has to appeal to "all-out" practical reasons.

13. See Woodward forthcoming for a suggestive discussion of the contrast between "difference-making" and "causal process" theories of causation. See also Steward 1997 and Hornsby 1993.

14. See Woodward 2003; see also Campbell 2007 for helpful discussion.

15. The case of imitation illustrates that teleology has the resources to conceive of reasons as "agent-specific." Although teleology appeals to worldly facts rather than the individual agent's mental states, this does not mean that two agents cannot have reason to perform different actions. One way in which different agents may be seen to have reasons to do different things is in virtue of their distinctive roles. Having just banged my toy a couple of times, I, currently performing the part of the model, have no reason to keep banging; but you, performing the part of the imitator, have every reason to bang your toy. Again, the very same objective purpose or value can be seen to yield different sorts of practical reasons, depending on the agent's skills and circumstances.

16. Of course, it is not obvious whether imitation is, or when it begins to be, tied up with explanation. Certainly to begin with, infant imitation may well be a more

primitive phenomenon than the ability to make rational sense of others' behavior. All we are saying here is that imitation provides compelling materials for teleological explanations. Acquiring a conception of intentional action may partly be a matter of learning to exploit such materials.

17. See Doherty 2009 for helpful discussion of the notion of engagement.

18. For a "grown-up" version of this point, compare John McDowell: "Finding an action or propositional attitude intelligible, after initial difficulty, may not only involve managing to articulate for oneself some hitherto merely implicit aspect of one's conception of rationality, but actually involve becoming convinced that one's conception of rationality needed correcting, so as to make room for this novel way of being intelligible" (McDowell 1998, 332).

19. See Williamson 2000, and especially Hornsby 2008, on the explanatory role of knowledge.

20. Davidson's gloss on "pro-attitude" bears repeating: "desires, wantings, urges, promptings, and a great variety of moral views, aesthetic principles, economic prejudices, social conventions, and public and private goals and values" (1963/ 1980, 4).

15   Action Theory Meets Embodied Cognition

Fred Adams

1   Introduction

In cognitive science, embodied cognition is sweeping the planet.[1] Interest
in this perspective on cognition is becoming wildly popular. Some of the
tenets of embodied approaches to cognition are compatible with the
received theories of action, but some aren't. In this essay, I will look at the
problem caused for the received view by the claim that much of embodied
cognition is situated and time-pressured in such a way that the received
view of how intentions work in the production of actions in these cases
cannot be correct. I shall defend a compatibility approach, arguing for the
view that even if action is time-pressured and situated, the requirements
of the received view can still be met.

2   Action Theory (AT)

There are theories of action that are not causal theories, but I will not
discuss them here because few (maybe no) sparks fly when combining
them with claims of embodied cognition. Potentially, sparks fly at the
intersection of causal theories of action and embodied theories of cognition, so in the spirit of generating light, we shall explore there.

Causal theories of bodily action[2] maintain that what makes a mere
bodily movement an action is its causal history. This is so regardless of
whether one considers the action the bodily movement (a *product* of the
right kinds of mental causes) that is brought about in the right way or
considers the action the very *causing* of the movement by those right kinds
of mental causes. On the product view (Mele 1992), my clenched fist opens
and is an action because I intended to open it and my intention produces
my open fist in the right way. On the causing view (Dretske 1988), my
action is my opening of my fist, where the opening is a causing of the

movement by my intention (in the right way). On the product view a relevant intention is not a constituent of the action, but on the causing view it is actually a component of the action.

On both views the important causal antecedents of actions are mental states and their representational (i.e., intentional) content. Not only must the proper mental states bring about the action in the proper way, they must represent the act as desirable, not impossible, and as one's intended goal for the action to unfold. So there is a constellation of desires (I want my fist to open), beliefs (I can open it), and intentions (I shall open it soon/now) in the background and production of the movement that constitutes the action. The representational details of the contents of these mental states are every bit as important as the details of their causing. The contents are essential to the determination of what is done. Two qualitatively identical bodily movements can be completely different actions if brought about by different intentions (with qualitatively the same bodily movements, Tom is scratching his itchy nose, Guido is signaling a mafia hit).

Among the shortcomings sometimes attributed to some versions of causal theories of action is that they are incomplete. Elisabeth Pacherie (2006, 2) puts it this way: "They account at best for how an action is initiated, but not for how it is guided, controlled and monitored until completion." Pacherie is surely right. This is why Al Mele and I (Adams and Mele 1989) modeled our accounts of action and intentional action on control models of goal-directed behavior generally. On our view a piece of behavior is goal-directed behavior only if it is behavior of a goal-directed system. A piece of behavior B is directed toward a specific goal G due to an information-processing network of control within the system S. S must be causing B and comparing information about whether B obtains (is about to obtain) with a representation of goal state G, and be prepared to monitor progress or make error-corrections as it detects that B is not going to match G. Thus a system S is a goal-directed system in its behavior B toward a goal-state G if and only if:

(1) S has an internal representational state R capable of fixing G as S's goal-state and S is capable of detecting G's presence or absence;

(2) Information about S's ongoing behavior B is fed back into the system as input and is compared with R;

(3) S's modification of output behavior B in response to comparison between S's present state and S's goal-state causally depend on the correction processes of (1) and (2).

All goal-directed behavior fits this model.[3] I (Adams 1986a, 1997) think[4] all intentional action fits a similar model that has come to be known as the "Simple View." So on my account, S does A intentionally only if: (1) S intends to A; (2) S does A; and (3) S's A-ing causally depends on S's intention to A (in the right way)—the intention guides and sustains S's A-ing via goal-directed feedback control systems. Here is how Mele and I (1989) described the role of intentions in their functional roles as motivators of action, initiators of action and sustainers of action.

Intentions are functionally specifiable mental states. The control model identifies the essence of the functional role of intentions. They must: (i) set the goal or plan of the action; (ii) be involved in causally initiating and informationally updating progress toward the action; (iii) provide a standard for determining error and correction or damage control when the plan goes awry; (iv) provide the criterion for goal-success (help determine when the intended action has been completed, disengage the plan's implementation, and so on; (v) play a crucial role in the counterfactual dependency of output behavior (bodily movement) upon intention and information input (the perception of present state as compared with one's intended goal-state). (Adams and Mele 1989, 514)

Mele and I (Adams and Mele 1992) later extended our discussion to include *trying*. We said that tryings were simply *intentions at work*. They do not involve special effort. They are not willings. Tryings exist in every case where an intention to A issues in an intentional A-ing. Trying is the agent's contribution to the action. Tryings are not mediators between proximal intentions (an intention to A here and now) and actions, in the sense that intentions cause tryings and then tryings cause actions. Instead, trying is a continuous unfolding of the intention's doing its work. Intentions are not ballistic. We put it this way:

For us, tryings are effects of the normal functioning of appropriate intentions. Roughly, trying to A is an event or process that has A-ing as a goal and is initiated and (normally) sustained by a pertinent intention. Successful tryings to A, rather than causing A-ings, are A-ings. . . . On the view to be defended, tryings begin in the brain. Their initiation is the immediate effect of the formation or acquisition of a proximal intention. Action begins where trying begins—in the brain. (Adams and Mele 1992, 326)

3   Embodied Cognition (EC)

There is a great deal of excitement in cognitive science these days over what has come to be known as *embodied cognition*. Before we get to specific claims, the general framework of embodied cognition is motivated by the idea that the mind and cognition are for action and consequently cognitive processing has its roots and grounding (Pecher and Zwaan 2005) in sensory (Barsalou 1999) and motor processing (Jeannerod 2006). The sensory and motor systems are not just input–output systems for cognition, contingently causally connected to cognition, but are constitutive of cognition (just how varies among the proponents). Hence, all concepts (their content and how they drive thought and action) can be understood properly only in relation to their sensory and motor origins. That's the positive side of the program. On the negative side is an urging away from theories of cognition that see concepts as arbitrary abstract symbols understandable (and functioning) independently of their contingent connections to perception or action (Turing, Fodor, Chomsky).

Much of the excitement is due to new empirical findings that link cognitive activity and behavior to sensory and motor priming, such that one unexpectedly finds faster cognitive reaction times when subjects are cognitively tasked with experimental paradigms that involve sensory or motor priming. In most cases, the conclusion drawn (Glenberg and Kaschak 2002) is that the best explanation for the empirical results is that cognition is not only grounded but happens in the sensory and motor systems. Some of the excitement is also due to the claims made that a paradigm shift to embodied cognition will even help us solve the symbol-grounding problem (Searle 1980; Harnad 1990).

Among the specific claims being made by proponents of embodied cognition (Wilson 2002), I will look mainly at those that have the most direct relevance for models of human action. Take the claim that cognition is situated. Here is how Wilson unpacks "situated":

Simply put, situated cognition is cognition that takes place in the context of task-relevant inputs and outputs. That is, while a cognitive process is being carried out, perceptual information continues to come in that affects processing, and motor activity is executed that affects the environment in task-relevant ways. Driving, holding a conversation, and moving around a room while trying to imagine where the furniture should go, are all cognitive activities that are situated in this sense. (Wilson 2002, 4)

Wilson points out that off-line cognition (planning, remembering, daydreaming) is not situated, on this understanding, and that this fact has been pointed out before (Clark and Grush 1999; Grush 1997). Such cognitive activity is also said to be "decoupled" from immediate interaction with the environment. She also points out that an argument could be made that:

situated cognition is nevertheless the bedrock of human cognition due to our evolutionary history . . . invoking a picture of our ancestors relying almost entirely on situated skills . . . obtaining food, avoiding predators. Thus, situated cognition may represent our fundamental cognitive architecture, even if this is not always reflected in the artificial activities of our modern world. (Wilson 2002, 5)

To her credit, Wilson finds such appeals strained. As she notes, it is likely that even our ancestors engaged in counterfactual reasoning about food and predators, while hunting and gathering or, while parenting, warning children about possible dangers to avoid. However, for our purposes, what matters is not whether all cognition is situated. The clear implication of the embodied cognition movement is that cognitive abilities arise as situated and never lose their connection to their sensory and motor origins. Furthermore, we will be interested mainly in action where the cognitive states involved in action may be seen as situated. The best case for this is in ongoing activity—where current cognitive states are causally involved in guiding and sustaining action. How much more situated can it get? We will be interested in what embodied cognition tells us about cognitive states driving situated action.

Closely associated with cognition's being situated is its being time-pressured. As Wilson puts it, "agents must deal with the constraints of 'real time' or 'runtime'" (Wilson 2002, 6). She continues:

These phrases are used to highlight a weakness of traditional artificial intelligence models, which are generally allowed to build up and manipulate internal representations of a situation at their leisure. A real creature in a real environment, it is pointed out, has no such leisure. It must cope with predators, prey, stationary objects, and terrain, as fast as the situation dishes them out. (Ibid.)

As with whether all cognition is situated, surely not all is time-pressured. Wilson points out that making sandwiches, paying bills, and working crossword puzzles don't fit the bill. Yet, as before, we can take the point embodied cognitive theorists make as that cognition has this property in its etiology. In addition, there will be cases where this feature will be needed to explain cognition's role in guiding and sustaining human activity. As Wilson notes, this will include cases from walking, to making skilled hand movements, driving in traffic, steering a plane in a dogfight, playing a sport, or just roughhousing with the kids or family pet.

Cognition is for action. This claim hits particularly close to home for action theory when embodied cognition considers how the visual system drives purposive behavior. Wilson nicely points out that the traditional view of perception has been that its cognitive role is to build up consciously accessible perceptual representations for the planning and guidance of action. However, recent empirical findings of Goodale and Milner (1992), Jeannerod (1997, 2006), and others threaten to unravel at least some of the traditional view because certain kinds of visual inputs prime for motor activity (Borghi 2005) types of grip (precision/power grip size, distance between index finger and thumb). And the activation of some perceptual and cognitive states fire motor neurons directly (even in the absence of task demands for the perceiver) (Gallese et al. 1996, Rizzolati et al. 1996). So the suggestion is that some connections between perceptions and motor activity are quite direct (literally "for" one another), going in both directions.[5] What is more, this can happen independently of conscious perceptual awareness by the subject. Wilson points out here (as elsewhere) that the claims are far from holding across the board, however. There is still, as she calls it, perception for perception's sake. Our visual processing, at least in the ventral stream, seems more flexible than this overall. Yet there is one more aspect of embodied cognition that is especially relevant to our attention here. Though normally ventral stream visual processing (sometimes called the "what" system generating a conscious visual field) and dorsal stream processing (now seen as a "how" processing system that guides actions such as reaching and grasping and that can guide behavior without a consciously accessible visual field) work together, they can come apart.[6] Indeed, as we will soon see, some of the most interesting cases for the meeting of action theory and embodied cognition are cases where purposive bodily movement is driven by dorsal stream visual processing and the motor system at several stages of remove (or dissociated) from ventral stream processing. How are these cases of behavior to be described, explained, and evaluated as actions?

It is mainly these aspects of embodied cognition that will occupy us here. Elsewhere (Adams and Aizawa 2008) I've dealt with some of the others including that cognitive systems off-load cognitive work to the environment, that the environment actually becomes a part of the cognitive system (the thesis of extended mind), and the claim that off-line cognition is body based (Adams manuscript).

4 Sparks, or Where AT Meets EC

At the intersection of action theory and embodied cognition is an important worry over the nature and role that representations (particularly intentions) are supposed to play in turning a bodily movement into an action. As described on the Adams–Mele control model of the role of intentions in actions (and tryings), intentions have a complex set of cognitive functions and they are causal antecedents of actions. The worry is that some of the constraints of embodiment placed on causal antecedents of bodily movement will turn out to disqualify those causal antecedents as intentions, at least as intentions traditionally conceived of as typical kinds of representations.[7]

Let's consider two features of embodied cognition that we have discussed, that cognitive states are *situated* and *time pressured*. Let's set aside whether all cognitive states are like this (presumably they are not). We are interested primarily in intentions. Surely not all intentions have these features. Pacherie (2006, 2008) nicely distinguishes three kinds of intentions with three kinds of intentional contents: future intentions (I will retire some day), proximal intentions (I will now type the letter L), and motor-intentions (and here is where it gets tricky . . . what is the content of a motor-intention?). Motor-intentions are sent in the here and now from various motor regions telling the body to move (specific muscles to contract or movement to be made in specific directions). What is the content of such a motor-intention? It doesn't represent a future state or movement, because, being an activated motor state, it is happening *now*. It is not a proximal intention for the very reasons imposed by the constraints of being situated and time pressured and updated in the flow of information being fed back during the process of moving. I'll explain more why this is so shortly. Does its content even involve concepts? What is its representational mood (indicative or imperative)? How can it have a mood, if it is not conceptual? Imperatives are like commands—do this . . . do that—where there are concepts of doing the "this"s and "that"s. How can it have a representational content if the thing it represents has not even yet happened, but is not so far ahead in the future that there is even room or distance between cause and effect? Normally effects (footprints in the snow) represent causes (feet making the prints). But feet don't normally represent the footprints they are about to make or are making. Motor-intentions, if they are representations, represent states of affairs they are involved in the act of bringing about at that very instant. So how can motor-intentions simultaneously fill the cognitive role they are supposed to fill on the control theory of action and satisfy the constraints of embodied cognitive states that are situated and time constrained? That's the question.[8]

Why do we need to appeal to these motor-intentions? There are several kinds of reasons, such as the result of experimental research on differences between dorsal stream visual processing and ventral stream processing. But others are more familiar from everyday experience with situated and time-constrained action. In the shower, I accidentally dislodge the soap from the soap tray. In a blink of an eye I bump it up against the wall of the shower, visually and tactileley track its trajectory, and catch it before it hits the shower floor. Catching it was lucky, but not accidental or unintentional. If it was purposive behavior, then action theory (AT, along the lines of Adams and Mele 1992) is committed to there being intentional and representational mental states active in the motivation, initiation, production, guiding, sustaining, and terminating of this bodily behavior.

Mark Rowlands (2006, 102–104) uses the term "deed" to designate activity that is both situated and time compressed. Two of his examples of deeds include catching a cricket ball, where "typically you will have less than half a second before the ball, which may be traveling in excess of 100 mph, reaches you." Another of his examples is playing Chopin's *Fantasie Impromptu in C# Minor*, where "your fingers have to traverse the keys in the sort of bewildering display necessary to successfully negotiate this notoriously difficult piece." Rowlands coins the term "deed" to cover these because he maintains that "they do not fit the strict conception of action." Specifically, he maintains that the direct antecedents of these deeds are not intentional or representational states, and he maintains that a general antecedent intention (to catch the ball or to play Chopin) is not sufficient for the relevant doings to be individuated properly as actions. What makes an action the action that it is cannot, thus, be the intentional content of a prior intention, because any number of deeds (online corrections) can be involved in satisfying an antecedent intention. He appeals to both phenomenology (we are not consciously aware of all the moves we make while carrying out these deeds) and science (research on dorsal vs. ventral stream processing supports the first point) to support his claim that the direct antecedents of deeds are not representational or intentional in the normal sense.

One might think, as I do, that motor-intentions can come to the rescue in just such cases. Rowlands does not, and he develops a view of deeds that gives these movements themselves the representational properties that the received view of action reserves for the intentional states that cause the bodily movements. Here is what Rowlands says about his rejection of motor-intentions:

We might explain the status of a deed in terms of its connection to a general antecedent intention, but then individuate the deed in terms of the motor representation that causally produces it. However, if this line is to be convincing, two questions need to be addressed. First, do motor representations possess content of a sort sufficient to individuate deeds? Second, if so, what is the source or basis of this content? In answering the second question, we will be required to tell a certain story about how motor representations come to satisfy the essential conditions of, or constraints on, representation: how they carry information about the environment, how they have the function of tracking environmental items, or enabling the organism to achieve some task in virtue of tracking such features, how they are capable of misrepresentation, and so on. (Rowlands 2006, 109)

Rowlands believes that the case for motor-intentions is no more compelling than the theory he develops on which it is the deeds themselves that satisfy these requirements for being representations.[9] In what follows, I want to try to explain how to answer the questions Rowlands asks. To do so, I will begin by reviewing a taxonomy of intentions offered by Elisabeth Pacherie.

Here are some of the ways Pacherie (2006) characterizes the role of motor-intentions[10] (M-intentions) versus present or proximal intentions (P-intentions): "P-intentions and M-intentions are both responsible for the online control of action, but whereas the time scale at which the former operate is the time scale of the consciously experienced present, the latter's time scale is that of the neurologically micro-present, which only partially overlaps the conscious present" (Pacherie 2006, 7).

Pacherie (ibid., 8) isolates three important characteristics of motor-intentions. These are normally associated with dorsal stream processing (vision-for-action system), which extracts visual information about properties of objects (situations) relevant to action and uses this information to build or elicit motor representations used in effecting rapid visuomotor transformations. First, objects and their properties are represented in a format that is relevant for immediate selection of motor routines. When I caught the falling bar of soap, my visual system represented the soap's spatial position in terms of the movements I needed to make to catch it (my reach, direction, grip size, and shape). Second, the representations of the necessary movements reflect implicit or tacit knowledge of the biomechanical constraints and the kinematics and dynamics of movement (none of it consciously accessed). Third, the motor representation normally codes for cascades of movements, where the goal of the action determines the global organization of the motor sequence. So, for example, the goal of a movement will partially determine the grip size and type of motor representation. One might catch a falling pen with a precision grip, if one were planning to use it to write . . . or with a power grip, if one were planning to use it as a weapon.

Echoing the worries of Rowlands, in a recent paper Shaun Gallagher (2008) forcefully challenges AT from the point of EC on whether there could be representations that fit the bill to both be representations with the appropriate intentional content and to be explanatorily useful. Being a representation-skeptic for what he calls "minimal representations," Gallagher thinks the AT model breaks down when it meets these situated, time-pressured types of cases. Gallagher is not totally a representation skeptic. When it comes to future (F-intentions) and nonsituated reasoning and planning, he is prepared to embrace them. But he would prefer a dynamic systems model free of representations entirely for explaining the types of actions minimal intentions are supposed to explain.

One important problem is that a majority of cognitive scientists continue to use the R-word and do so in ways that are often not clear. In the case of action it is nothing more than a handy, but often confused and misleading term, a bad piece of heuristics, an awkward place-holder for an explanation that needs to be cast in dynamical terms of an embodied, environmentally embedded, and enactive model. . . . It may take more energy to define and distinguish any legitimate sense of representation . . . than it would to explain the phenomenon in non-representationalist terms. And if one can explain the phenomenon in non-representationalist terms, then the concept of representation is at best redundant. (Gallagher 2008, 365–366)

I think the dynamic systems view cannot do without something that plays the role of representations, and I will explain why. I will also do my best to give an account of how motor-intentions get their representational content and what that content might be. For now, let's see why Gallagher thinks that no account of representation is likely to fit the bill for the kinds of situated, time-pressure actions we are considering.

To be sure we are talking about the same thing, paraphrasing Michael Wheeler (2005, 197) on "action-oriented representations" (AORs), here is what Gallagher says about these "minimal representations" (what we are calling motor-intentions). They are "temporary egocentric motor maps of the environment . . . fully determined by the situation-specific action required" (Gallagher 2008, 353). They don't represent a preexisting world via a type of internal image or neural pattern (a visual field from ventral stream processing, say). Instead, "how the world is is itself encoded in terms of possibilities for action" (ibid.). Sound familiar? This is very similar to the remarks of Rowlands, and involves the situated, time-pressured type of situation of EC applied to action-oriented representations. Gallagher adds that according to Wheeler, what is represented (in an AOR) is not knowledge that the environment is x, but knowledge of how to negotiate the environment. "AORs are action-specific, egocentric relative to the agent, and context-dependent" (ibid., 354). So, we are indeed talking about the same thing as Pacherie's M-intentions.

Now let's consider Gallagher's reasons for thinking that AORs or M-intentions cannot be representations. The first is decoupleability.[11] The argument is that representations are necessarily decoupleable and AORs aren't, so AORs can't be representations:

> According to . . . the standard definition . . . of representation, representation is decoupleable from x (I can represent x even if x is absent from the immediate environment). But once we do decouple . . . I suggest we are no longer talking about action in the same sense. Indeed, it is difficult to see how . . . acts can be decoupled from x . . . or the context without becoming something entirely different from an element of the action at stake, or an AOR. Off-line cognition, imaging, remembering, or even re-enacting an action decoupled from its original context and absent x may (or may not) require representation—but this says nothing about representation in action. (Gallagher 2008, 357)

Generally, it is true that if X represents Y, X and Y can come apart (decouple). I can take a picture of you and later look at it when you are not around. It still represents you. I can think about you, when you are not around. I can long for you when you are not around . . . and so on. Clear enough. First, is this an essential property of all representations? And second, is it true that AORs (M-intentions) cannot decouple?

Consider sensory states. If I touch you, you've got to be there. If I see you, you've got to be there. If I hear you, you've got to be there (somewhere causing my hearing). These token sensory states, when veridical, are coupled. Now one can be in qualitatively identical states and be uncoupled, as when one is hallucinating. When hallucinating, I only seem to be touching you (you are not really there but it feels exactly as if you were). I only seem to see you. I only seem to hear you. So, in the veridical cases, the coupling must be there. In the nonveridical cases, things may become decoupled. No one denies that such decoupled experiential states are representations. I don't think even Gallagher does. So if things are similar with motor-intentions (AORs), then they should count as representations as much as sensory states.

Searle (1983) reports cases performed by Penfield where the motor system is decoupled from the muscles. The subject does what he normally does when he makes a fist (but is unable to see if his hand closes and his arm is anesthetized . . . so he gets no proprioceptive feedback about his hand). Yet to some subjects it feels for all the world as though they did indeed close their hand (make a fist). It feels this way because they get *efferent copy feedback*. The motor system tells the brain that it sent the signal

that normally closes the hand. Signals received generate an actish experiential state in the subject. We might call it a hallucination of acting (not
unlike a hallucination of you that I might have as a sensory state, when
you are not actually there). If they don't actually cause a bodily movement,
does this mean that these are not genuine representations? I don't see why
that would be true of motor-intentions any more than it would be true of
a hallucination as of you, if you were not there. Hallucinations are representations, if anything is.

True, one would still have to explain where these AORs (M-intentions)
get their representational contents and what those contents are, if they are
representations. But the fact that they can decouple doesn't seem to mean
they can't be representations any more than the fact that I can suffer hallucinations of you means that when I actually see you, I am not in a state
that represents you. Gallagher[12] is right that off-line representations are
different from online ones. One type is veridical (seeing you) or a genuine
trying (I'm trying to catch the soap) precisely because it is online. Yet, this
does not mean that the same types of representations cannot in principle
decouple. Indeed, they can even still be tryings. When Penfield told his
subject to try to close his fist (while his efferent path to the muscles was
blocked) it would be false to say the subject didn't try because the subject
didn't succeed. He did try. His brain sent the signal. Penfield just blocked
it. The subject's motor-intention was decoupled, but it still was sent "to
the hand" and was telling the hand "to make a fist."

Today one can perform the same type of experiment with subjects using
transcranial magnetic stimulation (TMS) to stop the motor signals from
reaching the muscles. Subjects may be tapping with their fingers (to the
beat of a sound they are shadowing). When TMS interrupts their tapping,
the subjects report that they were trying to continue tapping but were
unable to produce the movement. This is a type of decoupling of motor
command from implementing a movement in the muscles. It is not exactly
"off-line." The subjects are not just "imagining" making the movement.
They were making them prior to the TMS activation and they continue
making them after the TMS activation is turned off, and the subjects didn't
do anything different in between (from their perspective).[13]

Okay, what's next? Gallagher mentions two other features[14] of representation that he thinks motor-intentions (or AORs) won't have. Discussing
why he thinks a dynamic system approach is preferable, he says: "Nothing
in this dynamically dissipating process amounts to a representation, if we
take representation to involve: an internal image or symbol or sign, a

discrete duration, and decoupleability" (Gallagher 2008, 362). We have discussed decoupleability, so it is on to the other two. Take discrete duration first. Gallagher doesn't really argue for this. At most he adds to the claim that they are not discrete that "it is more like a temporal, dynamic, and distributed process" (ibid., 364). He also does not explicitly argue that these are not internal images or symbols or signs. At most he adds that they extend "to include embodied environmental aspects . . . only 'weakly' neuronal" (ibid.). These are both argued for by Wheeler (2005) and Rowlands (2006) and accepted (but not argued for) by Gallagher.

So what are these two objections to motor-intentions being representations all about? They are about the rejection of a language of thought (LOT) model of cognition that EC is campaigning against. On the LOT model (or any naturalized[15] model of semantics), representations are thoughts, beliefs, desires, or future intentions. They are symbolic and language-like and propositional. They have a compositional syntax and semantics. They have discrete symbols that serve as the vehicles for their representational content. The vehicles might be different though their contents are the same (Frege puzzles).

For motor-intentions, Gallagher is suggesting that the LOT model cannot be right because the representations are situated and time-pressured and they are in the motor system. LOT does not portray the basic building blocks of thoughts, namely, concepts, as being in the motor system. So Gallagher is thinking of motor-intentions as pulses of electricity not unlike those the coil (or now computer) sends to the spark plugs to fire. No LOT there. No language-like representations there. No discrete symbols there. If the motor system works like this, then the LOT model does not apply to motor-intentions.

Gallagher agrees with Berthoz and Petit (2006) that the brain is an "organ for action rather than an organ for representation. They want to move away from a philosophy that puts language in first place and that models action on language-like representation, where action is equivalent to movement plus representation" (Gallagher 2008, 353). He also quotes Berthoz and Petit (2006, 23), saying "By applying this representational filter, everything in the external as well as the internal world appears frozen, fixed and stabilized by the projection of the propositional form, which implicitly structures representation." Gallagher agrees with Wheeler (2005) that "representations on the propositional model are discrete static structures, states of affairs that lack the kind of dynamics found in action. . . . what takes the place of representations in non-representationalist accounts of action is a form of perceptually based online intelligence which generates action through complex causal interactions in an extended-body-environment system" (Wheeler 2005, 193).

In reply to all of this, first notice that these are attacks on thoughts, beliefs, desires, and other such cognitive representations that on many views are likely to have symbolic elements with language-like structure. To lump these together with motor-intentions is to assume that motor-intentions have the same kinds of representational vehicles and representational contents as these other cognitive states. There is good reason to think that they don't. They are coming out of the motor system—not a central cognitive system. When in the dorsal stream, they are not even consciously accessible. And to some extent, motor-intentions are informationally encapsulated and not subject to the usual cognitive penetrability of rationality constraints (Bratman 1987).

There is little reason to think that they generate intensional contexts (Frege puzzles). If my motor-intention is trying to catch the bar of soap I dislodged from the shower tray and the bar of soap is the oldest bar of soap in the house, then my motor-intention is in the act of catching the oldest bar of soap in the house.[16] Very likely there are no differences in motor vehicles such that two different vehicles could share the same motor content and thereby generate intensional contexts (Frege puzzles).

They may even be nonconceptual. Jeannerod (2006) puts matters this way:

The visual percept . . . has a rich informational content about the object, but it has no conceptual content: it remains non-conscious and is ignored by the perceiver. If visual processing were to stop at this stage, as may occur in pathological conditions (Jacob and Jeannerod, 2003), the object could not be categorized, recognized or named. It is only at the later stage of the processing that conceptualization occurs. The representation of a goal-directed action operates the other way around. The conceptual content, when it exists (i.e. when an explicit desire to perform an action is formed), is present first. Then, at the time of execution, a different mechanism comes into play where the representation loses its explicit character and runs automatically to reach the desired goal. (Jeannerod 2006, 4–5)

So, if it is true that motor-intentions do not have conceptual content, it is probably true that motor-intentions are neither language-like, nor image-like, nor syntactic. This does not disqualify them from being propositional. Information can have propositional content and be coded in analog form (Dretske 1981). Whether the representations are distributed is relevant to their implementation level in the neurons, but it may not be relevant to their content one level up in description. My thought that today is Sunday has a discrete and propositional content. How it is realized or implemented in the brain is another story.

With respect to the motor system, as populations of neurons fire and sum together, a vector of electrical potential forms. Some of these vector summations become tuned to control specific muscles; some to control for specific directions (*directional tuning*) and configurations of hands or grip. An example of the latter is that you can write your name (however badly) with the pen in normal position, in your fist, in your opposite hand . . . maybe even between your toes or with the pen in your mouth. So for some vector summation there is commonality of direction and force, but no unique signal dedicated to specific muscles. Hence, some motor cells are representing types of movement and direction independently of which muscles are used to achieve this. This level of abstraction is an element of representation. The activation can also be contextual (fire in some sequences of activity, but not in others). This shows that there is something *representational* going on (not just a pulse being sent to a muscle as from the coil to the spark plugs). Therefore, that fact that there is no single discrete symbolic structure that implements a motor-intention does not disqualify motor-intentions from being representations.

Jeannerod (1985) has long noted that an act as simple as taking a book from a shelf is extremely complex and involves complex sensorimotor involvement at what he calls the "operational" level:

This consideration thus joins those concerning the *distributed* nature of the operational level. One can easily imagine that this level consists of different sensorimotor channels, each independent, each characterized by the type of sensory information it is capable of processing and by the type of movement it is capable of producing. The sensorimotor channel which processes "book thickness" information produces a movement that is adapted to this information, namely, contraction of the muscles which form a pincer grasp; the channel which processes the "distance with respect to the body" information produces movements which extend the arm, etc. In order to produce the correct movement to grasp a book, the different channels involved must be activated simultaneously. Simple observation reveals, in fact, the pincer grasp is forming at the same time as the arm is being extended, and that the fingers do not wait until they are close to the book before adopting the correct posture. The channels therefore function in a parallel fashion . . . because of their respective independence—an advantageous arrangement when a large quantity of information must be processed in a minimum amount of time, as is the case here. (Jeannerod 1985, 125–126)

Hence, a complex motor-intention (active in picking a book from a shelve) may be compositional in content, analog, distributed across several sensorimotor channels, and still satisfy the general nature of being a representation. I will now say more about why these motor-intentions are representations.

Earlier I said that the dynamic systems account that Gallagher prefers probably cannot succeed without representations. When I'm trying to catch the soap, something is still directing my reach *for the soap*, and this cannot simply be due to the causal influence of the soap itself and its structural properties impacting my sensory systems. Why not? Because what I do and how I shape my hand is dependent on my larger background goals (don't waste time in the shower, don't knock things from their proper places without trying to catch them) and so on. And as in reaching for a book, my goals are guiding the direction of my reach and the nature of my grip. The fact that these are not random but are being purposively coordinated by my motor system tells us that the elements for representation are there—nomic coordination and direction of a purposive movement.

There are two more matters to address, if motor-intentions are indeed representations. The first (earlier raised by Rowlands) is the matter of from where they acquire their representational content. The second is the format of their representational content. Let's consider the first matter. Motor-intentions function largely in service of proximal (P-intentions) or more distal future intentions (F-intentions). As noted earlier, my future and proximal intentions are normally conscious and constrained by considerations of rationality. As I plan to interact in the world and leave my mark, I consider all the possibilities of interacting with various goal objects and the array of goal states that I may desire to bring about. With a range of possibilities identified, I must go from the future intention (or what some call a distal intention, D-intention) to the more proximal intention, and then this must all be translated into the motor-intentions. Pacherie (2008) describes beautifully the cascade of content and dependency between these various intentions:

One can . . . distinguish two moments in the dynamics of M-intentions. The upstream dynamics lead to the selection of one among the typically several prepotentialized motor programs. When an M-intention is governed by a P-intention and inherits its goal from it, the presence of the goal tends to increase the salience of one of these possible pragmatic organizations of the situation and thus allow for the selection of the corresponding motor program. Forming a P-intention to act on an object, say reach for a pen, typically involves focusing one's attention on the object that is to be the target of the action. As Campbell (2002) points out, we need to explain how the motor system manages to connect to the very object identified on the basis of perceptual experience. Campbell proposes that "conscious attention to the object will include some awareness of the location of the object, and that the target for processing by the visuo-motor system can be identified as 'the object at that location'" (2002, p. 55). In other words, common location is the binding principle for perception and action, for objects represented at the level of P-intentions and objects represented at the level of M-intentions. The role of conscious attention is to define a target for the visuo-motor system. Once the target is defined, it is the job of the visuo-motor system to set the parameters for action on the object. . . . The guidance and monitoring functions of M-intentions are exercised as part of the downstream dynamics. They are responsible for setting the precise parameters of motor commands and for fine motor adjustments and rapid corrections during execution. (Pacherie 2008, 186–187)

In this Pacherie agrees with Jeannerod (1997, 2006) and MacKay (1981) that there is a hierarchy of motor representations such that the goals and parameters of acts coded for at the higher levels act as constraints on the lower-level representations.[17] The lower-level representations that drive the movement represent both the body in motion (a generator of forces) and a goal of the action encoded in a "pragmatic" mode, distinct from the "semantic" mode. For one, she cites his and other studies that suggest the "amount" of force needed for the movement is encoded. (On the subjective side there is a "sensation of effort" that accompanies this representation.) The representation of a goal represents both an object and a final state. Jeannerod suggests that these representations "fall between" a sensory function and a motor function. Pragmatic representations activate predetermined motor functions related to the specific objects and their affordances (Gibson 1979). Motor representations are relational, representing neither states of the body nor states of the environment, but states of the relations between the two: motor patterns that objects afford the agent. Pacherie adds that motor-intentions are at least partially modularly encapsulated and only moderately cognitively penetrable. However, some cognitive penetration is possible; how an object is grasped is not just a function of its size, but what we intend to do with it. So the systems and levels of intention have some degree of cross-talk. And the environment "affords" much more than the motor system responds to. So the response is determined by our other cognitive states (and thus there are limits to the encapsulation of M-intentions).

Subjects are not even always aware of what bodily movements their motor-intentions are producing. The role of F-intentions (or distal, D-intentions) is not lost, once an action begins. There must still be a causal dependency on the goal state represented in that D-intention. Pacherie puts it this way: "the relation between the three levels is not one of mere co-existence. They form an intentional cascade,[18] with D-intentions causally generating P-intentions and P-intentions causally generating in turn M-intentions" (Pacherie 2008, 188).

M-intentions inherit their representational content from distal and proximal intentions. As the agent forms goals (whether long-term or short-term) and plans how to achieve these goals, the other levels of intentions chain together and form an intentional cascade and a dependency of content working its way up and down the cascade. This helps explain why motor-intentions are context sensitive (e.g., changing grip posture to a precision grip or a power grip in time-pressured reaching depends on the goal of the use of the object being gripped). Hence there is a mechanism of dependency and inheritance of content that runs through the three types of intentions described by Pacherie.[19]

Now let's consider further the format of the representations that are motor-intentions. Consider the following types of acts. One might pick up: a needle, a pencil, a baby shoe, a bronzed baby shoe, a book, a copy of the OED, a bar of gold. Additionally, one might catch: a feather, a ping pong ball, a golf ball, a baseball, a bowling ball, an egg, a water balloon. fMRI studies show two things. If one is imagining doing these acts, the motor cortex is activated. What is more, just reading about them activates the sensorimotor areas that would be activated if one were to perform the acts. There is a first-person phenomenology of "what it's like" to do these acts that one can almost feel in just reading about or imagining them. And this neural imagining is just the sort of activity in the brain that one can use in brain–machine interfaces to learn to manipulate external robot arms and computer devices just by imagining acting.

Earlier I talked about "directional tuning" and other sorts of fine-tuning in the cortex that allow the brain to form correlations between firings of populations of neurons and bodily movements (whether muscle-specific or direction-specific types of movements). These types of movements are not innate. Yes, there are innate[20] types of motor routines, such as infant tongue protrusion and the ability to imitate shape of mouth (Meltzoff and Moore 1977), but these types of action listed above aren't some of them. These require a history of fine-tuning. That is, the agent has to make these movements, witness their outcomes, and then select for doing them again in order to set up a repertoire of abilities to make them. The movement types are learned, skilled.

What, then, is the format of the content of a motor signal that is sent? It is in the form of an imperative (Mandik 2005). It is in the form of a type of movement or type of direction of movement or sequence of types chained together (for complex movements).[21] The signals represent movement types: precision grip, power grip, move left, now up, now right, and so on.

Isn't this just the sort of thing that worried Gallagher? How can these be representations that are situated, time pressured, and coupled? These require a kind of representational particularity that falls short when a representation is run off-line or decoupled. The answer is that when it comes to *particularity* of representational content, this particularity is secured by causal connections. Consider perception. What makes my perception a perception *of you* (not your identical twin) is that I'm looking *at you* (not your twin). If you two look indistinguishably alike to me, it is not the qualitative content that secures particularity of my visual percept; it is causal origin that secures the particularity of content (Stampe 1977).

The same is true in the motor system. A signal that is sent to my index finger to contract might just as easily make my ring finger contract, if the signal were diverted to that finger. But what makes it a signal specifically directed to my index finger is that this is how the motor is wired to my body, to my hand. What makes it a signal to move my body to the right or left, open or close a hand or move a finger is that the signals are sent from an egocentric reference frame of my body and its connection to my brain. One's brain exploits the connections with which it comes packaged. The background conditions (channel conditions of the information flow) secure some of the conditions of the content that does not need to be sent in the signal itself (Searle 1983; Dretske 1981). So Gallagher's worry about particularity, about how this motor-intention can be about this token action, is solved. It is about this particular action (token) in virtue of being causally connected to this body—the body to which it has become finely tuned and to which it is causally connected.

There is, as Searle (1983) puts it, a world-to-mind direction of fit in the representations of motor-intentions. They are representations of types of movements and have an imperative force ("make *x* happen!"). They can be compared with sensory information to monitor the degree of goal-success or failure. Fed back through the sensory system will be representations of whether the particular movements are moving toward achieving one's goal (or have succeeded or have missed the mark and require a connection). And all of this will be a bit faster than the speed of thought in many cases.

Equally important, in order to fine-tune the motor system, one's brain must already be able to make the various movements. Then information is available via the sensory system about the type of movement the motor signal produced. So there are two systems of representation with different directions of fit (mind–world, world–mind) harnessed and working closely together—and both serving the purposes of the goal-directed system. Hence, motor-intentions (and their motor signals) become recruited by the brain for the types of movements they are able to make, based on past experience and "fine-tuning." As Mandik (2005) says, instead of being selected for their ability to indicate the way the world is (Dretske 1988) on the sensory side, these representations are being selected for the ability to perform various types of manipulations on the body and world.

5 Conclusion

As I set out to show, there is no incompatibility between the control-theoretic model of action and the fact that many actions are situated and time pressured—the fact that cognition is for action. The dependency between different types of intentions and their contents on the higher-level, consciously held goals of the agent and what Pacherie calls the "intentional cascade" explains the relation between future and proximal intentions and motor-intentions. Motor-intentions themselves are types of representation, and I have tried to map out the format of their content. Thus, I have provided a response to skeptics such as Gallagher and Rowlands who believe that motor-intentions are not representations and that representations are not needed in explaining the intentionality of "deeds" or situated and time-pressured purposive actions. Hence, on these matters there is compatibility between the claims of AT and EC. On other matters, I think there does turn out to be some incompatibility, but those matters will have to await another occasion for their airing.

Acknowledgments

Thanks to those who read and commented or corresponded helpfully on this essay. This is especially true of Ken Aizawa, Santiago Amaya, Steve Beighley, David Chan, Shaun Gallagher, Al Mele, Pete Mandik, Elisabeth Pacherie, Mark Rowlands, and Rob Wilson. I would also like to thank Richard Ivry for podcasting his Cognitive Science C127 on i-Tunes, where I learned some of the facts mentioned here about fine-tuning and the motor system.

Notes

1. Ken Aizawa says I'm understating the current influence of the movement.

2. Mental actions are interesting in their own right, but I won't discuss them here.

3. Mele and I (Adams and Mele 1989) realized at the time that there were many types of feedback that would be involved in these processes (Adams 1986b). Today Grush's (2004) work on emulators has done an excellent job of bringing things up to date. Our view does not require that things do not go "ballistic" at some point. Indeed, probably all bodily actions become ballistic at some point, but to be goal-directed they must be products of systems that have these goal-directed mechanisms and actions must originate in such systems.

4. Mele (1992) and I part company here, though his view, the "single phenomenon" view, is mainly a departure due to Bratman's (1987) attack on the Simple View. I have elsewhere explained why I don't find Bratman's attack persuasive, and Mele and I have skirmished in various journals over related points from time to time, but our views remain very close and we both accept the control model overall. For these differences with Mele, see Adams 1997, 1994a,b.

5. Aren't cases of "automaticity" of movement a problem for my view? I don't think so. There are actions and there is mere bodily movement. Cases of mere bodily movement can be triggered in the brain stem of hydraencephalic infants; another example is mere involuntary eye-blinks in normal human beings. These are mere behavior—things my body does, but not things I do. As in the view outlined for AT, actions will have intentional states with representational contents in their etiology. In fact, it is the worry that without this even involuntary movements could be cast as actions on a view like that of Rowlands (2006) (which puts the representational content in the movement itself) that keeps me from being persuaded by his view. More about this below.

6. Of course, though they can come apart, Goodale (2004, 1170) also says that "both systems are required for purposive behavior—one system to select the goal object from the visual array, the other to carry out the required computations for goal-directed action." It is in the latter instance that the motor system is involved and in which I will argue below that representations are involved.

7. David Chan (1995) introduces a new category of "nonintentional" actions for such cases. He does so because he thinks intentions have to meet rationality constraints, like those introduced by Bratman (1987). This means that for him mannerisms or habitual actions don't qualify as intentional actions, and we need a new category. I (Adams 1997, 2007) don't think all intentions do need to meet these "rationality" constraints, though most do. But "one-off" intentions, irrational intentions, or motor-intentions do not. As I'll explain below, motor-intentions can satisfy

the properties that Chan introduces to differentiate nonintentional actions from mere movements, viz., foreknowledge and an actish feel. So I don't think we need the new category. These are all tryings of various kinds, and tryings are intentional.

8. I'll say more below about how future intentions, proximal intentions, and motor-intentions are related on Pacherie's views and will try to answer this question about the content of motor-intentions. I'll also say why Searle's "intentions in action," though relevant, cannot give us the content of motor-intentions.

9. I won't here attempt to counter the theory Rowlands develops. Let me just say that if I can answer the questions he asks about motor representations, then I will have undercut some of the motivation for replacing the received view with this new view of "deeds."

10. The feature of being beneath the level of consciousness means that motor-intentions are not equivalent to Searle's (1983) "intentions in action." For Searle says a person correctly expresses the content of his intentions in action to raise his arm "quite precisely when he says 'I am raising my arm.'" (Searle 1983, 106ff). He adds that "if one wants to carve off the intentional content from its satisfaction he can say, 'I am trying to raise my arm'" (ibid., 107). All of this clearly takes place at the conscious level and is a type of processing that one may find in the ventral visual stream (not dorsal).

11. Gallagher (2008, 358) notes that Wheeler (2005, 219) gives up that AORs must be decoupleable, but Gallagher continues to press the point.

12. Gallagher considers but rejects that emulators (Clark and Grush 1999) might be the way to go. He rejects this because he thinks that once the representation and what it represents come apart, the game is over. The representation cannot then be guiding the action: "it ceases to be part of a forward motor control mechanism" (Gallagher 2008, 358). Actually this is not so. That is the beauty of emulators. They are part of the forward control. They anticipate what is happening before it does, so the system does not have to delay for feedback from the muscles and world. But even if Gallagher were right, the same is true for sensory states. Once you aren't there I'm not seeing you. The question is whether these representation types can decouple (in principle). It is not whether they can decouple while doing their cognitive work guiding an action or directly perceiving the world. No one thinks that for veridical perceptual states. So why hold motor-intentions to those standards? Curiously, Gallagher seems to agree that decoupled, emulator states and others may be representations when not guiding action. But he questions why they must be representations when coupled and guiding action. However, I think it would be far more curious if a representational state lost its representational status just because it became coupled to and began guiding and sustaining a purposive bodily movement.

13. There is a two-second window where what is to be sent is already "in the pipe-line." So for two seconds after the TMS is activated, subjects continue to tap normally. Then, after the two-second delay, their tapping is interrupted. What is more, research on brain–machine interfaces (neural prostheses) show that subjects can learn to send the proper motor signals to a machine to make a robotic arm move a device and serve a purpose. This shows that one can learn to transform a decoupled motor-intention (before one learns to make the robot obey) into a coupled motor-intention (when one learns to successfully drive a robotic device) from the motor cortex.

14. Actually, Gallagher gives six things that he thinks disqualify motor-intentions from being representations, but they are not all about EC—(1) they are not internal but extended into the environment, (2) are not discrete, enduring, (3) are not passive, but enactive, (4) are not decoupleable, (5) are not strongly instructional, and (6) are not homuncular, involving interpretation. I have dealt with extended mind issues elsewhere (Adams and Aizawa 2008). I will be addressing their being enactive in addressing their content. The whole point of a motor-intention is to be enactive. I won't here discuss the claim that they are not "strongly instructional." Gallagher doesn't either. He merely says that only EC can solve the frame problem and says representations would have to contain something like Searle's (1983) "background" to do so. I am working indirectly on this in thinking about closure and knowledge. If knowledge is not closed, it is precisely because there are channel conditions necessary for knowledge representations that contain information not contained in things they enable the subject to know (Adams, Barker, and Figurelli manuscript). And I won't discuss the homuncular objection because no one in the naturalized semantics camp thinks there is anything to "interpretation" of a representation that can't be reduced to purely natural causal networking. Gallagher doesn't argue for these so much as refer to others who have. Since I've addressed these other items elsewhere, I won't address them here.

15. See Adams 2003a,b.

16. Though I think there is nothing like a Frege puzzle in the motor system, Pete Mandik reminds me that there may be something similar to failure of existential generalization. For instance, when one TMS's the motor system (causing decoupling) and a signal is sent to the muscles "to move," the muscles may not move. Of course, this is not exactly a failure of existential generalization because these are imperatives, not indicatives. But there will be a failure of compliance conditions being met. If this counts as an intensional phenomenon, then there is intentionality even in the context of the content of a motor-intention. However, as soon as one backtracks up the intentional cascade to the proximal or future intentions, then one finds intensionality with a vengeance.

17. Al Mele points out to me that MacKay (1981, 630) also believes that motor schemas involved in handwriting extend to lower components of movements

representing neuromuscular activity to achieve the required results in the script being produced. For MacKay, too, the proximal intention forms an intentional cascade down to the level of the motor-intention.

18. Of course, Pacherie admits that some actions are performed "on the fly" and involve only the P-intentions and M-intentions (Pacherie 2008, 189).

19. Some may think that it is not necessary for the proximal intentions to cascade down to the level of the motor signals. For instance, Mele (1992, 222) suggests that the proximal intention to button one's shirt in the normal way may be sufficient to trigger the motor routines of buttoning, saying, "In normal cases, the plan is, by default, the agent's normal plan for that activity." But there is no normal plan for catching the bar of soap in the shower or deciding to catch the falling pen with a precision or power grip. Some of this is done on the fly and in compensation for changes in environmental contingencies. This tells me that there must be a cascade of information and representation downward through the layers of the control systems, as described by Pacherie, Jeannerod, and MacKay.

20. Gallagher (2005) thinks these might even by conscious, but does not argue for it. Both Pacherie (personal communication) and I think they are purposive and under control of feedback-controlled mechanisms. They are likely not consciously intentional. It turns out that this ability shows up in neonates, then diminishes, and then later returns. This is likely because the basal ganglia are inhibitory. In the interim between when this imitative activity starts and stops, the basal ganglia develop. When developed they only allow motor impulses that achieve a certain threshold to get through and cause these activities once again. At this later point, it is likely that the infants are indeed protruding their tongues voluntarily and perhaps fully intentionally.

21. Pacherie says these sequenced signals have a "grammar."

16 Intentions as Complex Dynamical Attractors

Alicia Juarrero

1 Background

What is the difference between a wink and a blink? Intuitively, we would say that a wink is intentional and a blink is not. From a philosophical point of view, answering the question, what *is* an intention and how does an agent's intention *cause* his or her behavior, has a long history. This "problem of action" dates back to ancient times. In the *Crito*, Socrates wonders how philosophers such as Anaxagoras or Anaximenes would explain his refusal to escape from prison. How could merely physical phenomena explain how his *reasons* for remaining keep him in jail? In the last half of the twentieth century, papers and books on action theory proliferated. Can *reasons* be causes? Doesn't the purposiveness or goal-directedness of action imply the occurrence of backward causation when an anticipated outcome plays a role in bringing about present behavior? If intentions are just brain events, how can they carry meaning such that it is the meaning or content of the intention that results in the appropriate kind of behavior?

From these few questions alone it becomes clear that the philosophical problem of action is fundamentally tied to the problem of causation: how *does* meaningful behavior come about? In this essay I will argue that a uniquely modern combination of views about causality—that only efficient causality is true causality, and that recursive or circular causality is impossible—is responsible for the impasse in which philosophical action theory finds itself. Elsewhere (Juarrero 1999; Juarrero-Roqué 1983a,b, 1985, 1987–88, 1988), I chronicle in detail those philosophical equivalents of epicyclic contortions designed to shoehorn the analysis of action into the modern notion of efficient causality, where intentional causes are understood as instantaneous forces that push the body into motion in billiard-ball-like fashion. For that reason alone none of these standard causalist theories of action succeeds. But then neither do the attempts that offer behaviorist or identity-theory reductions of the purposiveness of action. The impediment, I argued in those earlier works, is their inability to frame a scientifically acceptable way of understanding mereological (especially top-down) causality. I claim that concepts borrowed from complex dynamical systems theory can provide just such a theory-constitutive metaphor that makes intentional causation tractable.

During classical times it is left to Aristotle to provide a thorough analysis of the difference between voluntary, involuntary, and nonvoluntary behavior. As is well known, Aristotle accounts for all phenomena, not just intentional behavior, in terms of four causes. Suppose I intend to write a book. While my arm and hand movements serve as the *efficient* cause of the actual writing, the goal of producing a book functions as its *final* or purposive cause. Its *material* cause, the stuff from which it is physically constructed, includes the ink, paper, and so on. What makes the behavior a case of *writing a book*—instead of something else—is the *formal* defining or essential cause that sustains the behavior along that essential path and guides it to completion.

Less well known, however, is the role that another of Aristotle's principles plays in the history of action theory: the principle that there exists no circular or recursive causality; no self-cause. The concepts of *potentiality* and *actuality* lead to the conclusion that whatever happens is caused to occur because of something other than itself. Since nothing can be both potential and actual at the same time with respect to the same phenomenon, mover (actual) and moved (potential) cannot be identical. Even in the case of the (apparent) *self*-motion of organisms, one aspect of the organism *qua* active principle changes a second aspect from passive to active; this aspect, in turn, now *qua* active principle can move a third . . . and so on, until the animal moves.

By the time the intellectual giants of the seventeenth century and their followers got through changing the way philosophy and science are done, Aristotle's formal and final causes had been discarded as superstitious nonsense. With material cause left to one side, only efficient cause—the instantaneous, billiard-ball-collision-type causality of mechanistic science—qualified as *cause*. While discarding three of the four causes, however, modern science retained the Aristotelian thesis that nothing causes itself. When combined with the reductionist belief that wholes are no different from aggregates, the claim that anything that is caused must be caused by something other than itself—and only as a consequent of an *efficient* cause—produces an account of action that has bedeviled philosophy of mind and science for hundreds of years.

The inevitable philosophical upshot of this worldview is either a Cartesian substance dualism, or a thoroughgoing materialism. Either there exists a substance, the mind—along with its will—that because of its different (nonphysical) nature causes *actions*—winks, not blinks; or there must exist a *sui generis* physical process in the brain that triggers such behavior. The problem with the former disjunct is that it violates the laws of conservation of matter and energy: how can a nonphysical phenomenon such as an intention insert itself in (and alter) the physical space-time continuum to produce bodily effects without violating conservation laws? The central problem with the latter alternative, as Socrates questioned, is its inability to account for how a physical (say, neural) process can embody *meaning* and *intentionality* such that the intention's *meaningful content* causes, guides, and sustains behavior that terminates in action (Searle 1981). For nearly four hundred years, philosophical reflections relating to action theory have consisted in epicyclic contortions designed to circumvent these two main objections. Elsewhere (Juarrero 1999, chs. 2, 4, and 5) I chronicle these various attempts to fit the causes of action into a modern understanding of efficient cause. None succeeds.

More generally, the atomism and reductionism that pervaded modern science reduced integral wholes to mere epiphenomenal aggregates, and temporal processes to instantaneous snapshots. With the belief that only primary qualities such as mass are real, secondary relational properties too were stripped of their ontological status and labeled subjective. According to this framework, therefore, there is no way to conceive of how particles might interact to produce an emergent whole with qualitatively novel properties that can loop back down and affect the component parts. Even Immanuel Kant, who attributed his philosophical awakening to David Hume's influence, recognized that modern science's understanding of causality cannot account for living organisms. In the *Critique of Teleological Judgment,* Kant (1980) explicitly discusses this failure of mechanistic causality. As an example he mentions trees, which, because they produce leaves but are at the same time produced by the leaves, exhibit "a kind of causality unknown to us" (Kant 1980, 23, §65, AkV, 375). What was missing, Kant saw, was a scientific framework that explains mereological (part–whole, whole–part) relationships: (1) how numerous particles can interact to create wholes with emergent properties, and (2) how the novel properties of these organized wholes then can exert causal power so as to determine a different direction for the whole (Kant 1980; Juarrero-Roqué 1985). Neither the theory of evolution nor the classical thermodynamics of the nineteenth century provided solutions to these puzzles. Despite the fact that cosmological and biological evolution present us with increasing complexity and order over time, the second law of classical thermodynamics' continually reminded thinkers of the inevitability of dissolution and decay. What was missing, we can now say, was a conceptual framework that accounts for mereological interactions and provides a satisfactory explanation of causal relationships among levels of organization without reducing the higher to the lower—and is compatible with contemporary science.

2 Nonlinear Dynamical Systems Theory

Enter complexity theory. With the assistance of powerful desktop computers that could simulate nonlinear dynamic phenomena that were analytically intractable, by the last third of the twentieth century the phenomenon of turbulent flow, physical processes such as Bénard cells, and chemical phenomena such as the Belousov–Zhabotinsky (B-Z) reaction, showed that positive feedback loops among particles can result in self-organizing processes that, despite their superficially chaotic appearance, in fact embody very sophisticated degrees of order. These emergent higher-level phenomena, moreover, exert top-down influence on the very components that make them up (Belousov 1959; Zhabotinsky 1964).

Bénard cells appear when water is heated uniformly from below. At first, water temperature is close to thermal equilibrium, but as the water in the bottom of the pan becomes hotter a temperature gradient develops. At a certain temperature, convection begins, but the random fluctuations—the bubbles—are initially suppressed. Increasing the heat, however, causes the system to become unstable, and beyond a critical temperature any fluctuation can become reinforced such that it drives the system over the instability threshold and the dynamics suddenly switch: ordered macroscopic molecular flows abruptly form into visible rolling hexagonal columns—the Bénard cells. Suddenly, millions of previously independent water molecules synchronize into a complex, streamlined pattern that dissipates the temperature gradient and lowers internal entropy production.

What's important for our purposes is that once the rolling hexagonal convection columns appear, the behavior of each individual water molecule is no longer independent of the others; it is determined top-down by the cell in which it is caught up. Once each water molecule is entrained into the dynamics of a Bénard cell, that is, its behavior is constrained by its role in the overall rolling process. If one is willing to broaden one's understanding of causality and also to take causal potency so understood as the mark of the real, even in such elementary phenomena as these, and despite the claims of mechanistic science, dynamical processes provide empirical evidence that wholes can be more than just epiphenomenal aggregates reducible to the sum of their component parts. The newly organized arrangement shows emergent macroscopic characteristics that cannot be derived from laws and theories pertaining to the microphysical level; they also represent eddies of local order that exert active power on their constituents, top-down. Moreover, the integrity, identity, and characteristics of the overall pattern that constitutes a Bénard cell are decoupled from its material basis in the sense that different types of viscous fluids can present the same form of organization, which is no longer identified by the microarrangement of its constituents. Theories of individual identity based on token-identifications lose all relevance in these cases.

As intriguing as Bénard cells are, it is nevertheless undeniable that the conditions within which such dissipative structures appear are set from without: the rolling hexagonal cells form only because *we've* placed the fluid in a container of a certain size; because *we've* cranked up the heat that created the gradient that took the system far from equilibrium and precipitated the discontinuous transformation from conduction to convection. Other dissipative structures such as hurricanes and dust devils also form only because of the external metereological and atmospheric conditions. Clearly, in each of these cases, if the boundary conditions are removed the structure will disintegrate. Because the constraints within which the self-organization takes place are set externally, the type of emergence on display in these examples is only a weak form of emergence. Although such structures can therefore only be said to *self-maintain*—and not *self-create*—they nonetheless offer a "theory-constitutive metaphor" for rethinking autonomy and top-down causality in a scientifically respectable fashion.

Things get even more interesting at the chemical level, as Peirce, Mill, and other precursors of complexity theory recognized (see Juarrero and Rubino 2008). In the case of the B-Z reaction, the fourth step of the process, a positive feedback loop in which the product of the process is necessary for the process itself, represents precisely the type of circular causality forbidden since the time of Aristotle. As the fourth autocatalytic step iterates, the reinforced, accelerating hypercycle drives the system further and further from equilibrium until a threshold of instability is reached, at which point a random internal fluctuation or external perturbation can, once again and in a burst of overall entropy production, drive the system over the threshold of instability and cause it to reorganize at a higher level. The new regime, as always in nonlinear dynamical systems, is characterized by lower *internal* entropy production. What's novel in chemistry is that the dramatic colorful waveforms of the B-Z reaction are caused to occur by the dynamics of the process itself, in the sense that the constraints within which the new organization comes about are produced by the process's endogenous dynamics—the self-organization is precipitated by the far-from-equilibrium gradient created by the reinforcing loop. Because the constraints within which the reorganization takes place are in this sense *self-produced*, chemical processes truly *self-create*, not only *self-maintain* the way physical dissipative structures do. The term *autopoiesis—self-organization*—now applies, as does the term *strong emergence*.

3 Constraints

Borrowing from information and communication theory, and the work of Lila Gatlin (Gatlin 1972), I attempted in an earlier essay to analyze this kind of interlevel—mereological—causality in terms of context-sensitive constraints (Juarrero 1999). Doing so brings back a role for formal and final cause, but reworked in scientifically acceptable fashion.

Just as a gas-filled container at thermodynamic equilibrium can do no work, random taps on an old-fashioned telegraph device, or random pixels on a computer screen, can transmit no messages. Constraints that take the system away from equiprobability and equilibrium are necessary to perform work and communicate, respectively. Be it a piston in the first case or communication rules in the second, constraints represent or embody changes in probability distribution. A piston inserted into the container and moved to one side compresses more molecules to one side than the other. Pistons thus embody constraints that take the system away from randomness or equiprobability. In any language, some letters of the alphabet are more likely than others. Following Gatlin I called this kind of constraint *context-free* because it embodies the system's prior probability. The fact that different kinds of neurons fire at different intervals is an example of an innate context-free constraint, as are all innate propensities.

Context-free constraints, however, quickly reach a bottleneck that stifles communication because reliability of the information thereby produced is inversely related to message variety. At the limit, only one message would be transmitted with probability 1, all other alternatives being reduced to probability 0. By flashing at regular (nonrandom or nonequiprobabilistic) intervals, lighthouses signal "message, message, message." No pattern conveys no information; but the same pattern repeated time and again conveys no new information. Similarly, in nature, mitotic reproduction faithfully transmits "another, another, another" to a new generation. But the choke point of mitosis is that it allows no message variety except in error; and when errors do occur, the earlier biological information is lost.

As Shannon (1948) discovered, to ensure message variety as well as information transmission a different type of constraint is required, one that promotes message variety at the same time as it ensures reliable information content. *Enabling constraints* become necessary, in other words. Shannon's contribution to information theory was to demonstrate that reducing error was not incompatible with reliable message transmission if the message is encoded correctly using what can be called *context-sensitive constraints*. The key is making particles and processes interdependent by correlating and synchronizing them. Doing so establishes *conditional* probability distributions among the components.

Consider the following heuristic example, also from linguistics. In the English language, for example, in addition to the context-free constraints that make *a*s and *e*s more likely than *x*s and *q*s, the probability distribution of alphabet letters is also related to their interdependence: in English, *given* that the sequence of letters ...*tio* has already occurred, the probability that the next letter will be *n* is almost 1. The probability that the next letter will be *k* is almost nil. The likelihood of a particular letter's occurrence therefore depends not only on its own prior probability in that language; it also depends on the letter or sequence of letters that preceded it. When the appearance of the letter *q* (in English) increases the probability that *u* will appear next, the two become systematically related: they form an *i-tuplet*, a higher-level organization with *q* and *u* as components. As relations among *i-tuplets* themselves become contextually constrained, words become possible; further context-sensitive *syntactical* constraints on top of those then make sentences possible. And so on. Systems and systems of systems can emerge. This is true of any language: for instance, since Mandarin Chinese restricts words to only one or two syllables, differences in inflection are necessary to ensure message variety.

Words can say more than phonemes, sentences more than words. Since levels are screened off from each other, new levels of dynamical organization involve the appearance of novel capabilities at the uppermost level (Salthe 1985, 2002). Context-sensitive constraints are therefore generative;

they create information. The differentiation into a hierarchical system that is nevertheless dynamically integrated creates entirely new realms of meaning and possibilities. The overall system AB represents an enlarged phase space with more degrees of freedom than constituents A and B had separately: amino acids folded into a three-dimensional protein structure possess properties and capabilities that the linear sequences on their own do not, much less the individual codons; neural patterns can carry meaning that individual neuron firings do not, and so forth. In contrast to context-free constraints, which limit message variety, the closure of context-sensitive constraints thus opens up possibilities and increases Shannon entropy by freeing up previously unavailable message variety.[1] Context-sensitive constraints thus make complexity possible. By correlating and coordinating previously independent particles into a more complex, differentiated whole, context-sensitive constraints enlarge the variety of states the system as a whole can access.

It is important not to reify these dynamic "structures of process" (Earley 1981). I suggested earlier that context-sensitive constraints are conditional probability distributions that capture the interdependent relationships between the components. As just mentioned, they exercise top-down causal power by resetting the lower-level phenomena's context-free constraints—their prior probability, that is. Such "resetting" should not be understood as an exercise of efficient causality. The better analogy is with a game of cards: Whereas at the outset all four players have an equal likelihood of getting an ace, once one of the players has two aces the probability of any player being dealt an ace *ipso facto* alters. Their changed probability distribution just *is*—just embodies—the distribution of cards in the deck, combined with the dynamical interdependencies among the four players over the course of the game. These relationships—a higher-level phenomenon—constrain the particulate level, top-down; despite the claims of seventeenth-century thinkers, relationships can thus be more than just epiphenomenal.

Even in an artificial neural network this integration can precipitate the appearance of *semantics*.[2] A dramatic example of what positive feedback loops can bring about in nonlinear dynamical systems is found in word-reading neural networks (Hinton and Shallice 1991). Even though it is an artificial network, when the neural network is trained without feedback loops and subsequently lesioned, its output errors resemble those of surface dyslexia: If the word presented was *bed*, the erroneous output might be *bad*, or *bid*. But if the same network is trained with feedback loops and then lesioned below the feedback loops, the erroneous output mimics those of patients suffering from deep dyslexia: If the word presented was *bed*, the erroneous output might be *cot*; if the word presented was *orchestra*, the erroneous output might be *band*. The authors conclude that these remarkable results can be explained only by postulating that as a result of the circular loops, the network self-organizes a semantic attractor, that is, a high-dimensional dynamic pattern whose emergent properties embody semantic relationships. Circular causality is real, and it is responsible for a creative evolutionary spiral. Instead of representing *meaning* in a symbol structure, however, a dynamical neurological organization embodies meaning in the topographical configurations—the set of self-organized context-dependent constraints—of its phase space.

The trajectories of complex dynamical processes are characterized by so-called *strange* or *complex attractors*, patterns of behavior so intricate that it is difficult to identify an overarching order amid the variations they allow. Strange attractors describe ordered global patterns with such a high degree of local fluctuation that individual trajectories never quite repeat exactly, the way a regular pendulum does. Complex attractors are therefore said to be "thick" because they allow individual trajectories to diverge so widely that even though they are located within the attractor's basin, they are uniquely individuated. The width and convoluted trajectories described by strange attractors imply that the overall pathways they describe are multiply realizable. The butterfly-shaped Lorenz attractor is by now a well-known complex attractor.

Context-sensitive constraints are important not only for information transmission or in connectionist networks; they are also responsible for the creation of *natural* complexity. Feedback loops and chemical catalysts, as we saw in the B-Z reaction, are natural first-order context-sensitive constraints. As natural embodiments of first-order context-dependent constraints, catalysts are one example of how natural dynamics create complexity by interrelating and correlating what were heretofore independent particles. Reentrant loops in the nervous system are another. Once the catalytic loop achieves closure and a new level of complexity emerges, the lower-level constituents are henceforth characterized by *conditional* probability distributions different from that embodied in their prior probability. As distributed process wholes, complex structures such as Bénard cells and B-Z chemical waves thus impose what one might call *second-order contextual constraints* on their components by restricting their degrees of freedom. Particles behave differently once caught up in the higher-level organization than they would have as independent isolated particles. Whereas first-order contextual constraints are enabling and generative constraints that create novel global systems with increased degrees of freedom, second-order constraints are restrictive and limiting constraints that curtail the components' state space. The evolutionary payoff of restrictions at the particulate level, as mentioned earlier, is increased message variety at the global level, which can now do more and different things than the parts could on their own.

4   Top-down Constraints as Semiotic

Once top-down second-order contextual constraints are in place, energy and matter exchanges across an autocatalytic cycle's boundaries are regulated by the overall cycle, *in the service of the whole*. The organization itself determines the stimuli to which it will respond; doing so preserves and enhances its cohesion and integrity, its organization and identity. A sort of incipient *autonomy* therefore appears as control and direction is progressively turned over to the global level's needs by second-order contextual constraints that decouple and buffer the overall system from the merely energetic exchanges. It is important to emphasize that this selection process operates on the basis of criteria set at the higher level (Ellis 2007), on the basis of how well the higher-level operation is thereby executed. By altering the go of things at the lower level in the service of the whole, chemical processes thus display a self-direction and autonomy absent in those found at the physical level. Toward the end of this essay I will discuss the implications of these ideas for the thorny philosophical problem of free will.

Autocatalytic cycles degrade gracefully in large measure as a result of their robustness in the face of the addition and deletion of component particles. Autocatalytic cycles, that is, typically add, delete, and replace components such that the overall cycle's integrity, persistence, and efficiency are preserved and enhanced. Top-down causality described in this fashion is thus a process of selection, a kind of semiosis that interprets—from the point of view and for the benefit of the higher-level whole—*which* among all the possible component addition, deletion, or replacement alternatives best satisfies the requirements of the higher level. Cycle *abc*, over time, can thus be transformed into a cycle composed of molecules *def*, all the while remaining itself, that is, while continuing to function as the same *type* of process—while continuing to embody the same function (Ulanowicz 1997, 2005). A sort of incipient *selfhood* can therefore be said to emerge with complex dynamical systems. Indeed, insofar as a complex system acts from what can be called its own point of view, in its own benefit, an adaptive system's conatus toward continued organizational integrity and robustness is complexity science's answer to Aristotle's final and formal cause. And from chemistry onward, it is a product of a process of self-creation.

Complex systems also highlight the importance of interlevel contextual relationships and the relative unimportance of primary qualities—and thereby also introduce an element of normativity: it now becomes possible to *evaluate* the various microarrangements in light of the higher-level function they carry out. Some will do so better, or more elegantly, and so on, than others. In light of these remarkable processes, thorny philosophical topics such as the problem of *identity* suddenly need revisiting: Once a system's feedback loop extends into the environment and back in this manner, the environment is thereby brought into the phenomenon's very structure—into its very identity, in fact. Inside–outside distinctions become more difficult to specify. By making a system's current state and behavior depend systematically on its earlier trajectory, feedback loops also incorporate the system's history into its current state and behavior. Feedback, in other words, threads a system through both time and space, thereby allowing a system's temporal and contextual relationships to become a part of its very overall structure and identity, making a self-organizing network of components and its environment "in fact one system" (Rocha 2001, 97). More generally, once the chemical stage emerges from the merely physical, true chemical autopoiesis represents the advent of the *type–token* distinction, where multiple tokens can embody the same *kind* of phenomenon, a phenomenon that must be *type-identified* as, say, a particular chemical *function*.

Our current understanding of nonlinear dynamical phenomena thus allows us to appreciate that ontological categories can no longer be defined as in Newton's time, based solely on internal primary properties. No longer can one do science solely by isolating a phenomenon in the laboratory and analyzing its components. The concepts of essence and substance, identity and individuation, as just mentioned, must be rethought, but it is in any case undeniable that complexity theory effectively *reembeds* phenomena in context and history, thereby putting the lie to much of the atomistic flavor of modernity. When even a snowflake carries the trajectory it has traversed embedded in its very structure; when the trajectories of two pendulums—or the same pendulums swung at two different times—do not tend toward classic equilibrium but instead diverge dramatically despite virtually identical origins; when the context in which a genome is embedded alters its expression, causal relationships do not resolve simply into linear chains of efficient causes. And when self-organized systems create the very constraints that control matter-energy flows—when, in other words, the constraints that give rise to self-organization have been imported into the system, the capacity for "recursive production of structures becomes possible." This happens with the appearance of chemistry (Moreno 2008). It is thanks to the consequences of autopoiesis that a veritable explosion of structural variety becomes possible.

5   Mind as Complex Attractor

In earlier work I hypothesized that as a result of neural feedback loops (Edelman's *reentrant processes*), globally coherent wave patterns similarly entrain and self-organize into high-dimensional dynamic structures in the brain possessing emergent *mental* properties such as consciousness, intentionality (*sensu* Brentano), qualia, and so on.[3] Recent empirical research provides confirmatory evidence of a global workspace model of consciousness, dynamically understood in this way. Just a few months prior to this writing, Raphael Gaillard's team in France compared the way epileptic patients undergoing intracranial electroencephalograms consciously and unconsciously processed briefly flashed words using a visual masking procedure. Although neural activity in multiple cortical areas showed that the patients were processing masked words *nonconsciously*, these signals quickly degraded and the neural activity showed only local synchrony. In contrast, neural activity indicating *conscious* processing of unmasked words showed a sustained voltage increase, particularly in the prefrontal cortex. Even more distinctly, conscious processing showed long-range phase synchrony across different portions of the brain. Moreover, these widely distributed synchronized signals activate others, as evidenced by increases in long-range Granger causality. The authors conclude that the evidence supports Bernard Baars's theory of a global workspace model of consciousness: bottom-up propagation combined with top-down attentional amplification results in a whole-brain neural assembly and "*ignites* into a self-sustained reverberant state of coherent activity that involves many neurons distributed throughout the brain" (Gaillard et al. 2009.). "Consciousness is more a question of dynamics than of local activity," says Gaillard (2009, 7).

A self-organized neural state is representational and symbolic if its central features are given not by the configuration's intrinsic physical properties but by the *information* it carries (Wheeler and Clark 1999). Since feedback loops of nonlinear dynamical processes extend outward into the environment and back in time, it is also reasonable to maintain that mental phenomena are embodied processes with tentacles that extend outward to the environment and history. Although I will use language that refers primarily to neural or neurological processes, one must keep in mind that from a complex systems' perspective a mind's content is not just in the brain (Noë 2004).

If I am correct, moreover, mental phenomena should be describable mathematically as neural attractors. The more abstract and general a semantic category, the broader the neural attractor it describes; conversely, the more specific a semantic category, the narrower the attractor. Discovering high-dimensional patterns in the brain that lower local entropy production would provide confirmatory data for this hypothesis. Earlier I noted that in connectionist networks without feedback units, after a few training runs the connection weights of the intermediate neurons for *bid* and *bed* might be close, representing lexicographical relationships. In networks with feedback loops, on the other hand, the dynamic reconfiguration means that *bed* and *cot* are now nearer in semantic attractor space than are *bed* and *bid*. According to this view, then, *semantic closeness* in the mind too would be tantamount to relative location in dynamic space, a framework that, incidentally, would also account for the source of Freudian slips. I would not be surprised if the neural pruning that takes place in early childhood turned out to be a feature of this streamlining neural self-organization.

6   Intentional Action

Philosophical debates about top-down causality by supervenient mental states have invariably raised the following concern: If mental states have causal potency in virtue of being physical states, and one assumes causal closure of the physical realm, how can overdetermination be avoided? The type–token decoupling characteristic of complex systems points to a solution. A self-organized neural state can also be said to be causal *qua* representational and symbolic—*qua mental*, that is—if what matters is that the system's output is dependent on the neurological pattern, not because of the configuration's intrinsic physical properties but because of the mental content it carries (Wheeler and Clark 1999). The word-reading neural network and the fact that autocatalytic cycles select molecules for import on the basis of criteria determined at the global level are just two examples of how complex dynamical systems satisfy this requirement. The answer to the threat of causal overdetermination can thus be found in the reverse formulation: *Brain states can have causal efficacy in virtue of being (embodying,*

being entrained into) complex neural states with emergent mental properties.
That is, brain states can have causal efficacy in virtue of the mental content
they carry. The same brain states, token-identified, may have different (or
no) causal effects depending on whether or not they are entrained into a
mental attractor at all, or depending on whether or not they are entrained
in the same mental attractor, type-identified. On this view the microphysical configuration of the nervous system's dynamical network exercises its causal power and produces a particular output in virtue of
embodying the top-down context-sensitive constraints of emergent mental
properties.

Does this way of looking at the mind–brain problem resolve concerns
over causal overdetermination and conservation laws? Paul Humphreys
maintains that unlike aggregates, whose individual components retain
their identities, emergence happens only when microstates *fuse* (Humphreys 1997). When they *fuse*, particles comprising unified wholes "no
longer exist as separate entities and therefore do not have all their individual causal powers available for use at the global level." Because components "go out of existence" when they fuse, Humphreys maintains, worries
concerning causal overdetermination and the causal closure of the physical
are avoided and top-down causality is possible. Humphreys warns, however,
that fusion and multiple realizability are incompatible: any claim that
mental properties can be variously instantiated in components that do not
"go out of existence" reintroduces the threat of overdetermination, he
insists.

Complex systems have taught us that dynamic self-organization produces high-level emergents capable of top-down causation without thereby
violating conservation laws. Phase transitions, symmetry breaking, and
other forms of dynamic transformations entrain components into higher-
level wholes without thereby *fusing* the particles. Instead, the global patterns that emerge as a result of these qualitative changes are embodied as
the conditional probability distributions of the components. The operation
of *fusion*, a static notion that implies that once fused, there is no going
back, is unlike the operation of *integration,* despite the thermodynamically
irreversible nature of the latter.[4] Fusion is like the operation of context-free
constraints, which, as we saw, close off possibilities in a bottleneck that
prevents open-ended evolution. In contrast, bottom-up context-sensitive
constraints represent interactions that are Goldilocks-like—not too tight,
not too loose—and allow the same microarrangement token-identified to
take part in different global dynamics, type-identified, both synchronically
and diachronically. If the disruptive perturbation or fluctuation is strong

enough the global structure disintegrates, but while the constraints hold, the complex dynamics remain coherent over time (Ulanowicz 2005). The emergence of dynamical integration, I proposed earlier, is nothing but the effects of second-order context-sensitive constraints, embodied as a set of conditional probabilities that are invariant over time and that modulate and direct the behavior of particular—but now no longer independent— microphysical constituents in such a way that the mental content carried by the overall dynamics cascades into the action performed. In graph-theoretic terms, this unique balance between integration and differentia-tion can be measured in terms of a network's *causal density* (the fraction of interactions among nodes in a network that are causally significant). Analysis shows that high causal density is consistent with a high dynami-cal balance between differentiation and integration, and therefore with high complexity (Seth 2005, 2006; Seth and Edelman 2007). The robust-ness characteristic of complex systems is thus due to dynamics that are globally coordinated while component details remain distinct; compo-nents do not fuse, and yet the overall system displays a remarkable resil-ience and metastability in its functional powers despite radical differences in the arrangements of its component parts.

We are at last in a position to understand how top-down causality of the sort described above makes intention-caused actions possible. Accord-ing to this framework, *intentions* are similarly high-dimensional, neurologi-cally embodied long-range attractors with emergent properties. No doubt the billion-plus-neuron human brain possesses an indefinite number of imbricated dynamics. Intentions, by definition, involve motor attractors, as well as others embodying high-level properties of meaning (the semantic content of the intention), emotional valence, and so on. Aesthetic, ethical, or moral value judgments, I suppose, are embodied in even higher-level attractors, which self-organize later in both individual development and neurological evolution.

When intentions strongly entrain motor neurons such that they pre-cipitate a certain type of behavior with probability near 1, they constitute *proximate* intentions; when they merely prime the likelihood of future motor activity they embody *prior* intentions (Bratman 1987). Prior inten-tions restructure a multidimensional neural state into a new organization characterized by a new set of coordinates and a new dynamics; the context-sensitive constraints that partition a prior intention's contrast space carry emergent properties of meaning, emotional valence, and so on. On this account logical and syntactical relationships are also embodied in the higher-level relationships between the various attractors.

Dynamically, this means that once I form the prior intention to do *A*, not every logical or physically possible alternative remains open downstream, and those that do are contoured differently, probabilistically speaking. By imposing novel conditional propensities on available pathways, the dynamics of a newly self-organized semantic space constrain movements within it, top-down. Through the assignation of conditional probabilities, some act-types are eliminated, others are made more likely. Once I settle on the *prior* intention of going on a diet, say, the likelihood of certain future behaviors—such as gorging on cookies—recedes. (Other considerations such as the *robustness* of the agent's *character*, which can now be understood as the combined strength, stability, and resilience of the agent's mental attractor set, must also be taken into account.) As a result of further interactions among the prior intention, other internal dynamics, and the environment, one option from those weighted alternatives established by the new organization can become a proximate attractor. By strongly entraining motor dynamics to its own, this pathway in turn guides and constrains behavior in the immediate future. Formulating a *proximate* intention (do *A* now) can thus be understood as positioning a particular attractor just ahead of the system's immediate position in phase space and entraining the necessary motor attractors to execute the action. In this way the context-sensitive constraints that embody the meaningful content of intentions cascade into behavior top-down and carry out intentional behavior. And so the person acts. In recent years, nonlinear methodologies suitable to complex systems are providing increasing empirical confirmation that indeed intentions can be naturalized as soft-assembled context sensitive constraints operating as control parameters (Riley and Turvey 2001; Van Orden, Kloos, and Wallot 2009).

If I am right, one needs to be careful about conclusions drawn from the curious research on "choice blindness" (Hall and Johannson 2009). In a series of experiments, subjects were asked to select between, for example, two varieties of jam. Immediately after the volunteers made their choice, a different jar was substituted for the one selected. When asked why they chose the (substituted) jar, not only did the participants not notice the mismatch, they even offered "reasons" for their "choice." On my account, prior and proximate intentions can be more or less vague and ambiguous, or more or less specific and concrete; dynamically, the attractors will be more or less shallow and broad, or more or less narrow and deep. My proximate intention can be framed as either "stop at the next convenience store to buy something—anything—to eat for dinner," or "stop at the next 7-11 to buy a *Healthy Choice* brand frozen chicken dinner." The latter's attractor is represented by a much narrower and deeper well; the former's attractor would be embodied in a much shallower and broader basin. If my proximate intention had been formulated as the former, I would most likely not even notice that the item I selected from the freezer had been switched, no matter how conscious the decision. It seems to me therefore that Hall and Johannson's conclusion that "choice blindness drives a wedge between intentions and actions in the mind" follows necessarily only if the relationship between intention and action is conceptualized as billiard-ball causality between crisply defined objects (Hall and Johannson 2009, 27). One has to remain alert to how uncritical presuppositions about mechanistic causality can creep into the design of experiments and the conclusions we draw from them.

A similar caution applies to research that extrapolates from the timing of the appearance of the readiness potential to the reality of free will (Libet 2004). The Libet experiments went roughly as follows: participants were asked to perform activities such as pressing a button, or flexing a finger or wrist, within a certain time frame. Participants were also asked to note the position of the dot on the oscilloscope timer when "he/she was first aware of the wish or urge to act." The instant the button was actually pressed, or the finger flexed, was also recorded on the oscillator, this time electronically. By comparing the moment the button was pushed and time of the subject's conscious decision to act, researchers were able to calculate the time between the subject's initial volition and the ensuing action. The unexpected results showed that brain activity initiating behavior (the readiness potential) preceded (by up to 300 milliseconds) any conscious decision to act; even more remarkable, in their reporting the subjects often antedated the volition such that the intention and decision (was felt to) precede the action.

Since regulatory records operate in a time-independent mode and exert top-down causal influence on lower-level metabolic processes operating in a dynamic and time-dependent mode, arguments such as these purporting to refute the possibility of free will based on linear temporal relations between neural events and experience call for closer scrutiny. Libet's experiments clearly disallow mechanistic interpretations of the concept of free will that conceive of voluntary intentions as conscious representations distinctly separate from and preceding the actions they forcefully bring about as efficient causes. On such an account the subject's antedating is of course illusory, as is, a fortiori, any claim that the volition efficiently caused the behavior. But if one envisions top-down causality as the operations of second-order context-sensitive constraints, and one keeps in mind the fact that feedback loops embodied in those constraints extend outward into the environment and back in time, then the following alternative interpretation opens up: If the subject's intention is formulated in vague and general terms as suggested earlier—"I will press the button every so often"—the agent can then let the environment carry out the detailed movements without thereby obviating the higher level's control on the lower. Rodney Brooks calls the process "letting the world serve as its own model" (Brooks 1991). If I decide merely to "drive home" (as opposed to the more precise and specific "drive home along route X"), I can let the lay of the land—the traffic pattern or road conditions—determine for me whether to turn right on Oak Street or left on Poplar Street. A well-known example is the following: after driving home from work along our daily commuter route all of us have experienced the peculiar sensation of realizing that we can't even remember if the traffic light at Elm and Maple was red or green that day. Following Libet's reasoning, it is obvious that in such situations the actions of depressing the accelerator or brake bypass conscious decision making. But are they not therefore not constrained by awareness? I don't think so. Had a rabbit or a deer suddenly jumped in our path the automaticity would have been quickly replaced by consciously aware decision making.

The problem with the Libet-like experiments, on my view, is their reliance on a traditional understanding of causality as series of discrete events acting as efficient causes. In contrast, the thesis put forth in this essay has been that functional, informational, symbolic, and representational processes operate in the brain as top-down, second-order context-sensitive constraints. Unlike efficient causes, which have traditionally been understood to be instantaneous, atomistic events, the dynamics of higher informational regulatory systems—the genetic and neural systems, for example—often operate at a slower and longer time scale than that of their constituents; that these slower and longer dynamics can nonetheless constrain the lower-level dynamics that constitute them is an illustration of what Haken calls "slaving." Phase separations between levels of organization are often speed and time differences between levels of organization. Phases are clearly demarcated wherever crisp differences in time scales exist between the higher-level emergent dynamics and processes at the lower level; the Gaillard research mentioned earlier is just one of the most recent to show that dynamic phase separations are significant. Salthe (1985, 2002) notes that higher-level laws and principles can apply to dynamics that are slower and longer than those of the lower level; but the higher level is not always slower or faster than the lower: The regulatory genetic system operates faster than the metabolic system; the regulatory neural system works faster than the metabolic system. My point here is merely to point out that "there's more to heaven and earth than is dreamt of in your [mechanistic] philosophy, Libet," and so empirical research designed from a mechanistic framework may be chasing red herrings. Research on the role of timing in brain processing is still in its early stages (Carey 2008), but I am confident that future research into dynamic phase separation (such as that between alpha and beta patterns in the brain) will shed light on causal propagation and the process of top-down modulation control and regulation. In light of the discussion Libet's work has occasioned, further work on this feature of brain dynamics is warranted, especially phase differences between levels of neural organizations such as the regulatory informational system and the lower-level motor networks under the former's control.

Elsewhere I argued that the information-theoretic concepts of *equivocation* and *ambiguity* might help track the effectiveness of intentional constraints over the course of the behavior's trajectory. Newly developed techniques designed to capture the interdependencies between multiple time series should prove even more useful in determining the flow of information from one part of the brain to another. Granger causality, mentioned earlier in connection with the research on the distributed character of conscious processes in the brain, is one such technique that compares streams of data known as time series, such as fluctuations in neural firing patterns. Granger causality helps determine whether correlations are mere coincidences or reflect one process influencing another process. In one recent study,

Researchers gave volunteers a cue that a visual stimulus would be appearing soon in a portion of a computer display screen, and asked them to report when the stimulus appeared and what they saw. Corbetta's group previously revealed that this task activated two brain areas: the frontoparietal cortex, which is involved in the direction of the attention, and the visual cortex, which became more active in the area where volunteers were cued to expect the stimulus to appear.

Scientists believed the frontoparietal cortex was influencing the visual cortex, but the brain scanning approach they were using, functional magnetic resonance imaging (fMRI), can only complete scans about once every two seconds, which was much too slow to catch that influence in action. When researchers applied Granger causality, though, they were able to show conclusively that as volunteers waited for the stimulus to appear, the frontoparietal cortex was influencing the visual cortex, not the reverse. (Washington University School of Medicine 2008)

Because Granger causality only applies to pairs of variables, misleading results may occur when the true relationship involves three or more variables: If both variables tested are in fact being "caused" by a third, Granger tests may yield positive results even though the two variables have no causal relations with each other. In cases such as these a related test called *vector autoregression* (VAR) can be applied to better track information flow in the brain. Neuroscientists are currently using both techniques in their studies, whose purpose is to capture the conditional probabilities carried by context-sensitive constraints.

7 Autonomy

I would like to close with some thoughts concerning the implications that complex adaptive systems have with respect to the philosophically thorny subject of free will. I propose that these dynamical processes allow one to rethink autonomy and self-direction in a scientifically respectable way and with enough of a payoff to warrant the appellation *a kind of free will worth wanting.*

We saw earlier that the change from physical Bénard cells to chemical autocatalytic cycles occurs when the boundary constraints within which the organization takes place are created by the process itself—when, in other words, the production of the *order parameter* is brought inside the system itself, dynamically speaking. When the endogenous dynamics themselves control the overall process, the slack or *decoupling* between *type* and *token* that turns regulatory control and direction over to *type-identified criteria* provides a measure of self-direction and autonomy to chemical processes that is absent in merely physical ones.

Increased structural complexity through chemical catalysis production, however, in the end becomes brittle and reaches a bottleneck; chemistry soon reaches its limit, that is, at a choke point that prevents further evolution. As we saw earlier, because it relies solely on context-free constraints, mitotic biological reproduction quickly does too. Lila Gatlin, whom I cited earlier, argues that, evolutionarily speaking, the evolutionary bottleneck was breached and truly open-ended evolution made possible only after vertebrates discovered a way to retain *context-free* constraints stable while simultaneously allowing *context-sensitive* constraints to expand. The research team of Alvaro Moreno, Juli Peretó, and Kepa Ruiz-Mirazo at the University of the Basque Country (Spain) published a series of papers (Ruiz-Mirazo and Moreno 1998, 2000, 2006; Ruiz-Mirazo, Peretó, and Moreno 2004; Moreno 2008) individually and severally in which they expand on Gatlin's insight: open-ended evolution necessitated a way of preserving earlier evolutionary advances while at the same time continuing the process of catalytic creation. It required, in short, the creation of *hereditary* lineages. The appearance of what the Basque team calls *dynamic decoupling* guarantees both the open-endedness of evolution and the emergence of *strong autonomy*.

Robust and ongoing biological evolution becomes possible, that is, only when a second *type* of biological function appears that *preserves* prior evolutionary advances without interfering with the (ongoing) catalytic production from which those advances originated in the first place. This new type of functional component—of which DNA is a prime example—serves as what Moreno and his colleagues call a *register* (or *record*). This decoupling also results in the concomitant emergence of *strong autonomy*, because once again registers construct the constraints within which the ongoing catalytic function operates. The important point I want to make here is that when dynamic decoupling appears, the transformation that took place with the emergence of chemistry is taken one step further: with the appearance of registers the control and regulatory function is brought even further inside the system dynamics themselves. Constraints within which ontogenetic development is canalized not only embody phylogenetic information—they are now on board. Adding an additional set of internal top-down contextual constraints further decouples organisms from buffeting by energetic forces, thereby making it even more self-directing. As keeper of biological lineages, DNA faithfully preserves a relatively invariant record of phylogenetically earlier traits without thereby becoming involved in or interfering with those ongoing metabolic functions that allow variations to continue to appear over epigenetic time. Neuronal self-organization and the use of tools are other examples of this type of *dynamic decoupling*, claims the Basque team. As was the case in the emergence of chemical from physical processes, when register function decouples from catalyst function, the control and regulatory criteria that will direct the future course of events have been handed over even more so to the organism.

Because the two functions (registers and catalysis creation) cannot be directly linked, a novel, *information-type* of semiosis is required to translate between the two: "code-type information semiosis," of which DNA's *genetic* code is the prime example, is charged with this task (Moreno 2008). In my language, dynamic decoupling with indirect code-type information semiosis is a version of top-down causation in which semantic higher-level code regulates and modulates—constrains—lower-level energetic exchanges according to criteria set at the higher level. The law-like relations between the two phase-separated dynamics carry the code-type information transmitted.

I propose that the appearance of *consciousness* and related *mental* phenomena such as *intentions* constitutes the emergence of yet another register-type function, a function that once again serves as record or register—in this case of earlier ontogenetic experience. Having access to a conscious mental workspace while sensory mechanisms continue their ongoing work permits an explosive expansion of state space. It permits, that is, a new *dimension* of message variety, with trajectories regulated top-down according to *mental* content. The agent can now do a lot more and different things than before. Whereas with the appearance of DNA heredity became encapsulated in a new anatomical *structure*, the new conscious, mental workspace functions as a *dynamical register*, encoding mental content on a different dynamical scale (see Salthe 1985, 2002, on scalar and specification hierarchies; see Gaillard 2009). It is tempting to speculate whether emotions serve as the indirect information-type code that translates between the two. Freedman's research on the way olfactory stimulus simultaneously encodes meaning and emotion when remembered could be interpreted in this way (Freeman 1991).

What seems certain is that human *symbolic language* functions as the context-sensitive translation code between self-consciousness or long-term declarative memory on the one hand and ongoing sensory input on the other. The transformation of short-term memory into long-term declarative memory might turn out to be a component of this process. And when human language becomes entrained into culture and then recorded in written form, the added *sedimentation* of linguistic meaning encoded in dictionaries is an additional example of yet another high-level register (sensu Moreno) that enables cultural evolution to continue, and explosively so. The task of each new register is the same as DNA's: to preserve established information while allowing human beings to create new meaning as they experience new things. It should come as no surprise therefore that the meaning of concepts and even of "forms of life," as it becomes sedimented in dictionaries and moral codes, can bias the conditional probability distributions of patterns in individual nervous systems, both developmentally and phylogenetically.[5]

The process by which actions can be value-informed is therefore less mysterious once this framework is adopted. When from among the various alternatives presented to a potential agent she chooses one on the basis of very high-level value-infused criteria, behavior turns into ethical and moral action (moral as opposed to amoral, not immoral) in virtue of the axiological content the intention constrains, not the physical microarrangement of the neurological pattern that carries that content). Here again we have another example of a regulatory control function being "brought inside"—not structurally like DNA but dynamically—and therefore even more strongly decoupled from external, energetic control and direction.

The central thesis of this essay has been that the emergence, operation, and evolution of complex dynamical systems show how global systemic levels grow more and more self-directed as their capacity to constrain, modulate, and regulate their constituent levels is increasingly modularized and dynamically decoupled from merely energetic exchanges—in recent evolution by being split off as independent registers or records. Complex systems with this feature, which begins with biological heredity, are *strongly autonomous*. And they become even more so over the course of evolution with the emergence of consciousness, self-consciousness, values, and symbolic language. If mind and language are the most evolutionarily advanced dynamically decoupled *records* or *registers*; if decoupling from external buffeting is precisely the sort of trait one needs to determine autonomy; and if top-down context-sensitive constraints operating in complex adaptive systems can explain how the course of things can be regulated and modulated by higher-level criteria such as meaning and values; then it seems to me that nonlinear dynamical systems theory makes room for a *kind of free will worth wanting*.

Notes

1. It does not just activate previously existing potential; complexification creates heretofore nonexistent possibilities—and therefore new directions for the system.

2. See Wheeler and Clark 1999 for additional examples of new properties created by the *causal spread* of context-sensitive constraints.

3. These constraints are on top of those preexisting constraints, both context-free and context-sensitive, that present as innate predispositions or propensities—such as those embodied in mirror neurons, for example.

4. The irreversibility is provided not by unalterably fusing the micro-level components into a global structure, but by their historicity and context-dependence. These are embodied in the system's internal dynamics, which "carry on their back" the conditions under which the systems were created and the trajectory they have undergone. Even snowflakes, for example, carry in their very structure information about both the atmospheric conditions that caused them and those they traversed before reaching the ground.

5. Like DNA, however, and despite the claims of Foucault and other postmodernists, the top-down constraints of language are not completely rigid; instead they allow for the creation of new meaning accomplished through play and exploration.

17 The Causal Theory of Action and the Still Puzzling Knobe Effect

Thomas Nadelhoffer

One can test attempted philosophical analyses of intentional action partly by ascertaining whether what these analyses entail about particular actions is in line with what the majority of non-specialists would say about these actions. . . . [I]f there is a widely shared concept of intentional action, such judgments provide evidence about what the concept is, and a philosophical analysis of intentional action that is wholly unconstrained by that concept runs the risk of having nothing more than a philosophical fiction as its subject matter.
—Alfred Mele (2001, 27)

1 Introduction

It is a common assumption among philosophers that whether or not something counts as an intentional action depends on what was going on "in the head" of the agent at the time it was performed. On this view, intentional actions are events that are caused by a combination of antecedent conative and cognitive mental states such as wishes, desires, beliefs, reasons, decisions, and intentions.[1] And although the philosophers who adopt this kind of causal theory of action may admittedly disagree when it comes to the precise nature of the relationship between various mental states and human agency—for example, whether intentions can simply be reduced to pairs of beliefs and desires or whether intentions to x are necessary for intentionally x-ing—the orthodox view is that the proper etiological explanation of intentional action will be couched exclusively in mentalistic terms.

As intuitive as this view may initially appear, however, there is gathering evidence that folk ascriptions of intentional action are sometimes driven not only by judgments concerning the mental states of the agents in question but also by the moral valence of the outcome of the action. These findings—which are collectively referred to as the "Knobe effect" (Nichols and Ulatowski 2007, 348)—have led some philosophers to conclude that the concept of intentional action is inherently evaluative (Knobe 2003a,b). To the extent that this is the case, it potentially poses problems for the causal theory of action—at least if this theory is supposed to adequately capture the folk concept of intentionality.[2] After all, if an action can be intentional so long as its consequences are sufficiently bad even if the agent who brought it about neither desired, wanted, intended, nor tried to do so, the project of explaining intentionality solely in terms of the mental states of the agent is on shaky ground.

In this chapter, I am first going to briefly argue for the relevance of data on folk intuitions to the philosophical project of providing an account of intentional action. Then, I will examine some of the empirical research that has been done on this front—paying particular attention to Steve Guglielmo and Bertram Malle's recent attempts to resolve some of the puzzles that have arisen in light of Joshua Knobe's findings (Guglielmo and Malle n.d.a, n.d.b). More specifically, I will try to show that Guglielmo and Malle have yet to establish that the so-called Knobe effect is merely an artifact of an impoverished experimental design. In making my case, I will present the results of two new studies that suggest that even though Guglielmo and Malle have done much to advance our understanding of the folk concept of intentional action, they have yet to fully explain away Knobe's puzzling data.

At the end of the day, I will argue not only that philosophers of action need to pay close attention to the research on folk intuitions, but that this research potentially puts pressure on the common assumption that whether an action is intentional depends entirely on the mental states of the agent. That being said, it is admittedly too early in the day to determine the full extent of the threat. Plumbing these depths would require more data than we currently have at hand. As such, my primary goal in this chapter is merely to survey a small piece of the empirical terrain, present the results of two new studies, and consider some of the potential implications for the philosophy of action. Resolving all of the thorny underlying issues is an arduous task for another day that will require philosophers and psychologists to continue to work together on the important project of understanding the fundamental nature of human agency.

2   Folk Concepts and the Philosophy of Action

Oliver Wendell Holmes once famously remarked that "even a dog distinguishes between being stumbled over and being kicked" (Holmes 1963,

7)—a difference that permeates our ordinary judgments about responsibility and blame. In the event that someone accidentally or unintentionally harms you, this usually mitigates how much blame you think the person deserves for doing so. If, on the other hand, someone purposely and intentionally harms you under normal circumstances, this is grounds for judging the person to be fully morally (and possibly legally) culpable for the harm. In short, judgments about intentions and intentional actions lie at the heart of the sphere of our ascriptions of responsibility. Moreover, a standard direction of fit is commonly assumed to exist between the two— namely, judging whether an agent is fully responsible for x-ing requires one to first decide both whether she intended to x and whether she x-ed intentionally.

For present purposes, I am going to call this the *standard model* of intentionality and blame. In short, it is a *unidirectional* view whereby judgments about intentionality serve as inputs to judgments concerning responsibility, but not the other way around. Understandably, this seemingly commonsensical model has been adopted by philosophers and legal theorists alike. However, as intuitive as it may appear at first blush, this view has been called into question by recent data on folk ascriptions of intentional action. But before I examine the gathering evidence for the competing *bidirectional* model—the view that judgments concerning the badness of an action (or the blameworthiness of an agent) sometimes influence judgments of intentionality and not just the other way around[3]—I first want to briefly discuss the relevance of folk intuitions to the philosophy of action more generally.

The first thing worth pointing out on this front is that there is a storied tradition in philosophy whereby philosophers are in the business of analyzing folk beliefs, judgments, and concepts. Frank Jackson has arguably put forward the most thorough and persuasive recent defense of this position. On his view, "our subject is really the elucidation of the situations covered by the *words* we use to ask our questions—concerning free action, knowledge . . . or whatever" (Jackson 1998, 33). And given that ordinary language is often the proper subject matter of philosophy, "consulting intuitions about possible cases" is the proper method (ibid.). Although I entirely agree with Jackson's contention that philosophers should often focus on our ordinary beliefs and judgments,[4] his view is nevertheless based on the questionable assumption that the intuitions of analytic philosophers are representative of those of laypersons.

This is a problem that Jackson acknowledges when he says that he is "sometimes asked—in a tone that suggests that the question is a major objection—why, if conceptual analysis is concerned to elucidate what governs our classificatory practice, don't I advocate doing serious opinion polls on people's responses to various cases? My answer is that I do—when it is necessary" (ibid., 36–37). I, for one, agree with Jackson that when it comes to some issues such as free will, moral responsibility, and intentional action, people's ordinary intuitions are the appropriate starting point for philosophical investigation. However, I nevertheless believe that Jackson's method of getting at them—namely, armchair reflection coupled with *informal* polls of students and friends—is methodologically problematic. On my view, to the extent that philosophers are going to continue making claims concerning the contours of folk intuitions, the task of testing these claims should be attended to with the same carefulness and rigor one finds in psychology and cognate fields. In light of this concern, researchers working under the rubric of "experimental philosophy" have recently begun using techniques borrowed from the social sciences to get at folk judgments concerning a wide variety of philosophical issues.[5]

One topic that has received a lot of attention among experimental philosophers is the concept of intentional action.[6] After all, as Alfred Mele has correctly pointed out, any adequate philosophical analysis of intentional action should be "anchored by common-sense judgments" about particular cases (Mele 2001, 27)—even if it admittedly need not capture or reflect *all* of these judgments. On this view, one way of testing an analysis of intentional action would be to see whether it agrees with our pretheoretical intuitions. And the only method of determining what nonspecialists think about particular cases is to *actually ask them*. Having done so, if we find that an analysis of intentional action is entirely inconsistent with folk intuitions, we will be in a good position to suggest that it "runs the risk of having nothing more than a philosophical fiction as its subject matter" (ibid.).

Data about the folk concept of intentional action become all the more important for philosophers such as Hugh McCann who explicitly claim to be interested in ordinary concepts and not their philosophical counterparts (McCann 1998, 210). So, whereas those philosophers who are merely interested in technical concepts and other so-called "terms of art" may dismiss empirical data concerning folk intuitions *tout court*, philosophers such as Jackson and McCann, who are explicitly interested in analyzing our everyday concepts, are beholden to the results of the kind of research being done by experimental philosophers.[7] As such, even if experimental philosophy is admittedly not relevant to *all* philosophical projects, it is inescapably relevant to *some* of them.

Unfortunately, until fairly recently, there was a dearth of empirical research on how people actually think and talk about intentionality. Malle and Knobe tried to fill in this lacuna in their groundbreaking paper entitled "The Folk Concept of Intentional Action" (1997). In order to sketch the boundaries of ordinary judgments, Malle and Knobe ran a series of surveys. In light of their findings—the details of which need not concern us here—they developed the following five-component model of intentionality:

Belief   Desire

      ↘ ↙

    Intention

Skill   Awareness

     ↘ ↓ ↙

   Intentionality

According to this model, performing an action intentionally "requires the presence of five components: a desire for an outcome; beliefs about an action that leads to that outcome; an intention to perform the action; skill to perform the action; and awareness of fulfilling the intention while performing the action" (Malle and Knobe 1997, 12). Moreover, Malle and Knobe suggest that these five components are "hierarchically arranged, such that belief and desire are necessary conditions for attributions of intention and, given an *intention*, skill and awareness are necessary conditions for attributions of *intentionality*" (ibid., 15).

Malle and Knobe's five-component model has several strengths. First, it is based on controlled and systematic studies rather than armchair speculation or informal polls of students, friends, and colleagues. Second, by purportedly identifying all of the necessary components of the folk concept of intentional action, their model not only integrates a number of the past analyses of intentionality, but it also reveals where these previous analyses went wrong. However, despite the obvious advantages provided by Malle and Knobe's model, there is gathering evidence that when participants are given morally valenced vignettes, they often ascribe intentionality even though some of the conditions of the five-component model have not been satisfied. In light of this research, it appears that the aforementioned bidirectional view may better comport with the data on folk intuitions than its unidirectional counterpart. If true, this would not only put pressure on the standard model of intentionality, but it would also cast doubt on the causal theory of action more generally. But we are getting ahead of ourselves. Before we start worrying about the possible implications of these recent findings, we should first take a closer look at the findings themselves.

3 The Knobe Effect

In a series of recent studies, Knobe set out to determine whether folk intuitions about the intentionality of foreseeable yet undesired side effects are influenced by moral considerations (Knobe 2003a,b). Each of the 78 participants in the first of these side-effect experiments was presented with a vignette involving either a "harm condition" or a "help condition." Those who received the harm condition read the following vignette:

> The vice-president of a company went to the chairman of the board and said, "'We are thinking of starting a new program. It will help us increase profits, but it will also harm the environment.'" The chairman of the board answered, "'I don't care at all about harming the environment. I just want to make as much profit as I can. Let's start the new program'." They started the new program. Sure enough, the environment was harmed. (Knobe 2003a, 191)

They were then asked to judge how much blame the chairman deserved for harming the environment (on a scale from 0 to 6) and to say whether they thought the chairman harmed the environment intentionally. Of the participants, 82 percent claimed that the chairman harmed the environment intentionally. Participants in the help condition, on the other hand, read the same scenario except that the word "harm" was replaced by the word "help." They were then asked to judge how much praise the chairman deserved for helping the environment (on a scale from 0 to 6) and to say whether they thought the chairman helped the environment intentionally. Only 23 percent of the participants claimed that the chairman intentionally helped the environment (ibid., 192).

In another side-effect experiment, Knobe got similar results. This time each of the 42 participants received one of the following two vignettes:

Harm Condition
A lieutenant was talking with a sergeant. The lieutenant gave the order: "'Send your squad to the top of Thompson Hill.'" The sergeant said: "'But if I send my squad to the top of Thompson Hill, we'll be moving the men into the enemy's line of fire. Some of them will surely be killed!'" The lieutenant answered: "'Look, I know that they'll be in the line of fire,

and I know that some of them will be killed. But I don't care at all about what happens to our soldiers. All I care about is taking control of Thompson Hill'." The squad was sent to the top of Thompson Hill. As expected, the soldiers were moved into the enemy's line of fire, and some of them were killed (ibid.).

Help Condition

A lieutenant was talking with a sergeant. The lieutenant gave the order: "'Send your squad to the top of Thompson Hill.'" The sergeant said: "'But if I send my squad to the top of Thompson Hill, we'll be taking them out of the enemy's line of fire. They'll be rescued!'" The lieutenant answered: "'Look, I know that we'll be taking them out of the line of fire, and I know that some of them would have been killed otherwise. But I don't care at all about what happens to our soldiers. All I care about is taking control of Thompson Hill'." The squad was sent to the top of Thompson Hill. As expected, the soldiers were moved out of the enemy's line of fire, and some of them were saved (ibid.).

Once again, the two conditions yielded drastically different responses: 77 percent of the participants who read the harm condition said the agent intentionally brought about the negative side effect, whereas only 30 percent of those who read the help condition said the agent brought about the positive side effect intentionally (ibid.). When Knobe combined the praise and blame ratings from the two experiments, he got the following results: Whereas the participants who were given the harm condition said the agent deserved a lot of blame (M=4.8), those who were given the help condition said that the agent deserved virtually no praise (M=1.4). More-over, these results were correlated with their judgments about whether or not the side effect was brought about intentionally (ibid., 193).

Needless to say, philosophers and psychologists alike found these find-ings to be both surprising and puzzling. If nothing else, the results of Knobe's studies provided support for the bidirectional model of intention-ality while at the same time putting pressure on the more "valence-neutral" models that have traditionally populated the action theory literature.[8] However, although the asymmetry between participants' responses in the harm and help conditions is admittedly noteworthy, trying to fully explain it would take us beyond the scope of the present essay. Multiple explana-tions of the "Knobe effect" have been put forward in the literature and a number of follow-up studies have been run. Now is neither the time nor the place to examine either all of the existing data or the plethora of competing views that have been put forward to explain them.[9] For present purposes, the most important take-home lesson from Knobe's research is that in the harm conditions, participants judged that the side effects were brought about intentionally, even though neither the CEO nor the lieutenant cared at all about bringing them about. After all, these findings offer *prima facie* evidence against the view that Michael Bratman has dubbed the "simple view" (Bratman 1984)— the view whereby intending to x is necessary for intentionally x-ing.[10]

To see how the results of Knobe's studies put pressure on the simple view, we must first make a few initial assumptions. On the one hand, if an agent does not care at all about doing x (or bringing x about), then she lacks any desire to x. On the other hand, if an agent does not want or desire to bring x about, then she does not intend to do so. If these assumptions are correct, then Knobe's participants were willing to judge that the side effects were brought about intentionally even though the agents did not want—and hence did not intend—to do so. Thus, at first blush, Knobe has provided empirical evidence that calls both the simple view and the aforementioned five-component model of intentionality into question. More importantly, for present purposes, to the extent that folk ascriptions of intentional action are driven not only by judgments concerning the mental states of the agents but also by the moral valence of the outcome, Knobe's findings also create problems for the causal theory of action more generally.

Keep in mind that at least according to the aforementioned philosophical approach to action theory that is espoused by Jackson, McCann, and others, an adequate theory of intentionality will be one that comports with salient folk intuitions and judgments. As such, if it turns out that whether someone is judged to have done something intentionally depends not only on her mental states at the time but also on the moral valence of the outcome, then the causal theory of action falls short as a complete analysis of the folk concept of intentional action. Unsurprisingly, defenders of the more traditional valence-neutral model have not taken Knobe's findings lying down. Indeed, as we are about to see, recent studies suggest that perhaps the conclusions drawn by Knobe and others have been premature.

4 Resurrecting the Standard Model

In a pair of recent papers, Guglielmo and Malle set out to put pressure on Knobe's two central findings—namely, (a) the "side-effect findings," and (b) the "skill findings." The former—which potentially undermine the "intention" condition of Malle and Knobe's five-component model—purportedly show that people sometimes judge that an agent can bring about a side effect intentionally even if she neither wants, tries, nor intends to bring it about. The latter findings—which potentially undermine the skill condition of the five-component model—purportedly show that people sometimes judge than an agent can perform an action intentionally even if she does not exercise any salient skill in bringing it about. By my lights, Guglielmo and Malle's attacks on both findings are illuminating and important. However, for present purposes, I am going to limit my attention to their attempts to undermine the side-effect findings since these are the ones that potentially cast the most doubt on both the simple view and the causal theory of action. At the end of the day, if the latter two views are to be viable as accounts of the folk concept of intentional action, Knobe's side-effect findings would need to be explained away—which is precisely what Guglielmo and Malle try to accomplish. But since discussing all of the data they marshal forward is beyond the scope of the present essay, I will simply focus on the two studies that I take to pose the greatest potential threat to the Knobe effect.

In the first study, Guglielmo and Malle presented participants with versions of Knobe's earlier CEO harm vignettes. However, unlike Knobe's earlier studies, which forced participants to make simple dichotomous intentionality judgments, Guglielmo and Malle provided participants with more answer choices in the hopes that this would yield greater insight into how they actually viewed the CEO's primary actions. Upon reading a version of Knobe's CEO harm vignette, participants were first once again forced to make a yes/no intentionality judgment. Having done so, they were then provided with multiple action descriptions to choose from and asked to select "the most accurate description of what the CEO did." The choices were as follows:

1. "The CEO willingly harmed the environment."
2. "The CEO knowingly harmed the environment."
3. "The CEO intentionally harmed the environment."
4. "The CEO purposely harmed the environment."

Unsurprisingly, 73 percent of the participants answered the dichotomous intentionality question in the affirmative—which is roughly what one would expect based on Knobe's earlier findings. Surprisingly, however, across all four conditions of the study, only 1 percent of the participants deemed that "intentionally harmed the environment" was the most accurate description of what the CEO did. By contrast, 82 percent selected "knowingly harmed the environment," and 14 percent selected "willingly harmed the environment." On the surface, these results put serious pressure on the Knobe effect. After all, if the bidirectional model were correct, one would expect that the participants in these studies would find it most correct to say that the CEO "intentionally" or "purposely" harmed the environment. But contrary to this expectation, these were the two *least* popular options.

As Guglielmo and Malle point out, "this finding is particularly noteworthy because the same participants who first provided the forced-choice intentionality response afterwards picked a different label as the most accurate behavior description" (n.d.a). On their view, these results suggest that when participants "are freed from the forced dichotomous choice and have a chance to select a more subtle interpretation of the situation at hand," their answers no longer provide evidence for the Knobe effect (ibid.). In light of these findings, Guglielmo and Malle believe they have both undermined the bidirectional model while at the same time vindicating the valence-neutral five-component model. By their lights, people do not normally conceptualize the CEO as having intentionally harmed the environment. Instead, when people are given the choice, they view his behavior as "the intentional action of adopting a profit-raising program while fully knowing (and not preventing) that it would harm the environment." But insofar as this is the case, the Knobe effect starts to look like little more than an artifact of an impoverished experimental design. Indeed, the results of a follow-up study appear to further undermine the purported evidence for the bidirectional model of intentionality.

In this second study, participants were once again presented with Knobe's CEO harm vignette. They were then told that "this situation has certain ambiguities and leaves some questions open. How can we best describe what the CEO did? Please pick the most accurate description . . . then pick the second-most accurate description." The action descriptions available to participants this time around were as follows:

1. "The CEO intentionally harmed the environment."
2. "The CEO intentionally adopted an environment harming program."
3. "The CEO intentionally adopted an environment-harming program and a profit-raising program."
4. "The CEO intentionally adopted a profit-raising program that he knew would harm the environment."
5. "The CEO intentionally adopted a profit-raising program."

As Guglielmo and Malle once again correctly point out, if the bidirectional model of intentionality were correct, one would expect participants to select the first and second action descriptions as the most accurate. However, as was the case in the earlier study, only a minority of participants found these to be the "most accurate descriptions." In fact, the first two descriptions were selected as either the most or second most accurate by only 16 percent of the participants. Conversely, 83 percent of the participants deemed the fourth action description to be either the most or the second most accurate, while 20 percent selected the third description. In short, the results of this study provide evidence that "when people were asked to indicate which action the CEO performed intentionally, they showed striking agreement: He intentionally adopted a profit-raising program that he knew would harm the environment; he did not intentionally harm the environment" (ibid.). Guglielmo and Malle believe these findings lay to rest the bidirectional model of intentionality favored by Knobe and others. On their view, participants in earlier studies only judged that the CEO harmed the environment intentionally because they were forced to give a dichotomous intentionality judgment. However, once participants are given more choices, their intuitions no longer seem to provide any evidence for the bidirectional model. On the surface, these new findings admittedly pose a serious challenge to the Knobe effect. However, I don't think things are as straightforward as Guglielmo and Malle have assumed. By my lights, more work needs to be done before they "disconfirm" the claim that moral considerations sometimes influence folk ascriptions of intentional action.

Perhaps the biggest shortcoming of Guglielmo and Malle's new studies is that they don't actually directly test the Knobe effect. To see why, keep in mind that Knobe's key finding was that participants' intuitions were different in the harm condition than they were in the help condition—that is, participants judged bad side effects to be more intentional than good side effects. In order to fully explain away these findings, Guglielmo and Malle would have needed to include both harm and help conditions—something they failed to do. After all, even if their participants were admittedly less inclined than Knobe's participants to judge that the CEO harmed the environment intentionally, it is still possible that had they been presented with a help condition, their ratings of intentionality would have been even lower still. In short, Knobe's findings were relational. It wasn't just that participants in the harm condition overwhelmingly judged that the CEO intentionally harmed the environment. It was also that those in the help condition overwhelmingly judged that the CEO did not intentionally help the environment. To fully undermine this finding, Guglielmo and Malle would have needed to run both conditions.

Another worry arises with respect to the "multiple action description" method Guglielmo and Malle adopted. In short, just because participants did not select "intentionally harmed the environment" as the most accurate way of describing the CEO's behavior, it doesn't follow that they judged that the CEO did not harm the environment intentionally. All that follows is that participants thought it sounded more correct to state that the CEO knowingly harmed the environment. But insofar as knowing that doing x will bring about y is a necessary condition for intentionally bringing about y, it is unsurprising that participants may have deemed that it is more accurate to say that the CEO knowingly harmed the environment than it is to say that he intentionally harmed the environment. Consider, for instance, the following example: "Paige went to the beach to play volleyball. She ended up playing volleyball all afternoon." Now, imagine I gave you the following list of action descriptions and asked you to specify which one sounded the "most accurate":

1. "Paige willingly played volleyball."
2. "Paige knowingly played volleyball."
3. "Paige intentionally played volleyball."
4. "Paige purposely played volleyball."

If forced to select one of these as the most accurate, I suspect some people might judge that it sounds most accurate to say that she knowingly or willingly played volleyball. After all, both are presumably necessary conditions of intentionally or purposely playing volleyball. But this would not mean that they do not also think it is accurate to say that Paige played volleyball intentionally or purposely. Conversely, even if the majority of people selected "intentionally" (or "purposely") as the most accurate description of Paige's behavior, it wouldn't follow that they think it is in inaccurate to say that she played volleyball willingly and knowingly. By my lights, if one truly wanted to get at the salient intuitions in this case, one would need to provide participants with conjunctive choices as well such as:

5. "Paige willingly, knowingly, intentionally, and purposely played volleyball."

Had Guglielmo and Malle provided participants with both individuated and conjunctive action descriptions, they may very well have gotten results that were more in line with Knobe's earlier findings. But to the extent to which they failed to do so, they cannot rule out the possibility that participants judged that the CEO harmed the environment intentionally.

Of course, this criticism admittedly only applies to the first aforementioned study from Guglielmo and Malle. Their second study, on the other hand, is immune to this worry since it provides participants with precisely the kind of more fine-grained action descriptions I was lobbying for above. However, a closer look at the actual descriptions they used raises additional worries. To see why, consider once again the choices that were available to participants:

1. "The CEO intentionally harmed the environment."
2. "The CEO intentionally adopted an environment-harming program."
3. "The CEO intentionally adopted an environment-harming program and a profit-raising program."
4. "The CEO intentionally adopted a profit-raising program that he knew would harm the environment."
5. "The CEO intentionally adopted a profit-raising program."

By my lights, it is unsurprising that the majority of participants selected the third and fourth action descriptions as the most accurate since these contain more detailed and nuanced information than the other choices. As such, it doesn't follow from the fact that these were the two most popular choices that participants would not have judged that the CEO harmed the environment intentionally had they been provided with a more detailed description. In order to fully undermine the Knobe effect on this front, Guglielmo and Malle would have needed to provide participants with the option of selecting an "intentionally harmed the environment" action description that was just as detailed as the other lengthier choices. Consider, for instance, the following:

6. "The CEO intentionally adopted a profit-raising program that he knew would harm the environment. Hence, the CEO intentionally harmed the environment."

By providing participants with fine-grained action descriptions for the "knowingly but not intentionally" view without at the same time providing them with similarly fine-grained descriptions of the "knowingly and intentionally" view, Guglielmo and Malle may have unwittingly stacked the deck against the Knobe effect. As such, I believe that it is still too early in the day to proclaim a victory for the valence-neutral model of intentionality. Of course, determining whether the worries I have just raised about Guglielmo and Malle's studies are justified is an empirical affair.

Accordingly, I ran two new studies that were designed to put these worries to the test.

5   The Knobe Effect Revisited

Before I present my latest findings, I should first briefly summarize what I took to be the three main shortcomings of Guglielmo and Malle's aforementioned studies. First, they only used a harm condition rather than using both harm and help conditions. As such, they left open the possibility that participants could nevertheless have displayed the kind of asymmetrical intuitions identified earlier by Knobe. Second, the participants in Guglielmo and Malle's first study were given individuated action descriptions without also being given conjunctive action descriptions. As a result, it is quite possible that participants judged that the CEO harmed the environment intentionally even if they did not select this as the most accurate action description. Finally, the participants in Guglielmo and Malle's second study were given fine-grained action descriptions for the "knowingly but not intentionally" view but they were not provided with similarly fine-grained descriptions of the "knowingly and intentionally" view.

In light of these worries, I ran two new studies. In the first one, participants were 162 people who completed an online questionnaire.[11] Each participant was randomly assigned to one of two conditions—a harm condition (83 participants) or a help condition (79 participants). The two conditions were as follows:

The vice-president of a company went to the chairman of the board and said, "We are thinking of starting a new program. It will help us increase profits, but it will also harm [help] the environment." The chairman of the board answered, "I don't care at all about harming [helping] the environment. I just want to make as much profit as I can. Let's start the new program." They started the new program. Sure enough, the environment was harmed [helped].

This situation has certain ambiguities and leaves some questions open. How can we best describe what the CEO did? Please circle the number of the most accurate description:

1. The CEO intentionally adopted a profit-raising program that he knew would harm [help] the environment. Since he knew the program would harm [help] the environment and he intentionally adopted the program, the CEO intentionally harmed [helped] the environment.
2. The CEO intentionally adopted a profit-raising program that he knew would harm [help] the environment. Even though he knew the program would harm [help]

the environment and he intentionally adopted the program, the CEO did not intentionally harm [help] the environment.

In the harm condition, 77 percent of the participants judged that the CEO intentionally harmed the environment whereas only 23 percent judged that he did not intentionally harm the environment. In the help condition, on the other hand, only 19 percent of the participants judged that the CEO intentionally helped the environment whereas 81 percent judged that he did not intentionally help the environment. These results—which are in line with Knobe's earlier results—are statistically significant ($p < 0.01$, FET).

On the surface, these findings put pressure on the explanation of Knobe's studies put forward by Guglielmo and Malle. After all, on their view, people find it most natural to say that the CEO harmed the environment knowingly but not intentionally. However, at least with respect to this first study, participants were far more likely to judge that the CEO knowingly and intentionally *harmed* the environment than they were to say that he knowingly but did not intentionally harm it. Conversely, participants were far more likely to say that the CEO knowingly but did not intentionally *help* the environment than they were to say that he intentionally helped it. These results are precisely what one would expect based on the earlier side-effect studies run by Knobe and others.

Of course, one might worry that I may have unwittingly stacked the cards in favor of the Knobe effect given the specific wording of the two choices. For instance, in the harm condition, the first answer actually *explains* why one might deem the side effect intentional—namely, the CEO intentionally adopted a program that he knew would harm the environment. The second answer, on the other hand, did not provide participants with the reason why one might judge that the CEO did *not* intentionally harm the environment—namely, that he did not intend to do so. Instead, the second option once again provided participants *with the same reason for deeming the side effect intentional* that the first option provided. By my lights, this is a legitimate concern. Consequently, I ran another study that was designed to correct for it.

In the second study, participants were 130 people who completed an online questionnaire.[12] Each was randomly assigned to one of two conditions—a harm condition (59 participants) or a help condition (71 participants). Once again, the wording of the two respective vignettes—which were based on the original Knobe CEO studies—was the same but for the moral valence of the outcome. The two conditions were as follows:

The vice-president of a company went to the chairman of the board and said, "We are thinking of starting a new program. It will help us increase profits, but it will also harm [help] the environment." The chairman of the board answered, "I don't care at all about harming [helping] the environment. I just want to make as much profit as I can. Let's start the new program." They started the new program. Sure enough, the environment was harmed [helped].

This situation has certain ambiguities and leaves some questions open. How can we best describe what the CEO did? Please circle the number of the most accurate description:

1. The CEO intentionally adopted a profit-raising program that he knew would harm [help] the environment. Since he knew the program would harm [help] the environment and he intentionally adopted the program, the CEO intentionally harmed [helped] the environment.
2. The CEO intentionally adopted a profit-raising program that he knew would harm [help] the environment. But since he did not intend to harm [help] the environment, the CEO did not intentionally harm [help] the environment.

In the harm condition, 88 percent of the participants judged that the CEO intentionally harmed the environment whereas only 12 percent of the participants judged that the CEO did not intentionally harm the environment. In the help condition, on the other hand, only 25 percent judged that the CEO intentionally helped the environment whereas 75 percent judged that the CEO did not intentionally help the environment. Once again these results—which are statistically significant ($p < 0.01$, FET)—are perfectly in line with Knobe's earlier findings. Moreover, they put further pressure on the explanation of the Knobe effect that was put forward by Guglielmo and Malle.

Keep in mind that on their view, when participants are provided with the option of saying that the CEO knowingly harmed the environment but neither intended nor intentionally harmed it, they will not judge that the CEO harmed the environment intentionally. However, in my second study, participants were provided with both options but they nevertheless overwhelmingly preferred to say that the CEO both knowingly and intentionally harmed the environment. As such, it is unclear that Guglielmo and Malle have accomplished their goal of shielding the standard unidirectional view from Knobe's side-effect findings. Indeed, in both of my two latest studies, participants' responses provide new support for the bidirectional view while further challenging both the simple view and the causal theory of action. In light of these latest findings, I minimally believe that I have shown that more work still needs to be done before either side in this ongoing debate can claim a decisive victory. As it stands, I believe that the puzzling nature of the Knobe effect remains something that needs to be either further explained or further explained away.

That being said, it is worth mentioning that there are several lingering shortcomings with my two latest studies. First, as Guglielmo and Malle point out, nearly all of the studies on the folk concept of intentionality that have been run thus far share the limitation of using a vignette design. Mine are no different in this respect. I find their suggestion of using mock jury designs and visual stimuli very intriguing. The results of these kinds of studies would obviously shed important new light on the nature of folk intentionality judgments. Second, I did not collect data on the cognitive timing of my participants' responses to the vignettes. Guglielmo and Malle are apparently already running some reaction time studies, and I very much look forward to seeing the fruits of their labors. Finally, and most importantly, my studies admittedly did not address the "pro-attitude" hypothesis put forward by Guglielmo and Malle to partly explain the harm–help asymmetry. On their view, not caring about harming the environment is not on par with not caring about helping it. I entirely agree. Indeed, I voiced the same worry about Knobe's original vignettes in Nadelhoffer 2004b. However, for present purposes, my main goal was to test Guglielmo and Malle's "knowingly but not intentionally" explanation of the Knobe effect. Further testing their "pro-attitude" hypothesis is a task for another day. Hopefully, psychologists and philosophers will continue to work together on these issues in an effort to better understand the nature of our intuitions and beliefs concerning intentional action.

6   Conclusion

In this chapter, I set out to provide an overview of one of the more hotly contested recent debates in the philosophy of action. More specifically, I wanted to show that Guglielmo and Malle's recent attempt to lay the Knobe effect to rest falls short even if they have admittedly taught us many important lessons along the way. By my lights, it is clear that they have thrown down the gauntlet in defense of the standard model of intentionality (and the causal theory of action more generally). Their studies are both more sophisticated and powerful than the previous research that has been done on this front. As such, any subsequent work on the folk concept of intentional action must carefully take Guglielmo and Malle's insightful findings into account. Unfortunately, I was admittedly only able to scratch the surface of their research in this chapter. In the future, I hope to give their work the further attention it deserves. For now, I have merely tried to take a few small steps toward better understanding the still puzzling nature of the folk concept of intentionality. Whether people think I pushed the debate forward or backward remains to be seen.

Notes

1. One of the paradigmatic papers defending this view is Davidson 1963/1980.

2. In this chapter, when I use the term "intentionality" I am using it as shorthand for "intentional action." My usage is not to be confused with Brentano's notion of intentionality as the mind's "direction towards an object" (Brentano 1874) even if the two are admittedly related in some respects.

3. Though it need not ultimately concern us here, it is nevertheless worth pointing out that Guglielmo and Malle misconstrue Knobe's position throughout their work. In short, Knobe claims that the *badness* of the action—but not the *blameworthiness* of the agent—sometimes influences people's intentionality judgments. Moreover, he does not think that this influence ought to be viewed as a bias. Rather, Knobe claims that the folk concept of intentionality has an inherent moral component that gets implicated when people use the concept competently. My view, on the other hand, is that (a) blameworthiness as well as moral badness can influence folk ascriptions of intentional action, and (b) this influence represents an affectively driven bias or performance error. As such, Guglielmo and Malle (n.d.a) mistakenly lump our views together when they claim that we both believe that "intentionality judgments are biased by evaluative considerations, in particular by feelings or judgments of blame." In light of this mistake, many of their objections to Knobe's view are more directly objections to my own. As such, some of the evidence that they provide against what they call the "blame→intentionality" view fails to undermine Knobe's view even if this evidence admittedly puts pressure on mine. By my lights, the only general way to refer to both Knobe's view and my own without obscuring important differences between the two is to say that we both believe that moral considerations sometimes influence folk judgments of intentionality. Which moral considerations have this effect and whether this influence represents a bias or mistake are issues that are hotly disputed.

4. Two points of clarification are in order at this point. First, just because I think that data concerning folk intuitions are relevant to *some* philosophical debates—e.g., free will—it does not follow that I believe that these data are relevant to *all* philosophical debates—e.g., mereology. Second, just because I think that folk intuitions are *relevant* to some philosophical problems, it does not follow that I believe they *solve* these problems. To my knowledge, no experimental philosopher tries to move from "the folk think that *x* is the case" to "*x* is the case." Instead, to the extent that the folk intuitions are philosophically relevant, they serve as starting points and constraints to philosophical investigation and not final arbiters of philosophical truth.

5. For an overview of recent work in experimental philosophy, see Nadelhoffer and Nahmias 2007. For now, it is worth pointing out that the boundary between experimental philosophy and social psychology is admittedly blurry. This is partly because some scientists are interested in the same kind of intuitions that interest philosophers, and they, too, discuss the philosophical implications of their research—see, e.g., Carlsmith and Darley 2008; Damasio 1994; Darley, Carlsmith, and Robinson 2000; Greene 2003, 2007; Haidt 2001, 2003; Hauser 2006; Malle 2001, 2006; Nisbett 2003; Nisbett and Ross 1980; Wegner 2002. Because "experimental philosophy" is perhaps best viewed as a family resemblance term, trying to explicate the movement in terms of necessary and jointly sufficient conditions would be wrongheaded even if well intentioned.

6. See, e.g., Adams and Steadman 2004a,b; Cushman and Mele 2008; Feltz and Cokely 2007; Hindriks 2008; Knobe 2003a,b, 2004a,b), 2005a,b; Knobe and Burra 2006a,b; Knobe and Mendlow 2004; Leslie, Knobe, and Cohen 2006; Machery 2008; Malle 2001, 2006; Malle and Knobe 1997; Mallon 2008; McCann 2006; Meeks 2004; Nadelhoffer 2004a,b,c, 2005, 2006a,b,c; Nado forthcoming; Nanay forthcoming; Nichols and Ulatowski 2007; Phelan and Sarkissian 2008, 2009; Turner 2004; Wiland 2007; Wright and Bengson 2009; Young et al. 2006.

7. Indeed, McCann has actually run some studies of his own on the folk concept of intentional action (McCann 2006). For my response to his interpretation of the data he collected, see Nadelhoffer 2006c.

8. See, e.g., Mele 1992; Mele and Moser 1994; Mele and Sverdlik 1996; and Malle and Knobe 1997.

9. For two recent overviews of the action theory literature in experimental philosophy, see Feltz 2008 and Nado forthcoming.

10. Proponents of this view defend it on a number of grounds. First and foremost, the simple view purportedly captures our pretheoretical intuitions and coheres with our ordinary usage of the concepts of intending and intentional action (McCann 1998, 210). After all, in ordinary contexts it would admittedly sound strange for me to say that I dialed my friend's phone number intentionally even though I did not intend to do so. Second, given that the SV is the seemingly uncontroversial claim that *intending* to x is necessary for *intentionally* x-ing, the view has the virtue of being, well, simple or "uncluttered" (Adams 1986a, 284). Third, it "gives us reason to believe that our intentions causally guide our actions in virtue of their content" (ibid.)—thereby supporting our ordinary view of ourselves whereby the contents of our intentions to x play an important role in our intentionally x-ing.

11. Participants were recruited via this Web site: http://www.philosophical-personality.com/.

12. Participants were recruited via this Web site: http://www.philosophical-personality.com/.

References

Ackrill, J. 1978. Aristotle on action. *Mind* 87:595–601.

Adams, F. Manuscript. Embodied cognition.

Adams, F. 1986a. Intention and intentional action: The simple view. *Mind and Language* 1:281–301.

Adams, F. 1986b. Feedback about feedback: Reply to Ehring. *Southern Journal of Philosophy* 24:123–131.

Adams, F. 1994a. Of epicycles and elegance. *Canadian Journal of Philosophy* 24:627–636.

Adams, F. 1994b. Trying, desire, and desiring to try. *Canadian Journal of Philosophy* 24:613–626.

Adams, F. 1997. Cognitive trying. In *Contemporary Action Theory*, vol. 1, ed. G. Holmstrom-Hintikka and R. Tuomela. Dodrecht: Kluwer.

Adams, F. 2003a. Thoughts and their contents: Naturalized semantics. In *The Blackwell Guide to the Philosophy of Mind*, ed. T. Warfied and S. Stich. Oxford: Blackwell.

Adams, F. 2003b. The informational turn in philosophy. *Minds and Machines* 13:471–501.

Adams, F. 2007. Trying with the hope. In *Rationality and the Good*, ed. M. Timmons, J. Greco, and A. Mele. Oxford: Oxford University Press.

Adams, F., and K. Aizawa. 2008. *The Bounds of Cognition*. Oxford: Blackwell.

Adams, F., Barker, J., and J. Figurelli. Manuscript. Towards closure on closure.

Adams, F., and A. Mele. 1989. The role of intention in intentional action. *Canadian Journal of Philosophy* 19:511–532.

Adams, F., and A. Mele. 1992. The intention/volition debate. *Canadian Journal of Philosophy* 22:323–338.

Adams, F., and A. Steadman. 2004a. Intentional action in ordinary language: Core concept or pragmatic understanding. *Analysis* 74:173–181.

Adams, F., and A. Steadman. 2004b. Intentional actions and moral considerations: Still pragmatic. *Analysis* 74:264–267.

Aguilar, J. 2007. Interpersonal interactions and the bounds of agency. *Dialectica* 61:219–232.

Aguilar, J., and A. Buckareff. 2009. Agency, consciousness, and executive control. *Philosophia* 37:21–30.

Alvarez, M. 2005. Agents, actions, and reasons. *Philosophical Books* 46:45–58.

Alvarez, M., and J. Hyman. 1998. Agents and their actions. *Philosophy* 73:219–245.

Annas, J. 1978. How basic are basic actions? *Proceedings of the Aristotelian Society* 78:195–213.

Anscombe, G. E. M. 1963. *Intention*. Ithaca, N.Y.: Cornell University Press.

Anscombe, G. E. M. 1966. A note on Mr. Bennett. *Analysis* 26:208.

Anscombe, G. E. M. 1989. Von Wright on practical inference. In *The Philosophy of Georg Henrik Von Wright*, P. A. Schilpp and L. E. Hahn, eds., La Salle, Ill.: Open Court. Reprinted in *Human Life, Action, and Ethics*, ed. M. Geach and L. Gormally (Exeter: Imprint Academic, 2005).

Apperly, I. A., and S. A. Butterfill. 2008. Do humans have two systems to track beliefs and belief-like states? Unpublished manuscript, Department of Psychology, University of Birmingham, UK.

Aquinas, T. 1999. *On Human Nature*. Ed. T. Hibbs. Indianapolis: Hackett.

Aristotle. 1934. *The Nicomachean Ethics with an English Translation by H. Rackham*. Cambridge, Mass.: Harvard University Press.

Aristotle. 1978. *De motu animalium*. Trans. M. Nussbaum. Princeton: Princeton University Press.

Aristotle. 1983. *Physics*, Books III and IV. Trans. E. Hussey. Oxford: Oxford University Press.

Aristotle. 1999. *Nicomachean Ethics*. Trans. T. Irwin. Indianapolis: Hackett.

Armstrong, D. 1973. Acting and trying. *Philosophical Papers* 2:1–15. Reprinted in Armstrong 1980.

Armstrong, D. 1975. Beliefs and desires as causes of actions: A reply to Donald Davidson. *Philosophical Papers* 4:1–8.

Armstrong, D. M. 1978. *A Theory of Universals: Universals and Scientific Realism*, vol. 2. Cambridge: Cambridge University Press.

Armstrong, D. 1980. *The Nature of Mind*. Ithaca, N.Y.: Cornell University Press.

Armstrong, D. 1983. *What Is a Law of Nature?* Cambridge: Cambridge University Press.

Armstrong, D. 1997. *A World of States of Affairs*. New York: Cambridge University Press.

Armstrong, D. 1999. The open door: Counterfactual versus singularist theories of causation. In *Causation and Laws of Nature*, ed. H. Stanken. London: Kluwer Academic.

Astington, J. W. 1999. The language of intention: Three ways of doing it. In *Developing Theories of Intention: Social Understanding and Self-Control*, ed. P. D. Zelazo, J. W. Astington, and D. R. Olson. Mahwah, N.J.: Erlbaum.

Astington, J. W. 2001. The paradox of intention: Assessing children's metarepresentational understanding. In *Intentions and Intentionality: Foundations of Social Cognition*, ed. B. F. Malle, L. J. Moses, and D. A. Baldwin. Cambridge, Mass.: MIT Press.

Audi, R. 1993. Intending. In his *Action, Intention, and Reason*. Ithaca, N.Y.: Cornell University Press.

Baron-Cohen, S. 1992. Out of sight or out of mind? Another look at deception in autism. *Journal of Child Psychology and Psychiatry, and Allied Disciplines* 33:1141–1155.

Barsalou, L. 1999. Perceptual symbols systems. *Behavioral and Brain Sciences* 22:577–660.

Bartsch, K., M. D. Campbell, and G. L. Troseth. 2007. Why else does Jenny run? Young children's extended psychological explanations. *Journal of Cognition and Development* 8:33–61.

Bartsch, K., and H. M. Wellman. 1995. *Children Talk about the Mind*. Oxford: Oxford University Press.

Beebee, H. 2004. Causing and nothingness. In *Causation and Counterfactuals*, ed. J. Collins, N. Hall, and L. A. Paul. Cambridge, Mass.: MIT Press.

Bedau, M., and P. Humphreys, eds. 2008. *Emergence: Contemporary Readings in the Philosophy of Science*. Cambridge, Mass.: MIT Press.

Belousov, B. P. 1959. A periodic reaction and its mechanism. *Compilation of Abstracts on Radiation Medicine* 147:145.

Bennett, D. 1965. Action, reason, and purpose. *Journal of Philosophy* 62:85–96.

Bennett, J. 1988. *Events and Their Names*. Indianapolis: Hackett.

Bennett, J. 1995. *The Act Itself*. Oxford: Clarendon Press.

Bennett, J. 2008. Accountability (II). In *Free Will and Reactive Attitudes: Perspectives on P. F. Strawson's "Freedom and Resentment,"* ed. M. McKenna and P. Russell. Farnham: Ashgate Press.

Bentham, J. 1996. *An Introduction to the Principles of Morals and Legislation.* Ed. J. H. Burns and H. L. A. Hart. Oxford: Clarendon Press.

Berthoz, A., and J. L. Petit. 2006. *Phenomenologie et physiologie de l'action.* Paris: Odile Jacob.

Bishop, J. 1989. *Natural Agency: An Essay on the Causal Theory of Action.* Cambridge: Cambridge University Press.

Bishop, J. 2003. Prospects for a naturalist libertarianism: O'Connor's *Persons and Causes. Philosophy and Phenomenological Research* 66:228–243.

Bishop, J. 2007. *Believing by Faith: An Essay in the Epistemology and Ethics of Religious Belief.* Oxford: Clarendon Press.

Bittner, R. 2001. *Doing Things for Reasons.* New York: Oxford University Press.

Blackburn, S. 1998. *Ruling Passions.* Oxford: Oxford University Press.

Borghi, A. 2005. Object concepts and action. In *Grounding Cognition,* ed. D. Pecher and R. Zwaan. Cambridge: Cambridge University Press.

Brand, M. 1971. The language of not doing. *American Philosophical Quarterly* 8:45–53.

Brand, M. 1984. *Intending and Acting: Toward a Naturalized Action Theory.* Cambridge, Mass.: MIT Press.

Bratman, M. 1984. Two faces of intention. *Philosophical Review* 93:375–405.

Bratman, M. 1987. *Intention, Plans, and Practical Reason.* Cambridge, Mass.: Harvard University Press.

Bratman, M. 2000. Reflection, planning, and temporally extended agency. *Philosophical Review* 109:35–61.

Bratman, M. 2001. Two problems about human agency. *Proceedings of the Aristotelian Society* 101:309–332.

Brentano, F. 1874. *Psychologie vom empirischen Standpunkt.* Leipzig: Duncker & Humblot.

Brentano, F. 1995. *Psychology from an Empirical Standpoint.* London: Routledge.

Brooks, R. 1991. Intelligence without representation. *Artificial Intelligence* 47:139–159.

Buccino, G., L. Riggio, G. Melli, F. Binkofski, V. Gallese, and G. Rizzolati. 2005. Listening to action-related sentences modulates the activity of the motor system: A combined TMS and behavioral study. *Brain Research. Cognitive Brain Research* 24:355–363.

Buckareff, A. 2007. Mental overpopulation and mental action: Protecting intentions from mental birth control. *Canadian Journal of Philosophy* 37:49–66.

Buckareff, A., and J. Zhu. 2009. The primacy of the mental in the explanation of human action. *Disputatio* 3(26):73–88.

Byrd, J. 2007. Moral responsibility and omissions. *Philosophical Quarterly* 57:56–67.

Campbell, J. 2002. *Reference and Consciousness*. Oxford: Oxford University Press.

Campbell, J. 2007. An interventionist approach to causation in psychology. In *Causal Learning*, ed. A. Gopnik and L. Schulz. Oxford: Oxford University Press.

Care, N. S., and C. Landesman, eds. 1968. *Readings in the Theory of Action*. Bloomington, Ind.: Indiana University Press.

Carey, B. 2008. Anticipating the future to "see" the present. *New York Times*. June 10.

Carlsmith, K., and J. Darley. 2008. Psychological aspects of retributive justice. *Advances in Experimental Social Psychology* 40:193–236.

Carpenter, M., J. Call, and M. Tomasello. 2002. A new false belief test for 36-month-olds. *British Journal of Developmental Psychology* 20:393–420.

Chan, D. 1995. Non-intentional actions. *American Philosophical Quarterly* 32:139–151.

Charles, D. 1984. *Aristotle's Philosophy of Action*. London: Duckworth.

Chasiotis, A., F. Kiessling, J. Hofer, and D. Campos. 2006. Theory of mind and inhibitory control in three cultures: Conflict inhibition predicts false belief understanding in Germany, Costa Rica, and Cameroon. *International Journal of Behavioral Development* 30:249–260.

Child, W. 1994. *Causality, Interpretation, and the Mind*. Oxford: Clarendon Press.

Chisholm, R. 1964. The descriptive element in the concept of action. *Journal of Philosophy* 61:613–625.

Chisholm, R. 1966. Freedom and action. In *Freedom and Determinism*, ed. K. Lehrer. New York: Random House.

Clark, A. 1997. *Being There: Putting Brain, Body, and World Together Again*. Cambridge, Mass.: MIT Press.

Clark, A., and R. Grush. 1999. Towards a cognitive robotics. *Adaptive Behavior* 7:5–16.

Clarke, R. 1994. Ability and responsibility for omissions. *Philosophical Studies* 73:195–208.

Clarke, R. 2010. Intentional omissions. *Noûs* 44:158–177.

Clements, W. A., and J. Perner. 1994. Implicit understanding of belief. *Cognitive Development* 9:377–397.

Collins, J., N. Hall, and L. A. Paul, eds. 2004. *Causation and Counterfactuals*. Cambridge, Mass.: MIT Press.

Coope, U. 2004. Aristotle's account of agency in *Physics* III.3. *Boston Area Colloquium in Ancient Philosophy* 20:201–221.

Coope, U. 2007. Aristotle on action. *Proceedings of the Aristotelian Society (suppl. vol.)* 81:109–138.

Csibra, G., and G. Gergely. 1998. The teleological origins of mentalistic action explanations: A developmental hypothesis. *Developmental Science* 1:255–259.

Cushman, F., and A. Mele. 2008. Intentional action: Two-and-a-half folk concepts? In *Experimental Philosophy*, ed. J. Knobe and S. Nichols. New York: Oxford University Press.

Damasio, A. 1994. *Descartes' Error: Emotion, Reason, and the Human Brain*. London: Penguin.

Dancy, J. 2000. *Practical Reality*. Oxford: Oxford University Press.

Danto, A. C. 1963. What we can do. *Journal of Philosophy* 60:434–445.

Darley, J., K. Carlsmith, and P. Robinson. 2000. Incapacitation and just deserts as motives for punishment. *Law and Human Behavior* 24:659–683.

Davidson, D. 1963. Actions, reasons, and causes. *Journal of Philosophy* 60:685–700. Reprinted in Davidson 1980.

Davidson, D. 1967. Causal relations. *Journal of Philosophy* 64. Reprinted in Davidson 1980.

Davidson, D. 1971. Agency. In *Agent, Action, and Reason*, ed. R. Binkley et al. Toronto: University of Toronto Press. Reprinted in Davidson 1980.

Davidson, D. 1973. Freedom to act. In *Essays on Freedom of Action*, ed. Ted Honderich. London: Routledge & Kegan Paul. Reprinted in Davidson 1980.

Davidson, D. 1976. Hempel on explaining action. *Erkenntnis* 10(3). Reprinted in Davidson 1980.

Davidson, D. 1978. Intending. In *Philosophy of History and Action*, ed. Y. Yovel. Dordrecht: D. Reidel. Reprinted in Davidson 1980.

Davidson, D. 1980. *Essays on Actions and Events*. Oxford: Oxford University Press.

Davidson, D. 1985. Reply to Bruce Vermazen. In *Essays on Davidson*, ed. B. Vermazen and M. Hintikka. New York: Oxford University Press.

Davidson, D. 1987. Problems in the explanation of action. In *Metaphysics and Morality: Essays in Honour of J. J. C. Smart*, ed. P. Pettit, R. Sylvan, and J. Norman. Oxford: Blackwell. Reprinted in Davidson 2004.

Davidson, D. 2001a. *Essays on Actions and Events*, 2nd ed. Oxford: Oxford University Press.

Davidson, D. 2001b. The emergence of thought. In his *Subjective, Intersubjective, Objective*. Oxford: Oxford University Press.

Davidson, D. 2004. *Problems of Rationality*. Oxford: Clarendon Press.

Dennett, D. C. 1979. *Brainstorms: Philosophical Essays on Mind and Psychology*. Hassocks, Sussex: Harvester Press.

Dennett, D. C., and K. Lambert. 1978. *The Philosophical Lexicon*. Privately printed.

Doherty, M. J. 2009. *Theory of Mind: How Children Understand Others' Thoughts and Feelings*. Hove: Psychology Press.

Donagan, A. 1987. *Choice: The Essential Element in Human Action*. London: Routledge.

Dowe, P. 2000. *Physical Causation*. Cambridge: Cambridge University Press.

Dretske, F. 1981. *Knowledge and the Flow of Information*. Cambridge, Mass.: MIT Press.

Dretske, F. 1988. *Explaining Behavior: Reasons in a World of Causes*. Cambridge, Mass.: MIT Press.

Duff, A. 2004. Action, the act requirement, and criminal liability. In *Agency and Action*, ed. J. Hyman and H. Steward. Cambridge: Cambridge University Press.

Earley, J. 1981. Self-organization and agency: In chemistry and process philosophy. *Process Studies* 11:242–258.

Ellis, G. F. R. 2007. On the nature of causation in complex systems. *Royal Society of South Africa*. http://www.sabinet.co.za/abstracts/royalsa/royalsa_v63_n1_a6.xm.

Enç, B. 2003. *How We Act: Causes, Reasons, and Intentions*. Oxford: Oxford University Press.

Enç, B., and F. Adams. 1992. Functions and goal-directedness. *Philosophy of Science* 59:635–654.

Farahany, N. 2009. The interface between freedom and agency. *Stanford Technology Review*. http://www.stlr.stanford.edu.

Feinberg, J. 1984. *Harm to Others: The Moral Limits of the Criminal Law*, vol. 1. New York: Oxford University Press.

Feltz, A. 2008. The Knobe effect: A brief overview. *Journal of Mind and Behavior* 28:265–278.

Feltz, A., and E. Cokely. 2007. An anomaly in intentional action ascription: More evidence of volk diversity. In *Proceedings of the 29th Annual Meeting of Cognitive Science Society*, ed. D. S. McNamara and G. Trafton. Mahwah, N.J.: Lawrence Erlbaum.

Fine, K. 1982. First order modal theories III—Facts. *Synthese* 53:43–122.

Fischer, J. M. 1985–1986. Responsibility and failure. *Proceedings of the Aristotelian Society* 86:251–270.

Fischer, J. M., and M. Ravizza. 1998. *Responsibility and Control: A Theory of Moral Responsibility*. Cambridge: Cambridge University Press.

Fletcher, G. 1994. On the moral irrelevance of bodily movements. *University of Pennsylvania Law Review* 142:1443–1453.

Frankfurt, H. 1969. Alternate possibilities and moral responsibility. *Journal of Philosophy* 66: 829–839. Reprinted in Frankfurt 1988.

Frankfurt, H. 1978. The problem of action. *American Philosophical Quarterly* 15: 157–162. Reprinted in Frankfurt 1988. Page numbers refer to the latter edition.

Frankfurt, H. 1988. *The Importance of What We Care About*. New York: Cambridge University Press.

Frankfurt, H. 1998. *Necessity, Volition, and Love*. New York: Cambridge University Press.

Freeland, C. 1985. Aristotelian actions. *Noûs* 19:397–414.

Freeman, W. 1991. The physiology of perception. *Scientific American* (February):78–85.

Gaillard, R. 2009. "Consciousness signature" discovered spanning the brain. *New Scientist* 21:7.

Gaillard, R., S. Dehaene, C. Adam, S. Clémenceau, D. Hasboun, et al. 2009. Converging intracranial markers of conscious access. *PLoS Biology* 7:472–492.

Gallagher, S. 2005. *How the Body Shapes the Mind*. Oxford: Oxford University Press.

Gallagher, S. 2008. Are minimal representations still representations? *International Journal of Philosophical Studies* 16:351–369.

Gallese, V., L. Fadiga, L. Fogassi, and G. Rizzolati. 1996. Action recognition in premotor cortex. *Brain* 119:593–609.

Gatlin, L. 1972. *Information and the Living System*. New York: Columbia University Press.

Gibson, J. 1979. *The Ecological Approach to Visual Perception*. Boston: Houghton-Mifflin.

Ginet, C. 1990. *On Action*. Cambridge: Cambridge University Press.

Ginet, C. 2002. Reasons explanations of action: Causalist versus noncausalist accounts. In *The Oxford Handbook of Free Will*, ed. R. Kane. New York: Oxford University Press.

Ginet, C. 2004. Intentionally doing and intentionally not doing. *Philosophical Topics* 32:95–110.

Glenberg, A., and M. Kaschak. 2002. Grounding language in action. *Psychonomic Bulletin and Review* 9:558–565.

Goetz, S. 1988. A noncausal theory of agency. *Philosophy and Phenomenological Research* 49:303–316.

Goldman, A. 1970. *Theory of Human Action*. Englewood Cliffs, N.J.: Prentice-Hall.

Goldie, P. 2000. *The Emotions*. Oxford: Oxford University Press.

Goodale, M. 2004. Perceiving the world and grasping it: Dissociations between conscious and unconscious visual processing. In *The Cognitive Neurosciences III*, ed. M. Gazzaniga. Cambridge, Mass.: MIT Press.

Gopnik, A., and A. N. Meltzoff. 1997. *Word, Thoughts, and Theories*. Cambridge, Mass: MIT Press.

Goodale, M. A., and A. D. Milner. 1992. Separate visual pathways for perception and action. *Trends in Neurosciences* 15:20–25.

Gratch, G. 1964. Response alternation in children: A developmental study of orientations to uncertainty. *Vita Humana* 7:49–60.

Greene, J. 2003. From neural "is" to moral "ought": What are the moral implications of neuroscientific moral psychology? *Neuroscience* 4:847–850.

Greene, J. 2007. The secret joke of Kant's soul. In *Moral Psychology*, vol. 3: *The Neuroscience of Morality: Emotion, Disease, and Development*, ed. W. Sinnott-Armstrong. Cambridge, Mass.: MIT Press.

Grush, R. 1997. Yet another design for a brain? Review of Port and van Gelder (eds.), *Mind as Motion*. *Philosophical Psychology* 10:233–242.

Grush, R. 2004. The emulation theory of representation: Motor control, imagery, and perception. *Behavioral and Brain Sciences* 27:377–442.

Guglielmo, S. and B. F. Malle (n.d.a). Can unintended side effects be intentional? Solving a puzzle in people's judgments of intentionality and morality.

Guglielmo, S. and B. F. Malle (n.d.b). Enough skill to kill: Intentional control and the judgment of immoral actions. University of Oregon.

Haddock, A. 2005. At one with our actions, but at two with our bodies: Hornsby's account of action. *Philosophical Explorations* 8:157–172.

Haggard, P., and M. Elmer. 1999. On the relations between brain potentials and the awareness of voluntary movements. *Experimental Brain Research* 126:128–133.

Haidt, J. 2001. The emotional dog and its rational tail: A social intuitionist approach to moral judgment. *Psychological Review* 108:814–834.

Haidt, J. 2003. The emotional dog does learn new tricks: A reply to Pizarro and Bloom. *Psychological Review* 110:197–198.

Hall, L., and P. Johansson. 2009. Choice blindness: You don't know what you want. *New Scientist* 18:26–27.

Hall, N. 2004. Two concepts of causation. In *Causation and Counterfactuals*, ed. J. Collins, N. Hall, and L. A. Paul. Cambridge, Mass.: MIT Press.

Happé, F., and E. Loth. 2002. "Theory of mind" and tracking speakers' intentions. *Mind and Language* 17:24–36.

Harman, G. 1976. Practical reasoning. *Review of Metaphysics* 79:431–463. Reprinted in Mele 1997.

Harnad, S. 1990. The symbol grounding problem. *Physica D. Nonlinear Phenomena* 42:335–346.

Hart, H. L. A., and A. Honoré. 1959. *Causation and the Law*. Oxford: Oxford University Press.

Hauk, O., I. Johnsrude, and F. Pulvermüeller. 2004. Somatatopic representation of action words in human motor and premotor cortex. *Neuron* 41:301–307.

Hauser, M. D. 2006. *Moral Minds*. New York: HarperCollins.

Haynes, J., K. Sakai, G. Rees, S. Gilbert, C. Frith, and R. E. Passingham. 2007. Reading hidden intentions in the human brain. *Current Biology* 17:323–328.

Hempel, C. G. 1961. Rational action. In *Proceedings and Addresses of the American Philosophical Association*, vol. 35. Reprinted in N. S. Care and C. Landesman 1968, 285–286.

Higginbotham, J. 2000. On events in linguistic semantics. In *Speaking of Events*, ed. J. Higginbotham, F. Pianesi, and A. Varzi. Oxford: Oxford University Press.

Hindriks, F. 2008. Intentional action and the praise–blame asymmetry. *Philosophical Quarterly* 58:630–641.

Hinton, G., and T. Shallice. 1991. Lesioning an attractor network: Investigations of acquired dyslexia. *Psychological Review* 98:74–95.

Hobbes, T. [1651] 1994. *Leviathan.* Indianapolis: Hackett.

Hobbes, T. [1654] 1999. Hobbes's Treatise *Of Liberty and Necessity.* In *Hobbes and Bramhall on Liberty and Necessity,* ed. V. Chappell. New York: Cambridge University Press.

Hobbes, T. [1656] 1999. Selections from Hobbes, *The Questions Concerning Liberty, Necessity, and Chance.* In *Hobbes and Bramhall on Liberty and Necessity,* ed. V. Chappell. New York: Cambridge University Press.

Holmes, O. W., Jr. 1963. *The Common Law.* Boston: Little, Brown.

Hornsby, J. 1980. *Actions.* London: Routledge & Kegan Paul.

Hornsby, J. 1993. Agency and causal explanation. In *Mental Causation,* ed. J. Heil and A. Mele. Oxford: Clarendon Press.

Hornsby, J. 1997. Postscript: A disjunctive conception of bodily movements. In J. Hornsby, *Simple Mindedness: Essays in Defence of Naïve Naturalism in the Philosophy of Mind,* 102–110. Cambridge, Mass.: Harvard University Press.

Hornsby, J. 2004. Agency and actions. In *Agency and Action,* ed. J. Hyman and H. Steward, 1–23. Cambridge: Cambridge University Press.

Hornsby, J. 2008. A disjunctive conception of acting for reasons. In *Disjunctivism,* ed. A. Haddock and F. Macpherson. Oxford: Oxford University Press.

Hughes, C., and J. Dunn. 1997. Pretend you didn't know: Preschoolers' talk about mental states in pretend play. *Cognitive Development* 12:381–403.

Hughes, C., and J. Dunn. 1998. Understanding mind and emotion: Longitudinal associations with mental-state talk between young friends. *Developmental Psychology* 34:1026–1037.

Hume, D. [1748] 2007. *An Enquiry Concerning Human Understanding.* Oxford: Oxford University Press.

Hume, D. [1777] 1975. *Enquiries Concerning Human Understanding and Concerning the Principles of Morals.* Oxford: Clarendon Press.

Humphreys, P. 1997. How properties emerge. *Philosophy of Science* 64:1–17. Reprinted in Bedau and Humphreys 2008.

Hursthouse, R. 1991. Arational actions. *Journal of Philosophy* 88:57–68.

Imbens-Bailey, A. L., J. H. Prost, and W. V. Fabricius. 1997. Perception, desire, and belief in me and you: Young children's reference to mental states in self and others. Paper presented at the Biennial Meeting of the Society for Research in Child Development, Washington, D.C., April 3–6, 1997.

Jackson, F. 1998. *From Metaphysics to Ethics: A Defense of Conceptual Analysis*. New York: Oxford University Press.

Jacob, P., and M. Jeannerod. 2003. *Ways of Seeing: The Scope and Limits of Visual Cognition*. Oxford: Oxford University Press.

James, W. [1890] 1981. *The Principles of Psychology*, vol. 2. Cambridge, Mass.: Harvard University Press.

James, W. 1956. The will to believe. In *The Will to Believe and Other Essays in Popular Philosophy, and Human Immortality*. New York: Dover.

Jeannerod, M. 1985. *The Brain Machine*. Cambridge, Mass.: Harvard University Press.

Jeannerod, M. 1997. *The Cognitive Neuroscience of Action*. Malden, Mass.: Blackwell.

Jeannerod, M. 2006. *Motor Cognition*. Oxford: Oxford University Press.

Johansson, P., L. Hall, S. Sikstrom, and A. Olsson. 2005. Failure to detect mismatches between intention and outcome in a simple decision task. *Science* 310:116–119.

Juarrero, A. 1999. *Dynamics in Action: Intentional Behavior as a Complex System*. Cambridge, Mass.: MIT Press.

Juarrero, A., and C. Rubino, eds. 2008. *Emergence, Complexity, and Self-Organization: Precursors and Prototypes*. Mansfield, Mass.: ISCE Publishing.

Juarrero-Roqué, A. 1983a. Dispositions, teleology, and reductionism. *Philosophical Topics* 12:153–165.

Juarrero-Roqué, A. 1983b. Does level-generation always generate act-tokens? *Philosophy Research Archives* 9:177–192.

Juarrero-Roqué, A. 1985. Kant's concept of teleology and modern chemistry. *Review of Metaphysics* 39:107–135.

Juarrero-Roqué, A. 1987–88. Does action theory rest on a mistake? *Philosophy Research Archives* 13:587–612.

Juarrero-Roqué, A. 1988. Non-linear phenomena, explanation, and action. *International Philosophical Quarterly* 28:247–255.

Kamm, F. 1994. Action, omission, and the stringency of duties. *University of Pennsylvania Law Review* 142:1492–1512.

Kane, R. 1996. *The Significance of Free Will*. Oxford: Oxford University Press.

Kant, I. 1980. *The Critique of Teleological Judgement*. Trans. J. C. Meredith. Oxford: Oxford University Press.

Kim, J. 1989. Mechanism, purpose, and explanatory exclusion. *Philosophical Perspectives* 3:77–108.

Kim, J. 1993. The non-reductivist's troubles with mental causation. In *Mental Causation*, ed. J. Heil and A. Mele. New York: Oxford University Press.

Kim, J. 1998. *Mind in a Physical World*. Cambridge, Mass.: MIT Press.

Kleinig, J. 1976. Good Samaritanism. *Philosophy and Public Affairs* 5:382–407.

Knobe, J. 2003a. Intentional action and side-effects in ordinary language. *Analysis* 63:190–193.

Knobe, J. 2003b. Intentional action in folk psychology: An experimental investigation. *Philosophical Psychology* 16:309–323.

Knobe, J. 2004a. Folk psychology and folk morality: Response to critics. *Journal of Theoretical and Philosophical Psychology* 24:270–279.

Knobe, J. 2004b. Intention, intentional action, and moral considerations. *Analysis* 64:181–187.

Knobe, J. 2005a. Theory of mind and moral cognition: Exploring the connections. *Trends in Cognitive Sciences* 9:357–359.

Knobe, J. 2005b. Cognitive processes shaped by the impulse to blame. *Brooklyn Law Review* 71:929–937.

Knobe, J., and A. Burra. 2006a. The folk concept of intention and intentional action: A cross-cultural study. *Journal of Cognition and Culture* 6:113–132.

Knobe, J., and A. Burra. 2006b. Experimental philosophy and folk concepts: Methodological considerations. *Journal of Cognition and Culture* 6:331–342.

Knobe, J., and G. Mendlow. 2004. The good, the bad, and the blameworthy: Understanding the role of evaluative reasoning in folk psychology. *Journal of Theoretical and Philosophical Psychology* 24:252–258.

Kukso, B. 2006. The reality of absences. *Australasian Journal of Philosophy* 84:21–37.

Ladd, J. 1965. The ethical dimension of the concept of action. *Journal of Philosophy* 62:633–645.

Landesman, C. 1965. The new dualism in the philosophy of mind. *Review of Metaphysics* 19:329–345.

Leslie, A., J. Knobe, and A. Cohen. 2006. Acting intentionally and the side-effect effect: "Theory of mind" and moral judgment. *Psychological Science* 17:421–427.

Lewis, D. 1973. Causation. *Journal of Philosophy* 70:556–567.

Lewis, D. 1980. Veridical hallucination and prosthetic vision. *Australasian Journal of Philosophy* 58:239–249.

Lewis, D. 1986. Causal explanation. In *Philosophical Papers*, vol. 2. New York: Oxford University Press.

Lewis, D. 2004. Void and object. In *Causation and Counterfactuals*, ed. J. Collins, N. Hall, and L. A. Paul. Cambridge, Mass.: MIT Press.

Libet, B. 1985. Unconscious cerebral initiative and the role of conscious will in voluntary action. *Behavioral and Brain Sciences* 8:529–539.

Libet, B. 2004. *Mind Time: The Temporal Factor in Consciousness*. Cambridge, Mass.: Harvard University Press.

Libet, B., C. A. Gleason, E. W. Wright, and D. K. Pearl. 1983. Time of conscious intention to act in relation to onset of cerebral activities (readiness potential): The unconscious initiation of a freely voluntary act. *Brain* 106:623–642.

Louch, A. R. 1966. *Explanation and Human Action*. Berkeley: University of California Press.

Lowe, E. J. 2008. *Personal Agency: The Metaphysics of Mind and Action*. New York: Oxford University Press.

Machery, E. 2008. The folk concept of intentional action: Philosophical and experimental issues. *Mind and Language* 23:165–189.

MacKay, D. 1981. Behavioral plasticity, serial order, and the motor program. *Behavioral and Brain Sciences* 4:630–631.

Mackie, J. L. 1974. *The Cement of the Universe: A Study of Causation*. Oxford: Clarendon Press.

Malle, B. 2001. Folk explanations and intentional action. In *Intentions and Intentionality: Foundations of Social Cognition*, ed. L. Moses, B. Malle, and D. Baldwin. Cambridge, Mass.: MIT Press.

Malle, B. 2004. *How the Mind Explains Behavior: Folk Explanations, Meaning, and Social Interaction*. Cambridge, Mass.: MIT Press.

Malle, B. 2006. Intentionality, morality, and their relationship in human judgment. *Journal of Cognition and Culture* 6:87–112.

Malle, B., and J. Knobe. 1997. The folk concept of intentional action. *Journal of Experimental Social Psychology* 33:101–121.

Mallon, R. 2008. Knobe vs. Machery: Testing the trade-off hypothesis. *Mind and Language* 23:247–255.

Mandik, P. 2005. Action-oriented representation. In *Cognition and the Brain*, ed. A. Brook and K. Akins. Cambridge: Cambridge University Press.

Martinich, A. P. 2005. *Hobbes*. New York: Routledge.

Mathis, S. 2003. A plea for omissions. *Criminal Justice Ethics* (spring–fall):15–31.

McCann, H. 1975. Trying, paralysis, and volition. *Review of Metaphysics* 28:423–442.

McCann, H. 1998. *The Works of Agency: On Human Action, Will and Freedom.* Ithaca: Cornell University Press.

McCann, H. 2006. Intentional action and intending: Recent empirical studies. *Philosophical Psychology* 18:737–748.

McDowell, J. 1982. Criteria, defeasibility, and knowledge. *Proceedings of the British Academy* 62:455–479.

McDowell, J. 1998. Functionalism and anomalous monism. In his *Mind, Value, and Reality.* Oxford: Oxford University Press.

McGinn, C. 1982. *The Character of Mind.* Oxford: Oxford University Press.

McGrath, S. 2005. Causation by omission: A dilemma. *Philosophical Studies* 123:125–148.

McIntyre, A. G. 1985. Omissions and other acts. Ph.D. Dissertation, Princeton University.

McIntyre, A. G. 1994. Compatibilists could have done otherwise. *Philosophical Review* 103:458–488.

Meeks, R. 2004. Unintentionally biasing the data: Reply to Knobe. *Journal of Theoretical and Philosophical Psychology* 24:220–223.

Melden, A. I. 1961. *Free Action.* London: Routledge.

Mele, A. 1981. The practical syllogism and deliberation in Aristotle's causal theory of action. *New Scholasticism* 55:281–316.

Mele, A. 1992. *Springs of Action: Understanding Intentional Behavior.* New York: Oxford University Press.

Mele, A. 1997a. Agency and mental action. *Philosophical Perspectives* 11:231–249.

Mele, A., ed. 1997b. *The Philosophy of Action.* Oxford: Oxford University Press.

Mele, A. 2001. Acting intentionally: Probing folk notions. In *Intentions and Intentionality: Foundations of Social Cognition,* ed. B. F. Malle, L. J. Moses, and D. A. Baldwin. Cambridge, Mass.: MIT Press.

Mele, A. 2003. *Motivation and Agency.* New York: Oxford University Press.

Mele, A. 2006. *Free Will and Luck.* Oxford: Oxford University Press.

Mele, A. 2007. Reasonology and false beliefs. *Philosophical Papers* 36:91–118.

Mele, A. 2009. *Effective Intentions: The Power of Conscious Will*. Oxford: Oxford University Press.

Mele, A., and P. Moser. 1994. Intentional action. *Noûs* 28:39–68.

Mele, A., and S. Sverdlik. 1996. Intention, intentional action, and moral responsibility. *Philosophical Studies* 82:265–287.

Mellor, D. H. 1995. *The Facts of Causation*. London: Routledge.

Meltzoff, A. 1995. Understanding the intentions of others: Re-enactment of intended acts by 18-month-old children. *Developmental Psychology* 31:838–850.

Meltzoff, A., and M. Moore. 1977. Imitation of facial and manual gestures by human neonates. *Science* 198:75–78.

Menzies, P. 1989. A unified account of causal relata. *Australasian Journal of Philosophy* 67:68–69.

Moll, H., and M. Tomasello. 2007. How 14- and 18-month-olds know what others have experienced. *Developmental Psychology* 43:309–317.

Molnar, G. 2003. *Powers: A Study in Metaphysics*. Oxford: Oxford University Press.

Moore, M. 1988. Mind, brain, and the unconscious. In *Mind, Science and Psychoanalysis*, ed. P. Clark and C. Wright. Oxford: Blackwell.

Moore, M. 1993. *Act and Crime: The Philosophy of Action and Its Implications for Criminal Law*. Oxford: Clarendon Press.

Moore, M. 1997. Intentions and mens rea. In M. Moore, *Placing Blame: A General Theory of the Criminal Law*. Oxford: Oxford University Press.

Moore, M. 2006. Intention, responsibility, and the challenges of recent neuroscience. In *Does Consciousness Cause Behavior?* ed. S. Pockett, W. P. Banks, and S. Gallagher. Cambridge, Mass.: MIT Press.

Moore, M. 2009a. *Causation and Responsibility: An Essay in Law, Morals, and Metaphysics*. Oxford: Oxford University Press.

Moore, M. 2009b. Intentions, responsibility, and the challenges of recent neuroscience. *Stanford Technology Review*. http://www.stlr.stanford.edu.

Moore, M. 2010. Intentions as a marker of moral culpability and legal punishment. In *The Philosophical Foundations of the Criminal Law*, ed. R. Duff and S. Green. Oxford: Oxford University Press.

Moore, M. Forthcoming. Consciousness, brain states, and the causal efficacy of intentions. In *Conscious Will and Responsibility: A Tribute to Benjamin Libet*, ed. L. Nadel and W. Sinnott-Armstrong. Oxford: Oxford University Press.

Moreno, A. 2008. Organization and evolution: The principle of dynamic decoupling. Paper delivered at Complejidad 2008: 4th Biennial Conference on the Philosophical, Epistemological, and Methodological Implications of Complexity Theory. Havana, Cuba.

Moya, C. 1990. *The Philosophy of Action.* Oxford: Polity.

Mumford, S. 2009. Passing powers around. *Monist* 92:94–111.

Nadelhoffer, T. 2004a. The butler problem revisited. *Analysis* 64:277–284.

Nadelhoffer, T. 2004b. Praise, side effects, and intentional action. *Journal of Theoretical and Philosophical Psychology* 24:196–213.

Nadelhoffer, T. 2004c. Blame, badness, and intentional action: A reply to Knobe and Mendlow. *Journal of Theoretical and Philosophical Psychology* 24:259–269.

Nadelhoffer, T. 2005. Skill, luck, control, and intentional action. *Philosophical Psychology* 18:343–354.

Nadelhoffer, T. 2006a. Bad acts, blameworthy agents, and intentional actions: Some problems for jury impartiality. *Philosophical Explorations* 9:203–220.

Nadelhoffer, T. 2006b. Foresight, moral considerations, and intentional actions. *Journal of Cognition and Culture* 6:133–158.

Nadelhoffer, T. 2006c. On trying to save the simple view. *Mind and Language* 21:565–586.

Nadelhoffer, T., and E. Nahmias. 2007. The past and future of experimental philosophy. *Philosophical Explorations* 10:123–149.

Nado, J. Forthcoming. Effects of moral cognition on judgments of intentionality. *British Journal for the Philosophy of Science.*

Nanay, B. Forthcoming. Morality or modality: What does the attribution of intentionality depend on? *Canadian Journal of Philosophy.*

Nichols, S., and J. Ulatowski. 2007. Intuitions and individual differences: The Knobe effect revisited. *Mind and Language* 22:346–365.

Nisbett, R. E. 2003. *The Geography of Thought: How Asians and Westerners Think Differently . . . and Why.* New York: Free Press.

Nisbett, R. E., and L. Ross. 1980. *Human Inference: Strategies and Shortcomings of Social Judgment.* Englewood Cliffs, N.J.: Prentice-Hall.

Noë, A. 2004. *Action in Perception.* Cambridge, Mass.: MIT Press.

O'Connor, T. 2002. *Persons and Causes: The Metaphysics of Free Will.* Oxford: Oxford University Press.

Onishi, K. H., and R. Baillargeon. 2005. Do 15-month-old infants understand false beliefs? *Science* 308:255–258.

Pacherie, E. 2006. Towards a dynamic theory of intentions. In *Does Consciousness Cause Behavior? An Investigation into the Nature of Volition*, ed. S. Pockett, W. P. Banks, and S. Gallagher. Cambridge, Mass.: MIT Press.

Pacherie, E. 2008. The phenomenology of action: A conceptual framework. *Cognition* 107:179–217.

Parfit, D. 1997. Reasons and motivation. *Proceedings of the Aristotelian Society (suppl. vol.)* 71:99–129.

Peacocke, C. 1979a. Deviant causal chains. *Midwest Studies in Philosophy* 4:123–155.

Peacocke, C. 1979b. *Holistic Explanation: Action, Space, Interpretation.* New York: Oxford University Press.

Pecher, D., and R. Zwaan, eds. 2005. *Grounding Cognition.* Cambridge: Cambridge University Press.

Perner, J. 2004. Wann verstehen Kinder Handlungen als rational? In *Der Mensch—ein "animal rationale"? Vernunft—Kognition—Intelligenz*, ed. H. Schmidinger and C. Sedmak. Darmstadt: Wissenschaftliche Buchgemeinschaft.

Perner, J., B. Lang, and D. Kloo. 2002. Theory of mind and self-control: More than a common problem of inhibition. *Child Development* 73:752–767.

Perner, J., B. Rendl, and A. Garnham. 2007. Objects of desire, thought, and reality: Problems of anchoring discourse referents in development. *Mind & Language* 22:475–517.

Perner, J., and T. Ruffman. 2005. Infants' insight into the mind: How deep? *Science* 308:214–216.

Perner, J., P. Zauner, and M. Sprung. 2005. What does "that" have to do with point of view? The case of conflicting desires and "want" in German. In *Why Language Matters for Theory of Mind*, ed. J. W. Astington and J. Baird. New York: Oxford University Press.

Peters, R. 1958. *The Concept of Motivation.* London: Routledge.

Peters, R. 1967. *Hobbes.* Harmondsworth: Penguin.

Phelan, M., and H. Sarkissian. 2008. The folk strike back: Or, Why you didn't do it intentionally, though it was bad and you knew it. *Philosophical Studies* 138:291–298.

Phelan, M., and H. Sarkissian. 2009. Is the "trade-off hypothesis" worth trading for? *Mind and Language* 24:164–180.

Pietroski, P. 2002. *Causing actions*. Oxford: Oxford University Press.

Pink, T. 1997. Reason and agency. *Proceedings of the Aristotelian Society* 97:263–280.

Pink, T. 2004. Suarez, Hobbes, and the Scholastic tradition in action theory. In *The Will and Human Action: From Antiquity to the Present Day*, ed. T. Pink and M. Stone. London: Routledge.

Povinelli, D. J., and S. deBlois. 1992. Young children's (*Homo sapiens*) understanding of knowledge formation in themselves and others. *Journal of Comparative Psychology* 106:228–238.

Price, A. 2004. Aristotle, the Stoics, and the will. In *The Will and Human Action: From Antiquity to the Present Day*, ed. T. Pink and M. Stone. London: Routledge.

Prichard, H. A. 1949. *Moral Obligations*. Oxford: Clarendon Press.

Rakoczy, H., F. Warneken, and M. Tomasello. 2007. "This way!," "No! that way!"— 3-year olds know that two people can have mutually incompatible desires. *Cognitive Development* 22:47–68.

Rakoczy, H., F. Warneken, and M. Tomasello. 2008. The sources of normativity: Young children's awareness of the normative structure of games. *Developmental Psychology* 44:875–881.

Raz, J. 1978. Introduction. In *Practical Reasoning*, ed. J. Raz. Oxford: Oxford University Press.

Reid, Thomas. [1788] 1983. *Essays on the Active Powers of Man*. In *The Works of Thomas Reid, D.D.*, ed. W. Hamilton. Hildesheim: G. Olms Verlagsbuchhandlung.

Reingold, E. M., and P. M. Merikle. 1993. Theory and measurement in the study of unconscious processes. In *Consciousness*, ed. M. Davies and G. W. Humphreys. Oxford: Blackwell.

Repacholi, B. M., and A. Gopnik. 1997. Early reasoning about desires: Evidence from 14- and 18-month-olds. *Developmental Psychology* 33:12–21.

Richardson-Klavehn, A., and R. A. Bjork. 1988. Measures of memory. *Annual Review of Psychology* 39:475–543.

Riley, M. A., and M. T. Turvey. 2001. The self-organizing dynamics of intentions and actions. *American Journal of Psychology* 114:160–169.

Rizzolati, G., L. Fadiga, V. Gallese, and L. Fogassi. 1996. Premotor cortex and the recognition of motor actions. *Brain Research: Cognitive Brain Research* 3:131–141.

Rocha, L. M. 2001. Evolution with material symbol systems. *BioSystem* 60:95–121.

Rowlands, M. 2006. *Body Language*. Cambridge, Mass.: MIT Press.

Ruben, D. 1985. *The Metaphysics of the Social World*. London: Routledge & Kegan Paul.

Ruben, D. 2003. *Action and Its Explanation*. Oxford: Oxford University Press.

Ruben, D. 2008. Disjunctive theories of perception and action. In *Disjunctivism:Perception, Action, Knowledge*, ed. A. Haddock and F. MacPherson. Oxford: Oxford University Press.

Ruffman, T., W. Garnham, A. Import, and D. Connolly. 2001. Does eye gaze indicate implicit knowledge of false belief? Charting transitions in knowledge. *Journal of Experimental Child Psychology* 80:201–224.

Ruiz-Mirazo, K., and A. Moreno. 1998. Autonomy and emergence: How systems become agents through the generation of functional constraints. In *Emergence, Complexity, Hierarchy, Organization*, ed. G. L. Farre and T. Oksala. Acta Polytechnica Scandinavica. Espoo-Helsinki: The Finnish Academy of Technology.

Ruiz-Mirazo, K., and A. Moreno. 2000. Searching for the roots of autonomy: The natural and artificial paradigms revisited. *Communication and Cognition—Artificial Intelligence (CC-AI): The Journal for the Integrated Study of Artificial Intelligence, Cognitive Science, and Applied Epistemology* 17:209–228.

Ruiz-Mirazo, K., and A. Moreno. 2006. The maintenance and open-ended growth of complexity in nature: Information as a decoupling mechanism in the origins of life. In *Rethinking Complexity: Perspectives from North and South*, ed. F. Capra, P. Sotolongo, A. Juarrero, and J. van Uden. Mansfield, Mass.: ISCE Publishing.

Ruiz-Mirazo, K., J. Peretó, and A. Moreno. 2004. A universal definition of life: Autonomy and open-ended evolution. *Origins of Life and Evolution of the Biosphere* 34:323–346.

Russell, B. 1903. *The Principles of Mathematics*. Cambridge: Cambridge University Press.

Salthe, S. N. 1985. *Evolving Hierarchical Systems: Their Structure and Representation*. New York: Columbia University Press.

Salthe, S. N. 2002. Summary of the principles of hierarchy theory. *General Systems Bulletin* 31:13–17.

Sandis, C., ed. 2009. *New Essays on the Explanation of Action*. Basingstoke: Palgrave Macmillan.

Sartorio, C. 2005. A new asymmetry between actions and omissions. *Noûs* 39:460–482.

Sartorio, C. 2009. Omissions and causalism. *Noûs* 43:513–530.

Scanlon, T. 1998. *What We Owe to Each Other*. Cambridge, Mass.: Harvard University Press.

Schaffer, J. 2005. Contrastive causation. *Philosophical Review* 114:327–358.

Schroeter, F. 2004. Endorsement and autonomous agency. *Philosophy and Phenomenological Research* 69:633–659.

Schueler, G. F. 2003. *Reasons and Purposes: Human Rationality and the Teleological Explanation of Action.* Oxford: Clarendon Press.

Schueler, G. F. 2009. The Humean theory of motivation rejected. *Philosophy and Phenomenological Research* 78:103–122.

Schult, C. A. 2002. Children's understanding of the distinction between intentions and desires. *Child Development* 73:1727–1747.

Searle, J. 1980. Minds, brains, and programs. *Behavioral and Brain Sciences* 3:417–457.

Searle, J. 1981. The intentionality of intention and action. *Manuscrito* 4:77–101.

Searle, J. 1983. *Intentionality.* Cambridge: Cambridge University Press.

Sehon, S. 1994. Teleology and the nature of mental states. *American Philosophical Quarterly* 31:63–72.

Sehon, S. R. 1997. Deviant causal chains and the irreducibility of teleological explanation. *Pacific Philosophical Quarterly* 78:195–213.

Sehon, S. 2005. *Teleological Realism: Mind, Agency, and Explanation.* Cambridge, Mass: MIT Press.

Sellars, W. 1963. Philosophy and the scientific image of man. In *Science, Perception, and Reality.* New York: Routledge & Kegan Paul.

Seth, A. K. 2005. Causal connectivity of evolved neural networks during behavior. *Network* 16:35–54.

Seth, A. K. 2006. Causal networks in neural systems: From water mazes to consciousness. In *Proceedings of the 2006 Meeting on Brain Inspired Cognitive Systems*, ed. I. Aleksander et al. Millet, Alberta: ICSC Interdisciplinary Research.

Seth, A. K., and G. M. Edelman. 2007. Distinguishing causal interactions in neural populations. *Neural Computation* 19:910–933.

Shannon, C. 1948. The mathematical theory of communication. *Bell System Technical Journal* (July and October).

Shultz, T. R., and F. Shamash. 1981. The child's conception of intending act and consequence. *Canadian Journal of Behavioural Science* 13:368–372.

Simons, D. J., and C. F. Chabris. 1999. Gorillas in our midst: Sustained inattentional blindness for dynamic events. *Perception* 28:1059–1074.

Sirois, S., and I. Jackson. 2007. Social cognition in infancy: A critical review of research on higher order abilities. *European Journal of Developmental Psychology* 4:46–64.

Smart, J. J. C. 1959. Sensations and brain processes. *Philosophical Review* 68:141–156.

Smith, A. 2005. Responsibility for attitudes: Activity and passivity in mental life. *Ethics* 115:236–271.

Smith, M. 1998. The possibility of philosophy of action. In *Human Action, Deliberation, and Causation*, ed. J. Bransen and S. Cuypers, 17–41. Dordrecht: Kluwer Academic. Reprinted in Smith 2004.

Smith, M. 2003a. Rational capacities. In *Weakness of Will and Varieties of Practical Irrationality*, S. Stroud and C. Tappolet, 17–38. Oxford: Oxford University Press. Reprinted in Smith 2004.

Smith, M. 2003b. Humeanism, psychologism, and the normative story. *Philosophy and Phenomenological Research* 67:460–467.

Smith, M. 2004. *Ethics and the A Priori: Selected Essays on Moral Psychology and Meta-Ethics.* New York: Cambridge University Press.

Smith, M. Forthcoming. The explanatory role of being rational. In *Practical Reason*, ed. D. Sobel and S. Wall. New York: Cambridge University Press.

Smith, P. 1990. Contemplating failure: The importance of unconscious omission. *Philosophical Studies* 59:159–176.

Sodian, B. 1991. The development of deception in young children. *British Journal of Developmental Psychology* 9:173–188.

Sodian, B., C. Thoermer, and N. Dietrich. 2006. Two- to four-year-old children's differentiation of knowing and guessing in a non-verbal task. *European Journal of Developmental Psychology* 3:222–237.

Soon, C. S., M. Brass, H.-J. Heinze, and J. Haynes. 2008. Unconscious determinants of free decisions in the human brain. *Nature Neuroscience* 11:543–545.

Sorabji, R. 2004. The concept of the will from Plato to Maximus the Confessor. In *The Will and Human Action: From Antiquity to the Present Day*, ed. T. Pink and M. Stone. London: Routledge.

Sorabji, R. 1979. Body and soul in Aristotle. In *Articles on Aristotle*, vol. 4: *Psychology and Aesthetics*, ed. J. Barnes, M. Schofield, R. Sorabji. London: Duckworth.

Sorell, T. 1986. *Hobbes.* London: Routledge.

Southgate, V. 2008. Attributions of false belief in infancy. Invited Presentation at the EPS Research Workshop on Theory of Mind: A Workshop in Celebration of the

30th Anniversary of Premack and Woodruff's Seminal Paper, "Does the Chimpanzee Have a Theory of Mind?" (BBS 1978). Organized by A. Hamilton, I. Apperly, and D. Samson, University of Nottingham, September 11–12, 2008.

Southgate, V., A. Senju, and G. Csibra. 2007. Action anticipation through attribution of false belief by 2-year-olds. *Psychological Science* 18:586–592.

Stampe, D. 1977. Towards a causal theory of linguistic representation. In *Midwest Studies in Philosophy*, vol. 2. ed. P. French et al. Minneapolis: University of Minnesota Press.

Steward, H. 1997. *The Ontology of Mind*. Oxford: Clarendon Press.

Surian, L., S. Caldi, and D. Sperber. 2007. Attribution of beliefs by 13-month-old infants. *Psychological Science* 18:580–586.

Symposium on B. Libet. 1985. *Behavioral and Brain Sciences* 8.

Symposium on M. Moore's *Act and Crime* book. 1994. *University of Pennsylvania Law Review* 142: 1443–1748.

Tanney, J. 2005. Reason-explanation and the contents of the mind. *Ratio* 18:338–351.

Taylor, R. 1966. *Action and Purpose*. Englewood Cliffs, N.J.: Prentice-Hall.

Thalberg, I. 1977. *Perception, Emotion, and Action*. New Haven: Yale University Press.

Thomson, J. 1977. *Acts and Other Events*. Ithaca: Cornell University Press.

Thomson, J. 1996. Critical study on Jonathan Bennett's *The Act Itself*. *Noûs* 30:545–557.

Thomson, J. 2003. Causation: Omissions. *Philosophy and Phenomenological Research* 66:81–103.

Tomasello, M. 1999. *The Cultural Origins of Human Cognition*. Cambridge, Mass.: Harvard University Press.

Tomasello, M., M. Carpenter, J. Call, T. Behne, and H. Moll. 2005. Understanding and sharing intentions: The origins of cultural cognition. *Behavioral and Brain Sciences* 28:675–735.

Tomasello, M., and K. Haberl. 2003. Understanding attention: 12- and 18-month-olds know what is new for other persons. *Developmental Psychology* 39:906–912.

Tooley, M. 1987. *Causation: A Realist Approach*. Oxford: Oxford University Press.

Tuck, R. 1989. *Hobbes*. New York: Oxford University Press.

Turner, J. 2004. Folk intuitions, asymmetry, and intentional side effects. *Journal of Theoretical and Philosophical Psychology* 24:214–219.

Ulanowicz, R. 1997. *Ecology: The Ascendent Perspective*. New York: Columbia University Press.

Ulanowicz, R. 2005. A revolution in the Middle Kingdom. In *Micro, Meso, Macro: Addressing Complex Systems Couplings*, ed. H. Liljenström and U. Svedin. Hackensack, N.J.: World Scientific.

Ulanowicz, R. 2008. *The Third Window*. West Conshohocken, Pennsylvania: Templeton Press.

Van Mill, D. 2001. *Liberty, Rationality, and Agency in Hobbes's "Leviathan."* Albany: SUNY Press.

Van Orden, G. C., H. Kloos, and S. Wallot. 2009. Living in the pink: Intentionality, wellbeing, and complexity. In *Handbook of the Philosophy of Science*, vol. 10: *Philosophy of Complex Systems*, ed. C. Hooker. General editors D. M. Gabbay, P. Thagard, and J. Woods. Amsterdam: Elsevier BV.

Velleman, J. D. 1992. What happens when someone acts? *Mind* 101:461–481. Reprinted in Velleman 2000.

Velleman, J. D. 2000. *The Possibility of Practical Reason*. New York: Oxford University Press.

Vendler, Z. 1962. Effects, results, and consequences. In *Analytical Philosophy*, 1–15, ed. R. J. Butler. Oxford: Blackwell.

Vermazen, B. 1985. Negative acts. In *Essays on Davidson*, ed. B. Vermazen and M. Hintikka. New York: Oxford University Press.

Vihvelin, K., and T. Tomkow. 2005. The dif. *Journal of Philosophy* 102:183–205.

von Wright, G. H. 1978. On so-called practical inference. In *Practical Reasoning*, ed. J. Raz. Oxford: Oxford University Press.

Wallace, R. J. 1999. Three conceptions of rational agency. *Ethical Theory and Moral Practice* 2:217–242.

Walton, D. 1980. Omitting, refraining, and letting happen. *American Philosophical Quarterly* 17:319–326.

Washington University School of Medicine. 2008. Scientists adapt economics theory to trace brain's information flow. *ScienceDaily* (October 10). http://www.sciencedaily.com/releases/2008/10/081009185035.htm

Watson, G., ed. 1982. *Free Will*. Oxford: Oxford University Press.

Wegner, D. 2002. *The Illusion of Conscious Will*. Cambridge, Mass.: MIT Press.

Weinryb, E. 1980. Omissions and responsibility. *Philosophical Quarterly* 30:1–18.

Wellman, H. M., D. Cross, and J. Watson. 2001. Meta-analysis of theory of mind development: The truth about false belief. *Child Development* 72:655–684.

Wheeler, M. 2005. *Reconstructing the Cognitive World: The Next Step.* Cambridge, Mass.: MIT Press.

Wheeler, M., and A. Clark. 1999. Genic representation: Reconciling content and causal complexity. *British Journal for the Philosophy of Science* 50:103–135.

Wiggins, D. 1987. Claims of need. In his *Needs, Values, Truth.* Oxford: Blackwell.

Wiland, E. 2007. Intentional action and "in order to." *Journal of Theoretical and Philosophical Psychology* 27:113–118.

Williams, B. 1973. Morality and the emotions. In his *Problems of the Self.* Cambridge: Cambridge University Press.

Williams, B. 1981a. Internal and external reasons. In his *Moral Luck.* Cambridge: Cambridge University Press.

Williams, B. 1981b. *Moral Luck.* Cambridge: Cambridge University Press.

Williams, B. 1985. *Ethics and the Limits of Philosophy.* London: Fontana.

Williams, G. 1987. Oblique intention. *Cambridge Law Journal* 46:417–438.

Williams, B. 1995a. Acts and omissions, doing and not doing. In *Virtues and Reasons: Philippa Foot and Moral Theory*, ed. R. Hursthouse, G. Lawrence, and W. Quinn. Oxford: Clarendon Press.

Williams, B. 1995b. Internal reasons and the obscurity of blame. In his *Making Sense of Humanity.* Cambridge: Cambridge University Press.

Williams, B. 1996. Truth in ethics. In *Truth in Ethics*, ed. B. Hooker. Oxford: Blackwell.

Williamson, T. 2000. *Knowledge and Its Limits.* Oxford: Oxford University Press.

Wilson, G. 1989. *The Intentionality of Human Action*, 2nd ed. Stanford: Stanford University Press.

Wilson, G. 1997. Reasons as causes for action. In *Contemporary Action Theory.* vol. 1. ed. G. Holmström-Hintikka and R. Tuomela. Dordrecht: Kluwer.

Wilson, G. 2009. Debates about causalism in the theory of action. In *Philosophy of Action: Five Questions*, ed. J. Aguilar and A. Buckareff. London: Automatic/VIP.

Wilson, M. 2002. Six views of embodied cognition. *Psychonomic Bulletin and Review* 9:625–636.

Wimmer, H., and H. Mayringer. 1998. False belief understanding in young children: Explanations do not develop before predictions. *International Journal of Behavioral Development* 22:403–422.

Winch, P. 1958. *The Idea of a Social Science.* London: Routledge.

Wittgenstein, L. 1958. *Philosophische Untersuchungen*. Frankfurt: Suhrkamp.

Wittgenstein, L. 1972. *Philosophical Investigations*. Trans. G. E. M. Anscombe. Oxford: Blackwell.

Woodward, J. 2003. *Making Things Happen: A Theory of Causal Explanation*. Oxford: Oxford University Press.

Woodward, J. Forthcoming. Causal perception and causal cognition.

Wright, J., and J. Bengson. 2009. Asymmetries in folk judgments of responsibility and intentional action. *Mind and Language* 24:24–50.

Yablo, S. 1992. Mental causation. *Philosophical Review* 101:245–280.

Yaffe, G. 2009. Commentary on Moore's "Intention, responsibility, and the challenges of recent neuroscience." *Stanford Technology Law Review*. http://stlr.stanford.edu/2009/02/intention_responsibility_and_t.html.

Young, L., F. Cushman, R. Adolphs, D. Tranel, and M. Hauser. 2006. Does emotion mediate the relationship between an action's moral status and its intentional status? Neuropsychological evidence. *Journal of Cognition and Culture* 6:291–304.

Yuill, N. 1984. Young children's coordination of motive and outcome in judgments of satisfaction and morality. *British Journal of Developmental Psychology* 2:73–81.

Zhabotinsky, A. M. 1964. Periodic processes of malonic acid oxidation in a liquid phase. *Biofizika* 9:306–311.

Zimmerman, M. 1981. Taking some of the mystery out of omissions. *Southern Journal of Philosophy* 19:541–554.

Contributors

Frederick Adams   Professor of Cognitive Science and Philosophy, University of Delaware

Jesús H. Aguilar   Associate Professor of Philosophy, Rochester Institute of Technology

John Bishop   Professor of Philosophy, University of Auckland

Andrei A. Buckareff   Assistant Professor of Philosophy, Marist College

Randolph Clarke   Professor of Philosophy, Florida State University

Jennifer Hornsby   Professor of Philosophy, Birkbeck College, University of London

Alicia Juarrero   Professor of Philosophy, Prince George's Community College

Alfred R. Mele   William H. and Lucyle T. Werkmeister Professor of Philosophy, Florida State University

Michael S. Moore   Charles R. Walgreen, Jr. University Chair, Professor of Law and Philosophy, Professor in the Center for Advanced Study, and Co-Director of the College of the Law Program in Law and Philosophy, University of Illinois College of Law

Thomas A. Nadelhoffer   Assistant Professor of Philosophy and Contributing Faculty to Law and Policy Program, Dickinson College

Josef Perner   Professor of Psychology, University of Salzburg

Johannes Roessler   Senior Lecturer in Philosophy, University of Warwick

David-Hillel Ruben   Director of New York University in London and Professor, Birkbeck College, University of London

Carolina Sartorio Associate Professor of Philosophy, University of Arizona

Michael Smith McCosh Professor of Philosophy, Princeton University

Rowland Stout Senior Lecturer in Philosophy, University College Dublin

Index